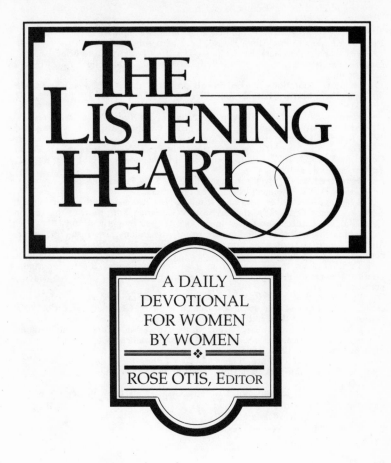

THE LISTENING HEART

A DAILY DEVOTIONAL FOR WOMEN BY WOMEN

ROSE OTIS, Editor

REVIEW AND HERALD® PUBLISHING ASSOCIATION
HAGERSTOWN, MD 21740

Bible texts credited to Amplified are from *The Amplified Bible*. Copyright © 1965 by Zondervan Publishing House. Used by permission.

Texts credited to Berkeley are from *The Holy Bible: The Berkeley Version in Modern English*. Copyright © 1969 by Zondervan Publishing House. Used by permission.

Scripture quotations marked NASB are from the *New American Standard Bible*, © The Lockman Foundation 1960, 1962, 1963, 1968, 1971, 1972, 1973, 1975, 1977.

Texts credited to NEB are from *The New English Bible*. © The Delegates of the Oxford University Press and the Syndics of the Cambridge University Press 1961, 1970. Reprinted by permission.

Texts credited to NIV are from the *Holy Bible, New International Version*. Copyright © 1973, 1978, 1984, International Bible Society. Used by permission of Zondervan Bible Publishers.

Texts credited to NKJV are from The New King James Version. Copyright © 1979, 1980, 1982, Thomas Nelson, Inc., Publishers.

Bible texts credited to NRSV are from the New Revised Standard Version of the Bible, copyright © 1989 by the Division of Christian Education of the National Council of the Churches of Christ in the U.S.A. Used by permission.

Bible texts credited to Phillips are from J. B. Phillips: *The New Testament in Modern English*, Revised Edition. © J. B. Phillips 1958, 1960, 1972. Used by permission of Macmillan Publishing Co.

Texts credited to REB are from *The Revised English Bible*. Copyright © Oxford University Press and Cambridge University Press, 1989. Reprinted by permission.

Bible texts credited to RSV are from the Revised Standard Version of the Bible, copyright © 1946, 1952, 1971, by the Division of Christian Education of the National Council of the Churches of Christ in the U.S.A. Used by permission.

Bible texts credited to TEV are from the *Good News Bible*—Old Testament: Copyright © American Bible Society 1976; New Testament: Copyright © American Bible Society 1966, 1971, 1976.

Verses marked TLB are taken from *The Living Bible*, copyright © 1971 by Tyndale House Publishers, Wheaton, Ill. Used by permission.

Manuscript editors: James Cavil, Laurie R. Gust, Penny Estes Wheeler
Designer: Bill Kirstein
Cover designer: Helcio Deslandes
Cover cloth: Marcus Brothers Textiles, Inc.
Typeset: 10/11 Sabon

PRINTED IN U.S.A.

98 97 96 95 94 93   10 9 8 7 6 5 4 3 2 1

R&H Cataloging Service
Otis, Rose, editor
    The listening heart.

    1. Devotional calendars—SDA. 2. Devotional
calendars—Women. 3. Women—Religious life.
4. Devotional literature—SDA. I. Title.
        242.643

ISBN 0-8280-0769-1

Biographical Sketches

Nora Agboka is married and has three daughters. She works at the Private Schools Unit of the Regional Education Office, is a board member of the Labone Preparatory and Secondary Schools, and is involved in family life programs. She loves children, flowers, and cooking. **Mar. 14.**

Deborah Aho lives at Riverside Farm Institute, a lay-operated Seventh-day Adventist training school in Zambia. She and her husband coordinate World Food Program to Prevent Malnutrition in their area. Deborah home-schools their three children, teaches sewing classes, and is in the process of organizing home industry for village women. **May 1, Sept. 10.**

Ginny Allen lives in Vancouver, Washington, with her husband, an academy Bible teacher. They have two married sons. She is a nurse in a public high school in Portland, Oregon. Ginny has spoken for retreats, seminars, and church weekends across the United States, Canada, Brazil, and Russia and cohosts a TV series on Christian concerns for 3ABN. **Sept. 7.**

Ellen Anderson is an associate professor of social work at Oakwood College, Huntsville, Alabama. She has academic and experiential competency in teaching, administration, grantsmanship, and research. She has touched and made a positive impact on thousands of lives and won hundreds to a new life experience in Christ. **Aug. 24.**

Nettie M. Anderson is an administrative assistant and editor and lectures concerning effective family relations. She is a minister's wife, has three daughters, and enjoys gardening, sewing, crafts, and reading. **Mar. 30.**

Chelcie Sterling-Anim is a secretary at the Trans-European Division. She is the wife of a minister and has one daughter. A trained Bible instructor and lay preacher, she enjoys working with young people and is actively involved in Pathfinder work. Her hobbies include badminton, music, reading, and needlework. **Feb. 7, June 18.**

Mabel Owusu-Antwi comes from Ghana, West Africa. She is studying for a master's degree in English literature at Andrews University in Michigan. Her husband is finishing his Ph.D. in religion. **June 24.**

Indrani J. Ariyaratnam is from Sri Lanka and writes from Pakistan, where she is the women's ministries director. She is a minister's wife, and has worked as a schoolteacher, editor, translator, secretary, cashier-accountant, and Bible instructor. **Feb. 15.**

Alma Atcheson, from Australia, is the mother of three children. She is the church communications secretary and assistant welfare leader. She was educated at Australasian Missionary College, now Avondale College, and served in denominational employment as a secretary until her marriage. Her interests are welfare work and gardening. **Dec. 5.**

Fern Gibson Babcock is a teacher and the director of the Teaching Materials Center at Southern College of SDA in Tennessee. She and her husband enjoy entertaining students in their home and telling mission stories about their years in Pakistan. In the pursuit of her writing hobby, Fern has published several books and dozens of articles over the past years. **Oct. 1**

Audrey Balderstone and her husband own and operate a garden landscaping company in England. She is active in her church and community in organizing flower festivals and fund-raising projects; she also conducts a bimonthly Home Fellowship group meeting and has two sons. She is president of the Adventist Business and Professionals Association (British ASI) and is the SDA representative on the Women's World Day of Prayer Committee. **Jan. 22, Oct. 14, Nov. 3.**

Lois Barker is a grandmother and great-grandmother who is retired and living in Holdrege, Nebraska. She spent 30 years in self-supporting ministry in the South. **Oct. 23.**

Mary Barrett is a minister's wife, mother, and homemaker in England. She is a published writer, public speaker, and evangelist. Her hobbies include cross-stitch, crafts, and reading. **Nov. 7.**

Michele Beach is the chairperson of the English Department at Takoma Academy in Takoma Park, Maryland, and also teaches French and journalism. She enjoys traveling around the world, ethnic entertainment and gourmet cuisine, medieval art and literature, tennis, skiing, and photography. **Nov. 17.**

Judi Wild Becker lives in California. Also a vocalist, she is a member of the Norman Steels Chorale of Pacific Union College as well as the Napa Valley Women's Ensemble. Her writings include articles in local newspapers, in the Loma Linda *Alumni News*, and several dental trade journals. **Apr. 26, May 22, June 20, Aug. 2, Dec. 3.**

Elizabeth Bediako is a native of Ghana. She and her minister husband and four children live in Maryland. She is an office clerk at the General Conference of Seventh-day Adventists and enjoys traveling, photography, cooking, and sewing. **Sept. 12.**

Joni Bell is a minister's wife, mother, musician, and nurse living in New York. **Sept. 2.**

Carol Booth writes from Huntsville, Alabama, where she is the assistant director of work education at Oakwood College. She is also a wife and mother of two sons. Carol enjoys sewing, reading, and working in youth ministries. **Aug. 19.**

Audrey E. Boyle is a theology graduate from Newbold College in England. Currently she is working as legal editor of the United Kingdom's top business magazine and also manages book publishing. In her spare time she is active in and runs seminars on child evangelism. **Aug. 14.**

Carol Bradfield was born to missionary parents to Africa. She and her husband have spent 40 years in mission service in five countries of Africa, and their three married sons are also in mission service. She is the chief accountant of the Southern Africa Union Conference, and is the local church treasurer and organist. Her hobbies include knitting, crocheting, and stamp collecting. **June 12.**

Carole Breckenridge is director of marketing for a chain of nursing centers in Maryland. She enjoys public speaking, writing, travel, reading, and nurturing friendships. **June 17.**

Ellen Bresee, the recently retired cofounder of Shepherdess International, has served with her husband in pastoral and evangelistic team ministry for many years and has taught elementary school. She is the mother of three sons and one daughter, and is a published writer, marriage counselor, and speaker. She and her husband just moved to Colorado. **Jan. 27, Mar. 1, May 17.**

Hortensia Bryce is a teacher, mother of three girls, and wife. She has been a language teacher for many years, and only recently left Mexico, where she taught English for four years, subsequent to which she obtained a master's degree in education at the University of Montemorelos. At the present time she teaches Spanish to Mexican-American children in the Weslaco Independent School District. **Nov. 25.**

Betty R. Burnett, from "Charlevoix the Beautiful," Michigan, works for the Department of Agriculture, has been married for 35 years, is a mother of five and grandmother of eight, and loves her church family and assists them by participating as an elder, adult Sabbath school teacher, women's ministries coordinator, and friend. She enjoys reading, crocheting, children, and walking in the fields and woods. **Oct. 20.**

Hazel Burns and her husband live in Kettering, Ohio, and have two grown children. She began a women's ministries program in her local church 10 years ago and is still actively involved in it. She is a homemaker, church and neighborhood Bible study leader, lecturer, and seminar instructor. Her interests include baking, quilting, painting, hiking, skiing, and family outings. **Oct. 18.**

Lena G. Caesar, along with her husband and two teenage children, lives in Montemorelos, Mexico. Besides directing the Modern Language Institute at Montemorelos University, Lena also consults and presents seminars in the area of child language development (she is a clinically certified speech/language therapist). She is originally from the West Indies, and enjoys traveling, reading, sewing, and poetry. **Dec. 19.**

Pam Caruso is retired but still actively involved in community service work. She enjoys reading, writing, classical music, walking, playing the piano, and helping with the very young children in her church. **July 13.**

Virginia Cason is a homemaker and public speaker. She and her doctor husband live in California and have four grown children. She has written programs and lessons for Vacation Bible School and Sabbath school, as well as songbooks for children. She teaches voice and is a radio DJ, a ham radio operator, and a private pilot. Virginia is the daughter of H.M.S. Richards, Sr. **Apr. 28, Aug. 31.**

Shari Chamberlain began her career as a health educator. She has been an associate in pastoral care for 10 years and a chaplain for five years. She is currently a chaplain with Hospice of Napa Valley of St. Helena Hospital in California. She enjoys mountain climbing, a good book, chatting with friends, and adventuresome travel. **Aug. 27.**

Lyndelle Chiomenti is the editor of the Easy English edition of the adult *Sabbath School Lesson Quarterly.* She is married and enjoys writing, reading, crocheting, antiques, history, water gardening, and biblical studies. **Jan. 9, Mar. 28, Dec. 23.**

Ginger Mostert Church is a marketing representative for the Review and Herald Publishing Association. She teaches seminars on possibility thinking, has had articles published in several church magazines as well as in local newspapers, and enjoys traveling, cross-stitching, reading, and writing. She and her husband have two grown sons. **Jan. 30, July 24, Nov. 8.**

Susan Clark lives in California with her husband and two active teenagers. She is a member of the local women's ministries council and enjoys leading a weekly women's Bible study. Her interests are quilting, gardening, reading, and supporting the music and sports activities of her children. **Mar. 20, June 5.**

Carel Clay lives in Napa, California, with her husband and daughter. She has two grown stepchildren. She teaches nursing at Napa Valley College and is currently completing her master's degree in nursing. She has taught cradle roll, youth, and adult Bible classes. Carel enjoys quilting, sewing, writing, public speaking, cats, and being a mom. **Oct. 29.**

Carole Spalding Colburn spent 25 highly rewarding years with her husband and family in the Far East. Taiwan, Indonesia, and Singapore all hold warm friendships and happy memories. Today their three children are grown and married, so the family includes six children and one precious little auburn-haired grandson. Carole works in the General Conference Treasury Department's international service section with furloughing missionaries and sponsored students from around the world. **Mar. 12, May 23.**

Cynthia Coston is mother of two preschool boys and office manager for her husband's veterinary practice in Virginia. She is a pianist, harpist, and vocal soloist. Children's and mother's ministries are her greatest interest at her local church. **Sept. 18.**

Judy Coulston has a Ph.D. in nutrition and a private practice headquartered in Fresno, California, where recently for nearly three years she hosted and coproduced a highly rated weekly television program. Her interests include singing in Spanish, gardening, public speaking, and holding church offices, but most of all she prefers the simple title of "soul winner and loving friend to all." **Sept. 20, Oct. 3.**

Celia Cruz is the administrative secretary in the Office of Women's Ministries at the General Conference. She is a pastor's wife, and mother of three adult children and two teenagers. She enjoys people, her family, teaching the 10- to 15-year-old children's Bible class at her church, assisting her husband with a young adult group, presenting seminars, and preaching. Celia spends her spare moments in needlework, reading, writing, and ceramics. **Apr. 14, Apr. 15.**

Phyllis Dalgleish, a receptionist, is the mother of three grown daughters, a widow, and a writer of children's stories. Her first book, *Hattie Hippo,* was published last year. She has worked in many of the children's departments in her church and enjoys crocheting, knitting, calligraphy, cooking, and writing. **Aug. 23.**

Shonna Dalusong is a wife, mother, and registered nurse. She and her husband are currently assisting in the nursery at their church, and helping with children's church and the youth activities. Among her hobbies are writing, and writing a monthly column for her church newsletter. **May 20, May 30.**

Laura Pascual Dancek is the director of speech/language pathology at a hospital in Port Charlotte, Florida, and an M.B.A. student. Husband Ed is the district manager for a financial planning company. Her hobby is music. **Dec. 25.**

Sandy Lee Betke Dancek, a literature evangelist, is a grandmother of four granddaughters, a published writer, and speaker. Originally from Pennsylvania, she and her husband, Ed, are making their home in West Virginia. Her interests are piano, organ, flower arranging, kids, and grandchildren. **Oct. 21.**

Enola Davis was raised in Brazil by missionary parents. As an adult, she spent more than 30 years in nursing, many of those in teaching and management, and seven years in nursing administration in the Philippines. Enola is retired and lives in northern California. Her greatest interests are "anything in nature" and "little children." **Mar. 23, May 16, Nov. 4.**

Ruth F. Davis is chair of the Oakwood College Home Economics Department. She is active in her church and community. She serves as superintendent of the Oakwood College Sabbath school and sponsors family life workshops for the college and community. **Aug. 6.**

Brenda Dickerson is a wife, mother, and homemaker. She writes from Lincoln, Nebraska, where she and her husband are caretakers of the campground owned by their church. Brenda enjoys gardening, sewing, and writing. **June 7, Sept. 9.**

Sandra Doran lives in Rhode Island with her pastor husband and two children. She is the administrator of a Montessori school, enjoys preaching and presenting seminars, has authored several books, and has written extensively for religious magazines. **Jan. 2, Apr. 13.**

Rita Eisenhower Duncan is a wife, mother, and secretary in California. Formerly a teacher, she enjoys reading and browsing in libraries, bookstores, museums, stationery stores, and antique shops. She sings in the church choir and helps in planning women's ministry activities for her local church. **Mar. 4, Apr. 22.**

Yvonne Minchin Dysinger is the author of *Adventist Tentmakers—Opening Doors Where Others Cannot* and has written for various publications. A retired nurse (M.P.H.), she is the mother of four children. She and her doctor husband have been missionaries in Cambodia, Tanzania, Singapore, and Pakistan. She enjoys sewing, travel, knitting, and backpacking (she climbed Mount Kilimanjaro in 1978). **Apr. 16, July 20.**

Crystal Earnhardt is an evangelist's wife, mother, and freelance writer. She has written two books published by the Review and Herald Publishing Association. Her articles and stories have appeared in *Adventist Review, Celebration, Insight,* and *Guide.* She lives in Misenheimer, North Carolina. **Sept. 19.**

Valerie A. Eccles is secretary to the education director at the Trans-European Division. A qualified teacher of information technology, Valerie also teaches vegetarian and vegan cookery in churches in her conference. Her interests/hobbies include current affairs, travel, badminton, floristry, and working with the wonderful children in the St. Albans Adventurer group. **Feb. 27.**

Shari Dancek Elder is the mother of two toddlers. She lives in Pennsylvania, where her husband works in advertising for a local newspaper. Shari is a full-time mom and a writer. Her hobbies include cross-stitch, outdoor sports, and remodeling her house. **Nov. 16.**

Christina Ennis is a medical technologist at the Veterans Administration Medical Center in Denver, Colorado. She has written several skits for young people and enjoys gardening and reading. **Dec. 17.**

Jocelyn Fay is alumni and public relations director at Atlantic Union College, South Lancaster, Massachusetts. She enjoys collecting antique blue-and-white china, growing herbs, and playing catch-the-calico-mouse with her cat, Mandy. **Dec. 28.**

Linda Hyder Ferry is a physician at Loma Linda University Hospital and teaches in the preventive medicine and family practice residency programs. Her current interest is studying the relationship between depression and lifestyle diseases. She and her husband are amateur ornithologists and conducted research on hummingbirds in southeastern Arizona for six years on their vacations. **June 14.**

Karen Flowers loves to read and knit and talk. Her treasures are counted in friends and family. She lives with her husband and two sons in a small town in Maryland on the edge of the city of Washington, D.C. She works with her husband as codirector of family ministries for the General Conference. **Jan. 20, May 14, July 3.**

Carol Foote is a registered nurse working at a small northern New York hospital in an alcohol and drug rehabilitation unit. She is active in her church, especially in women's ministries, and enjoys playing the piano and guitar. **Dec. 2.**

Heide Ford is a registered nurse and minister's wife living in Florida. She holds a master's degree in counseling and is the editor of *Shepherdessence*, the newsletter for the Florida Conference ministers' wives. Her special interests include reading, writing, different cultures, motorcycling, and skiing. **Mar. 5, June 22.**

Ruby E. Foster is the wife of a retired minister with two sons and one daughter, all grown and active members of the SDA Church. Mrs. Foster has worked closely with her husband during his ministry, and was the president of the Shepherdess Club in her conference for four years. **July 10.**

Mary Fowler, from India, is an elementary teacher. Born in an Adventist pastor's home, she is married to an Adventist minister and has two children and two grandchildren. **Apr. 11.**

Sharon Fujimoto is a sophomore at Pacific Union College majoring in international communication with a French emphasis. Her home is in Yokohama, Japan, where her parents have been missionaries since she was 9 years old. **Dec. 26.**

Linda Lane Gage writes from Walla Walla, Washington, where she is a mental health counselor in private practice. She has served as a pastor's wife, an associate pastor, and a chaplain. She is a mother of two and grandmother of three. **Dec. 15, Dec. 20.**

Cherryl A. Galley writes from Berrien Springs, Michigan, where she is working on her Ph.D. in counseling psychology. Her first devotional appeared in *Among Friends* in 1993. She is active in jail ministry and also enjoys writing, composing music, singing, piano, swimming, horseback riding, skating, racquetball, and photography. **Nov. 26.**

Sheryl Garrison is a single, and teaches kindergarten and first and second grades in a church school in Virginia. Her hobbies are photography, crafts, water sports, and puppet ministry. **June 10.**

Ada Gonzalez de Garcia is the director of counseling and guidance at the University of Montemorelos in Mexico. She and her husband have two sons and have coauthored a book about marriage. Her hobbies include music (she also teaches piano), sewing, knitting, and traveling. **July 21.**

Sonia Gazeta writes from Brazil College, where she teaches Portuguese for the Theological Seminary (SALT). She is also a translator and secretary of the Brazilian Ellen G. White Research Center. **Apr. 23, June 3, Aug. 9.**

Lila Lane George is a medical secretary and Arizona pastor's wife who enjoys her six grandchildren, oil painting, hiking, and reading. The church activity she finds the most fulfillment in is leading a 12-step support group. In 1988 she realized her dream of receiving her bachelor's degree (after a 30-year absence from college). **Mar. 19, Apr. 29, Apr. 30.**

Sarah Roddy Giang, her husband, and two young sons live in Rochester, New York. She is a pediatric neurologist at the University of Rochester. Her hobbies include sewing, orchid growing, bird-watching, and collecting books and hymnals. **Mar. 9.**

Evelin Gilkeson writes from Mississippi, where her husband is the principal of a boarding academy. She has two teenage daughters, teaches, and is working on a master's degree. **Sept. 14, Nov. 28.**

Bertha Appleton Glanzer taught church school and public school in southern California both in regular classrooms and as a special education teacher. She also directed the United Cerebral Palsy Center at Loma Linda University. Mrs. Glanzer, now 77 years of age, is retired and lives with her husband, Elder Ben Glanzer, in Yucaipa, California. **Nov. 18.**

Evelyn Glass is a homemaker, mother, and farmer. She is the women's ministries director for the Mid-America Union as well as a local church clerk and elder, and serves on the Maplewood Academy and the Minnesota K-12 boards. She has written articles for local and state newspapers and Christian publications. She enjoys folk painting, sewing, knitting, refinishing furniture, reading, speaking, and community programs and committees. **Aug. 20.**

Teresa Glass is a pastor's wife, mother, homemaker, and student living in Ogden, Utah. She enjoys skiing, reading, and people. **Mar. 17.**

Carmen O. Gonzalez writes from Auburn, New York. She is a single mother of one adult son. She taught many years in New York City public schools, and now teaches in Syracuse, New York. She has served as a church elder, superintendent, and head deaconess, and on the youth council. She is the Adventist Singles Ministries coordinator for the New York Conference of Seventh-day Adventists. Her interests include praising God, praying, writing letters, walking, bicycling, reading, people watching, playing with her nephew Danny. **Jan. 7.**

Kathryn M. Gordon works at Andrews University in Michigan and is currently working toward her master's degree in social work. She has served as an English teacher in Japan and Korea, and enjoys cross-country skiing, playing the flute, and baking pies. **June 9.**

Carrol Grady, a minister's wife, is a secretary and assistant editor in the General Conference Publishing Department. Among her many interests are writing, poetry, quilting, and music. **June 27, July 6.**

Ramona Perez-Greek is the assistant director of women's ministries for the North American Division. She has a Ph.D. in nursing, has been a university professor, is the first lady of the Gulf States Conference, a mother, and a writer. **May 26, Sept. 3.**

Lourdes E. Morales-Gudmundsson teaches Spanish language and literature at a university, is involved in her local church choir and as the personal ministries director, and leads a weekly Bible study group. She has written for various Spanish and English publications, has two books that are to be released this year, and is working with her husband to develop a Spanish television ministry that is scheduled to be aired this year. **Mar. 25, May 12, Sept. 17.**

Lillian R. Guild, wife of a pastor, evangelist, missionary, and administrator, is a nurse, Bible instructor, and literature evangelist. Before retiring, she was the administrative assistant to the director-speaker of the *Voice of Prophecy*, a radio program. She enjoys writing, walking, swimming, meeting people, and traveling. **Jan. 29, June 6.**

Laurie R. Gust is an advertising copywriter at the Review and Herald Publishing Association in Hagerstown, Maryland. Her special interests include skiing, traveling, canoeing, and hiking. **May 2.**

Melodie Gage Gustavsen lives in White Rock, New Mexico, with her physicist husband and 3-year-old son. She was an English major at Walla Walla College and got her master's degree in childhood development from the University of Washington. She enjoys homemaking, cooking, exercising, and her home quilting business. As a teenager she was fascinated with the ocean and wrote "God Is Like the Ocean." Later she and Rick were married at the Pacific seashore. **June 2.**

Heather Guttschuss is a registered nurse living in California. She spent several years as a missionary in Africa and has three books published by Pacific Press Publishing Association. She enjoys skiing and swimming. **Aug. 5.**

Patricia A. Habada has a doctorate in education curriculum and supervision and is a curriculum specialist for the General Conference Church Ministries Department. She is married, enjoys her daughters, has authored and edited countless instructional manuals, and has written numerous articles for denominational journals. Her hobbies include writing, boating, walking, music, and reading. **Feb. 5, Mar. 16, May 4.**

Cherry B. Habenicht is in youth ministry at Wisconsin Academy, where she teaches Bible and French 1, 2, and 3, and is guidance counselor and vice principal. She and her husband have served in ministry for 26 years, and have a daughter in college, a son in academy, and another son in second grade "to keep us thinking young!" She is a published writer who has been active in women's ministries. **June 25, Aug. 18, Dec. 31.**

Donna J. Habenicht is a professor of educational and counseling psychology at Andrews University in Michigan. She is a child psychologist who has conducted many workshops for children's ministries leaders and families, writes on parenting, and has published two books. She and her physician husband have two grown children and four grandchildren. Her hobbies include music, photography, traveling, reading, crafts, and being a grandmother. **July 8.**

Barbara Hales is a wife and mother living in New Carlisle, Indiana. She serves as a financial aid advisor at Andrews University, is a member of the Indiana Conference women's ministries committee, and lectures on women's issues. She enjoys writing, sewing, and cooking. **Feb. 1.**

Madlyn Hamblin and her husband own and operate a printing company in Tecumseh, Michigan. She is the author of the book *Promise in the Cornfield*, is actively involved in women's ministries, and enjoys volunteering for her local church. She is the mother of Kristy, a registered nurse, and Mike, a college student. **Dec. 1.**

Sali Jo Hand is a mother of three sons and has one daughter-in-law. She is a homemaker, artist, and senior pastor of two churches in southeastern Arizona. **Nov. 22.**

Lea Hardy, formerly an English teacher, now as a church elder promotes women's ministries, leads Bible study groups, and does some speaking. She is a published author and has written a Bible lesson series, "Women Discovering Jesus," primarily for overseas use. She writes for and acts in a local group called Maranatha Players. **Mar. 6.**

Beatrice Harris is a retired Bible instructor and church school teacher. She is a local church elder and an associate personal ministries leader, and has written articles for religious magazines. She has two grown children. **May 3, July 16.**

Peggy Harris is an elder and church growth director in her local church. She is also a musician, and is actively involved in ministering to women. She has her own business as an insurance agent and also presents biblical hospitality seminars. She and her husband have two children and grandchildren. **Sept. 24.**

Susan Harvey is the director of promotion and women's resources at the Review and Herald Publishing Association. She lives in Hagerstown, Maryland, with her husband, Rhea. Prior to joining the Review, she had a career as a professional interior designer and design teacher. She has two grown sons and enjoys keeping up with their creative and interesting lives, as well as reading, walking, and traveling. **May 24.**

Tessie Hatfield is a pseudonym. **June 16.**

Sue Hayford teaches at Parkview Junior Academy in Syracuse, New York. She enjoys gardening, reading, and traveling. She and her husband are ham radio operators. **Feb. 22.**

Edna Heise is a homemaker and seminar presenter in Australia. She and her pastor husband have three grown children. She has coauthored a book, *In Letters of Gold*, and written many articles for religious publications. Pencil and pastel drawing, gardening, and fund-raising are among her special interests. **Apr. 18, June 21.**

Lorabel Hersch is on the pastoral staff of the Collegedale church, where she serves as community chaplain. She is a former librarian and English teacher. She writes articles for religious magazines and has authored a number of Bible lesson quarterlies for earliteen- and junior-age young people. She is the mother of six adult children. She enjoys traveling with her husband, reading, writing, and getting acquainted with new people. **Sept. 8, Oct. 8, Oct. 30.**

Carolyn T. Hinson works in special education for Fulton County, Georgia. She teaches middle school students with learning disabilities. She has assisted her husband, a pastor, in evangelistic meetings as a Bible worker and bookkeeper, and is the women's ministries director for the South Atlantic Conference. They have three adult daughters. She enjoys reading, running, tending small house plants and tropical fish, and especially working with cradle roll-age children in her church. **Aug. 28.**

Kyna Hinson is a journalist and an assistant college professor. She is involved in women's ministries in her local church and conference and enjoys working with teenagers. She has written many articles for several religious magazines and enjoys embroidery, reading, and baking. **Feb. 16, Feb. 17, Feb. 18.**

Roxy Hoehn writes from Kansas, the geographical center of the United States. She's a trained teacher and has done quite a bit of writing for children, including several teen Sabbath school quarterlies. She is director of women's ministries for the Kansas-Nebraska Conference. **Nov. 2.**

Karen Holford is the mother of three small children. She is the wife of a pastor in Essex, England. Karen has written for a variety of denominational journals, including *Ministry*. She also designs Christian cross-stitch kits. **Jan. 19, Mar. 8, May 27, Dec. 21.**

Sharon Holmes is a mother, nurse, and musician from Connecticut. She is a published writer, enjoys sailing and travel, and performs with several singing groups and a string quartet. **June 13, Aug. 17.**

Lorraine Hudgins, a retired administrative secretary, has worked at Faith for Today, the Voice of Prophecy, and the General Conference of SDAs. She is active in her local church in Glendora, California, where she and her husband live. She enjoys her five children, 11 grandchildren, and writing. **Jan. 13, Feb. 9, Mar. 13, May 15, Sept. 13.**

Barbara Huff writes from Mound, Minnesota. She is the wife of a church administrator, a mother of two adult children, and a grandmother. She is a freelance writer and also the communication director and women's ministries director for the Minnesota Conference of Seventh-day Adventists. **Sept. 4, Oct. 2.**

Ruthie Jacobson, director of women's ministries for the Oregon Conference of Seventh-day Adventists, is a speaker and published writer. She and her husband, Don, both enjoy serving the people of Oregon, their home and garden, and reading. **Oct. 25.**

Anna Johansen is originally from Iceland but writes from Cyprus, where she and her husband are in mission service. They have three adult children who live in Denmark. Her interests are reading, music, embroidery, and crossword puzzles. **Nov. 11.**

Dolly Alexander-Johnson served the Adventist school system in Canada and in Africa for 13 years before earning a doctorate in linguistics and taking up residence in the United States. A published author and active in her church, she writes from Pacific Union College in Angwin, California, where she has directed and taught in the English language program for the past five years. **Sept. 21.**

Madeline S. Johnston writes from Berrien Springs, Michigan, where she and her husband make their home. She is a freelance writer, part-time secretary, advice columnist for *Guide* (has answered more than 1,000 letters), and mother of four grown children. She has served overseas as a missionary, and written several books and numerous articles. Writing, knitting, genealogy, Scrabble, photography, and bird-watching are among her special interests. **Jan. 21, Apr. 9, Apr. 21.**

Marianette Johnston is the treasurer for Planned Assistance for Troubled Children (PATCH). She and her pastor husband spent 42 years in ministry; several of those were in mission service. Her special interests are family, her grandchildren, cross-stitch, and quilting. **July 11, July 12.**

Jeanne Jordan, a retired teacher, lives in Michigan with her husband. They have been married for 44 years, served as missionaries for 12 years, and have two grown children. She has authored three books and countless articles in church magazines, and enjoys reading, traveling, and words. **Sept. 25.**

Collene Kelly is an elementary teacher by profession but a homemaker by choice. She enjoys spending time with her minister husband and two preschool boys. Collene also likes gardening, walking, writing, trying new recipes, and attending family gatherings. **Sept. 1, Nov. 23.**

Birthe Kendel is from Denmark and writes from St. Albans in England. She is a minister's wife and the happy mother of two teenage daughters. She is the director of children's ministries and women's ministries for the Trans-European Division of Seventh-day Adventists. **Feb. 13, June 15.**

Marilyn King writes from Oregon, where she and her husband are enjoying a busy and rewarding retirement. For many years she worked as a registered nurse. Her hobbies include working with the young people at their church, staying in touch with friends, and enjoying her children and grandchildren. **Sept. 16.**

Marg Kinney is the secretary in the Art Department at the Review and Herald Publishing Association, and is the wife of Robert Kinney, the president. She has three grown children. Her special interest is working with young children. Marg enjoys poetry, reading, scrapbooks, and camping. **Dec. 16.**

Fylvia Fowler Kline, a third-generation Adventist, completed her undergraduate and graduate degrees in Pune, India. She now lives in the United States and works as the administrative secretary for the General Conference Media Services; however, she considers motherhood her primary occupation. **July 22.**

Linda Klinger's 20-year career as a pastor's wife has confirmed the calling she felt at the tender age of 8—her passion for ministry intensifies with each passing year. She shares a story from her own experience. **Sept. 28.**

Betty Kossick is a freelance writer, wife, mother, and grandmother. She has been very active in her church as a church elder, Bible worker, teacher, church secretary, and receptionist. Her personal philosophy is "others." Betty and her husband live in Ohio. **Aug. 1, Nov. 30.**

Karen Kotoske is a dental hygienist and the director of the Amistad Foundation. She and her husband and two cats make their home in California. She enjoys reading, photography, gardening, and linking people up with other people or organizations for mission projects. **July 1.**

Andrea Kristensen, a single parent of a teenage son, is the editor of *Junior* and *Teen* Sabbath school lesson quarterlies and *Junior/Teen Program Helps*. Answering complex questions from her worldwide readers is her volunteer project. She lives in Maryland and enjoys biking, rafting, reading, writing, cooking, and attending concerts and living-history events. **Jan. 18, Mar. 7.**

Teresa Gay Hoover Krueger is an associate pastor for church life and counseling. She and Harry, her husband, are currently raising a 3-year-old son while she pursues an active schedule of pastoral counseling, especially with women, discipling ministry, and praise music. Teresa enjoys the outdoors, particularly hiking (she has hiked the Grand Canyon four times). **Feb. 6, Mar. 11, May 11, Aug. 11.**

Kay Kuzma writes from Tennessee, where she and her husband make their home. Kay is founder and president of Family Matters, and hosts a daily radio feature and weekly television program for families. She is a public speaker and author of numerous books, and the mother of three grown children. **Sept. 6.**

Ifeoma I. Kwesi is a recent graduate from the Theological Seminary at Andrews University in Berrien Springs, Michigan. While completing the requirements for the Master of Divinity degree, she served as associate pastor of the All-Nations Seventh-day Adventist Church. An avid reader, political activist, and sports enthusiast, Ifeoma lives in Columbus, Ohio, with her husband and will begin her doctoral studies in the area of ethics shortly. **Feb. 23.**

Doris Kennemer Langham and her husband live in California and have two adult children. She is a secretary to the senior chaplain at St. Helena Hospital and enjoys her grandchildren, gardening, walking, and helping people. **June 8.**

Eileen E. Lantry is from north Idaho. She is a librarian, teacher, homemaker, minister's wife, and Bible worker. She spent 14 years as a missionary in the Far East. Eileen has authored 13 books, and loves nature, gardening, hiking, and cross-country skiing. **Jan. 6, Mar. 24, Apr. 2, Sept. 27.**

Lillian Lawrence is retired from teaching church school and managing a supervisory home for adults. For 60 years she was church pianist and organist, and held most church offices. Many of her poems and several articles were published in hometown newspapers years ago, as well as by church magazines. She raised seven children, including Lorna Lawrence. **Aug. 7, Sept. 30.**

Lorna Lawrence, an internationally known choral conductor and concert soloist, is presently completing a Ph.D. program in crisis counseling. Her special interests include travel, writing, musical composition/performance, and counseling. Her reputation as a humorist (original songs and readings) has kept her in demand as a performer. Currently Lorna teaches elementary school in northern California. **Jan. 5, Mar. 3, Apr. 25, Nov. 19.**

Gina Lee, an accountant, is a published writer of more than 300 stories and has contributed to two books. She makes her home in California with two dogs and four cats and is actively involved in animal protection, environmental protection, vegetarianism, and collecting books. **Feb. 3, Apr. 5, June 4.**

Irma R. Lee is a freelance writer living in Ithaca, New York. She has an adult son who attended Oakwood College. Irma is working toward a degree in human services at a local college. **Feb. 8, Sept. 22.**

Kathie Lichtenwalter is the daughter of missionaries, and a minister's wife. She and her husband and four sons live in Berrien Springs, Michigan. She plays and teaches violin, and also enjoys writing. Her special interests are being a mother, supporting her husband in his ministry, and music. **Jan. 10.**

Cheryl Linn, wife, homemaker, and mother of two boys, ages 3 and 5, lives in Colorado and works in a health-care institution in the patient business office. Her interests include herb gardening, quilting, and mountain biking. **May 19.**

Joyce Hanscom Lorntz, Ph.D., is a nationally featured presenter, an associate pastor of the Fletcher, North Carolina, SDA Church, a national certified counselor, a licensed pastoral counselor, a licensed clinical professional counselor, and a member of the American Counseling Association. Dr. Lorntz is married to Pastor John Lorntz, and they have two daughters. **May 13.**

Aileen Ludington and her husband are both physicians and have a medical practice in Loma Linda, California. She has been a regular contributor to *Signs of the Times* for the past five years, and has had two books published. She is the mother of six children, grandmother of 11. She enjoys writing, reading, hiking, and walking. **Oct. 19.**

Evangeline Lundstrom and her family live in Dayton, Ohio. She is the wife of a physician practicing internal medicine, and has twin 16-year-old sons. She has a B.S. degree in nursing, and is currently working as a church secretary. Evangeline is a local church elder, and enjoys traveling and music. **Sept. 5, Oct. 10.**

Pat Madsen is a homemaker living in California who is also a published writer of poems, songs, and stories. She has served as Sabbath school superintendent and is involved in a Bible study group. Her hobbies include walking, music, poem writing, gardening, traveling, and the study of herbs. **Feb. 19, Apr. 24, May 28.**

Anita Marshall lives with her husband in England, where she is a writer and computer typesetter for Stanborough Press. She is actively involved in Vacation Bible School, has written a manual on VBS, has had many articles published in magazines, and has written two books for teenagers. **Mar. 21, June 19, Aug. 21.**

Selma Chaij Mastrapa is a psychologist who lives in Maryland. She is a church elder, teaches a Bible class at her church, and is chair of the Women of the Year Committee. She enjoys the study of different cultures, music, reading, walking, and traveling. **Aug. 29.**

Betsy Matthews is a treasurer in California, where she and her husband host a television program called *Lifestyle Magazine.* They have three grown sons and one granddaughter. Betsy enjoys music, sewing, flower gardening, reading, and traveling. **Mar. 22, Apr. 10.**

Jamisen Matthews is a transcriptionist for a nursing agency in New Haven, Connecticut. She is the mother of two teenage daughters, has a ministry for the deaf, and also assists in distributing food in the community. **Oct. 17.**

P. Deirdre Maxwell lives and works in California's Napa Valley. She has two grown children. Last year she served as adult superintendent at the Pacific Union College church. She enjoys her small flower garden, but prefers to read and go to concerts. Most of all, she likes to learn about new things, places, and people. **July 18.**

Wilma McClarty is an English and speech professor at Southern College of SDAs, a wife, and a mother of two. She is a public speaker and writer who has received many honors and awards, one of the most recent being the Sears-Roebuck Teaching Excellence and Campus Leadership Award for 1991. **Oct. 4, Oct. 5, Oct. 6.**

Frances McClure, wife, mother, homemaker, and secretary, lives with her minister husband in the Washington, D.C., area. She has three adult children and two grandchildren. Frances enjoys flower gardening, crewel stitchery, cooking, entertaining, organizing, traveling, the outdoors, and witnessing to neighbors. **Mar. 29, May 6.**

Norma McKellip is a junior accountant in the General Conference's Transportation and International Personnel Service (TRIPS). She lives in Laurel, Maryland, and is active in her local church as an elder, Bible teacher, and small group leader. She enjoys gardening, walking, reading, sewing, and people. **June 9.**

Gloria C. McLaren is the mother of five children (three are young adults; two are deceased). She is the chaplain for the Hospice of the Florida Suncoast in Largo, Florida. Her hobbies include writing, sewing, cooking, knitting, crocheting, and gardening. **Jan. 15.**

Marge McNeilus is a homemaker, mother of four children, and grandmother of four. Her husband owns McNeilus Auto and Truck Parts, and she works as his bookkeeper. Her hobbies include traveling, grandmothering, photography, crafts, writing, and music. **Dec. 9.**

Marilee McNeilus is a homemaker and mother of three adult children, and has five grandchildren. She and her husband live in Minnesota, where they own a manufacturing business and are active in church projects around the world. Marilee is a shell collector, scuba diver, gardener, and local church treasurer. **Aug. 4.**

Myrna Melling and her husband live in northern California, where she is administrator for Dr. Dean Ornish's Preventive Medicine Research Institute. The mother of three grown children, Myrna enjoys singing with the Napa Valley women's ensemble. Other hobbies include cooking and traveling—often to visit her four grandsons. **Sept. 26, Oct. 15.**

Darlynn Mello is from northern Maine. She is a writer, minister's wife, and mother of four. Darlynn is actively involved in recovery ministry and works with women survivors of sexual abuse. Quilting, music, and solitary meanderings rejuvenate her. **Aug. 25.**

Barbara Mittleider works as travel coordinator at the General Conference of Seventh-day Adventists. She has served with her husband in evangelism and administrative work in both the United States and Africa. Special interests include Sabbath school work, evangelism, and the development of young ministerial couples. **Mar. 10, July 26.**

Lois Moore is a public health nurse in Caldwell, Idaho. She is head elder in her church, and teaches a weekly adult Bible study class. She served as a missionary in Indonesia and in South Korea before her marriage. She has two stepchildren. **Feb. 2.**

Rowena Moore has been employed at the General Conference of Seventh-day Adventists since 1977 as an administrative secretary. In 1993 she spent July in Moscow, Russia, helping set up the secretarial procedures for the Euro-Asia Division office, and served as a recording secretary for the Annual Council meetings held in Bangalore, India, in October. She is a single mother, having adopted Elizabeth from India in 1981. She enjoys reading, needlepoint, and traveling. **May 5.**

Marie Munro writes from Sydney, Australia. She is a certified nurse and works with her husband in his medical practice. They have three adult children. She is an elder in her church, and enjoys her computer and preaching. **Apr. 19.**

Lillian Musgrave and her husband have for more than 30 years made their home in northern California, where they own their own business. They have three children and three grandchildren. Lillian enjoys reading, writing, music, church work, cooking, needlework, and family activities. **Dec. 30.**

Diane Musten is a secretary in the General Conference Ministerial Association. She serves in a local church as a "Stephen minister" (caregiver). She moved to Maryland with her husband and young daughter in 1974 when he was in publishing work. Having been raised in a nonreligious home and baptized at the age of 21, Diane carries a heavy burden in her heart for souls. Some of her favorite activities are connected with Bible study, reading, art, music, traveling, horticulture, and the great outdoors. **Apr. 6.**

Beatrice S. Neall is a professor of religion at Union College. She and her husband served as missionaries for 17 years in Southeast Asia. Her hobbies are gardening, growing African violets, and writing. **Feb. 25.**

Joan Minchin Neall was born in Australia, lived in England, and now makes her home in Dayton, Tennessee, where she is a registered nurse. She and her husband have four grown children. She is the women's ministries leader at her local church. She enjoys nature, sewing, journalism, and her grandchildren. **Jan. 31, Mar. 15, Apr. 7, May 18.**

Bienvisa Ladion-Nebres writes from Lubumbashi, Zaire, where she works as an office secretary in the Africa-Indian Ocean Division Auditing Service. She enjoys music, stamp collecting, teaching, and helping in her church. **Aug. 16.**

Joyce Neergaard lives in Cyprus and works with her husband in ADRA as assistant for project development and as Shepherdess coordinator in the Middle East Union. She is a nurse and enjoys working with her local church in community health promotion programs and junior-teen Sabbath school. Singing, reading, writing, snorkeling, and skiing are some of her leisure-time pleasures. **Jan. 4.**

Ora Newton, Alabama-born, now living in Yaounde, Cameroon, is the wife of Leonard G. Newton, president of the Central African Union Mission. She is the mother of five adult young people. Ora enjoyed teaching church school in the United States and now teaches English to Cameroonians. **Aug. 8.**

Karen Nicola is a wife and mother living in the foothills of northern California. She is a member of a local Toastmaster club, communication secretary for her church, and a published writer. Karen and her husband lost a 3-year-old son to leukemia, and she has since published a book on grief recovery. **Dec. 14.**

Sheree Parris Nudd, a vice president of a 243-bed hospital in Rockville, Maryland, is also an accomplished speaker and published author. She is the youngest alum to have established an endowed scholarship fund at her alma mater, a college in Keene, Texas. She and her husband have two daughters. **Jan. 1, Mar. 26.**

Katie Tonn-Oliver makes her home in California. She is a creative and commercial writer and a seminar presenter who has written 11 books and numerous articles. Katie is a recovering victim of child abuse who currently has four major writing projects on the subject. **Nov. 1, Nov. 27.**

Salome Omanya, a citizen of Kenya, is a Women in Development project manager for ADRA in Kenya. Previously she taught school for 18 years, was a social worker for 10 years, and a secretary for two years. Salome has eight children and five grandchildren, and is working on a master's degree in public health. **Dec. 13.**

Blanche Orser, previously administrative secretary with Adventist Health Systems' corporate offices (Glendale, California) and executive secretary for six years with the Ukiah Valley Medical Center, writes from Ukiah, California, where, after a four-year career change, she once again works at Ukiah Valley, as Physical Therapy Department secretary. She is the mother of three adult children and the sister of Celia Cruz, administrative secretary to Rose Otis. **Dec. 10.**

Norma Osborn is an educator/administrator's wife, mother of two children, and an associate pastor at Sligo church in Maryland. She was formerly an elementary teacher and enjoys reading, sewing, quilt making, and decorating. **May 31.**

Rose Otis is the director of the Women's Ministries Department of the General Conference, a department created at the 1990 General Conference Annual Council. Prior to her present election, Rose spent two years working with her husband representing the General Conference in the former Soviet Union, helping to organize the church into a division and negotiating with government officials. She and her husband have two grown children. **Jan. 11, Apr. 8, May 9, Dec. 22.**

Revel Papaioannou is English, born in India, and married to a Greek pastor. She writes from the biblical town of Berea, Greece, where she and her minister husband make their home. She has four adult sons and two grandchildren. She teaches English part-time, teaches a youth Bible class, gives Bible studies, preaches, and does some translating. Her hobbies include stamp and coin collecting and walking. **Dec. 8.**

Norma Jean Parchment and her minister/administrator husband make their home in Ontario, Canada. Norma is a pioneer for women's ministries in the Canadian Union Conference of Seventh-day Adventists. **Dec. 24.**

Rachel I. Patterson is an editorial assistant in the North American Division Church Ministries Department and the NAD coordinator of Shepherdess International. She and her minister husband have two grown children. Rachel has written numerous articles for Christian magazines and enjoys writing, reading, antiques, and traveling. **Aug. 26.**

Julia L. Pearce is a nursing instructor and a consultant in women's health services, and has written articles regarding women's health issues. She makes her home in California, and is the coordinator of women's ministries in her local church. She enjoys women's history, reading, sewing, and giving women's medical presentations. **Jan. 16, Feb. 24, Aug. 13.**

Lois Pecce, a happily married mom of three young adults, lives in Centerville, Ohio, with her college professor husband. She is a freelance writer, and cofounder and president of Dayton (Ohio) Christian Scribes, a writers' group. Lois is active in nursing home ministry, writing to prison inmates, and her local church. She enjoys gardening, sewing, reading, knitting, and snorkeling. **Oct. 28.**

Lori Peckham is the first woman editor of *Insight* at the Review and Herald Publishing Association. She and her husband live in Falling Waters, West Virginia. Lori enjoys traveling, snorkeling, and jet skiing. **Aug. 3.**

Christene Perkins, a registered nurse with a master's degree in nursing, is presently on sabbatical to help care for her 88-year-old mother. She has written articles on health-related topics and made contributions to books on pathophysiology. Chris is actively involved in her local church and enjoys people, reading, bird-watching, gardening, sewing, baking, woodworking, and travel. **May 29.**

Eunice Peverini is a homemaker and mother of three adult children and grandmother of two. She and her husband, the speaker/director of the *La Voz de la Esperanza* radio ministry, live in California. After working for 22 years for *La Voz* and the *Voice of Prophecy*, she currently assists with the work at the *VOP* gift shop. She enjoys interior decorating, flower arrangement and crafts, gardening, sewing, reading, and community work. **Jan. 12, Aug. 12.**

Julianne Pickle is a young stay-at-home mom. She has authored the popular little cookbook *100 Percent Vegetarian: Eating Naturally From Your Grocery Store*. Currently she is working on writing Christian Bible poetry books for young children. **Nov. 10.**

Birdie Poddar is from northeastern India. She and her minister husband live in Poona, India. Birdie has three adult children and two grandchildren, and worked as an elementary teacher, cashier, cashier accountant, and statistician before retiring in 1991. **Dec. 7.**

Edelweiss Ramal is a nursing instructor at Montemorelos University. She previously taught at Pacific Union College, and was the director of Kanye Hospital's School of Nursing in Botswana, Africa, where she and her minister husband and two children served as missionaries. Edelweiss is involved in youth ministries at her local church. **July 25.**

Sylvia Renz is a minister's wife, mother, and homemaker living in Darmstadt, Germany. She is a published writer of articles, radio programs for Adventist World Radio, and books. She loves reading and discussing issues with young people. **Jan. 28.**

Dawn L. Reynolds is a musician and educator in the state of Maryland. She plays the piano, organ, ukulele, and recorder. She is a published writer, seminar presenter, and an advocate for nurturing young children with music. Spare-time activities include needlework, writing, and reading. Dawn has been active in her church since age 9 as assistant church pianist, working with youth, and serving on the local conference committee. She is the mother of one lovely adult daughter. **Sept. 29.**

Julie Reynolds is a registered nurse who practiced maternity nursing for seven years. She is now a full-time homemaker and mother living in North Carolina. She is a pastor's wife and is active in the children's division at her local church. She loves reading, hiking in the mountains, singing, camping, and visiting the ocean. Julie plans to pursue her career as a hospital chaplain. **Dec. 11.**

Kay D. Rizzo is a freelance writer living in Gresham, Oregon. She is the author of 13 books. **July 30, Aug. 15, Sept. 11, Nov. 15, Dec. 29.**

Emilie Robertson, a minister's wife for 30 years, is a photojournalist. She has held numerous church offices, including serving as the communication secretary for different churches for more than 25 years. She is currently the activities director, head cook, and assistant manager of the retirement village at Eden Valley Institute in Colorado. Emilie enjoys writing, exploring, sewing, drawing, and painting. **Dec. 18.**

Mindy Rodenberg is a nursing student. She has lived in Indiana, Alberta, Virginia, Maryland, British Columbia, and Washington State. Her hobbies include writing, sewing, cross-stitch, swimming, waterskiing, and traveling. Her dorm room is like a magnet, drawing friends in for foot, back, neck, and shoulder massages, haircuts, or just a good chat. **Apr. 20, Nov. 5.**

Jeanne Rudatsikira and her husband are missionaries in Burundi, Africa. She is a pharmacist and the women's ministries director of the Burundi Association of Seventh-day Adventists, and loves spiritual music. **Jan. 14.**

Terrie E. Ruff is an instructor in the Behavioral Science Department at Southern College. She works with the youth Sabbath school class and as assistant superintendent in her local church. She also volunteers in the community with such agencies as Senior Neighbors and is proud to be a "Big Sister" with the Chattanooga Big Brother/Big Sister Association. She has a master's degree in social work. She loves to work with people and also enjoys singing for the Lord. **Feb. 4, Apr. 3.**

Leona Glidden Running is a retired professor (emeritus) of biblical languages at Andrews University, where she still teaches several ancient languages. Three books she has written have been published, and she enjoys swimming, reading, knitting, and crocheting. **Nov. 21.**

Deborah Sanders is a mother, housewife, and writer. She and her husband and two children make their home in Canada. She has written a collection of poetry and goes by the pen name "Sonny's Mommy," and enjoys doing community service work. **Apr. 12.**

Sheila Birkenstock Sanders, a speech therapist, is a transitional counselor for retarded adults in California. She is a widowed mother of two and stepmother of four children, Sabbath school superintendent, and teacher. She has contributed to the *Collegiate Quarterly* and enjoys photography, travel, reading, sewing, and singing. **Oct. 12, Oct. 13.**

Cheri Schroeder, whose father was an American Indian, came out of spiritualism and the occult. She is an apartment building manager and home schooling mother living in New Hampshire, teaches an adult Sabbath school class, and gives Bible studies. She enjoys painting, needlework, reading, hiking, and gardening. **Nov. 9.**

Susan Scoggins works for the Computer Department of the General Conference. She is a wife and mother and has spent more than 20 years supporting her husband in the church work in several U.S. conferences, Lebanon, and Rwanda. **Feb. 26, Mar. 31.**

Jean Sequeira, born in England, now lives and writes in the United States. She has worked as a Bible instructor, teacher, and office manager. She spent 18 years as a missionary in East Africa with her minister husband and two children. Her interests are calligraphy, flower gardening, photography, and writing. **June 26, July 14, Aug. 22.**

Roberta Sharley and her husband, Lawrence, are retired—both from the health field. Roberta was an R.N., Lawrence a sanitarian (health inspector). They have lived all their lives in the northwest U.S. Roberta is active in her church. **Sept. 15, Dec. 4.**

Penny Shell is a chaplain at Shady Grove Adventist Hospital in Maryland. She has been a hospital chaplain for 10 years and an English teacher for 14 years. She has learned a lot from her students and her patients. Penny enjoys writing, and many of her articles have been published in magazines. She also enjoys puttering around her home in Maryland. **July 5.**

Carrol Johnson Shewmake worked with her husband in the ministry for 43 years, and as a school librarian for 15 of those years. She is the mother of four adult children and grandmother of seven grandchildren, has written numerous articles and two published books and will soon have two more ready, and conducts seminars on prayer. Her hobbies are nature, writing, reading, speaking, dolls, sewing, and people. **Aug. 30.**

Karen Kinney Shockey is the administrative assistant to the vice president for finance at the Review and Herald Publishing Association in Hagerstown, Maryland. The publishing ministry is dear to her heart. The daughter of Robert Kinney, president of the Review and Herald, she grew up in the publishing house family and began her service to the church there as a student at age 16. **July 27.**

Iris Shull is an administrative assistant in the Marketing Department at the Review and Herald Publishing Association. Iris is married and has a son, 3-year-old Matthew. She is active in her local church, currently working in the cradle roll department. As a member of the Hager chapter of Professional Secretaries International, Iris earned the certified professional secretary rating in 1987. Her pastimes include music (singing or playing her flute), reading, travel, and embroidery. **June 23.**

Esther Simbayobewe is a pastor's wife in the Butare district of the Rwanda Union Mission. **Oct. 16.**

Alice Smith writes from her retirement home in Fletcher, North Carolina. For many years she was the representative at the General Conference level for the profession of nursing through the ASDAN office. Her hobbies include gardening, traveling, and staying in touch with family and friends. **July 17.**

Cherilyn J. Smith is a wife, mother, and administrative assistant to the academic vice president at Southern College of Seventh-day Adventists. She is a deaconess, active in both adult and children's Sabbath schools, and involved in a hurting parents' ministry. She enjoys baking, walking, reading, and cross-stitching. **Jan. 24.**

Janice R. Smith, the mother of four preschoolers, is an elementary teacher (not presently employed), homemaker, and recording artist, and plans to home-school her children. She is involved in ministry to families and is the kindergarten leader at her local church in Canada. She enjoys outdoor activities with her family, sewing, craft making, and music. **Nov. 6.**

Peggy Janelle Smith is an alumna of Southern College of Seventh-day Adventists and is now back teaching there in the Office Administration Department. She is a single mother with two children. She is also very active in family life ministries at the Collegedale church. Her hobbies are reading, music, and needlework. **July 9.**

Marie Spangler, founder of Shepherdess International (a support system for ministers' wives on the General Conference level), is a retired teacher, mother of two grown children, and a minister's wife. She is a published writer whose special interests include music, memory books, people, pastors' wives, and early childhood development. **Oct. 11, Nov. 14.**

Glenice Linthwaite Steck writes from northern California, where she lives with her husband and two children. She works as an administrative secretary at St. Helena Hospital, and is actively involved with the children's department at her church. Her hobbies include walking, and collecting Dickens' Village lighted miniatures. **Feb. 10.**

Ardis Dick Stenbakken was an active Army chaplain's wife for 23 years; however, her husband retired to serve at the General Conference. She is most proud of their adult son and daughter. Ardis is concerned about women's issues and enjoys church work, crafts, reading, travel, and public speaking. **Jan. 23, Mar. 27, Apr. 4, May 10.**

Beulah Fern Stevens writes from Portland, Oregon, where she is the director of pastoral care at Portland Adventist Medical Center. She is a chaplain and nurse and has written and taught internationally in the specialty of spiritual care in nursing. **July 2, July 29.**

Ursula Strasdowsky, a native of Germany, and her husband have been in mission service in Africa and the Far East for 16 years, and now live in Switzerland. She presents seminars on marriage and the family and has written articles and radio scripts in German. They have three married daughters. **Aug. 10.**

June Strong, homemaker, author, and speaker, counts being elected her church's first woman elder as one of the greatest challenges and highest honors of her career. She has written six books and for 18 years has had columns in religious magazines. June enjoys gardening, people watching, tole painting, and reading. **June 1, July 4.**

Laura Lee Swaney is presently studying to be a certified alcoholism counselor and plans to counsel adult survivors of incest. Her goal is for a ministry in helping battered women and people with drug addictions find freedom in Jesus. She and her family reside near the Ithaca, New York, area. She and her husband are both new writers for Christ. **Dec. 27.**

Loraine Sweetland is director of the library at the General Conference. She writes book reviews for *Library Journal*, is a director and editor of the newsletter of her local Rotary Club in Laurel, Maryland, and is vice president of the board of Oasis, a mental health group. She taught church school for 14 years and has served as personal ministries director for her church, as well as holding many other church offices. She enjoys reading, antiques, gardening, and computer work. **Oct. 26.**

Arlene Taylor, an internationally known speaker, is president and founder of Realizations, as well as director of Infection Control/Risk Management at St. Helena Hospital. Dr. Taylor is a published author, a church organist, and a talk show host on radio. She and her husband make their home in the Napa Valley of northern California. **Jan. 17, Jan. 25, Mar. 2, Nov. 21, Nov. 24.**

Audre B. Tayor is an administrative assistant for ADRA International and serves as a local church elder. Her hobbies are writing and choral conducting. She is a published writer, and NBC in Washington, D.C., awarded her an Angel Award in national competition for one of her choral performances. She is also a practicing psychotherapist in the Washington metropolitan area. **July 28.**

Monica Stocker Taylor is a homemaker. She and her husband make their home in Wayland, Iowa. She is the personal ministries director and superintendent in her local church, and enjoys cooking, baking, sewing, writing, reading, animals, and meeting people. **Oct. 31.**

Sylvia Taylor, a nurse, lives in active retirement with her husband in Elanora, Australia. She and her husband were both previously widowed, and she is the mother of two grown children and grandmother of four. She is a published writer and enjoys reading, cooking, gardening, and traveling. **Nov. 29.**

Edna Thomas, a missionary, is a native of Memphis, Tennessee. She is currently living and teaching primary school in Freetown, Sierra Leone, West Africa. **Feb. 11.**

Stella Thomas is a homemaker and mother of two children, a daughter and a son. She is from India, but was born in an Adventist home. She works as an administrative secretary in the Global Mission office at the General Conference of Seventh-day Adventists. **Apr. 17.**

Nell B. Thompson lives in Santa Rosa, California, where she is retired from nursing. A widow (her dentist husband died in 1986), she is committed to personal and spiritual growth. Her hobbies have included "anything connected to athletics." **May 7.**

Peggy Tompkins is a church administrator's wife, mother of two grown children, grandmother of four little boys, and a homemaker living in Nebraska. For the past eight years she has compiled the magazine *The Heart of the Home* for the encouragement or affirmation of mothers who choose to work at home. She enjoys working on many different types of crafts. **Nov. 20.**

Margaret Turner, a retired hospital chaplain and nurse, is living in Dayton, Ohio, with her husband. She is the mother of three adult children and is a local church elder. She enjoys gardening, reading, bird-watching, and genealogy. **Nov. 13.**

Janis Vance is president and founder of Take Heart retreats, a ministry devoted to spiritual healing for women who have been sexually abused in childhood. She is a registered nurse and a licensed rehabilitation counselor with a master's degree in education. She teaches an adult Bible class at her local church. Janis and her husband live in California and are the parents of three grown children. **Oct. 27.**

Junell Vance is the Atlantic Union Conference women's ministries director. She is married and has two children and 10 grandchildren. Junell is a registered nurse, writer, musician, vocalist, and speaker. Besides her interest in her family and women's ministries, she is also interested in prison ministries. **May 8, Oct. 7.**

Corrine Vanderwerff, a missionary and freelance writer, manages REACH child sponsorship projects in Zaire, where her husband is the ADRA director. She has two new book releases, one being the 1994 junior devotional book. **Feb. 21.**

Nancy Van Pelt, a family life educator, certified home economist, author, and internationally known speaker, has written 17 books on family life. Her newest release is a prayer notebook for an organized prayer life. She and her husband make their home in California and are the parents of three grown children. Her hobby is quilting. **Jan. 8, Feb. 12, Feb. 28, Mar. 18, July 7.**

Nancy Cachero Vasquez is an administrative secretary in the North American Division office, wife of the vice president of the North American Division, and mother of three young adult children. Her special interests are reading, writing, crafts, shopping, and baking. **May 21, July 19.**

Sabine Vatel, R.N., is an English major at Southern College. She calls Altamonte Springs, Florida, home. **June 30.**

Nancy Vyhmeister is a professor of mission at the Seventh-day Adventist Theological Seminary at Andrews University in Michigan. She has written various articles for religious publications and textbooks. Nancy enjoys homemaking, writing, friendships, and her grandson. **Dec. 6.**

Norann Cubberly Waller lives in Connecticut with her husband and two cats. She is a communication/public relations consultant and the assistant communication director for her local conference. Norann loves people and especially enjoys caring for children and the elderly. Her other special interests include media outreach, singing, songwriting, swimming, reading, nature, traveling, and gardening. **July 15, Dec. 12.**

Elizabeth Watson, mother of three young people, is an associate professor of social work and the director of a single-parent program at Andrews University. She is a local elder in her church, enjoys child evangelism, and tells and writes children's stories. She is a frequent contributor to the *Message* Junior section of *Message,* and is one of the authors of a new members' book, *Stepping Stones.* **Apr. 27, May 2, June 11.**

Dorothy Eaton Watts, a freelance writer and speaker, is a conference president's wife in Canada. She was a missionary for 16 years, founded an orphanage, taught elementary school, held various other positions in the denomination through the years, and has written eight books and numerous articles in religious publications. Her hobbies include bird-watching, gardening, and hiking. **Jan. 3, Apr. 1, July 23.**

Kit Watts is an assistant editor of the *Adventist Review.* She has been a pastor, teacher, and librarian. Kit lives in Silver Spring, Maryland, and her interests are traveling and photography. **Feb. 14.**

Veryl Dawn Were writes from South Australia, where she is a homemaker. She is a nurse by profession, served as a missionary for eight years, is the mother of one grown son, and has written articles for various religious publications. Currently she is involved in community service work with her husband and enjoys gardening, bird-watching, stamp collecting, and knitting. **July 31.**

Penny Estes Wheeler, acquisitions editor for the Review and Herald Publishing Association, works behind the scenes on the development of book manuscripts. She and her husband have four (almost) adult children who have scattered themselves hither and yon around the world. She enjoys the organized confusion of an English garden and spends her spare time trying to create the illusion around her home. **June 28.**

Carlene Will teaches seminars on home organization and personal devotions. She is the women's ministries leader for her local church. She is the mother of four boys, and works in her opthalmologist husband's medical office in Issaquah, Washington. **Nov. 12.**

Debby Gray Wilmot, a registered nurse, homemaker, piano teacher, pastor's wife, and mother of two, lives in California. She is the church choir director, an accomplished accompanist, and a coordinator for the Northern California Conference Shepherdess organization. Debby enjoys acrylic painting, flower gardening, and composing music for voice, keyboard, and guitar. **Feb. 20.**

Halcyon Wilson is the pastor for family life and counseling at La Sierra University church, Riverside, California. She is an author and speaker, and enjoys reading and writing. She and her husband bask in the friendship of their six children and 11 grandchildren. **Jan. 26.**

Ronna Witzel and her husband live in northern California and have three grown children. She began a women's ministries program in her church more than eight years ago and is still actively involved in it. Her interests include wildflowers, gardening, sewing, and grandparenting. **May 30, Sept. 23.**

Marcedene V. Wood is a retired secretary, copy editor, and Bible instructor. She worked in Kansas, Hawaii, the western United States, and the Washington, D.C., area. At the present time she is leader in the children's department for ages 7-10 in her church in Kansas. Her hobby is working with these young children. **Oct. 9.**

Wilma Zalabak is a budding listener while she completes her Master of Divinity degree, after which she will return to the Georgia-Cumberland Conference as a Bible instructor/evangelist with church planting duties. **Oct. 22.**

A Continuing Christmas

Love the Lord your God with all your heart and with all your soul and with all your mind. Matt. 22:37, NIV.

My 4-year-old looked up at me and asked, "Mommy, is it still gonna be Christmas?"

Knowing what she meant, I replied, "Well, honey, Christmas is over, and today is the first day of the new year."

"But I want it to be Christmas!" Lauren persisted.

"You like Christmastime, don't you?" I asked gently.

After a thoughtful moment she countered, "But it *is* gonna be Christmas, because I said, 'Dear Jesus, please help it to be Christmas *all* the time.'" She said it with an air of finality and a tone meant to convince herself as well as me.

I thought of the words I had spoken that very morning to my husband of 10 years: "I wish Christmas would last longer." What I meant was that by the time we got the cards mailed, the shopping finished, the house decorated, the packages wrapped, the food cooked, the baking done, and the house cleaned up all over again, I was as worn out as the proverbial "partridge in a pear tree."

I wanted Christmas to last longer so I could sit by the fire and rest up a bit, so I could relish the tastes (oh, the calories) and the smells (especially cinnamon) of the season. I wanted more time at Christmas to do some serious and thoughtful well-wishing. I agreed with Lauren. Christmas was definitely over too quickly.

Why, I hadn't even had time to roast the fresh chestnuts that my husband's parents had lovingly gathered. I thought wistfully of the Chinese chestnut tree in their yard in upstate New York. Just steps away is their apricot tree, which tries to obliterate the entryway to the house each summer by literally dropping its fruit on the porch steps.

I also wanted more time to contemplate the true meaning of Christmas, even if that phrase has itself become a cliché. Do we really remember and rejoice over the birth of a baby? Is there a way to celebrate a continuous Christmas?

A little girl's precious question interrupted my reverie.

"Mommy, do you know what I'm going to give Jesus for His birthday?"

"What?"

She patted herself at her heart. I hugged her.

"Me, too, honey. Me, too." Yes, dear Jesus, help us to make it Christmas all the time.   SHEREE PARRIS NUDD

On the Nature of Inspiration

The breath of the Almighty . . . makes for understanding.
Job 32:8, NRSV.

I turned on the car radio today, and the strains of "Morning Has Broken" brought me back to my college days. I was suddenly sitting in chapel, listening to Dr. Sauls's talk of gardens and freshness and beginning anew. I was inspired again, sitting there in my car, and when the song ended I felt refreshed, the traffic around me fading in importance to my inner renewal.

The difference between being in college, I decided, walking into my office, and being enmeshed in the world of work, home, and family is quite basic. In college our inspiration is delivered to us all in one place, all in one time. We sit in early-morning classes and read of prophets, talk of poets. We gather in libraries and calculate common problems. In the evening we gather up astronomy books and gaze at stars.

And then we graduate.

Our inspiration does not end then, but becomes more diffused, less concentrated in one place. There suddenly exists no campus, no instant forum for ideas, no professor doling out large realities.

And our inspiration, when it comes, must be recognized, seized for what it is, savored and stretched, else we lose it. Our work, then, is to look beyond the cliché of our everyday existence for the new thought, the new idea.

In some places, and at some times, it is easier than others. As a nursery school teacher, I found inspiration easier to grasp in sand and water, clay and paint, than in the finance meetings, board committees, and paperwork that I face as an administrator. Removed from the raw elements of the earth, separated from the process by the branches of an "internal structural tree," I stretch backward for a glimpse that will urge me forward.

And perhaps that is the key in seeking inspiration. The stretching backward. Back to lively lectures and star-splashed evenings. Back to childhood romps on beaches and endless questions. Back to ancient scrolls and dusty prophets. Back to dust in a garden.

Anne Morrow Lindbergh, in her book *Gift From the Sea*, talks about the "art of shedding," the ability to find "how little one can get along with, not how much." Describing the cottage from which she writes, she says: "I am content. I sit down at my desk, a bare kitchen table with a blotter, a bottle of ink, a sand dollar to weight down one corner, a clam shell for a pen-tray, the broken tip of a conch, pink-tinged, to finger, and a row of shells to set my thoughts spinning" (p. 34).

Inspiration comes, it seems, from the single-syllabled elements that call out to us beneath the complex levels with which we layer our lives. Shells. Sand. Sun. Sky. Break of morn. Cry of bird.

For the inspired ideas are not the complicated but the simple. In the midst of an information explosion and the entangled web of intricately detailed lives, we seek not the solution of more complexity but that of the single metaphor. We seek, in essence, to lose our lives so that we might gain them. We seek the strains of "Morning Has Broken" in the midst of the commute to make sense of the journey and of no consequence the blaring horns and hazards along the way. — SANDRA DORAN

JANUARY 3

No Use Pretending

Be sure your sin will find you out. Num. 32:23.

Our family was enjoying a weekend holiday in Ootacamund, a resort area in the Nilgiri Hills of southern India. On Sunday morning we planned to eat masala dosai at a restaurant. We were about to leave our pet monkey, Bosco, in the hotel room when 12-year-old Stephen noticed a broken windowpane through which Bosco could escape. He would have to go with us.

However, at the hotel entrance a sign said "No pets allowed."

"Lock Bosco in the car," my husband ordered.

"He'll get out!" 8-year-old David protested. "He knows how to roll down the windows." A leash wasn't the answer either, for Bosco knew how to untie knots and undo hooks.

"Mom, you'll have to baby-sit Bosco while we eat," 11-year-old Esther suggested. "We'll bring something back for you."

"Hey! That's no fair!" I complained. "I know what we can do. I'll hide him inside my sweater."

I buttoned the bulky knit red sweater all the way down the front and stuffed Bosco inside. Crossing both arms over my middle, I said triumphantly, "Now, there! Nobody will know we have a pet!"

Bosco began to squirm.

"Sssh! Bosco!" I warned. "Be a good monkey!"

Bosco did his best.

"OK, we're ready!" I whispered. "Let's go! Now walk in as though everything is normal."

Ron walked in first, followed by our three children. The only vacant table was on the far side of the room. Bosco smelled food and began clawing for an opening. I spread my hands and pressed him tighter against my stomach.

Suddenly all talking in the restaurant stopped. Everybody was staring at me! I looked down. There hung two feet of monkey tail right down the center of my skirt!

Just then Bosco popped a button and stuck his head out to see what was happening. Everyone burst out laughing! It was no use pretending any longer. I brought him out for all to see.

A waiter headed my way, and my embarrassed family tried to act as if they had never seen me before. Fortunately the gracious management let Bosco stay with us. Afterward I wondered why I had tried so hard to pretend he wasn't there.

Every once in a while I'm tempted to button up my sweater to hide my mistakes inside, hoping people will not discover what kind of person I really am. I think that if I can just cover my failings no one will know that I'm not really the super-perfect Christian I pretend to be. But sooner or later the tail of my sin slips out for everyone to see.

"Lord, help me today to stop pretending. Make me open and transparent, with nothing to hide."   DOROTHY EATON WATTS

JANUARY 4

New Year, New Heart

A new heart will I give you, and a new spirit will I put within you: and I will take away the stony heart out of your flesh, and I will give you an heart of flesh. Eze. 36:26.

We all make resolutions. Some are formulated on paper; some are intentions firmly set in our minds. Usually these promises for change fall into the self-improvement category. However, as worthy as these intentions to improve ourselves are, they do not get to the heart of our spiritual life. Do we give as much attention to resolutions with eternal consequences?

Consistent study of God's Word, a deeper prayer life, and motivation and sensitivity in sharing our faith are resolutions that strengthen our relationship to God. Although most of us aspire to improve in these areas, we find excuses to procrastinate until a more "convenient" time.

Our human natures certainly do get in the way of our resolves, but what do we do if we fail? Give up? Stop making resolutions? Wait for another new year so we can start over again? No. The problem of broken resolutions is not solved by a new year rolling around. The solution lies in receiving a new heart.

I have heard it said that to have a new heart is to have a new mind, new purposes, and new motives. As much as we may desire to have such a change in our lives, we cannot generate a new heart in ourselves. The transformation comes through God's power alone, but we must choose to serve Him. Following are some suggestions for maintaining this new heart: (1) request His working in your heart to change the stone to flesh; (2) daily, hourly, give yourself to God's control; (3) when you fail because of your human frailty, acknowledge your sin. Then ask for forgiveness and continue on.

In this new year, let God make your heart new again every day.

JOYCE NEERGAARD

JANUARY 5

Gifts With a Personal Touch

There are different kinds of gifts, but the same Spirit. There are different kinds of service, but the same Lord. There are different kinds of working, but the same God works all of them. 1 Cor. 12:4, NIV.

Any memories the little girl had of her mother would have to last her a lifetime. For when her parents divorced, her father, whom she lived with, prevented her from contacting her mother. Unfortunately, the mother died before the child was old enough to make contact on her own.

I had known this mother when we were both children. Now, suddenly, here I was talking to her grown daughter, trying to answer the many questions that had burned within her for years. She begged me to tell her anything that I could recall. What did she look like? What had she been like? Was she this or that?

We talked together for some time—I, trying to recall as much as I could; she, trying to piece together unsettled memories and fragments of stories. Just as I was running out of memories to recount, she asked me a startling question. "Was she someone you would have selected for your friend?"

Wincing inwardly, I had to admit that I wouldn't have. While we had spent considerable time together in our rural community, we really had no interests in common. Not wanting this response to be a total letdown, I began to share several things that I had learned from her mother. The more we talked, the more it became apparent that her mother was a valuable part of my life.

Reflecting upon our conversation, I realized that each person who enters our life is not of necessity a friend—but each person is of value as one of God's unique creations and has something to offer that can benefit us.

Some people touch our lives for only a few moments. We need to challenge ourselves to find the uniqueness in them. This realization has caused me to look at others differently, to observe with care, to listen with an ear tuned toward growth, to find the gift from God through each one.

With intent, we can learn to admire individuality, look for a special gift, thank God for even chance encounters, and cherish the insights we receive. Otherwise we might miss a gift that God is sending our way. In yet another facet of life we can say with King David, "The Lord be exalted!" (Ps. 40:16, NIV).   LORNA LAWRENCE

JANUARY 6

This Is the Day!

This is the day which the Lord has made; we will rejoice and be glad in it. Ps. 118:24, NKJV.

Our home in north Idaho is built on the edge of a bluff that drops steeply 500 feet to the winding Kootenai River. Across the valley, against a backdrop of two mountain ranges, spreads the fascinating drama of sunrises and sunsets, changing weather moods, and eagles soaring on the air currents. Coyotes howling at night send tingles down our spines. We spy through our telescope on nesting Canadian geese at the river's edge or deer meandering through the meadow. Closer, yellow Union Pacific locomotives emerge from a tunnel 250 feet below on a branch line to Canada. God has given us a magnificent backyard!

Maybe you're like me. God's gift of beauty is not just for looking. I must touch it, smell it, hear it, hike on it. So I approached my husband: "Let's make a trail to the railroad tracks."

"You want to dig through those rocks and bushes?" he objected. "The abrupt incline demands many switchbacks."

"Please," I pleaded. "It will be so much fun in the years to come."

Soon he joined me in laying out the trail by pounding stakes on our precipitous five acres. We worked an hour each day with shovel and hoe for about a month. Now almost every morning I talk to my heavenly Father as I hike that trail.

When it's snowing I need ski poles to keep from slipping. I praise God for the sunrise, tell Him how much I like spring's wildflowers and the fragrant bushes in bloom. Sometimes I thank Him for the dark clouds that cover the mountains or the fog that hides everything. I imagine that He stops with me to admire each new wildflower, from the yellow buttercups and pink prairie stars of early March to the purple asters of October. I thank Him for the towhee's trill, the chickadee's call, and the lovely bluebirds. Sometimes I'm so absorbed in life's problems that I miss the beauty. Then I just tell Him how I feel and ask Him to use one of His thousands of ways to solve my problems.

These morning walks with God have become a must in my life. Even when I'm far from home I find a place to walk so I can talk with God.

You too can enjoy these exciting times with God. You can choose to take 365 hikes a year with the Father who loves you. He's ready to share His secrets. He always has time to listen. Tell Him your plans, your joys, or what's bothering you. Wherever you live, enjoy a daily hike with your Father. — EILEEN E. LANTRY

Back on Track

It is of the Lord's mercies that we are not consumed, because his compassions fail not. They are new every morning: great is thy faithfulness. Lam. 3:22, 23.

Did you ever wake up and find that even before you opened your eyes your mind was flooded with a million and one things you needed to do that day? Did you become discouraged at the thought that there was no possible way you could get them done, but that you had to try? Did you feel tired even before you got started? If you answered yes to any of these questions, join the club. I often feel that I am the founder, president, and promoter of that club! We need to get back on track.

One cold January morning I awoke at 5:20. I tried to go back to sleep, but I was unable to. Within minutes I had managed to write an endless mental list of chores and errands that needed to be done. Some were more important than others; nevertheless, I thought each was a top priority. I was anxious not only about the day, but about an upcoming singles retreat I had been coordinating. I was also facing a major operation within a few weeks and wanted to do many things in preparation for it and for the weeks of recovery thereafter. Needless to say, I was overwhelmed and discouraged. Mingled with those worries was the reminder that nothing would get done without the Lord to help me. Resisting the temptation to skip my worship (after all, I needed all the time I could get), I turned to the Lord in desperation. I realized how incapable I was without His power and direction. I prayed and pleaded to be delivered from the pressure. I wish I had thought of Matthew 6:34, which would have reminded me to "take therefore no thought for the morrow: for the morrow shall take thought for the things of itself. Sufficient unto the day is the evil thereof."

As I began my worship, I opened my Bible with the intention of going over some verses that my prayer partner and I had agreed to look at during the week. That's when I came across the text for today, Lamentations 3:22, 23. What a wonderful promise and reminder! As I read it, I was filled with great joy. My eyes swelled with tears in appreciation. Not only had the Lord known the very thing I needed, but the burden was lifted. I thanked the Lord with words of praise and tears of joy. I encourage you to look into God's Word for the water of life, for the wonderful words of life. It is a fountain for our comfort, knowledge, strength, and assurance. His great and precious promises will put us back on track.

CARMEN O. GONZALEZ

New Life for Your Prayer Life

Do not be anxious about anything, but in everything, by prayer and petition, with thanksgiving, present your requests to God. Phil. 4:6, NIV.

Do you ever feel like your prayer life is dull, boring, or your prayers never go higher than the ceiling? You can bring new life to your prayer life through a prayer notebook.

It is often overwhelming and confusing to pray for every need every day of the week. Prayer can often lose its effectiveness and become little more than vain repetitions. It can even produce a discouraged spirit in the pray-er. To simplify prayer and yet adequately cover all prayer requests without getting discouraged, I teach women in my Personal Devotions seminar to organize prayer requests around a plan.

Each day of the week a different topic is prayed for. For example, on Monday pray for personal matters—concerns about yourself as a wife, mother, and homemaker, and your career and spiritual growth; on Tuesday pray for your husband or significant other; Wednesday, family—children, grandchildren, and parents; Thursday, prayer requests from friends, work associates, and church and women's ministry; Friday, pray for world church, missionaries, and literature evangelists as well as for heart and home readiness for Sabbath; on Sabbath pray for your pastor and local church endeavors; and on Sunday pray for our country and government. These prayer topics should be personalized to fit your individual needs and lifestyle.

Assigning topics to days of the week divides the responsibility into manageable portions. For example, on Wednesday I pray for every family member by name regarding their marriages, spouse, career, health, and their personal, spiritual, and financial needs. I pray for each grandchild by name—about character development, behavior, friends, their teachers, grades, and spiritual development. Notice, this plan allows me to become very specific as I intercede with God on behalf of my loved ones. If I were to pray for every family member every day, I would likely rattle off their names and concerns in a rapid, rote manner.

If you will get in the habit of jotting down your prayer requests in a prayer notebook, it will keep you on track. I'm so convinced that a prayer notebook enriches prayer life that I wrote one. It's called "My Prayer Notebook." Now you will have a place to jot prayer requests as well as answers to prayer. I find it is not necessary to write out my prayers word-for-word. All that I need are a few words to jog my memory. When the prayer is answered, write the answer in a different color. Answers will then stand out as a vivid and visual testimony that God is answering your prayers and actively working in your life day by day.

Keep your wants, your joys, your sorrows, your cares, and your fears before God. You cannot burden Him or tire Him. He who numbers the hairs on your head is not indifferent to your prayers. His heart of love is touched by your problems. Nothing is too great for Him to bear. Nothing that concerns your peace is too small for Him to hear and no problem is too difficult for Him to unravel (see *Steps to Christ*, p. 100).

Why not practice prayer in this manner this week and see what God can do?   NANCY VAN PELT

Transformation

You, O Lord, keep my lamp burning; my God turns my darkness into light. Ps. 18:28, NIV.

His coveted box had finally arrived. It protected the material for a water lily Tiffany-style lampshade. Uroboros, the name of the glass that would fashion this shade, was supposed to be some of the most exquisite glass ever crafted. Surely, with such an exotic name, it would ripple with color. But when my husband opened the box, I found it difficult to mask my disappointment. The blues and greens for the water were muddy in tone and rough in texture. The only glass I could muster enthusiasm for were the pinks that would compose the water lilies. Because it was his hobby, I bit my tongue to prevent negative words from escaping my lips. But how could I remain silent when it came time to put the finished product where he wanted it—in the family room right next to where I usually sit? I decided, however, to worry about that dilemma later, for he predicted it would take six months to complete in his spare time.

During the next two months I was away from home. But I received weekly reports that always included an update on the shade. "Since you're not here, I'm really making great progress," one report went. Did that mean that he missed me, or that my usual presence hindered his creativity? I chose to believe the former. But my real concern was that he would finish sooner than he thought, and I would have to decide sooner than I thought what I would say about the shade's final resting place.

I am home now. And the last progress report I received solved my dilemma. It was Friday evening when I noticed an unusual glow in the dining room. As I entered the room, I blinked in disbelief. There on the table sat a lamp base, lighted and crowned with the Tiffany shade. The light had transformed the murky blues and greens into hues that shimmered like water. The lilies floated serenely (and somewhat smugly). After the shade is cleaned and polished it will glisten even more. And we will place it *across* from where I usually sit in the family room so I can look at it often.

What a difference light made in the presentation of the glass. I now know that the thickness and folds of Uroboros glass are designed specifically to catch, hold, and reflect the light. Just as we are designed to reflect Christ in our lives. Without Him our lives are like the dark, lifeless glass as it first came from the box. Without Him our lives are muddy and rough. But when we invite Him to live in our hearts, His truth will transform us. His love will shine forth. And we will reflect the rainbow hues of mercy that surround His throne.   LYNDELLE CHIOMENTI

Tassel Fashion

Make tassels on the corners of your garments, with a blue cord on each tassel. You will have these . . . to look at and so you will remember all the commands of the Lord, that you may obey them and not prostitute yourselves by going after the lusts of your own hearts and eyes. Then you will remember to obey all my commands and will be consecrated to your God. Num. 15:38-40, NIV.

This morning I stood inside the clutter of closet paraphernalia and fingered through the short row of empty sleeves that make up my wardrobe. Nothing I own has tassels on blue cord. But then, I'm not an Israelite.

Considering how fickle, how easily distracted they were, tassels were a good idea for them. A quick glance and the whole world knew where you came from, whom you belonged to, whom you claimed to be following, how you should be living, where you were planning on going. Tassels were the designer label for the wilderness generation, a kind of trademark claim. No one even needed to say a word.

That's because tassels were meant to be seen. Hanging, dangling. On the outside, not the inside. Noticeable. Concrete. Either you wore them or you didn't. Either you were an Israelite or you weren't. A tassel on blue cord verified all the difference. If it was a profession, it was also a relentless reminder.

I wonder if I'd feel comfortable wearing tassels. Would I wear my identity proudly? everywhere? Would I really need the reminder that I'm not like the rest of the world? Would I mind looking different? Would I be willing to dress for God's name, or am I so used to dressing for my own? And what about the instant assumptions, the high expectations that come with any trademark? Anonymity has its comfort, you know. And license. Just ask a prostitute.

Maybe that's the point of tassels. My commitment to God. How I look is an unmistakable means of registering my relationship with Him. It's an instant picture worth a thousand words. If I leave confusion in anyone's mind as to whom I belong to, I'm flirting with my own unfaithfulness.

That's because the way I dress is not just a witness to the world. It's a protection to my soul. God understands fashion; what a woman looks like has a powerful impact on her identity. And He never, never wants me to forget that I'm the slave girl He brought out of the wilderness of my own making and the daughter He's taking up to the Promised Land.

I haven't decided what to wear this morning. Yet. I need to find something that carries the trademark of the One who created tassels on blue cord. Because I want the unmistakable evidence of His touch on everything I wear.

Of course I know that the way I look will never save me. But it does label my life with the Designer who wants to.

KATHIE LICHTENWALTER

JANUARY 11

One Hundred Years From Now!

So we fix our eyes not on what is seen, but on what is unseen. For what is seen is temporary, but what is unseen is eternal. 2 Cor. 4:18, NIV.

Recently, when my husband and I moved into our new home, we went through the house room by room hanging window shades, arranging furniture, and unpacking what seemed like an endless trail of boxes. We promised each other that before we'd move again we'd have a gigantic yard sale!

We managed to settle the house quite nicely before Christmas arrived, and none of our holiday guests were aware of the stack of boxes hidden away in the basement. We planned to tackle them during our vacation between Christmas and New Year's. One day we got up our courage and began to sort through the boxes. I noticed that not a few of them had remained sealed through more than one move. The names of rooms had been written with a marker on the tops of the boxes, instructing the movers where the box was to be put. In previous moves a box might have been marked "family room." But now the word "basement" was written like a judgment decree across that same box. That one word said it all! The once-precious contents had been relegated to the basement—the last stop before the garage sale or, worse yet, a trip to the dumpster.

It wasn't long until a pile destined for the neighborhood

dumpster began to mount. But before tossing out a cloth tote from the 1990 General Conference session, I ran my hand around inside its pockets. From an outside pocket I pulled a manila folder with the word "rush" written on its cover in bold red letters. *Horrors!* I thought, almost afraid to open the folder to see what crisis I had neglected! Inside I found three letters that had seemed important at the time. But now, standing in the middle of the basement, I realized that the world had kept turning even though the contents of this folder had been out of sight and out of mind for more than two years. Ceremoniously I dropped the folder in the trash pile.

That simple incident prompted me to do a little mental exam as I folded the empty boxes and stacked them under the stairwell. "Rose, why do you usually begin your days by making lists for yourself that are next to impossible to complete? Why do you set yourself up for unwanted stress by creating too many 'rush' folders?"

While I was growing up, my mother would occasionally help me put things in perspective by saying, "Honey, a hundred years from now this isn't going to make a bit of difference!"

"Lord, in this brand-new year, help me to focus on the things that will make a difference a hundred years from now."   ROSE OTIS

JANUARY 12

The Privilege of Service

Serve one another in love. Gal. 5:13, NIV.

Tablecloth—a piece of cloth of any color used to cover a table to protect it. It can be made of cotton, linen, polyester, or lace. It can be intricately embroidered, or appliqued, or perhaps come in a cheerful print. It can be very expensive, or everyday and ordinary. A tablecloth can be totally clean, or have tiny stains on it from earlier use. It can be carefully starched and ironed, or quite wrinkled. It may be new, or very worn.

I have seen tablecloths used in many ways: as Mary's cloak in a Nativity play; as a skirt for a Christmas tree—meant to look like snow; or placed temporarily in a window to serve as a curtain. It may be used to cover a filo pastry to keep it from drying out, or it may be laid out on a lawn for a picnic. Sometimes it may be covering a pile of unfolded laundry, or it may become a child's imaginary dragon, mountain, or tent to camp in.

Tablecloths seem to have a "humble and loving heart," allowing themselves to be used in whatever way their owners wish: folded in half, hung up, put on the floor, or elegantly laid out on a table set with the best china and silverware.

I thought of all this as I was putting our new dark-green tablecloth on our table for our family's Christmas dinner. Then I thought, *What if we were as humble and as willing to be used by the Lord as a tablecloth is to be used by its owners? Surely then we would all be ready to sit together at the great banquet table of the Lamb, in the kingdom of heaven.*

May our lives be like a tablecloth: embroidered lovingly by the Holy Spirit and by communion with our Lord, washed and made white by the blood of the Lamb, and prepared carefully to meet Him on that glorious day. — EUNICE PEVERINI

JANUARY 13

Commitment

I love them that love me; and those that seek me early shall find me. Prov. 8:17.

I've overslept again," I said, and quickly took my shower.
In haste I dressed and scurried to redeem the fleeting hour.
No time for worship now, I mused, as hurriedly I ate,
Then bolted out the door for work—I'd never yet been late!

No time to thank my precious Lord, or ask for His protection;
No time for basking in His love, or seeking His direction.
It seemed I'd left Him standing there alone—His arms outspread;
I knew He'd never let me down—and off to work I sped.

God doesn't seek revenge, and so my day did not go badly,
But deep within I knew my Lord was disappointed sadly.
That night I knelt beside my bed to thank Him for His care.
He warmed me with His presence in those moments spent in prayer.

His love, so overwhelming, drew me gently to His side;
At once I proffered Him my heart, my stresses, and my pride.
Late hours once filled with duties, I've relinquished and agreed
To let Him govern; now I've time for everything I need.

My rising time is absolute; I make God first each day.
He's waiting in the stillness for me as I kneel to pray.
And in those early hours alone, before the world's astir,
I've grown to know my Saviour, and my heavenly Comforter.

All that I have belongs to Him; He holds and turns the key
To heaven's storehouse for His gift—bought at Gethsemane.
The mountains often loom before me just as in the past,
But I've met the Mountain Mover, and I know He'll hold me fast.

LORRAINE HUDGINS

An Immeasurable Love

*So he got up and went to his father. But while he was still
a long way off, his father saw him and was filled with
compassion for him; he ran to his son, threw his arms
around him and kissed him. Luke 15:20, NIV.*

In general, people love only those who love in return. It is not the
same with Jesus. While He was on earth He welcomed everyone.
To His detractors who criticized Him by saying, "This man
welcomes sinners and eats with them," He replied with the parable
of the prodigal son that we find in Luke 15:11-32.

Each time I read this parable I am deeply touched by the
extraordinary reaction of the father toward his son who had left
him. "While he was yet at a distance, his father saw him and had
compassion, and ran and embraced him" (RSV). He did that even
before his son had confessed. The father was so delighted by the
return of his son that all the evil he had done was as nothing. That
is to say, he had always waited for him favorably and tenderly. He
always hoped to see his son return despite the time that passed, and
it is for that reason that he recognized him while the other was still
far away. What a pleasant surprise this was for this son. I am sure
that was an unforgettable day in his life.

It is extremely important to have the firm assurance that in the
same way our heavenly Father loves us and waits for us. He has an
immeasurable love for each person He has created. It suffices only
to turn around and look toward Him for Him to forget all the evil
we have done. Ah! How marvelous that is! When I think of it, my
heart is filled with indescribable joy. I know that neither hunger,
nor sickness, nor death can separate me from His love. I know that
all that He permits to happen to me is for my good, according to
what is written in Romans 8:28.

Let us surrender our lives to Jesus so that He will direct us and
we will be immersed in His great love each day.

JEANNE RUDATSIKIRA

Riding the Waves With Jesus

And he said, Come. And when Peter was come out of the
ship, he walked on the water, to go to Jesus. Matt. 14:29.

I've never been waterskiing and never will. The whole idea scares
me! You'd think I'd love water sports, having been raised on an
island, but the truth is, I never even learned to swim. Relaxing on
the sandy beach and wading in the still, blue water was enough for
me.

But I admire the brave and daring Peter. Imagine with me for a
moment the incredible experience he had on the water that stormy
night. Jesus, having just fed the multitude, had sent His disciples to
the other side of the Sea of Galilee and gone to a quiet place to pray.
The sun was going down, and night was beginning to fall. All was
still and peaceful as the disciples rowed along.

Suddenly the elements became angry—wind, rain, blackness—
and an angry sea caused the disciples great fear. Where was Jesus?
Panic! Yes, the worst kind of panic, and to add to their fear, they
saw a figure walking on the water, on the wave-tossed sea!

I imagine they all cried out as one voice filled with fear. Then
they heard that familiar voice. "Be of good cheer; it is I; be not
afraid." The so-called brave Peter challenged Jesus. "Lord, if it be
thou, bid me come unto thee on the water." Jesus returned the
challenge. "Come," He said. What did Peter do? He stepped out
and was riding the waves with Jesus.

What a sight that must have been. Those moments were high
achievement for Peter. But then Peter let go of the faith that was
sustaining him, and he began to sink.

But the One who was just a hand's length away stretched out
His hand and grasped Peter's, saving him from the raging sea.

As I labor with Him each day I'm reminded that in every
situation He bids me "Come! Just trust Me, and experience what I
will do for you today." His invitation is for all of us—His children.
He was up in the mountain praying, but He never forgot His
disciples. He saw their plight and came to the rescue, and at the
same time taught them a valuable lesson: "I am your all in
all."

Now He is up in heaven, but He still watches over us. We are
so dear to Him, and we need not fear the difficulties of the day,
because with Him holding our hands the experience is like skiing.
The power of the water, His Spirit, buoys us up. "O thou of little

faith," He said to Peter, "wherefore didst thou doubt?" We must depend on God always, for He is able.   GLORIA C. McLAREN

Guardian Angels and Ministering Spirits

Are not all angels ministering spirits sent to serve those who will inherit salvation? Heb. 1:14, NIV.

I have friends who believe very differently from me about angels. One doesn't believe in angels at all. Others believe in all the varieties of New Age mystical beings. I have been comforted my whole life by the thought that angels do guard us and rescue us. Mission stories and other stories of danger and disaster have quickened my resolve that angels indeed minister to our needs.

What I am trying to figure out is how to tell my friends who aren't accustomed to Bible language why I am so sure about angels. Do they have any clue about those who are "heirs of salvation"? Would they believe Psalm 91:10, 11, "For he orders his angels to protect you wherever you go" (TLB)? Or the stories of Peter in prison, Daniel in the lions' den, and Elijah and the chariot of fire? In this age of laser light shows and *Star Trek*, wouldn't we love to show, just once, our angels and a chariot of fire?

But in this media age, more than ever, we need to sense God's presence and peace and have the special comfort of knowing that God's Word has told us of these ministering spirits. That they are surrounding us and not just for protection in a physical sense, but to keep us from evil influences and to strengthen our ability to live for God. As we seek to live in God's way, to follow the plans to bring good to those around us, we can think of the special gift of ministering spirits sent to help us minister to others.

JULIA L. PEARCE

Adopted

He planned, in his love, that we should be adopted as his own children through Jesus Christ. Eph. 1:5, Phillips.

They came running up to me. "Guess what?" Melissa asked excitedly. "Angie just found out that she is adopted!" The little girls, hands entwined, looked at each other and smiled. Then two little faces turned soberly toward me, and Melissa whispered, "Is being adopted good or bad?" I groaned inwardly. Melissa's questions were seldom simple or easy to answer.

"I suppose adoption is like many other things in life—partly good and partly bad," I replied. "How did you come to be adopted, Angie?" She told me that her parents had been killed in a car accident and because there were no relatives who could take the baby, she had been placed in an orphanage.

I explained that it was "bad" that Angie's biological parents had been killed (and then I had to define biological!), but that it was "good" her adoptive parents had chosen Angie to be their child. My explanation must have impressed Melissa, because her mother called me a few days later—slightly nonplussed. Melissa's birthday was approaching and the child wondered if my present for her could be an "adopt-a-doll."

Melissa and I went shopping. Selecting a doll to adopt took a very l-o-n-g time, and then there were the "adoption" papers to complete. On the way home, Melissa insisted that I save her present until her actual birthday dinner.

A few days later we all watched Melissa open her adopt-a-doll. Cradling the new addition in her arms, Melissa looked over at Angie and said, "I think I know how your mother felt when she brought you home. Here, you hold the 'baby' and pretend that she is you." Eventually Melissa and Angie went into the playroom to have a tea party.

Sometime later I realized that Melissa was introducing her new addition, Amaryllis, to the other dolls and stuffed animals. "And," she was saying, "I want to help you understand [oh dear, that was one of my phrases!] that while it is too bad little Amaryllis could not live with her biological [she said each syllable separately] family, I have adopted her into my family. This is a *good* family and—'it doesn't get any better than this' [a phrase her father sometimes uses after finishing a particularly yummy slice of home-made rhubarb pie]." The girls clapped and went on with their play.

I chuckled to myself and then realized how true her words were. We all have biological families—none of which can provide us with everlasting life. Fortunately, the King of the universe wants to adopt all of us as His children (see 2 Peter 3:9). God's family is a *good* family, and—"it doesn't get any better than this."

Because of Melissa I understood this concept more clearly. The girls would understand about the family of God, too. I headed for the playroom—to invite myself to a tea party.   ARLENE TAYLOR

Slaughtering Not-so-sacred Cows

Thou wilt keep him in perfect peace, whose mind is stayed on thee: because he trusteth in thee. Isa. 26:3.

Sometime back in my adolescent daze I adopted the slang phrase "to have a cow." It meant roughly "to be thoroughly upset about something," as in "Tom's folks had a cow when he flunked math" or "Suzy will have an absolute cow if that creep asks her to the party." Now, my friends, who at that time were as busy "calving" as I was, probably threw off that bit of agrarian nonsense years ago, but it clung to me, as barnyard by-products sometimes do.

Thus it happened that even after I became a married mom with a toddler, I still tended a herd of cows of my own creation. Seized one blistering midsummer day in suburbia by the desire to freeze 18 dozen ears of corn for winter, I sallied forth across the chartless Illinois prairie to the Broadview Academy farm with 3-year-old Kent in tow. All went smoothly as I corralled the corn and a gargantuan zucchini in my car trunk and began the trek homeward.

Chuckling to myself in anticipation of regaling the guests at an upcoming baby shower with my gag gift of a huge beribboned squash and a "Now that you're eating for two . . ." card, I swung my car from the rutted dirt lane of the farm onto the country road and glanced at my watch. "Horrors!" I shrieked. "How did it get so late? I'm about to miss the shower!"

With that I promptly abandoned my plan to retrace my certain but circuitous route and sped recklessly along a shortcut to doom. Familiar landmarks dissolved. Endless flat acres of tall shimmering corn stretching to the horizon lined both sides of every roadway I raced madly down. Kent gazed at me innocently. "Mommy," he queried wide-eyed, "are we having a cow yet?"

A cow? More like a herd of cattle! In full stampede. How often

I need to remember that "nothing that in any way concerns [my] peace is too small for Him to notice" (*Steps to Christ*, p. 100).

Does my obstinate colleague at work strew obstacles in my path? Don't have a cow! Does the room of my hormone-crazed teenager altogether obscure the path? Abort that cow! Does my husband wonder what I do all day every day since our new baby arrived? Does my ex-spouse cut off child support? Slay those cows! Does my aged parent's inability to recognize me anymore underscore my own intimations of mortality? Kill that cow! Does everything cost more money and take more time and energy than I have? Do I feel helpless to address the overwhelming problems of humanity? Slaughter those cows too!

With fixed trust in the heavenly Herdsman, I resolve not to let people and events stampede me into "having a cow," but to allow *Him* to regulate the production of livestock and keep me in perfect peace. ANDREA KRISTENSEN

JANUARY 19

Creative Corners

Search me, O God, and know my heart; test me and know my anxious thoughts. See if there is any offensive way in me, and lead me in the way everlasting. Ps. 139:23, 24, NIV.

I love to make beautiful little things. Small pieces of embroidery, tiny quilts, a few dried flowers in a basket. It's fun to think up a new design and figure out how to make it a reality. I like to find interesting things other people have made and fill every nook and cranny of our home with special things. But I have a friend who thinks all this is a waste of time and energy. She scorns all the little extras in my home as "just more junk to dust." She tells me that I should do more useful things with my time than make cross-stitch samplers.

Maybe she is right. But for me, craft is one of the only forms of relaxation that I have. It's great to sit down after a day of caring for three preschoolers, sew a few stitches, and feel I have achieved something concrete! But her words often nag away in my mind, making me feel that it really is a waste of time to stencil the walls of the upstairs room where visitors rarely go or to make a pretty arrangement on a bedroom shelf.

Then the other day I saw a nature program about all the creatures that live deep in the sea. Many had never been seen by human beings until quite recently, and they could be viewed only through special cameras sent miles below the sparkling waves. Some of the sea life was fantastically exotic, but for thousands of years only God knew it was there.

I thought of the many other places in the world tucked away from human sight, yet filled with God's creativity. God needn't have made so many different roses. But He did. He filled this world with beautiful things, tucking them into every corner regardless of whether they would be seen or not. Was it because He just loved being creative too? Did He delight in the idea of making a lovely secret corner that no one else would ever see, merely for the satisfaction of being able to pronounce everything good?

And what about our own lives? Do we beautify only the bits that are seen? What do we do with that dark alcove, that space under the bed? Do we fill it with rubble and junk and things no one wants? Or do we spend time working on the hidden corners and secret places known only to ourselves and God, filling them with the fragrant flowers of love, contentment, peace, and joy? It will take some effort and creativity, prayer, and even pain, and maybe no one else will ever notice, but you and God will have a secret delight that will make it all worthwhile. — KAREN HOLFORD

JANUARY 20

Loving the Longing

I love the Lord, for he heard my voice; he heard my cry for mercy. Because he turned his ear to me, I will call on him as long as I live. Ps. 116:1, 2, NIV.

To be human is to crave wholeness. We yearn to be significant, to find meaning and purpose in life. To have experiences that offer fulfillment for more than a fleeting moment. Brenda Hunter in her book *Where Have All the Mothers Gone?* asks the question: "Is there a woman anywhere who has not at some point in life cried out, 'There must be more to life than this'? Who has not voiced this cry in the quiet of early morning or in the despair of midnight or just after sex or when the momentary joy of success has palled?" (p. 172).

Augustine, knowing the answer, put it this way: "Our hearts are restless until they rest in Thee." But there is a sense in which even when we have found Jesus, there will always be the longing. I am learning that this is not a problem to be remedied, not a sickness to be cured. Rather I am learning to love the longing. It is this

41

yearning, this incompleteness, this lack of fulfillment that God implanted in my heart to call me back to Him continually. It is not incompatible with love and hope and growth. It's just a thirst created in the warp and woof of my being that keeps me coming back again and again to draw from the fountain.

Gerald May, in his perceptive book *Addiction and Grace*, speaks of this inborn longing as "our true treasure, the most precious thing we have. It is God's song of love in our soul" (p. 180). Fulfillment is in making it a duet.　　　　KAREN FLOWERS

The Remote Dream

So do not throw away your confidence; it will be richly rewarded. Heb. 10:35, NIV.

In childhood, more than 50 years ago, my husband and I dreamed of a faraway land called Russia. We read about it in elementary geography books—vast, timbered, with steppes and lakes and mountains, formidable in its Siberian cold, impressive with its cathedrals and museums. It fascinated Bob particularly, and he longed to visit there.

I thought of *matrushka* dolls that nest inside each other, borscht that satisfies the stomach, and balalaikas that cheer the soul. Sites like the Kremlin and Red Square seemed to abound with history and intrigue.

Yet it all seemed utterly remote, untouchable. Dreaming of a visit to Russia was like dreaming of a visit to the moon—a fantasy, fun to play with but never to become reality.

As we grew older, fearsome stories of Stalin's madness were added to the picture. We prayed for fellow believers we knew we'd never see.

Still later we worked in South Korea. We were now in East Asia but still totally separated from Russia. Just a few miles from our home the demilitarized zone between us and North Korea reminded us of the clear demarcation between Communist neighbors to the north and anybody else. Sputnik had just recently roared into the news, and Western reaction was frantic. We watched from a Korean beach one evening as one of America's answers to Sputnik moved through the heavens above.

Nevertheless, a few months ago my husband and I spent a month in Russia, teaching at Zaokski Seminary. Our gracious hosts took us sightseeing in Moscow, Tula, St. Petersburg, and Kiev. As we stood in Red Square with the sunlight of a perfectly clear day gleaming off the golden domes of the cathedrals there, watching the changing of the guard at Lenin's tomb, eyeing the vast walls of the GUM department store, we kept saying, "It doesn't seem possible that we are actually here."

Likewise, as a friend guided us through the Hermitage and other palatial museums of St. Petersburg, with wooden floors of intricate parquetry design, with sculptured and decorated ceilings that demanded neck-stiffening awe and appreciation, with paintings and sculpture from the world's greatest artists, and with gold and other precious metals and gems in all the walls and pillars and displays, we could only in wonder repeat, "I can hardly believe we're actually here, seeing all this in person."

And yes, we ate borscht, bought *matrushka* dolls for our grandchildren, and even got a balalaika for our musician son for Christmas.

We've been hearing about heaven for a long time. Does it seem so remote that we've assumed we'll never actually go there? Will we be surprised when suddenly the opportunity opens up?

MADELINE S. JOHNSTON

JANUARY 22

"Simply Good"

Charm is deceptive, and beauty is fleeting; but a woman who fears the Lord is to be praised. Prov. 31:30, NIV.

Today we buried our friend. Every Monday night since her illness had been diagnosed, some of us had gathered to pray for her and her family. We longed for a miracle but prayed, "Thy will be done." The church was packed with so many who had similarly prayed. The blessed hope was our only comfort.

Later, when telling a friend what a big funeral it had been, I was asked, "What did she do?" The truth was Airwyn didn't *do* anything. She just *was*. Her Christianity was so much a part of her that it permeated every aspect of her life. She wasn't an "up-front person," but she worked with the children and as a deaconess; she supported every endeavor, and her loving, gentle influence was felt throughout the church.

She was always the first to be concerned, to be helpful, and above all to be cheerful. Even during her illness her thoughts were always of others, and it was an inspiration to visit her. When she heard that one of the young people was to be baptized, she wrote

43

a letter of joy and encouragement. That young person will never forget that example of selflessness and true Christian caring.

During the funeral service one of the pastors spoke of "the incredible impact of a simply good life." Airwyn was simply good. One had only to look at those who attended the funeral to see the number of lives she had touched. There were old and young, church members and nonmembers, colleagues, neighbors, and friends, as well as the relatives, to whom she is irreplaceable. The words of Proverbs were very fitting for this devoted wife, mother, and grandmother: "Her children rise up and call her blessed; her husband also, and he praises her" (Prov. 31:28, RSV).

It would have been easy today to have been bowed down with sorrow and disappointment. As well as our own immediate grief, there is so much evil, sin, and suffering in the world that we sometimes wonder if we can make any difference. The truth is that we can make a difference in our world. This new year we have a message of hope for the world. We know that sin, suffering, and sadness are soon going to be replaced by the joy of seeing Jesus return to reunite us with our loved ones and to take us home. Let's determine to put our hand into the hand of God. As He leads us safely into the unknown, let us be open to every opportunity He presents to make a difference in the lives of those we meet. If we will allow Him to make us "simply good," we will be the loving and lovable Christians who will touch the lives of others and so introduce them to the greatest of all friends—Jesus Christ!

AUDREY BALDERSTONE

JANUARY 23

I Hate Housecleaning

Create in me a clean heart, O God; and renew a right spirit within me. Ps. 51:10.

I hate cleaning house. As far as I am concerned, there are at least a million more interesting things that need to be done first. A clean house is important to me—I don't like messes or dirt. But I just don't like to do the cleaning myself. In the 23 years that my husband was in the Army, I jokingly said that I either had to clean house or to move, so I moved. Well, it was half jokingly. I remember the first time I told my mother that I hated cleaning house. She had taught home economics for many years and thought she had raised me right. She looked at me in shock. "But why?" Well, it's just that it has to be done all over again the next week.

Nothing new; just do it again. And again and again. Over and over.

I think God knows how I feel. Can't you just see Him in His apron with His cleaning bucket? "Oh, no," He says, "I just cleaned up that mess last week, and now I have to do it again." Or: "She asked for help out of that predicament just the other day, so I helped her, and now she's in it again." Or maybe it goes, "Seventy times seven. This is now 489, but she really wants to be forgiven, and I do love her. Here comes the cleaning solution." Again and again. Over and over He cleans up my quagmire.

Of course there is a difference. I don't think God really complains or tries to get out of the cleanup job. In fact, Jesus volunteered to do it and applies His own blood of cleansing. "Thank You so much, God, and please help me to want to stay clean." ARDIS DICK STENBAKKEN

JANUARY 24

The Answer

I sought the Lord, and he answered me, and delivered me from all my fear. Ps. 34:4, RSV.

Someone I loved was in trouble. Spiritually adrift, she experimented with things that could harm her physically, alienate her from family and friends, and emotionally scar her for life. I felt drained from the constant worry and stress.

Pleading daily with God for help, I determined one morning to be like Jacob and not let go until God revealed to me that He cared about and was involved with my problem. I needed hope. It was during this session that I read Psalm 34:4: "I sought the Lord and he answered me, and delivered me from all my fear." This was the answer!

For months I repeated this verse to myself. It soothed my frayed nerves and reinforced the concept of an involved God. No longer paralyzed by anxiety, I focused on the individual's needs and tried to be a tool in God's hands.

But things didn't improve for my friend as I had expected. If God had "answered" me, why wasn't the situation resolved? Why hadn't my friend turned away from the things that were destroying her? What point had I missed in the practical application of this verse? Should I ask for something else, or ask in a different way? The verse said to seek God, and I had. It promised that He would answer me, but I sensed no resolution. After all, everything was still the same.

While kneading bread dough one Friday, I contemplated the verse. Suddenly I realized the promise *was* true. God had answered me and had taken my fear away. The following word picture helps illustrate the insight I gained that day.

In my mind, my friend and I are walking down a path beside a beautiful creek when suddenly, seeking a thrill and ignoring the possibility of drowning, she jumps in to ride the rapids. I run along the bank, frantically screaming for someone to save her as she is pulled through the water. She is feeling free and having fun, but I sense impending disaster. Suddenly Someone is beside me. He has heard my cries and is responding to my pleas for help. Together we run along the bank calling to my friend. My Companion is much stronger than I am and has equipment to assist in the rescue, but even He cannot pull her out of the water until she wants help. We are united in our efforts to help my friend, and His presence strengthens and encourages me.

"Thank You, Lord, for giving me the answer."

CHERILYN J. SMITH

JANUARY 25

What Is in Your Hand?

Whatever your hand finds to do, do it with all your might. Eccl. 9:10, NIV.

I closed the book with a gentle thud, my mind still centered on the story. For an 11-year-old with a fertile imagination, books were the stuff of which dreams were made. How I loved to read—especially the reading course books. Every Sabbath I would stop by the church library and bring home something new to peruse that afternoon.

"How I wish I had a great talent," I said to my father (Leslie Warren Taylor), who was reading across the room from me. "I wish I could do something exceedingly outstanding" (I enjoyed using long words!).

Dad chuckled as he asked, "What story did you read today, Arlene?"

I told him about Florence Nightingale, who had (basically singlehandedly, mind you) changed the image of professional nursing forever. "I would like a talent like that," I mused.

"You do have one," my dad said. "The parable of the talents makes it very clear that every individual has at least one outstanding talent" (Matt. 25). "I once heard a minister preach a sermon on that topic," my dad continued. "He said that many people never accomplish anything because they are waiting to accomplish something great. Instead we simply need to identify 'what is in our hands.' Regardless of how humble we might think our talent, we can 'bring our nothings to the Lord and let God make them into somethings.' "

We talked about Bible characters who had used whatever was in their hands. Moses, who had a rod in his hand; Mary, an alabaster box of perfume; Samson, a donkey's jawbone; the widow, two mites; Gideon, a trumpet and a pitcher; Dorcas, a needle and thread. There were so many examples!

Over the years I have thought of that conversation many times. I can still see the picture in my mind's eye as Dad leaned a bit farther back in his chair and asked, "What is in your hand, Arlene?"

"Nothing," I replied, not realizing that he was speaking metaphorically.

"Then ask God to show you what is in your hand and use it with your might."

It was excellent advice. I have seen individuals who have not had the benefit of advanced formal education or great opportunities use whatever they had in their hands to wonderful advantage. Some have had the outstanding gift of speaking a word aptly, which the book of Proverbs says is like apples of gold in settings of silver (see Prov. 25:11).

This year, ask God to show you what is in your hand. Then use it with your might!

ARLENE TAYLOR

JANUARY 26

Prayer

Call on me in the day of trouble; I will deliver you, and you shall glorify me. Ps. 50:15, NRSV.

In the days when my children still did naughty things, my oldest daughter was taken to the back bedroom for a reprimand. For the rest of us the atmosphere became tense. We were not willing to say anything or look anyone in the eye. No noises were coming from the back bedroom when my 3-year-old, in her husky voice, yelled, "Jan, call upon the Lord in the day of trouble!" Needless to say, laughter on everyone's part interrupted any discipline that may have been needed.

Is that what prayer is to us? Asking for help when we are in trouble? "Prayer is the opening of the heart to God as to a friend. Not that it is necessary in order to make known to God what we are, but in order to enable us to receive Him. Prayer does not bring God down to us, but brings us up to Him" (*Steps to Christ*, p. 93).

"You are my friends," says Christ (John 15:14, RSV). Can anything be more wonderful than having a friend I can trust, speak freely to, and open the deepest recesses of my heart and mind to, knowing I will be understood and accepted? We have such a friend in Christ. I like to compare our relationship with Christ to that of a healthy growing human relationship, whether it be marriage, parent/child, sibling, or a very good friend. Prayer is more than talking with or to God. It is a relationship, a true friendship. Friendship implies open communication, acceptance, and love. Prayer redeems us from isolation, for it builds a relationship with God, and when we pray with and for each other we strengthen friendships. We need not be alone!

"If we keep the Lord ever before us, allowing our hearts to go out in thanksgiving and praise to Him, we shall have a continual freshness in our religious life. Our prayers will take the form of a conversation with God as we would talk with a friend. He will speak His mysteries to us personally. Often there will come to us a sweet joyful sense of the presence of Jesus" (*Christ's Object Lessons*, p. 129).

The thought that I can have a continual freshness in my spiritual life is very exciting to me. My prayer life will enrich my spiritual life, and surely my spiritual life affects my attitudes, my behavior, my very being. Who I am!

We may think, at times, that prayer is getting something from God, which He may hesitate to give, but which persistent prayer will bring about. But prayer is not to get from God what we want, but rather to help us accept what we have. It is not necessarily to relieve us of pain, but to help us bear it. It is not to attempt to change God's mind, but to help us accept God's mind. Prayer is an endeavor not to outline some plan of action for God to follow, but to help us understand what God's plan is. It is to ask not that God's will be changed, but that God's will be done.

Calling upon the Lord in the day of trouble is a very acceptable prayer. Prayer always connects us with God, giving us a continual freshness in our spiritual lives.

HALCYON WILSON

Trusting

Now mine eye seeth thee. Job 42:5.

My husband and I were just beginning to experience the joy and freedom of our newly retired lifestyle. It started with a relaxing trip to Cancún, Mexico, where we swam in the warm turquoise Caribbean. Snorkeling brought us into the world of a gorgeous array of fish painted by the Master Artist Himself. We loafed on sunny beaches, viewed Mayan ruins, and browsed in quaint little shops.

We shivered a little on returning home, but the brisk fall days provided a perfect opportunity to bring out the dusty tennis rackets and hit a few balls. Long walks amid fall colors brought us more enjoyment.

Everything seemed to be going great. Then the sky fell in!

We were exploring the woods and creek below our house one morning after a rainfall. The fallen leaves were slippery and thick, but I was being careful—I thought. Ascending the last hill, I stepped on something hidden under the slippery leaves that rolled as I stepped. I fell with a thud, landing on my twisted ankle.

Excruciating pain pierced my very being. I lay moaning and digging my fingers into the soft wet earth. Efforts to stand were hopeless. On hands and knees I painfully dragged myself to the top of the hill, where my husband was able to carry me "piggyback" to the house.

In the hospital emergency room and on the X-ray table I prayed, "Please, God. Please don't let my ankle be broken." But broken it was. With a heart heavier than the cast that enveloped my leg, I headed home.

As I lay helplessly staring at my elevated leg, the tears trickled down. How could God allow more pain in my life and still love me? I was already fighting cancer. Wasn't that enough? Our house was in the process of selling. It was time to pack. I needed to do my Christmas shopping. My to-do list was longer than my cast.

Fortunately, I had been studying Job in my personal devotions, and the Bible story started speaking directly to me. God didn't explain to Job why he was being afflicted, why Satan was allowed to take away his blessings. Job sank to the depths of discouragement. Circumstances tempted him to doubt God's love. Friends even misinterpreted God's purposes.

The most difficult thing for Job to handle was that he felt

rejected by God. Only when Job decided to trust God implicitly, only when he decided to believe that God loved him no matter what happened to him, did he begin his gradual ascent from despair to hope and happiness.

After studying Job, I too began to realize I had been looking through a fog of misunderstanding about God's love toward me. The only way for the mist to clear was for me to trust His love even when I couldn't understand it—to trust Him according to what He is, rather than how I feel. Then I began to rise from despair to confidence and could say with Job, "Now mine eye seeth thee."

ELLEN BRESEE

JANUARY 28

His Last Letter

But let all those that put their trust in thee rejoice: let them ever shout for joy . . . let them also that love thy name be joyful in thee. Ps. 5:11.

My dear church members, I have got bad news for you. They have arrested me once more, and this time I fear the worst. I am waiting for the indictment, and it looks bad. I have no money to hire an able attorney. They will not even let me out on bail.

"My cell is situated in the basement, so I cannot see the sun. It is wet down here, the walls are moldy, the floor is formed of tamped earth, and there are muddy puddles everywhere.

"And the worst thing of all: there are rats here! I dare not fall asleep, for last night one rat tried to gnaw my toes. The table I'm writing on totters frightfully.

"This is probably the last letter I'll be able to write to you, because I don't have any more paper and the candle is already burnt down to a tiny stump of wax. I probably won't order any more, as it no longer appears to be worth the effort.

"Maybe there are a few days left for me to live, maybe just a few hours. Don't forget me, you dear folks at Philippi! Your tired old Paulus."

I am happy such a letter was never mailed. Instead of this, Paul wrote: "Rejoice in the Lord alway: and again I say, Rejoice" (Phil. 4:4).

Paul followed his own advice and concerned himself with beautiful and positive thoughts. He never allowed the problems to blind his eyes to the most important things in life. He did have sufficient reason to complain. But in spite of the facts, he was thankful and gave expression to his joy. And this was no hypocrisy, for such joy is more than a fleeting feeling. It is one of the fruits of the Holy Spirit, the result of a lifestyle rooted in a living and loving God.

I would like to try this today. The next time I feel like complaining, I'm going to express joy and return thanks instead!

SYLVIA RENZ

The Lamb of God

He is brought as a lamb to the slaughter, and as a sheep before her shearers is dumb, so he openeth not his mouth. Isa. 53:7.

What impressed you most on your recent trip from Australia and New Zealand?" a friend asked me on our return.

It was not the cruise through the majestic mountains on the fjord of New Zealand's Milford Sound that impressed me most. Nor the helicopter ride over the soaring, craggy peaks surrounding snow-clad Mount Cook.

Not the blazing beauty of Australia's brilliantly colored birds. Nor the cuddly koalas.

Not the expansive white sand beaches, framed in brilliant turquoise waters with roaring waves crashing on the treacherous rocks. Nor the lush rain forests of giant eucalyptus trees, dwarfing fern trees as they reached as much as 50 feet into the deep-blue sky.

All these beauties were wonderful to behold, but they were not what impressed me most.

What made the greatest impression on me was seeing a sheep sheared. There are about 165 million sheep in Australia and only 17 million people, so it is a common sight to see a sheep being sheared. But for me it was very special, a spiritual experience I shall never forget.

I watched intently as a giant bruiser of a fellow picked up a big sheep and sat it down on its rump. As the shearer took the clippers and began shearing, the sheep didn't struggle at all. It didn't even let out a "baa." It was totally obedient and submissive to its master.

As I sat there watching, Isaiah's description of Jesus at the cross flashed into my mind: "He is brought as a lamb to the slaughter, and as a sheep before his shearers is dumb, so he opened not his mouth" (Isa. 53:7).

Like that submissive sheep, Jesus submitted to His Father's will.

And like that silent sheep before its shearer, Jesus did not open His mouth—even when He was taunted and abused while pinned to the cross.

As I watched that submissive sheep being sheared, I received such an intense glimpse of what Jesus did for me on the cross that I could hardly keep back the tears. Jesus, a helpless babe born in a manger, became a totally surrendered man. At the cross Jesus could not have saved Himself and saved me, too!   LILLIAN R. GUILD

JANUARY 30

Love in Action

Many, O Lord my God, are Your wonderful works which You have done. Ps. 40:5, NKJV.

The other day I read a sentence that challenged me through and through. Let me share it with you. Read it silently and then reread it aloud: "Attempt something so great for God that it's doomed to failure unless God is in it." You can't stop with once—read it again!

Then another sentence almost knocked me off my feet. "Never tell anyone it can't be done . . . God may have been waiting for centuries for somebody ignorant enough of the impossible to do that very thing" (J. A. Holmes).

Could it be that often I fail to get really involved, make a difference, because I'm afraid I'll fail? Could I be guilty of causing others to fail, or—worse still—not even get started? Perhaps I'm seeing impossibilities instead of opportunities to work more closely with God.

Instead of praying for God to use me, I've been cowering behind a screen of fear, laziness, or maybe just plain lack of faith. Could it be that my eyes have even been blinded by the things (glitter, good times, or the weight of everyday living) of this world?

God made me to look beyond all this. I'm His child and created for a purpose. Look again at our text for today. I'm beginning to want to reach out and reach the sky—and beyond.

Let me share one more challenge. Read it daily. Weave it into the fiber of your being.

I like to think of a goal as a target. The bull's eye is 100. Concentric rings are 80, 60, 40, and 20. I aim for 100, but sometimes I hit 80 or even 20. But if I didn't aim for 100, I would probably hit zero or miss every time. Someone said, "I would rather attempt to do something great for God and fail than to do nothing and succeed."

Encourage each individual in your family to set high goals. Each one aims at becoming more caring, more active. Each will live these goals.

Do dreams come true? If they're God's dreams, they can't fail—even when we hit only 20. "Lord, increase my vision, my faith. Multiply my goals until my goals are those of Yours. Let the impossible begin with me—to glorify You."

GINGER MOSTERT CHURCH

JANUARY 31

God's Polishing Process

That our daughters may be as corner stones, polished after the similitude of a palace. Ps. 144:12.

What is more beautiful than an exquisitely polished object, and what is more unsightly than a corroded one? God's desire for us as His daughters is to be as polished stones.

Rust is a common form of corrosion. How does it happen? It happens slowly, imperceptibly at first, as a reddish-brown substance that corrodes and weakens the metal as it is exposed to the elements. It can be prevented by coating the object with oil or grease, but once it is there it can be removed only by hard work with a grindstone or emery cloth.

It happens to people, too, slowly, imperceptibly. Once, after an extended illness, I returned to my job, only to be told that my skills had gotten "rusty." Time, stresses, and disuse had weakened the metal of the polished tools of the trade.

It happens also in our relationship with God. Slowly, imperceptibly at first, but we realize it when doubt, discouragement, and fear take the place of faith and trust. It happens by neglect, by long periods of time away from the oil of God's Word, which will prevent the formation of rust. But if rust has formed, God may have to use the grindstone or emery cloth of trial to remove the corrosion.

God's desire for us is to be as daughters polished after the similitude of a palace. Today may our souls be bathed in the oil of God's Word. But if corrosion has still developed, let's be willing for God to polish us no matter how hard the process.

JOAN MINCHIN NEALL

Spaghetti for Supper

And it shall come to pass, that before they call, I will answer; and while they are yet speaking, I will hear. Isa. 65:24.

It was a hot and humid Friday afternoon as I drove eight miles into town to the grocery store. Mission accomplished, I headed my car out of the parking lot. To my left I noticed a man carrying a sign that read "Work for Food." *That's strange,* I thought. *Have times gotten that bad? Is he homeless? Was that old car parked nearby his? If he's got money for gas, why can't he buy food?*

"Now, Barbara," I said to myself, "how would you feel in that situation?" *What should I do?* I wondered. *I don't have any extra money. . . . I guess I could get him something to eat. . . . Does he have a wife and kids? I guess I could take him to the Community Services center . . . but that might not be safe.*

By now I had driven a half mile from the store. I turned the car around and drove back. He was still there. If I hurried, I could get something from the food pantry and be back in 15 or 20 minutes.

With the food box on my car seat, I pulled into the store parking lot, but he and the old car were gone. I wondered if someone had helped him. *Maybe he went across the street to the other store,* I thought. *I'll go see.* But he wasn't there. I checked the shopping center down the road, but he wasn't there either. I drove through the neighborhood, but didn't find him anywhere. *Now what do I do, Lord? I don't want to take this food back. Should I have told him that I was going to get him something to eat?*

As I pondered what to do, I noticed the apartments across the street. One of our missing church members lived there, and I wondered if she could use the food. I parked the car, ran to her door, and knocked. When she opened the door, I told her that I had some food I needed to give away, and asked if she could use it. She looked surprised, then said, "Yes." After I brought the food box in from the car, she told me this story.

It was the last day of the month, and she was down to her last dollar. Her daughter, who would be home from school within the hour, had been wanting some spaghetti to eat, but they did not have the ingredients to make it. Her dollar would purchase the spaghetti or the sauce, but not both. When I knocked on her door, she was praying about their food situation. Imagine her gratitude to have her prayer answered so speedily. And there was pasta *and* sauce in the box—spaghetti for supper!

Maybe that man was an angel in disguise sent to set me in motion to help someone else. I can't say for sure, but I am certain of one thing. If you're willing to ask God to use you and to help you listen to the Holy Spirit's prompting, He'll let you share an exciting part in answering others' prayers. BARBARA HALES

From the Wastebasket

The Lord . . . is my strength and my song. Isa. 12:2, NIV.

On January 4, 1993, the front cover headlines on *Newsweek* screamed "A Pattern of Rape—War Crimes in Bosnia." The article's recitation of the atrocities committed by Serbs against the Muslim women in Croatia still churned in my head as I threw a bunch of stuffed animals into the washing machine. "Before I give them to any child, they have to at least look clean," I said to myself.

I felt sort of sick and disappointed as I pulled them out of the machine at the end of the washing cycle. One of them, a little lamb, had a rip in a seam that I hadn't noticed, and its stuffing was now all over the other animals! I removed the offending lamb from the washer, pulled off as much of the plastic and cellulose stuffing as I could from the others, and threw them into the dryer. Just before I threw the little lamb into the wastebasket, I noticed that it had a wind-up mechanism. Unthinkingly I wound it up, and, not at all to my surprise, there was nothing. *What else could I expect from the poor, traumatized little lamb?* I thought. I left it in the trash can.

After the other animals were dry, I proceeded to pick off more of the plastic stuffing and drop it in the wastebasket. I must have kicked it or something, for all of a sudden I heard "rockabye" music. I looked at the animal I was picking the stuffing from—no wind-up on it. The music continued, then slowed, and nearly stopped before I identified the source—the discarded little lamb!

One ear was missing, half its stuffing was gone, and it'd been through the wash, but still that little lamb was singing! I wanted to jump on a plane and fly to Croatia! I wanted to tell those mutilated, abused women: "The Lord could be your strength and song!"

I can't afford to fly to Croatia, but I can let the Lord be *my* strength and *my* song! I too get mutilated and torn at times. But Jesus, my Lamb, can give me a song—His song—to sing. LOIS MOORE

Coming Home

They are not of the world, even as I am not of the world. John 17:16.

When I was a child, my family relied largely on our fireplace to heat the living room on cold winter nights. During hot summer days when winter seemed far away, we searched the paper for advertisements giving away free firewood. Then we would all pile into a truck and drive to the address given to collect the old lumber. We brought it home and stacked it up right next to the house so that the fuel would be partially sheltered by the eaves.

As I walked home from the school bus during the winter months, I would come down a hill and be greeted by the sight of all the wood piled up outside the house, and I knew that inside the snug home there would be a warm fire and a hot meal waiting for me.

I like to think that going to heaven will be like coming home from school and seeing that woodpile. The world can be a cold place, but Jesus is waiting at home for us with all the warmth of His love.   GINA LEE

Let Go—Let God

Delight yourself in the Lord and he will give you the desires of your heart. And my God will meet all your needs according to his glorious riches in Christ Jesus. So do not fear, for I am with you; . . . I will uphold you with my righteous right hand. Ps. 37:4, Phil. 4:19, and Isa. 41:10, NIV.

In my singleness I have learned to trust and depend on God to fill the loneliness I feel at times. There are times when I am tempted to do things my own way and take charge (because, of course, God is moving too slowly!), but I realize that God will work all things out for my good if I allow Him. In my alone time I have learned about faith as the substance of things hoped for—the evidence of things not seen (see Heb. 11:1). I have learned of the virtue of patience, the true character of God, and of loyalty and commitment in the face of compromise. I have learned to treasure quiet time, and I have learned more valuable lessons about myself. I have learned to stop making plans without God. I have learned to "let go and let God" take complete control of my total life. And that includes my marital status. I rest in the promise of God supplying *all* my needs and giving me the desires of my heart. I am secure in knowing that God is always here for me and will never leave me; therefore, I am never alone.

I believe that as a Christian woman I should believe and be satisfied. I should strive to be contented with my life. There are times, however, when I am discouraged and down—times when I'm simply tired of being alone. There are times when I want to recapture a sense of family that I've lost through the death of my parents. In these times I must remember that only God can mend my dreams that have been broken; only He can satisfy my desires.

To "let go and let God" is to live life full of excitement, hope, and dreams! "Our heavenly Father has a thousand ways to provide for us of which we know nothing" (*Our Father Cares*, p. 67). I dare to dream, take courage under God, and make it come true. "For I know the plans I have for you," declares the Lord, "plans to prosper you and not to harm you, plans to give you hope and a future" (Jer. 29:11, NIV).

Hang tough, sisters! Trust the Lord. Commit your way to Him. Wait patiently on the Lord. Let go . . . let God!   TERRIE E. RUFF

1-800-HEAVEN

Call upon me, and I will answer. Ps. 91:15.

Talk about the worst of times—it was. The week had been a disaster—personal illness, car trouble, no heat from the furnace—one catastrophe after another. Discouragement consumed me. Even the sun refused to shine as we set out for church in the rain on Sabbath morning. I was convinced that God was busy elsewhere.

"Lord," I prayed as we pulled onto the interstate highway, "I need to know that You are with me. Show me in some way today that You care."

We drove on in silence, Paul's eyes on the road, mine gazing into familiar fields searching for grazing deer. Minutes later an

18-wheeler passed us on the right, obstructing my view. I started to complain, then noticed the sign on the truck's back door.

"Tired of it all?

Why not make the best of things?

Call 1-800-HEAVEN."

Chagrined and somewhat astonished at the immediate response to my prayer, I whispered, "Thank You, Lord."

"Did you say something?" my husband asked, glancing in my direction.

I turned and showed him my first smile of the day. "It's a beautiful morning, isn't it?" I asked.

And so it was, after all.   PATRICIA A. HABADA

FEBRUARY 6

My Bear Story

God is love. Whoever lives in love lives in God, and God in him. . . . There is no fear in love. But perfect love drives out fear. 1 John 4:16-18, NIV.

On my first solo backpacking trip I had the great fortune of encountering a bear. I was thrilled! Even as a child, my favorite stories were by naturalists who proclaimed the wonders of God's creation. Now it was my turn to experience it firsthand, and I stood motionless. The bear was in a large dense oak tree above me. I did the "not-moving-a-muscle, not-swatting-a-mosquito" thing until I got tired of not being able to see the creature as it wandered around in the treetop, bouncing the branches and making acorns fall all around me.

I spent way too much time standing under that tree, straining, trying to see. I finally gave up. I was cold and hungry and had a destination to reach before dark. And since the bear didn't seem to care if I was there or not, I took off my pack and got out a granola bar. Big mistake!

Now the bear had no trouble seeing me! It shot down the tree and came out over me on the closest branch. Its nostrils flaring and breath heavy, it was less than five feet away! When I looked into its beastly eyes, I was sure it wanted only one thing. I had to get out of there.

I grabbed my pack and ran down the trail, looking back only to see how much lead I had. That bear came down the tree trunk like a firefighter down a pole. In sheer terror I ran on, daring to look over my shoulder again. Now the bear was running just as fast as it possibly could—in the opposite direction! My adrenaline-fueled laughter was rich, full, and free. I still laugh today as I picture that terrified little bear running for its life away from my fleeing figure.

I think about that bear often. Sometimes it's when I want to ask someone to pray with me, or tell what the Lord has done for me. There are times when I am so inspired by the joy of a song that I want to raise my hands toward heaven and the God who has shown me so much love. But I am ruled by the fear of scorn and rejection. I am afraid of offending someone. I'm so sure I already know how others will react. I wonder if God laughs or cries.

Peter and John were also faced with very real threats, yet they prayed, "Now, Lord, consider their threats and enable your servants to speak your word with great boldness. Stretch out your hand to heal and perform miraculous signs and wonders through the name of your holy servant Jesus" (Acts 4:29, 30, NIV).

"Dear Father, the next time I am afraid of what someone will think, remind me of the little bear, and give me strength to reach out in love. Amen."   TERESA GAY HOOVER KRUEGER

FEBRUARY 7

Let Him Direct Thy Path

Trust in the Lord with all thine heart; and lean not unto thine own understanding. In all thy ways acknowledge him, and he shall direct thy paths. Prov. 3:5, 6.

During one summer while away at college, I found a temporary job with a small firm that I had done work for before. One day the manager asked if I would follow her home that evening to pick up some documents to take to the office since she was leaving town the next day. As we pulled out of the parking lot, she asked me to follow her. I did for most of the way, but then we got on a dual lane highway, and the traffic began to build up in the left lane. Since the traffic was moving faster in the right lane, I passed her. I had been to her house before and I dislike traffic jams, anyway. Soon I reached her house and pulled into the driveway. I waited and waited. *Why did she stay in that slow lane*? I wondered.

Finally she arrived, and I got out of my car smiling broadly. I was feeling proud of the fact that I had avoided all that traffic and arrived there before her. Imagine my embarrassment when my manager told me she did not live there anymore! This was the reason she had asked me to follow her. Now we had lost precious minutes because I thought I knew the way.

Our Christian experience is sometimes like that. So often we get impatient with God. May God help us to trust Him and allow Him to guide our paths, so that when we reach our final home, we're at the right address. — CHELCIE STERLING-ANIM

Nothing Blocks His View

My frame was not hidden from you when I was made in the secret place. When I was woven together in the depths of the earth, your eyes saw my unformed body. Ps. 139:15, 16, NIV.

Finally the entourage pulled into the stadium. The excitement in the air heightened. The crowd swelled to more than 10,000 people. We'd waited three hours in the hot sun for this moment to arrive. Now there was movement on the platform.

With camera in hand I jockeyed for a favorable position. There were hundreds of people in front of me. I prayed that the new zoom lens that I'd purchased the day before wouldn't let me down. The roped area that spectators were advised to stay behind kept us a great distance from the platform—I wanted a closer view.

I don't know how I managed it, but as Nelson and Winnie Mandela approached the microphones on the platform, I was no longer behind the roped area. I was now positioned with the media corps. When I held my camera up and looked through my viewfinder, I nearly fainted with delight. Winnie Mandela's beauty far exceeded the photos I'd seen of her. Their radiant faces were so close, I felt I knew them well.

God doesn't need a pair of binoculars or a zoom lens to see us clearly and up close. Nothing blocks His view. His built-in seeing apparatus is never out of focus.

Often we suffer in silence, thinking that no one knows what we're going through—and that no one cares. We hesitate to share our burdens with others for fear of being misunderstood or even rejected.

But God knows us well. He knows when we are hurting. His all-seeing, loving eyes are focused on us when we shed tears in the wee hours of the night. God watches as we pace the floor—broken with despair. Our heavenly Father isn't kept at a distance from those He loves so dearly. There are no crowds blocking His view of you and me.

God is with us in the midst of our darkness, bringing with Him Jesus' message, "I am the Root and the Offspring of David, and the bright Morning Star" (Rev. 22:16, NIV).   Irma R. Lee

FEBRUARY 9

To Move God's Arm

Like as a father pitieth his children, so the Lord pitieth them that fear him. For he knoweth our frame; he remembereth that we are dust. Ps. 103:13, 14.

Our Glendora church had just finished another Revelation Seminar class, and the 62 townspeople had gone home. Juice pitchers were empty, the cookie plate lay bare. Enthusiastic members remained to discuss events of the evening.

But our exuberance was short-lived, for just then a 9-year-old girl burst through the door, panic written on her flushed little face. I knew her only as one of the children in the church.

"My little sister is lost!" she blurted as she burst into tears. "Please pray that they'll find her!" My husband jumped to his feet and was out the door. Impulsively this little girl I hardly knew threw her arms around me and sobbed out her grief.

The sprawling church campus is bordered on the north by the San Gabriel Mountains. Children's classrooms, the fellowship hall, the parsonage, and the sanctuary are spread around its perimeter, where the main street of this quiet little city dead-ends. A California oak spans an area wide enough to seat 100 people under its branches. But an ever so pleasant church campus can take on eerie aspects at night when a child is lost. Thoughts of abduction and other tragedies can crowd reason into a corner. We recalled the recent sighting of a mountain lion nearby and the Doberman it had overcome.

Everyone had joined in the search—everyone except the grieving child with whom I was praying and a distraught mother on her knees beneath a campus light. While I prayed, the little girl clung and wept. Periodically our eyes scanned the busy scene.

Suddenly, from across the campus, my husband's voice rose clear and distinct. "She's found!" My prayer halted with "Thank You, Lord," and I watched the mother hasten to her 3-year-old. But my little friend, still absorbed in her grief, didn't hear the message.

I repeated the glad news in her ear, and she was gone to join her precious little sister.

But something happened to me that night. The need of a little girl I hardly knew twisted my arm, and drew me to her forever.

That's the way it is with our heavenly Father. Too often we take His presence for granted. Maybe we don't even know Him "all that well." But when a crisis causes us to implore His help, His strong tender arms enfold us and His yearning heart is moved to respond.

If I, a struggling human being, could be so touched by the tears of a little girl I hardly knew, I will never doubt the compassion our heavenly Father feels when we cry out to Him!

We can actually move the arm of God! Our faith can stir His great heart of love! The pen of inspiration assures us, "By your fervent prayers of faith you can move the arm that moves the world" (*The Adventist Home*, p. 264). That's a promise!

LORRAINE HUDGINS

FEBRUARY 10

Joy Comes in the Morning

In the morning I lay my requests before you and wait in expectation. Ps. 5:3, NIV.

Once again I was in the hospital. This time I was sitting beside the bed of my father, holding his hand as I had done so often in the past. For the second time in his life he was scheduled to undergo open-heart surgery. This time, however, he was 78 years old, and the doctor explained to us frankly that Dad's chances of survival were not as great as they had been 15 years ago.

We visited him frequently, those few days before surgery, and I learned many valuable lessons. For example, my 13-year-old daughter was there with me on one occasion and my dad, noticing the tears on her face, asked the reason. "Grandpa," Bonnie said in such an open and forthright manner, "I'm afraid you're going to die." Inwardly I winced, and then I realized that she had verbalized what all of us had been afraid to say. Now we could talk about it.

Memories flooded my mind. I thought of the hours he had spent reading to me when I was a child; how many times he had read and reread my favorite Uncle Arthur stories. There were all the happy times I had spent tagging along with him while he worked at the college poultry farm. Even now I treasured our weekly rendezvous when the two of us went grocery shopping together.

I had often begged my dad for favors as a child; many times I'd asked him to give me something special. Sometimes the answer had been yes; other times, no. How quickly I had learned that when Dad said, "We'll see," it usually meant "Yes." I felt in much the same position now.

"Dear heavenly Father," I breathed, "please let me keep my dad a little bit longer. Please, if it is Your will."

The hours dragged by during surgery. The tears rained down my cheeks unbidden as I struggled with wanting my dad to live and yet trying to prepare myself to accept the possibility that God might say no this time. Finally the surgeon appeared, clad in those operating room scrubs that hint of life-and-death drama behind closed doors.

This time the answer was yes! After long hours in the recovery room, my dad was still alive and gaining strength. What joy our family felt that morning. In fact, I experienced such acute and grateful relief that it was almost painful. Like King David, I could say that God had filled me with joy; I had taken refuge in Him and was glad! (see Ps. 5:11; 16:11).　　　GLENICE LINTHWAITE STECK

FEBRUARY 11

Not Seeing Yet Believing

Therefore I say unto you, What things soever ye desire, when ye pray, believe that ye receive them, and ye shall have them. Matt. 11:24.

I was standing with the congregation in a school hall where a small church group met for worship. While singing a hymn, I looked up at the dusty rafters, seeking to make my heart susceptible to the Holy Spirit's filling. Suddenly the Holy Spirit spoke to me: "Your presence here is a result of your late mother's desire from the Lord in her lifetime."

Tears welled up in my eyes, for I was in a foreign country 6,000 miles from home where I had come as a missionary, married a national, and made my permanent home. Standing with my husband and two sons, I reflected how as a child I tagged behind my mother to a small Methodist church congregation where she was the pianist and once a cofounder. I and my brother had to sit by the piano in the simple services in an attitude of service not looking to be served.

My mother wanted to serve the Lord in a special way, and I often questioned why she had died of cancer at 51, before her children, her life's focus, had fully entered their life careers. She had molded our futures, and although she may not have meant for me to be a missionary in Africa, specific things she did fit me uniquely for the call I received, unsought but confirmed by prayer and minor miracles from the Lord. I feel she would not have wanted *me* to go so far away from home alone, but she would have loved it to have happened to her!

That was the revelation to me. I was fulfilling her dream for herself. And the Lord was showing me that as Moses saw the Promised Land and was not able to enter, and David could gather the materials for the building of the Temple but yet not build, the Lord was fulfilling my mother's dream in me although she did not see it in her lifetime.

The Lord God lives not in time but in eternity. He sees and knows all, and cares about all of our desires and is willing to fulfill them. But we are bound by time in a sinful planet, so we must grasp the Lord's promises and by faith receive them. "For now we see through a glass, darkly; but then face to face: now I know in part; but then shall I know even as also I am known" (1 Cor. 13:12).

Praise the Lord! EDNA THOMAS

FEBRUARY 12

A Tranquilizer for Problems

A cheerful heart is good medicine, but a crushed spirit dries up the bones. Prov. 17:22, NIV.

Most of us are overworked and underlaughed. Yet laughter is a wonderful tranquilizer for problems.

Dr. Joyce Brothers writes that humor "lets us detach ourselves from our troubles, laugh at them, and eventually overcome them." She says that "studies indicate that those who lack a sense of humor are short on emotional stability, self-confidence, and the ability to endure stress. Those with a good sense of humor tend to be more resilient and are able to cope better." Medical research suggests that laughter may help reduce the risk of heart disease, high blood pressure, and stress-producing emotions.

Yes, a good belly laugh has been scientifically proven to react positively on our body systems. In his book *Laugh After Laugh*, Dr. Raymond Moody tells of a clown performing for seriously ill children in a hospital. One small girl giggled with delight as he approached. There was immediate excitement from the hospital staff. The clown learned that this child had been catatonic and unresponsive for months. Laughter became the breakthrough.

Norman Cousins, in *Anatomy of an Illness*, tells how he discovered the benefits of laughter in treating his own serious illness. After watching funny television programs, such as *Candid Camera*, he experienced less pain. Ten minutes of mirthful laughter resulted in two hours of pain-free sleep.

Humor helps us keep the stresses of life in perspective. I believe humor is a matter of survival for stressed women. That's why I use lots of it in my seminars. Humor is a blessing.

One of my favorite stories is of the newly married wife who, after her shower, bounded into the living room—stark naked—to surprise her husband with a hug and a kiss. To her horror, he was not alone. The pastor had stopped by for a visit. With a shriek she fled into the bedroom. Other women might have found a new church home, but she marched up to her pastor the very next week and said, "Hi, I'm Jan. I wasn't sure you'd recognize me with my clothes on." Together they shared a good laugh, and the awkwardness passed.

If something doesn't go exactly the way you think it should today, try laughing about it rather than coming unglued. It will take the sting out of a situation and put a smile on your face.

And remember it's scriptural. Bildad encourages Job by saying, "He will yet fill your mouth with laughter and your lips with shouts of joy" (Job 8:21). And David describes a return to prosperity with the words "our mouths were filled with laughter, our tongues with songs of joy" (Ps. 126:2).

Someone has said, "If you are happy, notify your face." Good advice. Start today with a smile and take it from there.

NANCY VAN PELT

FEBRUARY 13

God's Perfect Gift

Every good gift and every perfect present comes from heaven; it comes down from God. James 1:17, TEV.

When I was young I had three goals for my immediate future: to marry, to have children, and to live happily ever after. Today, 27 years later, I can truthfully say that I have reached my goals.

As soon as my husband and I were married, we looked forward to welcoming the first of the four children we had planned. However, as the months and years passed without any sign of an increase in our family, I did my best to persuade God to fit into my plans. Instead He fit me into His.

One day we received a call to the mission field to step in for another family who had to return home because of illness. We accepted and soon found ourselves in a leprosy hospital in West Africa. Four years passed, and one day a little girl was born at the hospital—unwanted by her biological parents. As I cared for this little girl, my prayers changed. "May we keep her, Lord?" I asked. "And if not, please find some other home for her before we get too attached to her."

After five months I felt confident that God wanted her to be ours, and therefore I was devastated when late one evening the biological mother approached me and wanted to talk. Because I had to come back the next morning with an interpreter, I had lots of time to think and pray. By this time we had come to love "our little daughter," and I remember telling God how disappointed I was that it had taken Him five months to "make up His mind" just to give us another disappointment. In the middle of my complaining I suddenly heard a voice saying: "The baby is going to stay with you. The biological mother will ask only for clothes."

I repeated that assurance in my mind as I walked down to the hospital ward the next morning with an interpreter. God kept His promise. The biological mother had no interest in the baby, and asked only for clothes. Our daughter had come to stay. Two years later another little girl made our family complete.

If you are a young woman praying for a child of your own and think adoption is a "second best," remember that with God there is no second best, only the very best. Today, 20 years later, we still thank God for answering our prayers His way. We will never know how our life would have been had God chosen to answer our prayers differently. All we know is that "every good gift and every perfect present comes from heaven; it comes down from God."

BIRTHE KENDEL

FEBRUARY 14

Not Just for Lovers

A friend loveth at all times. Prov. 17:17.

Valentine's Day struck my fourth-grade class with a storm of preadolescent emotion charged with giggles, shyness, and uncontrollable blushes.

We brought punch-out cards portraying furry animals and

cartoon children billowing balloons of sentiment. Then, with eyes riveted upon the valentine box, we waited for true love or terrible disappointment.

Some questions still linger in my mind. Did Del sign other girls' cards with "love"? Did Donnie inscribe my card with more Xs and Os than the ones he sent to Linda and Sharon?

In academy, Valentine's was the season for 8″ x 10″ photos, banquets, and hand-holding in the dark across the aisle of the school bus. On my Seventh-day Adventist college campus, February 14 sparkled with new watches, unique symbols of engagement when worn on a young woman's right wrist.

When my friend Aileen once paid my way to an expensive special event in the midst of the sea of ordinary days far from Christmas and my birthday, I was dumbfounded. "It's Friends' Day," she announced with as much authority as Abraham Lincoln in establishing Thanksgiving.

Friendship is worth celebrating. After all, is it not a friend's love that sustains us when a romance fades, a lover is false, or a marriage fails?

But friendship is more than an insurance policy for our romantic mishaps. Consider how friends function in our lives. When we are recalcitrant or frightened, who but a friend can persuade us to think a new thought? When we falter at opportunities to grow, who but a friend can understand our fragile ego, our need to succeed? Who but a friend really accepts us as we are?

Friendship is a sacred thing. In the final conversation with the disciples before His death, Jesus said there was no greater love than when one friend laid down his or her life for another (see John 15:13).

Valentine's ought not to be just for lovers. Let us celebrate those who in our joy or sorrow are truly with us and whose love restores our souls.   Kit Watts

FEBRUARY 15

Stranded in Elephant Country

Let this mind be in you, which was also in Christ Jesus: who, being in the form of God, thought it not robbery to be equal with God: but made himself of no reputation, and took upon him the form of a servant, and was made in the likeness of men. Phil. 2:5-7.

We were headed for the bird sanctuary in Sri Lanka, and had already passed through beautiful areas of lush greenery. In one area our car passed within a safe distance of a herd of more than 60 elephants. In another area we passed by deer grazing peacefully on the green grass, and a peacock that spread out its beautiful tail as though to greet us.

Our hearts were merry as we drove along, and we had high expectations that the birds we would see would be even more beautiful than those we had already seen. Suddenly there was a big "bang!" as we drove over a large rock, and the engine stopped. No amount of trying would get it started again. We decided that the timing chain in the engine must have broken. We sat and waited, wondering what to do in this lonely place. The few people around us were hurrying in the opposite direction. We asked them where they were going and why the big hurry. They said that herds of elephants often pass through here, and that if we stayed we would probably be trampled to death.

Here we were stuck in the middle of elephant country with our son and two daughters and a broken car. Would the elephants really come and kill us? We prayed, committing ourselves to God's all-powerful hands, then set up camp and started a fire.

"Daddy, you sit up half the night and keep the fire going, then I will look after it for the rest of the night. Don't worry; God will protect us," said our 12-year-old son, who had always found joy in trusting God.

To our surprise, we soon heard the sound of a motor. We looked, and saw a tractor coming. Someone had reported our plight to the rangers. Soon they had us in safe quarters, and they even promised to help repair our car.

This experience reminds me of our Great Ranger, Jesus Christ, who found us when we were lost! We were sunken in sin, and eternal death was our natural reward. He sought and found us, and was willing to give up His life to save us. The rangers came to save us because it was their duty, but Jesus came because of His great love for us. Let's determine each day to stay close to Him so that His sacrifice won't be in vain. INDRANI J. ARIYARATNAM

FEBRUARY 16

Real Friendship

By this everyone will know that you are my disciples, if you have love for one another. John 14:35, NRSV.

Have you ever enjoyed the blessing of having a best friend? A *real* best friend? There's nothing like having one, whether you're 6 or 60.

My best friend in first and second grade was Gloria. We shared our lunches and our snacks. We loved to practice writing our letters and numbers together. We took turns pushing each other at the swings during recess. I was always full of energy; Gloria was quiet and introspective. When feelings were inevitably bruised or hurt, we always quickly made up. There was so much fun in being together and no fun at all being apart. We knew the real love of friendship beat in our 6-year-old hearts—and it still does today.

Although years have passed, I don't believe the dynamics of true friendship have changed that much—even from the beginning of time. The human heart will always crave love and companionship—God made it that way. But the heart craves the real thing, and that's what a true friend brings. Gloria and I knew that, and the elements of our friendship are still relevant today.

While it was fun to "pool resources" in first grade, the secret ingredient that made our food taste so good wasn't just the meal, but the sharing. Half a sandwich or cookie was always better if my little buddy was enjoying it with me. And now it's good to remember that no object, however valuable, is more precious than a person. A person is not an acquisition. Such friendship is a gift. If we want to know others because of what they *have* and not just for *themselves*, we're on the wrong track!

Nothing makes completing a difficult or disagreeable task better than having a friend to help, and nothing adds more joy to a happy time than having a good friend with you. Are you still able to work together and have fun together with friends the way children do? If not, it may be time to slow down, take stock of things, and rearrange priorities.

It's easiest to relax and have fun, or just plain relax, when you know you're accepted. A good friend will take pleasure in you without trying to give your personality a "makeover," or worse, a complete overhaul! At times constructive criticism may be necessary, but the more reluctant the giver and the more gentle the message, the better. When you do clash, trust each other to find a way back to the things that made you friends in the first place! Don't be afraid to make room for mutual forgiveness when feelings are hurt and there are misunderstandings.

Everything comes down to mutual trust and confidence. This is not blind loyalty, but an honest belief in others, and a hope for the best for them. It takes a certain maturity to handle the extremes as well: to cheer friends on in times of great success, to genuinely share their joy, or to stand by them in times of tragedy, in the dark days of bereavement or loss. God gives the special insight to see that when the human heart is open, it is most fragile. We must learn to handle these open hearts with an ever-gentle touch. He does. He is our ultimate best Friend, and we can learn so much from Him.

KYNA HINSON

FEBRUARY 17

Mentoring Friendships

Bid the older women likewise to be reverent in behavior . . . and so train the young women. Titus 2:3, 4, RSV.

I like the term mentor more than role model, because mentoring calls for a relationship! The women of the Northwest Bible church in Dallas, Texas, have created a beautiful, brilliant strategy to make their women's ministry come to life. They call it the Heart-to-Heart plan. In their own words, they describe it like this:

Heart-to-Heart is "a program that has been successful in developing supportive friendships between older and younger women. Titus 2:3-5 places the responsibility for teaching and disciplining younger women upon mature, godly women. There are important reasons for this. First, women understand women. They have gone through [some of] the same experiences and felt the same emotions. Moreover, sympathetic listening and godly counsel often diffuse tense situations before they escalate into crises.

"Second, the immorality that is disqualifying Christian workers from the ministry would be avoided. Ninety percent of these situations start with men counseling women. To fill this role, spiritually mature women should have a biblical perspective of life, a sound working knowledge of the Scriptures, and a solid track record of godly conduct. . . .

"The following guidelines are suggested: 1. Make a one-year commitment to the relationship. 2. Contact each other once a week and meet at least once a month. 3. Pray for each other. 4. Do things together, whether it be Bible study, shopping, learning a new skill, or just going to lunch. Each set of partners is free to do what they want as long as they work on the relationship" (Vickie Kraft, *Women's Ministries, an Overview of Philosophy and Ministry*, p. 6).

The Heart-to-Heart program has a good plan to match the women, all volunteers, according to their needs. Young women get the benefit of wisdom without the parental overtones they might get from their mothers, since they meet as friends. Older women with extra time get eager recipients of their wisdom and care, and the benefit of new friendships when their own children may be grown and living on their own. This strategy works even in churches that don't have a plan as highly developed as the Northwest Bible church's.

I have become more and more grateful to the mature Christian women I know. They have shared their experiences—what it was like to live in hardship, to have their faith stretch to God, and to have that faith rewarded. They have lived through the deaths of dear ones, through loss of property, through threats and taunts. They have stood faithfully by husbands, or struggled with families in the wake of death or divorce. They have made brave strides into the world, some with God only to guide them. Many have plunged into studies in new fields, encouraging their children as they all worked side by side. While life has been no bed of roses for many of them, they can all tell of sweet moments and share the fragrance with those of us who will only listen. The mentoring friendship— God bless you as you search for one and keep you if you've found one. It's a rare, precious gift! KYNA HINSON

FEBRUARY 18

Being Your Own Friend

Say to wisdom, "You are my sister," and call insight your intimate friend. Prov. 7:4, RSV.

In her interesting book *Your Personality Tree*, Florence Littauer tells us that there are four personality types. She explains that the sanguine is sunny and loves interacting with people; the melancholy is contemplative and likes to work behind the scenes; the choleric likes to be right up front, running things; and the phlegmatic simply wants peace and quiet with the least possible fuss!

Wherever you fit in this scheme, or in any combination of the temperaments, do you like yourself? It may seem to be a light question, but really, it gets to the heart of Christianity. There is nothing like redemption, because when it comes to our lives, we are reminded of our creation as well. God made us, and then died to redeem us. Time and time again, when we see Him at work in Scripture, He demonstrates His great love for sinners. He does not care about all the ground-in dirt that has accumulated in humanity over thousands of years. He cares about you and me! He cares about our lives and the quality of our lives. He cares about us when we think we're absolutely right and when we're dead wrong. He loves us even though He knows everything about us, and He wants us to turn to Him for help, for strength, and for resources in times of plenty and times of trouble.

Ultimately, when we are comfortable with Him, we become most comfortable with ourselves. Oh, that does not eliminate loneliness—the human heart will always yearn for company. But people—family members and friends—will take on a different value to us. We won't feel the urge to clutch at them so possessively, to be so demanding, or to close our circles to others selfishly. We will welcome, not demand, their friendship and their love when it comes to us, secure enough in ourselves to give the same freely. Does this sound too lofty? Well, it won't be easy. It's never easy to grow. But becoming friends with Jesus, through quiet times, through prayer, and through meditation, can make us most "at home" with ourselves, and ideally, most like Him. KYNA HINSON

FEBRUARY 19

Walking in His Steps

To this you were called, because Christ suffered for you, leaving you an example, that you should follow in his steps. 1 Peter 2:21, NIV.

Have you ever tried to walk in deep, dry sand? It can be a rather slow-going situation. Recently while we were out on the beautiful Oregon coast, I found myself having to cross a considerable amount of deep, dry sand to get out to the refreshing ocean. As I struggled along, it seemed that it was going to be impossible for me to make it all the way. I was sinking in and sliding all over, and at times almost falling down. Then I made a discovery: if I walked right in my husband's footsteps, I could go along almost as easily as I could walk on wet sand. I found, however, that I had to hurry or the wind would obliterate his footprints. If I wanted to do my own thing, like pick up driftwood or shells, then I had to plow my way through the sand by my own power!

In our spiritual life a lot of us choose to do our own thing. We have a perfectly beautiful set of footprints to follow. Jesus laid them out for us and gave us the option of walking in them or of blundering and plowing along, trying to make our own set of prints. We are told that when we follow Him, we can take hold of His divinity and enjoy heaven right here on this earth. Should we have any question about what to do? "Christ is our model; imitate Him, plant your feet in His steps" (*Testimonies*, vol. 5, p. 345). PAT MADSEN

"Stressed or Rest"

*Come to me, all you who are weary and burdened, and I
will give you rest. Matt. 11:28, NIV.*

Traveling is such an interesting adventure. The discovery of
sights, sounds, and smells captures my attention around each
new bend. However, the mode and mind-set in which I travel makes
a big difference not only in what I enjoy along the way, but how I
feel after arriving at my destination.

This idea is well illustrated by contrasting a trip in which stops
and activities are included in the daily plan with one during which
you drive nonstop, ignoring everything but the need for pit
stops.

Life is also like a journey. With which type of trip does your
sojourn compare? Is it exciting, interesting, and enjoyable, with
refreshing stops along the way? Or is it better described by the
bumper sticker that commands, "Get in, sit down, hold on, and
shut up"? At the end of a hectic day do you arrive frazzled and
tired, wondering how and why you ever got involved with all this
in the first place?

Have you noticed how places associated with refreshment for
weary travelers have the word "rest" included in their names—rest
stop, restroom, restaurant? Now notice some other words that,
when applied, can help in coping with life: restoration, restraint,
restitution, and maybe just plain rest!

Life in the fast lane can exact a heavy toll. Despite the fact that
Jesus didn't live in the space age, He well knew through experience
how draining everyday living can be. I'm so glad He empathized
with our predicament and lovingly provided the needed remedy.
Talking to His disciples, as well as to us, He entreated, "Come with
me by yourselves to a quiet place and get some rest" (Mark 6:31,
NIV).

In the hassle of our daily schedule we need to find the time to
take advantage of Christ's stress prescription. He's waiting to give
us just what we need.

Are you tired of the struggle,
Does it seem that life has been unfair?
The temptations, the burdens overwhelm you,
It feels like no one cares.

But there's One who's beside you
To supply everything you'll ever need.
Take a moment to listen
And you'll hear His voice softly plead.

"Come unto Me, you who are tired, and I will give you rest.
Take My yoke upon you. I'm gentle and humble.
In Me you will be blest."

If the whole world forsakes you
Jesus offers His love constantly.
When life's problems confront you
The solution He will always be.

You're of infinite value,
More than sparrows or flowers so rare.
Hear Him whisper this promise
As you come to Jesus in prayer.

"Come unto Me, you who are tired, and I will give you rest.
Take My yoke upon you. I'm gentle and humble.
In Me you will be blest."

DEBBY GRAY WILMOT

FEBRUARY 21

Stand on Your Feet

Now get up and stand on your feet. I have appeared to you to appoint you as a servant and as a witness of what you have seen of me and what I will show you. Acts 26:16, NIV.

In her prolific writings Ellen White says that there are three ways in which the Lord reveals His will to us: (1) in His Word, (2) by His providential workings, and (3) through appeals of His Holy Spirit making impressions upon our hearts.

His voice "will be recognized," she further writes, "if we do not separate our souls from Him." She then counsels that if we are in doubt about any subject that we should first consult the Scriptures.

When military and political unrest forced our temporary evacuation from Zaire in late 1991, I was working on a manuscript for a junior-aged devotional. My husband, Date, and I decided that I'd go to North America to work on the book while he would stay close to the border and reenter the country as soon as possible. My good friend Dianne was temporarily managing a hotel property and gave me a quiet, comfortable room—an ideal place to write.

Having been evacuated in a hurry, I carried little besides a few clothes, my computer, and a Bible. All my reference books and notes were at the mission, and without them I felt lost.

Staring at the blank computer screen a few mornings later, I didn't know how I could possibly finish the manuscript by press deadline. "God," I said, "I need some tangible evidence that You'll help me."

God, I believe, prefers closer communication than for us simply to open the Bible and take the first text seen as His message for the day. Just then, though, I did open my Bible at random and began scanning the page. Paul was telling his story to King Agrippa. "Now get up and stand on your feet," I read. "I have appeared to you to appoint you as a servant and as a witness of what you have seen of me and what I will show you."

Those words immediately translated into a direct command. "Start writing. Tell what you know about Me. I'll show you the rest." And I went to work claiming that as a promise. Each day ideas did come. Friends shared stories and reference materials, and I met the press deadline.

I continue to claim that promise for my writing, and God continues to give direction—through the Bible, by providence, and through impressions of the Holy Spirit. Corrine Vanderwerff

FEBRUARY 22

Promises

For no matter how many promises God has made, they are "Yes" in Christ. 2 Cor. 1:20, NIV.

I have a real problem with promises. I must make at least 20 of them some days. I'm not talking about the big promises, like promising to "love, honor, and cherish till death do us part." I made that promise once and I intend to keep it for a lifetime. No, I'm talking about promises that involve the little day-to-day things. I promise myself that I'll get up right when the alarm goes off at 5:00 a.m. so that I'll have time for a big leisurely breakfast. I promise my husband that I'll be home before 5:30 that evening. I promise my students that I'll have their essays graded by the end of the week—for sure!

Then comes "tomorrow." The alarm goes off—and the quilt feels so warm. A few more minutes of comfort suddenly seem much more important than a good breakfast. I really plan to leave school before 5:00, but a student needs extra help with an assignment—and I still have all those essays to grade. I don't get into my car until 6:00. Or I might leave school on time, and tell my students they'll have to wait one more day to get their essays back.

Such promises are easy to make. It's amazing how difficult they can be to keep! Even though I try to be careful and think before I make such promises, sometimes circumstances change. Sometimes I have to change my plans—and in the process I break promises.

That's one reason I find today's text so remarkable—and so comforting. It has been estimated that there are more than 7,000 promises by God found in the Bible (*All the Promises of the Bible*, p. 10). If I were to make that many promises, I don't think I could remember them all, much less keep them all! But God's Word says that no matter how many promises He makes to us, He keeps every one of them!   SUE HAYFORD

FEBRUARY 23

He's Big Enough

But my God shall supply all your need according to his riches in glory by Christ Jesus. Phil. 4:19.

Children can present such challenges and insight for living that I now look forward to "hanging out" with them on occasion. It seems to me that my niece, Christina, is constantly sharing fresh perspectives and new understanding in realms that would otherwise lie dormant.

Just before I left home to begin seminary studies, I asked Christina if she wanted to spend the night with me. She jumped at the opportunity, and we spent the evening doing our favorite things. But like most 5-year-olds, when it was time for bed she manufactured many reasons to prolong that inevitable fate. Having given her a bath, I told her a story and listened as she prayed before tucking her in. And here our story begins.

First, she needed a drink of water, "or juice, if you have any," and so I brought her something to drink. Of course, this led directly to her needing to go to the bathroom, and so I allowed her to get up for that. Next she announced that she was afraid of the dark, and so I scurried around for a few minutes to locate a night-light. That settled, I went back downstairs to resume my packing, hoping that she would now fall asleep. But it wasn't very long before her voice summoned me again.

"I'm still scared," she said. "Can't you come to bed with me?"

I proceeded to explain that I had many things to accomplish before I could come to bed, but that she shouldn't be afraid. I reminded her that she had prayed and that Jesus would take care of her.

Imagine my shock and dismay as she retorted, "Humph! He can't take care of Himself." Appalled, I sat down on the bed next to her and asked, "Why would you say that, Christina?"

"Well, He's just a little baby," she explained.

"No, He's not!" I countered.

"Yes, He is. My teacher said so and that He was wrapped in swaddling clothes and lying in a manger," she insisted.

Breathing a sigh of relief and with a smile on my face, I began assuring this precious little girl that, in fact, Jesus was all grown up, big and strong, and truly able to take care of her.

"I'm glad He's big enough . . . aren't you?" she asked just before she fell asleep. This final comment caused me to consider and appreciate more fully that which I had taken for granted. We don't serve a baby God or a puny God that is limited in His capacity to take care of us. We are promised that our "God shall supply all [our] need according to his riches in glory by Christ Jesus," and that which God has promised, He is able to perform.   IFEOMA I. KWESI

FEBRUARY 24

Free at Last

You will know the truth, and the truth will set you free.
John 8:32, NIV.

Released! What does it mean to a hostage to be set free at last? While glued to the TV to watch hostages coming home, we still cannot imagine their real feelings. But we rejoice. We thrill at the thought of their freedom.

What about the rest of us? When God gives us freedom from the captivity of ignorance and the misery of bad relationships or bad habits, what do we do? With our spiritual release, how are we to live? Do we really know that we are released and from what? Do we feel empty like the house that was cleaned out in Matthew 12:44 and eventually filled with more evil? Or do our spirits soar with great elation, love, and peace, ready to take action? Do we think what it might really mean to be with God, home at last? We can be at home with God now in this world because of the promised Holy Spirit who will abide with us and teach us. Many of us continue to be bound by conflicts and demands, little realizing that we can have freedom from the rush and the press of duties by connecting with the Comforter who will dwell with us. A number of times Jesus talked about truth and freedom. If the truth sets us free, if the truth is the Word, if the Comforter is the Spirit of truth, then having the Comforter and the Word will bring us release and freedom. In John 14:26 Jesus talked about the Comforter teaching us, and the very next words are "Peace I leave with you" (verse 27).

Some of us know a lot about being depressed or down in the pit of despair. We feel discouraged, incapable of getting out of our everyday burdens—school problems, poor grades, criticism, and low self-esteem. What do you mean, spirits soaring? The only spirit I have is a disenchanted spirit, weary and heavy. How many of us need peace, freedom, and comfort!

But what hostage would say, "Oh, I've become accustomed to these four walls and the chains, so I might as well stay; I understand the routine"? No. No. No. We have to say we would rush out into the light and air, hugging our loved ones close—totally savoring the moment, the feeling of release.

Let us ask God to free us from our pits of routine and depressing thoughts and put us on a higher plane of thinking. Let us ask for the Comforter to bring us peace, teach us the Word, and dwell with us so that we may be released to feel the joy of freedom in God's love. JULIA L. PEARCE

FEBRUARY 25

Cherie Crosses Some Bridges

A little child shall lead them. Isa. 11:6.

When the Neall family first went to Cambodia in 1957, our 5-year-old Cherie created a sensation wherever she went. The people stroked her blonde hair. "Does she paint it?" they asked. Looking into her blue eyes, they marveled, "She has blue and white eyes!" They pinched the fuzz on her arms and exclaimed, "She has fur like a monkey!" Cherie reveled in all the attention.

One day Ah Huay, our helper, took Cherie to her village for

the weekend. When I found out about it I was beside myself with worry. I could just see my little girl in a dirt-floor hut surrounded by dirty, naked children. Would she eat unclean meat? Would she drink river water? Would she get lonesome when night came and she had to sleep on a bamboo bed with several other people? When they tried to comfort her, would she understand a word they said? Would she worship in a Buddhist temple looking at idols?

I insisted that we go and get Cherie. "Now, this is a fine fix to be in," said my husband. "Forty-two kilometers one way on an abominable road—all on a Friday afternoon." We set off in the dust and heat of the day, the paved road giving way to dirt. And we began to cross bridges—26 thunderous, splitting, loudly protesting bridges. My heart was brightened by the prospect of rescuing Cherie. "Poor little thing! How thrilled she'll be to see us," I mused. I could just see my sad-faced little girl running up and hugging me.

"Look at all those people in the road," said Ralph as we neared the village. "There's a blonde head—it's Cherie!"

Cherie, in triumph, was perched atop Ah Huay's big bicycle, while a large procession of children surrounded and followed her. She was queen for a day, her dusty feet and dirty dress topped off with a bright-red hibiscus in her hair. Ralph tried to capture the moment on film, but the crowd dissolved before the camera.

Then I ran and grabbed Cherie.

"Did you miss me?" I cried.

"No," she answered quite frankly.

"Did you know Ah Huay wants to keep you here for the weekend?"

"No [excitedly]. Am I going to sleep here?"

"Do you want to?"

"Yes, that would be fun!"

"Have you eaten yet?"

"Yes, I had a good dinner."

"What was it?"

"I drank water out of a coconut. And I had candy and a big piece of French bread."

I wasn't too thrilled.

Just then Ah Huay came up, quite embarrassed by the turn of events. "She's very happy here," she kept telling me. And then I realized we had a diplomatic problem on our hands. The family and the neighbors had considered it quite an honor to entertain an American girl, and now we were coming to take her away.

Lamely I hit on a solution. "We'll all come soon and stay overnight," I promised. We said goodbye and once more started off on the bumpy, dusty ride home. It wasn't long before our dirty Cherie was sound asleep on the back shelf of the car.

As we rumbled over the bridges once more, it occurred to me that Cherie had crossed many bridges that day. Bridges that I had anticipated in misery, she barely noticed—bridges of language, diet, sanitation, and religion. These people were her friends. She loved them, and love crosses all bridges.   BEATRICE S. NEALL

Perspectives

In every thing give thanks: for this is the will of God in Christ Jesus concerning you. 1 Thess. 5:18.

Rain poured onto the Peugeot as it wound along the shores of the Mediterranean, making its way north. The road was good, and the rain, though heavy, was not intolerable. At least it wouldn't have been intolerable if the car's windshield wipers had been in working order. Howard peered ahead, trying to keep on course. Rain coursed down the windshield, distorting images, and the frustration level became tangible in the car.

Little Amy, riding beside her daddy, studied the situation with all the sensitivity of a 7-year-old. She looked at her daddy's squinted eyes and tense, leaning body, then looked at the blinding windshield, looked again at his eyes, and again at the windshield. "Daddy," she finally said in a tone of both sternness and incredulity, "don't look at the windshield. Look at the road."

A grin spread across Howard's face as his focus involuntarily changed and the road became at once easier to navigate. It didn't take him long, either, to realize the significance of what his little daughter had just taught him, not only for driving safety, but for living.

Circumstances had not improved: same place, same time, same broken wipers, same rain. But a little girl's perspective had turned a tense, trying situation into no more than a demanding one.

Life is not a smooth-running machine. There will always be traffic jams and supermarket lines, red traffic signals and ill-timed phone calls, sick children and worn-out car brakes, troubled and troublesome people, and just plain bad days. How circumstances affect us depends largely on a matter of perspective. We can make up our minds to be content even amid life's little problems, to see through the rain to the road ahead.

My children are used to my "perspective template." It's been worn out on them. Laid up against the most difficult situation, it usually changes perspective. It goes like this: if this is the worst thing that ever happens to me, I shall be very fortunate.

Boiled-over kettle of soup? If that is the worst thing that ever happens to me I shall be very fortunate. Lost in a new town? Frustrating, yes, but if it's the worst thing that ever happens to me, won't I be happy. The undeserving target of someone's slanderous tongue? Hard as that is to take, if it's the worst thing that ever happens to me . . . Flight delays, flu, even something as bad as broken bones—"if it's the worst thing . . ." seems to throw my vision into a clearer mode. I can give thanks that I can see the road in spite of the rain blocking my view.　　　　　Susan Scoggins

God's Hands on the Wheel

Fear thou not; for I am with thee: be not dismayed; for I am thy God: I will strengthen thee; yea, I will help thee; yea, I will uphold thee with the right hand of my righteousness. Isa. 41:10.

A few months ago I traveled to the north of England to an area known as the Peak District in Derbyshire. It is not exactly a mountainous region, but it certainly has some very high hills! For some reason I took the wrong exit off the freeway, and found myself on the wrong side of the Peaks. It was by now quite dark, and my route would take me across country. The road wound its way out of the small town of Macclesfield and began to rise up above the town steadily. The vehicle in front of me was an ambulance. Under normal circumstances this would have been cause for complaint, as they do not travel that fast. However, on that particular night it felt good to be following those lights. Still the road went higher and higher, and now it was totally dark, with nothing on either side but moorlands and hills. Suddenly the ambulance signaled right and disappeared down what seemed like an old trail. I realized what a comfort it had been having that vehicle in front of me. Now I was totally alone, and it seemed as if I were heading straight for the clouds! There was not another vehicle in sight, and I could feel the fear building up.

What a place this would be to break down! What would I do—stay with the car? Although I had prayed at the start of my journey, I again asked God to protect me.

I could see the road ahead disappearing into what looked like clouds or a very heavy fog. Then, just yards in front of me, the ambulance rejoined the road, and we both entered the fog together! I had no concern for anything to the side or behind me—there was only one thought—keep your eyes on those lights. And that's just what happened for three fourths of a mile up on that mountainous road. As long as I kept my eyes on the ambulance, I would not get lost or be left up there alone. Does that sound familiar? Soon we started to descend, and just as we came into the town of Buxton, the ambulance turned right, and I turned left, safe at my destination. I knew what it was to have the Lord send His angels to guide and protect me. What a providence. What a great God!

VALERIE A. ECCLES

FEBRUARY 28

Discover Prayer

So I say to you: Ask and it will be given to you; seek and you will find; knock and the door will be opened to you. Luke 11:9, NIV.

I have always believed in the principle of prayer, but until a few years ago it was not a priority in my life, nor had I ever experienced the power of prayer. It was not a rebellious spirit I exhibited, just ignorance about prayer power. Some people may accidentally discover the right way to pray. But most of us pray in a haphazard manner and accept disappointing results. No one had ever introduced me to the incredible, exciting, and life-changing results of talking daily with the living God of the universe.

Then one day I came face-to-face with the biggest problem I have ever faced. The usual "window-shopping" or "I-don't-really-expect-anything-to-happen" prayer would no longer do. When window-shopping, you aren't serious about purchasing anything and come home empty-handed after hours of shopping.

Suddenly I recognized that I had spent hours (perhaps even years) in window-shopping prayer. I rarely got down to specifics. I expected little from prayer and received little. Now that I needed much, I was totally unprepared.

It was out of such an experience that a pattern for personal devotions and prayer took shape for me. My daughter, Carlene, introduced me to a plan that made sense even in the midst of chaos.

Organization is my middle name. I could organize *anything*—a home, files, drawers, a husband (well—sometimes!), books, seminars. But no one had ever even hinted that one's prayer life needed structure and organization. All I'd ever learned about prayer was "present your requests before God daily." I did, and it seemed like vain repetition and a series of jumbled requests that boiled down to little more than asking God for whatever I could remember on that day.

But it was here in the midst of personal crisis, with the help of a prayer notebook and a little organization, that I learned to pray. I noticed that as I wrote out specific requests, God answered. Even in the midst of crisis God was working all around me.

You too can discover that rather than being another dreary task to complete, a prayer notebook offers structure, organization, and best of all, hope. It will beckon you each morning, remind you of your heart's desires, and encourage you. It will speak to you daily of your real needs and call you to accountability before God.

Why not write out several prayer requests right now?

NANCY VAN PELT

MARCH 1

I Talked to God Last Night

How precious also are Your thoughts to me, O God! How great is the sum of them! If I should count them, they would be more in number than the sand; when I awake, I am still with You. Ps. 139:17, 18, NKJV.

I woke up in the black of the night, reached out to touch my husband, and he wasn't there!

Loneliness overwhelmed me as I realized where he was—thousands of miles away on a foreign continent. I couldn't go back to sleep, so I began thinking about God and His relationship to me. Did He really know I was lying there in the dark, quiet house alone? Did He really care?

Then I thought about my years as a mother of four small children. Never did one cry out in the night without my coming to my child's side. And am I not one of God's children? A mother can be depended on to come any time her child cries in the night. Surely God, who said He was more dependable than even the mother of a nursing child, can be counted on to come when I cry out in the night.

It was then that I became aware that I was not alone in my

darkly curtained house. I felt His presence so close I could almost feel His touch on my hand. I felt cozy and comfortable, and it seemed I could hear Him say, "Ellen, you are not alone. I'm right here by your side whether you're asleep or awake. I will never leave you!"

I was awed with the thought that our magnificent God can be by my side and yet by yours, too. I don't understand it all, but I know it's true, because He is always there when I reach out to Him.

I have awakened in the night on other occasions and have learned to cherish these quiet times and little conversations God and I have together. Sometimes He offers a gentle rebuke, sometimes a "Well done," and sometimes just a comforting presence in a lonely situation.

Next time you awaken in the night and can't sleep, don't waste the hours. Take some time to talk with Him. He is waiting to hear from you. He wants to bless you with His presence.　　ELLEN BRESEE

MARCH 2

Run to Jesus

They will see His face. Rev. 22:4, NIV.

We sat together in the deepening twilight—four women in my mother's little retirement center apartment. It had been a time of remembering. Eva had recalled that more than 50 years ago my mother and father had courted each other in the Caseys' living room. How we had laughed at her description of "courtship back then."

The autumn wind gently rustled the leaves near the open patio door as Eva got up from her chair and prepared to return to her own room down the hall. Pausing a moment with her hand on the doorknob, she spoke of her own husband, Claude, who had died several years before. "Oh, Kathleen, I can hardly wait for heaven," she said. "I shall *run* to Claude." The door closed, and she was gone.

My mother slowly got up from her chair and walked across the room to gaze at a picture of my father, who had died the year before. In a voice that was vibrant with love and hope she said, "I shall run to greet your father, too, Arlene. Oh, yes! I will *run* to Warren." I could picture the scene. My mother, the toils and troubles of this life forgotten, running toward my dad, standing there in vigor and health, arms outstretched to greet her.

Tears filled my eyes. *How wonderful*, I thought. Both of these women are acting out Paul's words recorded in 1 Thessalonians 4:13. They are grieving with hope, carrying a picture of their loved ones in their minds—the present loss balanced by the anticipation of future reunion. Heaven was not simply an ethereal concept to them. It was a real place seen by the eye of faith—a place where we will recognize others and be recognized (see 1 Cor. 13:12). We will run to greet each other without our infirmities; we will run free from the pain of loss; we will run exuberantly with the joy and energy of eternal youth.

In the silence that followed, I looked at Ellen and felt a twinge of discomfort. Having never married, she had neither husband nor children. *What was she feeling right now*? I wondered. Almost as if reading my thoughts, Ellen said quietly, "I shall run to Jesus. I shall run to greet my Best Friend." What a beautiful picture those two sentences created. The words of a song by John W. Peterson flashed through my mind: "I want to see my Saviour first of all." Despite what our lives on earth may have held in terms of human relationships, and regardless of who else we want to see, heaven is a place where there is a special Someone we can run to greet, knowing that within those welcoming arms of everlasting love there is room for us all.

The twilight deepened, and I prepared to leave. Driving home, I smiled to myself; it was fun, this looking forward to heaven with an enhanced dimension. I could just picture myself hurrying forward with Ellen to greet our Best Friend. Yes, I will *run* to Jesus.

ARLENE TAYLOR

MARCH 3

Songs of Experience

I will sing a new song to you, O God; on the ten-stringed lyre I will make music to you. Ps. 144:9, NIV.

Over the years I have taken the words of King David as a challenge and have composed many new songs to the Lord; songs born from my own experiences. While I did not have a 10-string lyre, I did have a guitar that substituted admirably.

The process of composing gospel songs has been as varied as the songs themselves. Some took a long time to complete, requiring much finishing and polishing over a period of weeks or months. Others were completed within 15 minutes, the lyrics and melody almost writing themselves.

One time a friend of mine requested that I write a special song for her wedding. I happily accepted, knowing that I had six months in which to complete the music. This time, to my surprise, the process was a struggle. I tried this and that and began to feel somewhat panicky as the wedding date drew near. I finally realized that I was having difficulty because this was not my life, my experience, or my special occasion. If there was going to be a song, it would have to be born out of her life experience.

We visited together, and I asked about her feelings concerning this person to whom she was committing her life. As we talked, I was able to catch her joy, the sense of excitement, the positive commitment—and a picture began to form in my mind. Within days I had a song that the bride told me expressed exactly what she wanted to say; a song that has since been sung at numerous weddings.

As human beings, creations of God, we each have songs to sing; stories of our own to tell. God wants us to sing our unique songs so that those who hear us will understand our great Lord from another point of view. If we fail to sing—literally and metaphorically—a part of God's universal symphony will be missing. As our lives change, as the stories of our lives deepen and expand, our songs will change.

Let us sing to the Lord a new song, a song that expresses our deepening knowledge of His love and care. I want to hear your song so I can add it to my repertoire of thanksgiving; I want to share my song with you. "I will sing with my spirit, but I will also sing with my mind" (1 Cor. 14:15, NIV).   LORNA LAWRENCE

MARCH 4

The Name of the Lord

The name of the Lord is a strong tower: the righteous runneth into it, and is safe. Prov. 18:10.

A group of college students had gathered in a faculty home for vespers. Suddenly that peaceful setting became a panic situation for me when someone announced that we would go around the circle and share a favorite Bible verse. Having little experience with such an activity, I found that the only verse my terrified mind offered was John 3:16—which I knew someone else would use before my turn came.

In the 30 years since this event, I have forgotten the other details, such as who was there and what text I managed to mumble.

But memory has freeze-framed the moment when a Bible verse became vibrant—the verse that Miss Babcock shared.

Alice Babcock was an English professor whose Introduction to Poetry class opened many windows of joy and understanding to me. When her turn came, she quoted Proverbs 18:10, "The name of the Lord is a strong tower: the righteous runneth into it, and is safe." Then she talked about the cities of refuge in Old Testament times. These walled cities were set aside as havens where a person fleeing from danger could be safe. As she spoke, my imagination saw the back of a person in flowing robes and sandaled feet running desperately down a dusty road toward the open gate of a distant fortress. In that moment of my little personal panic, the strong tower of the Lord was particularly appealing!

As I have reread this verse through the years, I have considered not only the safety it promises but also the name of the Lord that provides the safety. Bible writers used many names for God. Isaiah builds the concept of the strength that is in the Lord's name by listing some of His titles: "His name shall be called Wonderful, Counsellor, The mighty God, The everlasting Father, The Prince of Peace" (Isa. 9:6). Whenever I read or hear these words, my mind automatically plays the music of Handel's *Messiah*, but during a second time through I can focus on the Lord's attributes. He is wonderful, mighty, and everlasting. He is not an abstract god, but a counselor and father. He is the Prince, not just of a kingdom removed from me in time and place, but of peace, which He can give me at any time in any place. I can feel safe when I run to such a God.

Miss Babcock never knew how she made a Bible text come alive for me. I cannot thank her for this gift, but I offer her text to you today with the prayer that the name of the Lord will be your strong tower too.   RITA EISENHOWER DUNCAN

MARCH 5

Self-esteem and Mary Magdalene

You are precious and honored in my sight, and . . . I love you. Isa. 43:4, NIV.

One evening while I was scrubbing my bathtub, my mind began searching for answers to the pervasive problem of poor self-esteem. I wondered who in the Bible had struggled with a low self-worth. Scouring away like a good Martha would do, the Bible character that actually came to mind was her sister, Mary

Magdalene. Think for a moment about her life. What kind of self-worth did Mary Magdalene have?

We know her story. Simon the Pharisee, a respected religious teacher, led her into sin. She was deeply wronged by him. Eventually this resulted in a life of prostitution. What kind of self-worth do you think a prostitute would have?

For women especially, lovemaking is more than just a physical act. It involves the giving of our very being, our total emotions. For prostitutes to debase lovemaking and sell their womanhood for money, I would imagine they must have some of the lowest levels of self-worth.

So here is Mary Magdalene with an extremely low self-esteem. What changed her? How did she ultimately realize her worth?

The answer is embodied in the man Christ Jesus. Seven times she heard His strong cries to the Father in her behalf to free her from the demons that controlled her heart and mind (see *The Desire of Ages*, p. 568). She perceived that He knew her past, yet also knew her struggling heart, her love, her devotion.

I think one reason that she sat at His feet so often (even at the displeasure of her sister) was that she needed continual reminders and assurances of God's love and the high value He placed on her.

Jesus says, "Look at the birds of the air and the flowers of the fields—our heavenly Father cares for them. He will care for you—you are much more valuable than they" (see Matt. 6:26-29).

In Isaiah He says, "You are precious . . . in my sight, and . . . I love you" (Isa. 43:4, NIV).

Have your parents or family continually put you down? God exclaims, "Though your father and mother forsake you, I will receive you" (see Ps. 27:10, NIV).

If you feel depressed, He empathizes—"A bruised reed [I] will not break and a smoldering wick [I] will not snuff out" (Isa. 42:3, NIV).

The thoughts God thinks toward you are "thoughts of peace and not of evil, to give you a future and a hope" (Jer. 29:11, NKJV).

When you are plagued by doubts and low self-worth, do as Mary Magdalene—sit at Jesus' feet and soak in all the affirmation, love, and reassurance He so much wants to give you, the high worth He places on you.

We are not worthy in ourselves, yet He has chosen to place worth on us. Choose to believe it. When in doubt, do as Mary—hear it again, read it again.

Write your favorite promises of love and affirmation on small cards and keep them in your purse or car, or on your refrigerator. When self-doubt rises to overwhelm you, pull that card out—read it and reread it. Then choose to believe it, whether you feel like it or not.

In time, by absorbing Jesus you will become changed. You will begin to feel it, as well as to believe it. HEIDE FORD

God Made Me a Woman

So God created man in his own image, in the image of God he created him; male and female he created them. . . . And God saw all that he had made, and it was very good. Gen. 1:27-31, NIV.

God made me a woman; it was by no mistake,
no error in production,
    that life came to me
        in the form of a girl;

No accidental blend of
    genes and chromosomes
        provided me with a heart
            full of love and sensitive femininity.

God designed that I should be
    His woman, His servant
        here on earth. He gave
            me a woman's body with which to serve Him.

Just as He made our mother, Eve;
    No second-class creation
        was this, no accidental
            afterthought in His eternal plan.

God gave me a woman's mind.
    He designed it Himself;
        He intended that I should have
            the skills to live a fruitful life.

He gave me hands to do a woman's work,
    but never limited them
        to washing dishes, changing diapers, sweeping floors,
            although these things are good.

He asks my service, desires my heart,
    carries my burdens, creates in me

the yearning to do His will,
to be all that He designed me to be.

God made me a woman; I rejoice in that.
I praise Him for the time He gives
to carry out His purpose.
God made me a woman, and I am glad.

LEA HARDY

MARCH 7

Holocaust in the Nuclear Family

Weeping may endure for a night, but joy comes in the morning. Ps. 30:5, NKJV.

I grew up in what has become a sign of a bygone era—a happy, loving nuclear family. My mom baked a mean apple pie, and my dad at least toyed with the idea of brandishing Old Glory on the Fourth of July. Together they produced the requisite 2.0 healthy American kids.

With the exception of my brother (whose room defied the conventional wisdom of "a place for everything . . ."), our family lived in a tidy dwelling that clung to a craggy California hillside. It was no terrain for a white picket fence, but my dad did contribute several black toenails to the effort to tame the wilderness when he periodically skidded downhill into his mower.

I had two arrogant quasi-Persian cats, Fluffy and Smoky. Regularly scolded by the blue jays and family members they routinely ignored, they seemed less oblivious to Bowser, my brother's fox terrier, who never established a clear preference for chasing cats across the DMZ, slobbery tennis balls across the tarmac, or peas popped straight from the pod across the kitchen linoleum.

Occasionally feline/canine rapport provided a testy microcosm of sibling relationships, but no one *ever* feared a nuclear holocaust in our family. It was a safe and supportive house. Solid. Stable. Sound at the core. Unthreatened by meltdown and far from a blasting zone.

Not until my own home stood at ground zero and I witnessed a burst of blinding power obliterate my son's childhood innocence, vaporize our family life, batter us with continuing shock waves, overshadow our future, blight our spirits, wither our green hopes, and decay our life force did I fully understand and appreciate the inestimable value of a parental heritage, or legacy, of peaceful coexistence. How often we fail today to bequeath that to succeeding generations.

In broad human terms, nuclear-family *holocaust*, from a Greek word meaning "burnt whole," does just that, and its fallout has a long half-life. The fleeting, fertile promise of eternal spring, with its bustle, warmth, light, and chlorophyll-laden tufts of grass in someone else's turf, ends in the sterile, blasted landscape, silence, chill, and darkness of perpetual nuclear winter. Permafrost in the heartland.

Why does God hate divorce (see Mal. 2:16), a will-o'-the-wisp that beckons us to doom, a siren song that lures us to ruin on the rocks? He has many reasons, and if we are wise, we won't try to experience them firsthand. If we already have (either as adults, or as children) been denied our birthright, our proper inheritance, of an intact nuclear family, we need to remember His assurance that someday soon our bleak, scorched desert of alienation and dislocation, bounded then by a white picket fence if we wish, "shall rejoice, and blossom as the rose" (Isa. 35:1). No chimera. No mirage. No unmet great expectations. We will "dwell in the house of the Lord *for ever*" (Ps. 23:6). "And there shall be no night there" (Rev. 22:5). ANDREA KRISTENSEN

MARCH 8

When You Get to the End of Your Rope

My grace is sufficient for you, for my power is made perfect in weakness. 2 Cor. 12:9, NIV.

Once there were two people who were at the end of their ropes. There was Elijah, sitting hungry and parched by the dried-up brook . . . at the end of his resources . . . at the end of his road. And there was a widow . . . at the end of her flour . . . at the end of her oil . . . at the end of her hope. By themselves they could do nothing. Each looked doomed to die. Both must have glimpsed a little despair and wondered what God could possibly do to save the situation.

Apart, their lives seemed hopeless. But God brought them both together there outside the village of Zarephath. Elijah was almost fainting from fatigue and hunger; she may have been weeping as she collected the twigs together to fuel her last meal. God brought them together and gave them hope. Even though they may have reached rock bottom from an earthly perspective, they still clung to their faith in God.

Elijah needed faith to leave the safe haven of the brook. The widow needed faith to believe that if she fed this strange man first, there would still be food for her own family. And through their faith they were preserved. But they also needed each other. God provided for them both in a way that made them interdependent on each other, as the flour and oil continued to flow from the widow's earthenware jars till the famine finally ended.

Sometimes we come to the end of our ropes, our brooks, our oil jars. We may feel, as the widow may have, that the last thing we need is another mouth to feed. Or we may feel like Elijah and not want to leave the comfort of the brook and face the dangers of the world again.

Famines may touch our lives. Emotional famines. Spiritual famines. Just at the times we feel we have nothing left to give, God may bring us into contact with another "starving" person. Our natural instinct may be to withdraw, to preserve whatever we have left for our own use.

But even in our times of famine, God can use us to be an instrument of His blessings to others. Our own weakness and lack of personal resources can mean that we are more open to being used by God to help others in need. And He will not let us down. He will make sure that there is always just enough oil and flour in our storage jars until the famine in our lives has passed once more.

KAREN HOLFORD

MARCH 9

God's Great Sadness

How can I give you up? Hosea 11:8, NIV.

Several years ago while searching for an African violet show in a local park, I wandered into an orchid show by mistake. The main showroom was filled with hundreds of blooming orchids of all colors and varieties. They were so gorgeous that I returned the next day to see them again. Before I left, I stopped by the salesroom and purchased a beautiful pink phalaenopsis. Orchid growing had become my new hobby. I joined the orchid society to learn how to raise orchids. I found they were really not hard to grow. I could actually keep them alive and even get them to bloom for weeks at a time. Over the next few years I ordered orchids from catalogs and purchased others at shows. Soon they would not fit in the windows.

My father enclosed part of the basement and built light tables. My husband and I experimented with thermostats, heaters, and fans to provide the best growing conditions. Each time I opened the door to the orchid room I was greeted with a soft puff of warm, moist air and the sight of scores of blooms. Even in the midst of an upstate New York winter, the orchid room looked like a snapshot of Hawaii.

One day this past spring I noticed that two newly purchased orchids had yellowish-brown spots on their leaves. Over the next few weeks the leaves turned brown. The spots appeared on other plants. Blooms fell off. I realized with horror that a plant virus had infected my orchids. Plant viruses are incurable, and infected plants die. I sadly watched my orchids, which had once lent such beauty to the world, destroyed by an invisible virus.

This experience made me realize the infinitely greater sadness God feels as He watches His once-perfect creatures destroyed by sin. Sin has the same effect on us as the virus did on my orchids. Its onset is insidious, and initially there may be no recognizable effects. However, allowed to run its course, it separates us from God and destroys us. I never hated my orchids because they had a virus. I hated the destruction caused by the virus, just as God hates the destruction sin produces in His creatures.

Unlike plant viruses, the virus of sin has a cure. God offers us a relationship of trust with Himself—the source of everlasting life. Even when we sin, God longs for us to turn to Him for healing. He does not force His love on us. Yet He does not want to give us up to the destruction that results from sin. His love for each of us leads Him to say, "How can I give you up?" Knowing what a caring God we have, how can we say no to His healing power?

SARAH RODDY GIANG

MARCH 10

Love One Another

Let us love one another, for love comes from God. Everyone who loves has been born of God and knows God. Whoever does not love does not know God, because God is love. 1 John 4:7, 8, NIV.

I hadn't slept well, for the events of the past week had mentally exhausted me. It had been a long night, so I got up early, dressed, and went outside to take a walk around the campus of Africa's

Solusi College. It was so peaceful, and some of this peace pervaded my own soul.

As I looked around the campus, I noticed people on the verandas of many of the faculty homes. I wondered what they were doing so early in the morning. As I walked closer to the first home I could see the women arranging bouquets of flowers, and then I noticed that the same thing was happening at the other homes. Tears came to my eyes when I realized what they were doing.

The day before, we had driven to Solusi through the area where the Battle of Bulawayo was being fought. We had witnessed a torrential downpour as we entered the area where the soldiers were fighting, and believed it to be an answer to our prayers for protection as we made our way by convoy to Solusi.

A few days earlier two of our missionaries, Don and Ann Lale, from Great Britain, had been brutally murdered. They were teachers at Inyazura Secondary School in Zimbabwe. After a service at the Highlands church in Harare, we had made plans for a second service at the Solusi College church and would then have interment in the Pioneer Cemetery on the college campus.

The political situation in Zimbabwe was such that firm plans didn't always materialize. We had arranged for the flowers from the first service to be sent with the caskets on the plane to Bulawayo, but plans had gone awry and there were no flowers on the plane when it arrived.

Now our sisters were making sure that there were wreaths and bouquets for the service and were showing their love for the fallen missionaries who had made the supreme sacrifice.

Hundreds of us formed an honor guard and sang as the hearse entered the campus and the caskets were taken to the front of the church. Then after the memorial service we sang hymns of hope and assurance as we escorted our fallen companions to their final resting place.

Many times I have thought back to that day, remembering not the sadness and loss we felt, but the honor, respect, and love displayed.

I wish we could display that love to others each day and not just at times of great loss. Let's be loving and kind to all we come in contact with, and may they see by our actions that we have a relationship with the Lord that is the guiding principle of our lives.

BARBARA MITTLEIDER

Amazing Love

Behold what manner of love the Father has bestowed on us, that we should be called children of God! 1 John 3:1, NKJV.

Jiggers was a delightful dog, a perfect pet, and a beautiful beagle. Although the family had acquired her when I was just 1 year old, she eventually became "my" pet and my best friend. She slept in the middle of my bed while I curled up on my pillow. When I wanted to stretch out, I would kick her, and she would growl while we competed for a comfortable position. Jiggers and I would explore frozen creekbeds, run through cornfields, and sit in her doghouse together while I read her stories. I would tie her ears over her head, and she would sit on me. We were buddies.

When she was 12 years old, the signs of old age became obvious. She got too feeble to make it outside in time, so Mom and Dad said she would have to stay outdoors for the sake of the carpets. She lived in her little house, and as the winter became bitterly cold, we gave her a heating pad to sleep on. Every morning before school I would go out to feed her and warm her frozen water.

Then one morning she didn't lift her head as I came out the door. She looked funny, and there was ice on the carpet by her mouth. I began to scream her name, and turned and fled in grief and terror into my dad's waiting arms.

Many years later I was thinking about that day, and for the first time wondered about my dad. I called my mother on the phone, and asked her how Daddy just happened to be there that morning. Her answer went something like this: "Daddy knew Jiggers couldn't last much longer, and he was worried about how it would affect you. Every morning when you went out to feed her, Daddy would stand at the window and watch. The day that Jiggers died, Daddy could tell just by looking at you. He ran to the door and went to you even before you could get back to the house."

Many of us have known the love of earthly fathers, and yet our heavenly Father's love is so much greater. "For your Father knows what you need before you ask him" (Matt. 6:8, NIV).

"Almighty Father, I stand in awe of the love You have shown us by giving Your only Son in death before we even knew our need. I love You, Lord. Amen." TERESA GAY HOOVER KRUEGER

Everyday Miracles

Are not two sparrows sold for a penny? Yet not one of them will fall to the ground apart from the will of your Father. And even the very hairs of your head are all numbered. So don't be afraid; you are worth more than many sparrows. Matt. 10:29-31, NIV.

It was one of those cozy little Bible study groups that most of us have been a part of at some time or another in our Christian journey. Call them prayer bands, cell groups, or TLC circles, they offer warm fellowship and Christian encouragement to every climber on the path to Canaan.

This evening we were talking about miracles. It seemed that each of us had seen God work in a special, undeniable way that week, and we were excitedly telling about it. Marcia had had her lost purse returned to her with all her money and credit cards intact. Jane's brother had phoned to mention that he had been back to church that week; she had prayed for years that he would return. Betty's son had received a large sum of money he desperately needed but had no reasonable hope to ever collect. This had been an unusual and faith-building week.

It was then that the newest member of our group, Marilyn, quietly spoke up. "You know," she said, "I see miracles every day when I remember to look for them."

I have discovered since then that Marilyn is right. God does work miracles every day for me—everyday miracles, if you please. Not only keeping me breathing or giving me eyesight. No, I mean special little things that He makes happen just for me, things that remind me that He loves me, that I am special to Him. But I do need to be looking for them, I've learned; otherwise I blindly credit them to good luck or right living. Things like the dime on the floor in the supermarket checkout line and the total for my groceries being exactly what I have in my purse—if I include that dime! I feel all warm inside as I realize that God knows how embarrassed I would have been not to have had enough money to pay my bill, especially with that long line of harried commuters impatiently pressing behind me.

Sometimes God covers over my thoughtless mistakes. Like the day I faxed a message to another church office and then realized, after I had punched the transmit key, that one line I had included might be misunderstood by the fax operator. Without a doubt she would read it on her way to deliver it to its intended recipient. "Dear God," I breathed, "don't let Jean be hurt; I didn't mean it the way she is going to take it." Moments later, for the first and only time in years of sending faxes to that office, the machine flashed the message "communication error." My fax had not gone through.

God's everyday miracles—my heart is warmed each day by their reminders of celestial love. Some days these reminders come in less memorable ways, but always they are there when I think to look for them. God works them for you, too. Watch for yours today.   CAROLE SPALDING COLBURN

The Miracle Word

Inasmuch as ye have done it unto one of the least of these my brethren, ye have done it unto me. Matt. 25:40.

Our Boeing 747 was crowded as it lifted from Hong Kong International Airport. It was 9:45. City lights twinkled in the distance and faded. Hopefully we could sleep a little before arriving in San Francisco 11 hours later.

My husband sat at my left in the four-seat center section of the plane. On my right was a man of slight stature, and beside him was his small son of about 4 years. Across the aisle sat the child's mother and sister. Our cultures were different. I could not speak their language, nor could they speak mine.

The child's boundless energy was exceeded only by his piercing voice. "Like father, like son," I observed as the father repeatedly stood upright on the seat and stepped over his son to the aisle. The stench from his feet penetrated the air. I could only hope they would settle down soon.

My husband was asleep. Turning toward him, I sunk my head into my pillow in an effort to doze off, but frequent elbow jabs in my back kept me tense and wakeful. After what seemed hours both father and son were finally asleep, and to my dismay, the child's head was now squarely in my lap. It annoyed me.

Suddenly my mind went back to the manger, and the little head I held seemed to belong to the Christ child. How could I, the mother of five children, have been so vexed! Fully awake now, I glanced at the father. His sleeping form was contorted uncomfortably across both their seats as he lovingly held the restless little fellow close to himself.

Both were unaware when I slipped my pillow carefully under the little boy's head. For the rest of the night I adjusted it to their movements, and each time it warmed my heart. I thank God for the prompting of the Holy Spirit that night and for the words in Matthew 25:40 that kept running through my mind.

Morning came. The piercing little voice roused us all, but this time I could smile. The father discovered the use I had given my pillow, and patted it. "Nice!" he beamed. "Nice!" I have never been thanked more sincerely.

Soon our breakfast trays came. Once more the little man's smile beamed my direction. Pushing their two containers of fresh fruit onto my tray, he motioned that neither he nor his son wanted them. In charade fashion I thanked him with my smile, and he understood.

I was still reflecting on all that had happened as our plane came to a full stop in San Francisco. I watched that little family of four walk ahead of us into the terminal—strangers in a strange land. My heart went out to them as they turned and waved goodbye before blending into the crowd. Then a great surge of concern swept over me. I hoped the people in this, my country, would treat them kinder than the citizens of this earth treated our Lord when He, who had no place to lay His head, came to this lost, uncaring world.

That text has given me a whole new concept. I've concluded that however small our kindness, the blessing we receive in exchange is far too great to miss! "Inasmuch"—it's the miracle word!   LORRAINE HUDGINS

MARCH 14

Sin: Minor or Major?

But I say unto you, That whosoever looketh on a woman to lust after her hath committed adultery with her already in his heart. Matt. 5:28.

For verily I say unto you, Till heaven and earth pass, one jot or one tittle shall in no wise pass from the law, till all be fulfilled. Whosoever therefore shall break one of these least commandments, and shall teach men so, he shall be called the least in the kingdom of heaven. Matt. 5:18, 19.

In certain parts of Nigeria a species of snake is regarded as royal. Therefore, whenever it pays a courtesy call to a home, it is accorded royal treatment. The Hindu regards the cobra that inhabits his house with reverence. Some Ghanaians will chase all pests out of their rooms with vigor. But not the wall gecko! It is literally called "landlord." It is at liberty to roam wherever it pleases. I consider these customs absurd.

Very often people regard certain sins as minor and overlook them. But remember: sin is sin. My Bible confirms this by saying that "sin is the transgression of the law" (1 John 3:4) and breaking one commandment is like breaking all ten. According to Romans 6:23, "the wages of sin is death." Yes, we may regard our sin as minor, but to God the wages of *any* sin, minor or major, is death. This is an alarming thought.

It is my fervent prayer that people would know this and stop condoning sin in any form. A prolific writer, Ellen G. White, says, "The greatest want of the world is the want of men [and women] . . . men who do not fear to call sin by its right name . . . men who will stand for the right though the heavens fall" (*Education*, p. 57). If only we can learn to do just that! This indeed would be a sure step toward repentance and salvation. Let us then say with Job: "Make me to know my transgression and my sin" (Job 13:23).   NORA AGBOKA

MARCH 15

Trust in the Lord

Those of steadfast mind you keep in peace . . . because they trust in you. Isa. 26:3, NRSV.

Recently I was scheduled for minor surgery and was confident and upbeat until the day prior to the event. It had been planned for some months, and I told myself, "There's nothing to it." I had busied myself with plans and preparations for the coming year-end holidays. After all, the surgery performed a year before was much more extensive and involved. It was done on an emergency basis, and I had not had time to think about or plan for it. This was merely a follow-up. No problem.

I awakened that morning to a barrage of negative thoughts flooding my mind like the waters of a flash flood. I became immobilized with fear. What if I get an overwhelming infection? What if I don't wake up from the anesthesia? What if this is my last day? What should I say to my family? What if . . . ? The waters of the flood were about to engulf me as I struggled for air.

"Lord," I cried, "where are You? Why this terrible fear?" His soothing voice came back to me as I took my Bible and, going to my quiet place, slowly read, "Thou wilt keep him in perfect peace, whose mind is stayed on thee: because he trusteth in thee" (Isa. 26:3). "Peace I leave with you, my peace I give unto you" (John 14:27). "What time I am afraid, I will trust in thee" (Ps. 56:3). "My God; in him will I trust" (Ps. 91:2).

"Yes, Lord, I trust You. Give me Your peace. Thank You, Lord, for this gift."

The floodwaters slowly and quietly receded as my fears were quelled. I entered surgery the next day with a trust in His promises and awoke to a good report.

"Lord, give me Your peace as I place my hand in Thine and trust You for whatever You allow to come to me today. Amen."

JOAN MINCHIN NEALL

MARCH 16

The Driver's Seat

Teach me thy way, O Lord, and lead me in a plain path. Ps. 27:11.

We had been studying the first few chapters of Genesis in Bible class, and I wanted the children to reflect on the awfulness of sin, so I asked them to draw a picture to show what happened to Adam and Eve after they ate the forbidden fruit. The children set to work with crayons and large sheets of paper.

As I moved quietly around the room to watch their progress, I saw pictures that clearly indicated the Garden of Eden, angels, Adam and Eve in their "new" clothes, fields of weeds growing profusely, and animals being sacrificed on stone altars.

Then I came to Billy. "What is this, Billy?" I asked. "I don't recall any cars in the Bible lessons. Tell me about it."

Proudly Billy held up his picture for all to see. His drawing showed a very large open red convertible that filled the lower half of his paper. He called our attention to the two people in the back seat, then pointed to the driver and explained: "This is God. He's driving Adam and Eve out of the garden."

Silly? Sassy? Smarty? No, none of these. Billy had simply fulfilled one of the cardinal rules of learning. He had related new data to prior understanding. His understanding of the word *drove* was related to traveling in an automobile—something he did every day. When I told the class that God *drove* Adam and Eve out of the garden, Billy pictured God in the driver's seat!

And maybe that's not such a bad image. If we could picture God "in the driver's seat" of our lives, perhaps we could come closer to the destination He wants us to reach! PATRICIA A. HABADA

MARCH 17

The Essence of Value

Look at the birds of the air; they do not sow or reap or store away in barns, and yet your heavenly Father feeds them. Are you not much more valuable than they? Matt. 6:26, NIV.

When I arrived home from anatomy class I had a message waiting for me: "Please pick up my children from school. I am going to commit suicide. Tina." My mind raced, *If only I had been home when she had called! Should I call 911? Where is she? Does her counselor know this? And where is her husband, Mike?*

I developed a massive headache from my suppressed anger. I was angry at Tina's uncle who had sexually abused her as a child. I was angry at her once-pastor father, who justified his conditional love to her mother, brother, and sisters. I was angry at anyone out there who would take the part of an evil messenger by trumpeting that personal value comes from who we are, what we are, and what we do. I was angry because I was in serious danger of losing a precious friend.

Eleven o'clock that night Mike called to tell me Tina had returned home, and I was truly grateful. Throughout the course of the day I had come to realize even more that performance has little to do with value. I wanted Tina to live even if she never spoke to me again, or if she never cleaned her house, or if she never read to her kids, or if she never, ever came to church again. Tina believed she had to do all these things and a lot more to be worth anything. But Tina has value to me and to God because she is a human being—and that is enough.

In the book *The Desire of Ages* (p. 316) we can read about a delegation of elders being sent to Jesus to urge Him to help the centurion because he was worthy: he had done so much for the nation of Israel—he had built a synagogue! The author affirms how far this attitude is from the spirit of the Gospel. The Centurion's value had nothing to do with his performance. Jesus healed his servant, but not because of anything the centurion had done.

Today, like then, the messages are whirling at us (and too often from us) that what we do puts us in a better position for value. To believe that, however, could lead us to where my friend Tina has been for so long: if you don't perform, you have no value. I thank Jesus that there is no better position for salvation than to recognize our great need (see *The Desire of Ages*, p. 317), and that there is no better claim for value than being human.　　　TERESA GLASS

MARCH 18

Facing Personal Pain

Cast all your anxiety on him because he cares for you.
1 Peter 5:7, NIV.

Have you been hurt, battered, the victim of divorce or desertion, or suffered the death of a loved one? When faced with personal pain, people frequently look for a scapegoat upon whom to heap all blame. They often search for escape into a world of alcohol, the euphoria of drugs, TV, or affairs. Sometimes such people try to run away, hide from God, or blame others. Often they think that no one else has experienced what they are going through. This simply is not true. Granted, each of us is a distinct individual and our pain may be unique, but many problems do show similar aspects. No one can solve all the problems you face today or take away your personal pain, but you can be helped toward change if you can be challenged to action.

It takes courage to change—to admit you may have been part of the problem, to stop blaming others even when you are a victim, to stop nursing your hurts, to work through complex issues of rejection, confronting what is fair and what is not. All of this can become bearable, however, when you recognize that life is full of challenges. The price may be high, but it is possible to work through chaos.

Obviously a plan is needed to become a fulfilled person regardless of what has transpired prior to this time. The following plan has assisted many who seek renewal and personal growth.

1. Commit yourself to God every morning. God's power to change you is infinite! But a one-time superficial prayer of "God help me" won't do. In order to change deeply ingrained habits, you will need to maintain an hour-by-hour connection to heavenly power.

2. Release the hurts of the past. You can choose to keep alive every agonizing, torturous detail of the past, or you can break free. The desire for revenge frequently keeps the past alive. Let someone else hate, hurt, and become bitter (see Eph. 4:31, 32).

3. Select a motto to reprogram your mind. Such a motto might be "I can do all things through Christ which strengtheneth me" (Phil. 4:13). Print your motto on a small card and place it in a prominent spot on a mirror, refrigerator, desk, or dashboard. Repeat it aloud every time negative thoughts enter your mind.

And remember: Don't let yesterday use up too much of today. The past is past. Today you have a fresh opportunity to approach God and move forward. With Paul, forget what lies behind and reach forward to what lies ahead (see Phil. 3:13). Allow Him to work in your life today. NANCY VAN PELT

MARCH 19

Letting Go

Casting the whole of your care—all your anxieties, all your worries, all your concerns, once and for all—on Him; for He cares for you affectionately, and cares about you watchfully. 1 Peter 5:7, Amplified.

None of us reach adulthood with all our childhood dependency needs met. Our well-meaning parents were not always able to give us the level of time, attention, patience, and security we needed. Those unmet needs have been described as a "black hole" deep within that we try to fill with people, work, food, religiosity, activities, chemicals, being compulsively caught in performance traps, and/or trying to control others. As we allow Jesus to work deep within our core, He brings His healing touch and helps us to deal with the pain of the past so it no longer has power over us.

Sometimes we have trouble trusting God to handle a problem, situation, habit, attitude, or person in our lives. We hang on tightly, but there is great freedom in letting go. Is there something you need to release to your totally trustworthy and caring Father?

A slogan in Twelve-Step Recovery Groups that speaks eloquently of trust is "Let go, and let God." I am indebted to an unknown author who writes:

"Letting go does not mean to stop caring;
    it means I can't do it for someone else.
Letting go is not to cut myself off;

it's the realization I can't control another.
Letting go is not to enable;
    but to allow learning from natural consequences.
Letting go is to admit powerlessness;
    which means the outcome is not in my hands.
Letting go is not to try to change or blame another;
    it is to make the most of myself.
Letting go is not to fix, but to be supportive.
    It's not to judge, but to allow another to be a human being.
Letting go is not to be in the middle arranging the outcome; . . .
Letting go is not to be protective;
    it's to permit another to face reality.
Letting go is not to deny, but to accept.
Letting go is not to nag, scold, or argue, but instead
    to search out my own shortcomings and correct them.
Letting go is not to adjust everything to my own desires;
    but to take each day as it comes and cherish myself in it.
Letting go is not to criticize and regulate anybody; . . .
Letting go is to fear less and live more."

Lila Lane George

MARCH 20

Dirty Windows

For since the creation of the world [God's] invisible attributes, His eternal power and divine nature, have been clearly seen, being understood from what has been made, so that [men] are without excuse. Rom. 1:20, NASB.

Recently my husband and I bought a 40-year-old house. This house, built in 1950, had been painted only once—in 1950. Forty years of dirt had accumulated on the walls, ivy engulfed the house, spiders and bugs were everywhere. And the distinct smell of an uncared-for house permeated the air.

An entire month was spent cleaning out the garbage, scrubbing, priming, painting the walls and ceilings, and scrubbing ceramic tile. (Can you imagine what the bathroom shower looked like?) We scraped 40 years of hard water mineral deposits out of the tub. The stove alone took an entire day!

Finally we moved in. But the windows were still dirty—very dirty. Eventually I tackled them, and we could actually see out of them! The sky was blue and the trees were green. Nature beckoned us. There was a world out there!

As Christians we are like those windows. The world sees us every day. We might even be getting a bit overgrown and ragged-looking on the outside (stress, overcommitment, etc.). The inside probably could use some TLC.

At our spiritual birth we were sparkling new, but have we done a thorough revamping of the heart since then? Not necessarily a remodeling, but just a thorough cleaning. The rest of us can be sparkling and clean, swabbed with bleach and Lysol, but what about those windows? We need to see out of them because that's our avenue to the Creator. We are held accountable for what light God has shown us. Our windows must be clean—no streaks—in order to see what He has revealed. We can't afford to put it off because something else is happening. We need to see clearly, right now. We need to be without excuse in our understanding.

Look out of the windows of your soul right now. Reflect. If you cannot see clearly, why not ask God to begin a thorough cleaning?

SUSAN CLARK

MARCH 21

The Silence of Zechariah

And when he came out, he could not speak unto them.
Luke 1:22.

When I was a child, I can remember saying to my brother, "Isn't it funny how silence whistles?"

"It doesn't" was all he said, but I knew he was kidding me, because I'd been hearing it whistle for as long as I could remember!

It wasn't until about 12 years ago that I discovered my brother had spoken the truth. It seems I've had a mild form of tinnitus (noises in the ear) all my life.

Once I went to a meeting about tinnitus. We listened to reproductions of the sorts of noises other people have to live with, and I came away grateful I had only a "tiny whistling kettle" in my head!

I'm still fascinated by absolute silence, since apparently I've never heard it. And the silence of Zechariah fascinates me too.

Was it a punishment from God for not believing what the angel said? It sounds like a punishment: "Because you did not believe my words . . ." (Luke 1:20). But wasn't nine months a bit severe? Surely nine days would have made the point.

But Zechariah knew he'd sinned in not believing the angel, so he did not shrink from his punishment. At least the gospel gives no indication to the contrary.

And then, almost as fascinating as his silence, comes a veritable flood of praise after the naming of his son (see Luke 1:68-79). Obviously his nine-month silence had done his spiritual life no harm!

Of course, during those nine months he'd gone about his daily business, and his priestly term had been completed. When you're not spending time talking you have a lot of time to think. I think the most beautiful thing about Zechariah's silence is that he and God had obviously been communing deeply.

So was it a punishment, or was it God's way of getting Zechariah's full attention in preparation for the great task He had given the priest and his wife? Only God sees into the heart. Maybe He saw that Zechariah needed time out to think. One thing it confirms is that God's punishment is nothing to be afraid of.

But we are afraid of silence, aren't we? Everywhere we go noise fills the air. Every moment must be given over to sound busyness. We're in danger of losing a great gift.

If nothing else, the story of Zechariah's silence makes the point that sometimes God has to step into our lives and create the conditions in which we are more likely to hear His still small voice.

So Zechariah's silence was actually a gift from God.

I pray that we too might be given that gift, at best regularly, and at least occasionally. And if we're not, then we really should try to make our own quiet times when the voice of God can be heard.

ANITA MARSHALL

MARCH 22

A New Home

Let not your heart be troubled: ye believe in God, believe also in me. In my Father's house are many mansions: if it were not so, I would have told you. I go to prepare a place for you. And if I go and prepare a place for you, I will come again, and receive you unto myself; that where I am, there ye may be also. John 14:1-3.

John 14:1-3 was the text for the sermon at my home church last week. It was a special day because we celebrated the twenty-fifth anniversary of our congregation. The sermon was presented by the minister who was pastor when our family transferred our membership to the church.

His title was "The Smile I'm Waiting For." He shared his experience of returning from the service during World War II and of meeting his wife when he was discharged. That reminded me of a homecoming my husband and I shared recently upon his return from more than five weeks in Russia presenting evangelistic meetings. Our separation was certainly not as long as the pastor's. But when my husband left Los Angeles International Airport, five weeks seemed like forever.

About a week before his return, my husband called to ask if I would be meeting him at the airport. I still wonder why he even questioned, except that his arrival was midday and he may have felt I couldn't get off work. My answer was "Of course." I was at the airport early (naturally the plane was late!). Finally after watching literally hundreds of people come up the ramp from clearing customs, I saw my husband. All of a sudden the five weeks that had seemed interminable were over, and I saw his smile.

My recent experience is nothing compared to what the homecoming will be like at Christ's return. Nothing compared to seeing the smile on His face. But my experience provides me with some idea of what the Second Coming will be like.

During our congregation's special weekend we shared the phrase that we were "25 years nearer home." How wonderful. And each day brings us one day closer to that wonderful day.

BETSY MATTHEWS

MARCH 23

How Much Does It Cost to Give?

If you forgive [others] when they sin against you, your heavenly Father will also forgive you. Matt. 6:14, NIV.

I was 12 years old, and my father had been appointed president of the Rio-Minas Mission in central Brazil. There was only one catch—he had "inherited" a problem. There had been a disaffection movement in the mission, and although my parents had nothing to do with the affair, they were viewed as enemies by some of the people.

The way in which my parents handled the conflict made a profound impression on my mind. My father traveled most of the time throughout the mission and treated all members amicably, whatever their reaction was to the situation.

At home our next-door neighbor had been a leader in the disaffection movement. Because of the location of our home on a dead-end street, this man and his wife had to walk in front of our house every time they left theirs. Both my parents never missed a chance to wish each of them a good day as they walked by, but for months there was no response. They would not even look in our direction.

That didn't deter my parents, however, and sure enough, about a year later there was a thaw in the cold front, and we were actually invited into their home.

I sometimes wondered how my parents could be so gracious in the face of all the problems, but they both believed that a gentle answer turns away wrath (see Prov. 15:1, NIV).

In another instance, a national worker had been dropped from employment. He was ill, and his wife was expecting a child. My mother went to visit this family soon after our arrival in Brazil, but was not welcomed. Nevertheless, she made some clothes for the expected baby and took them over to the home.

Later when the man died, Mother offered to sew the mourning dress for the widow—and her offer was accepted. She also helped prepare and serve food on the day of the funeral. Gradually the family became more friendly, although they soon moved away and we heard little of them.

Thirty-two years later I again visited Rio de Janeiro. Imagine my surprise to discover that my host had invited that same woman and her son (now grown) to have dinner with us. It was refreshing to realize that time had healed old wounds, and I enjoyed listening to them recount pleasant memories of their association with our family.

Truly Dr. Luke was right: "Give, and it will be given to you. A good measure, pressed down, shaken together and running over, will be poured into your lap. For with the measure you use, it will be measured to you" (Luke 6:38, NIV).　　　　ENOLA DAVIS

MARCH 24

Dead as the Dodo

You appointed [them rulers] over everything you made; you placed [them] over all creation: sheep and cattle, and the wild animals too; the birds and the fish and the creatures in the seas. Ps. 8:6-8, TEV.

We had only two days to explore the small island of Mauritius in the Indian Ocean before our plane took us to Johannesburg. Our first discovery saddened us.

About 350 years ago a large gentle bird called the dodo flourished here. Imagine meeting thousands, maybe millions, of these unusual birds in the only place they lived in all the world! Related to the pigeon and about the size of a well-fed turkey, they stuffed themselves in late summer and autumn on palm fruits and seeds lying on the ground. Then, living on fat reserves, they gradually lost weight during the leaner months.

Their stubby wings, like decorative little stumps, couldn't lift their plump bodies off the ground. They didn't need to fly, for no predators harmed them. If you'd walked on the beach, they'd likely waddle up to you on their short legs, harmless and friendly. You might laugh at their enormous, wide, down-turned beaks of yellow and green and the three ridiculous curly plumes sticking out of their tails. Maybe you'd stroke their soft blue-gray feathers as their black eyes looked at you.

But you can't No, *never*! European sailors and Dutch colonists who settled on Mauritius clubbed the last dodo to death about 1680. They often killed the dodo for the sheer sport of killing a defenseless bird. Imagine having fun killing this remarkable creature! Their hogs, rats, and dogs ate the meat and destroyed the eggs. Many dodos were shipped to Europe to be exhibited in zoos. Some lived for years, but no one thought to breed them in captivity in safe, protected areas.

As I looked at the only dodo left on the island, stuffed in a glass case in the museum at Port Louis, I thought God must be crying too. He trusted us with this beautiful bird, but because of cruelty and stupidity the world lost a unique creature forever.

How sad our heavenly Father must be! He sees the cruelty and thoughtlessness of people whom He appointed to be kind and loving to everything He created—animals, friends, family, everybody. God placed each of us here to reveal His love and kindness to others. Do you show His character by being thoughtful, caring, and considerate, or are you thoughtlessly killing those around you with your words and actions? EILEEN E. LANTRY

Forgive and Live

Forgive us our debts, as we forgive our debtors. Matt. 6:12.

In the January 1993 issue of the popular health magazine *Prevention* there is a little news clip entitled "Forgive and Live," with a subheading that reads: "Holding a grudge can hinder your heart."

The clip goes on to say that "researchers have found a direct connection between anger and immediate, harmful changes occurring in [the] heart." Cardiac patients who were asked to remember an event that made them feel angry experienced a measurable change in the efficiency with which their hearts pumped blood. People with heart disease were counseled not to get angry or hostile.

Easier said than done, right? And yet this counsel applies to all of us. How otherwise could Paul ask us to rejoice in all circumstances and "let your moderation be known unto all men" (Phil. 4:5)? Keeping our cool is not only good spiritual advice, but sound physical counsel. But how do we achieve that equanimity in the midst of situations that fairly scream for our vengeance?

Forgive. After you have kicked and screamed, threatened, and turned on the silent treatment, try forgiving. Nobody says it will be easy. Forgiveness has its price. But it's much less a price to pay than hanging on to your anger. In fact, forgiving is like a generous rebate. You invest a tiny act of the will, and the returns can be monumental.

Someone once defined forgiveness as the fragrance flowers breathe when they are trampled upon. You may feel like that delicate flower that has given, time and again, only to be disdained, humiliated, or rejected. You have only two options: cultivate the hurt or let it go. If you choose to nurture the hurt, remember that that poisonous plant is growing inside you, not your enemy. Someday it will bear its deadly fruit to your mortal, and possibly eternal, detriment. If you choose to let it go, the only loss you will experience is that of a suffocating burden that has been lifted from not only your shoulders but your life. LOURDES E. MORALES-GUDMUNDSSON

MARCH 26

First-Time Fliers

For the Lord himself will come down from heaven, with a loud command, with the voice of the archangel and with the trumpet call of God, and the dead in Christ will rise first. After that, we who are still alive and are left will be caught up together with them in the clouds to meet the Lord in the air. 1 Thess. 4:16, 17, NIV.

Mommy, we're higher than a beagle!" Lauren's incredulous expression tells me more than her words.

It is her first flight on an airliner. At least it is the first that she will remember. The last time she was on a plane she was just a toddler.

Then we had flown to visit my mother at her paradise home in Hawaii. Lauren was afraid of the waves. She preferred to sit on the beach and perform the ancient child ritual of sand-eating.

I remember many things about that trip: the delicious tastes and smells, the beauty of the water, the weightless feeling of snorkeling, and the rainbow colors of friendly fish looking for a handout. I also remember discovering another of the hundreds of "new" things that new parents learn—the stark reality that a vacation with a child along resembles more an expedition or an endurance test than a respite!

Now Lauren is 5, and her baby sister, Jaime, is the toddler in tow. Jaime is trying to keep her father from getting bored on the flight by alternating gymnastics with jumping jacks on his lap.

"What did you say, honey?" I try to hear the meaning hidden by her words.

"We're higher than a beagle!" She repeats the assertion.

"Oh, now I understand. But I think you might mean 'higher than an *eagle*.' " I try to say it matter-of-factly, as though it is a common misconception held by all first-time fliers.

Her sparkling eyes are like exclamation points in her expression. She smiles ever so slightly and processes the change in her mind. Then she turns back to the window to watch the ground drop below us. The jigsaw of plowed and planted fields recedes into two-dimensional color and texture.

It is easy for me to feel her excitement and sense her new discovery. It is easy because she is my child.

When I look out the window this time I see through *her* eyes, and it is as if I am flying for the first time too. I watch her delight and fascination, and revel in the rise of parental satisfaction within me.

It is the kind of feeling that I imagine my heavenly Father must feel when He sees His children comprehending and learning and thrilling to new awareness of His love.

My eyes are carried beyond hers to the disappearing earth, and I think of our conversation earlier that week about how Jesus will come in the clouds and how we will travel to heaven with Him.

First the small dark cloud will grow and grow, until it is as bright as sunlight. The earth will groan as marked and unmarked graves release their long-held prisoners. Angels and more angels escort us through the skies.

On that trip there won't be seat belts to fasten or crash-landing procedures. There won't be bags to pack or baby diapers to remember. No bargain tickets or boarding passes. No seat assignments or emergency exits.

On that trip there will be no first-class, coach, or standby status.

Instead, there will be singing and thanksgiving as we board the ultimate space shuttle for the ultimate journey.

On that trip we'll both be "first-time fliers," Lauren and I.

And as this earthly sphere falls away, I'll scoop her up in my arms and shout, "Hallelujah, we're higher than a beagle!"

SHEREE PARRIS NUDD

MARCH 27

No Women Allowed

Jesus . . . got up from the meal, took off his outer clothing, and wrapped a towel around his waist. After that, he poured water into a basin and began to wash his disciples' feet, drying them with the towel that was wrapped around him. John 13:3-5, NIV.

When I first realized that there were no women present at the Last Supper, I felt left out. Well, even more than that, I felt depressed. Why would Jesus, who was so good to women, have left us out completely? Was there significance to this omission? I think there was.

You see, if women had been present in that upper room, it would have ruined a very large portion of the lesson that Christ had to teach. If even one woman had been there, she would never have allowed the etiquette lapse; she would automatically have been the servant. She was used to serving. Washing feet was ordinary, everyday stuff. She was already considered to be on the same level with servants, yes, a possession. She would have grabbed the basin out of Jesus' hands, I'm sure, horrified at the whole idea of His serving anyone. She would never have thought herself too good to serve.

"Jesus said to them, 'The kings of the Gentiles lord it over them; and those who exercise authority over them call themselves Benefactors. But you are not to be like that. Instead, the greatest among you should be like the youngest, and the one who rules like the one who serves. For who is greater, the one who is at the table or the one who serves? Is it not the one who is at the table? But I am among you as one who serves' " (Luke 22:25-27, NIV). No wonder the women loved and followed Jesus—they could

112

identify with Him. In fact, the only record of anyone supporting Jesus financially in His ministry is of a group of women (see Luke 8:3).

I am no longer depressed by this story. I like the idea of following a Saviour who identified like that with me—Emmanuel.

ARDIS DICK STENBAKKEN

MARCH 28

The Potter

But now, O Lord, thou art our father; we are the clay, and thou our potter; and we all are the work of thy hand. Isa. 64:8.

I will take the cup of salvation, and call upon the name of the Lord. Ps. 116:13.

My husband and I share a mug collection. And it's heresy to suggest that it's gotten out of hand. Heresy because we have yet to find the perfect mug. Heresy because the most charming of all potter's studios surely must be in the next hollow. Heresy because mug shopping is fun and brings us in contact with interesting people—potters, studio owners, and other "muggies."

Every mug we have is our favorite. There is the huge mug that rests on two flat feet. And there is the demure porcelain mug painted with a hummingbird, one wing "flying" above the rim. There is a mug shaped like a pink Cadillac that rides along on four wheels. And the mug with our wedding vows etched on it. I could go on for two more cupboards.

Some of our favorite potters and studios include an artisan who set up shop in an old mill he discovered one day while buying peanut butter. On his business cards he writes, "Mugs are as essential to life as the liquid they hold." Then there is the potter who resides in a Victorian house nestled in the Appalachian Mountains of Virginia. Her dog, she says, is her best critic. To get to Fox Cross Pottery, one must drive a country path where foxes cross more often than cars. And once we get there we can't decide which we like better—the potter's mugs or his llamas that graze in the meadow adjacent to the studio.

There is one potter's studio that utterly fascinates me, despite the fact that his techniques are too painstaking, his clay too rough, his wheel too slow. His finished wares, however, glint with glazes I have never seen, inner fires no other potter duplicates. And as they burn, it always seems to me that no one could ever offer him

113

enough for all his trouble. I stopped in for a brief visit the other day. Brief because his techniques were still too painstaking, his clay still too rough, and his wheel still too slow. And there were other potters down the road I thought I might like to visit. As I turned to leave, he handed me a sketch. "Especially for you," he indicated. "That is, if you're interested."

"But your clay is so inferior," I answered, glancing at his rough, work-worn hands.

"Ah, but my glazes," he replied. "The inner fires no other potter knows."

"But I don't have enough money with me right now," I countered.

"A gift," he smiled, the smile drawing me to his face for the first time, really.

And upon seeing his face, I decide. The other potters can wait. Despite this clay, His glazes are superior.

LYNDELLE CHIOMENTI

MARCH 29

Unsolicited Counsel

Dear children, let us not love with words or tongue but with actions and in truth. 1 John 3:18, NIV.

As a young pastor's wife who had to adapt to frequent moves in order to survive, I was not surprised to find our little family on the go again. We were being sent to help with an evangelistic series. This time, however, the move would be more complicated. I had just given birth to our first child, a baby girl, five days earlier. The call was to another part of Florida, where summers were hot and air conditioners were almost nonexistent. The three of us moved into a stifling apartment surrounded by lively university students, and to make matters worse the baby had colic and cried incessantly.

My evangelistic duties were to greet the people and hand out supplies. In addition my husband and I were asked to provide transportation for those needing a ride to the meetings. This assignment led to another bothersome frustration.

One of the dear saints, who was a passenger in our car, became a self-appointed child expert in spite of the fact that she herself had never had children. Immediately upon situating herself in the car, she would begin to counsel me regarding my baby's crying; the proper way to burp the child; whether or not the baby was dressed too warmly; whether or not the formula was the right temperature, etc., etc. When I listened to her I felt that I wasn't even capable of holding the baby right. What was I to do? The child was mine, and she didn't come with a set of instructions. I would do the best I could! Even when I tried to comply with the woman's counsel she would often change her advice. She even continued her training program during the daytime hours by telephone.

Despite my best efforts, it seemed that nothing I did was right. I'd never met a person like this well-meaning sister of mine. Finally I'd had enough! I was discouraged and tired. This lady had all the answers. She could tell others what to do, but her unsolicited advice brought me only confusion and discouragement. Finally I mustered all my courage and kindly but firmly told her that I was the mother of my child and I would decide what was best for her. I would be her friend—minus her counsel.

There are young and old all around us who need our unreserved support. They need to know that we care for them even if we think we have a better way of doing things. Their inexperience and blunders will not bring censure, but love and acceptance as one member of the body cares for another.　　FRANCES McCLURE

MARCH 30

Red and Yellow, Black and White

For God so loved the world that He gave His only begotten Son, that whoever believes in Him should not perish but have everlasting life. John 3:16, NKJV.

When I was a small child, my sister Helen carried me to school on her hip. There were advantages to being the eleventh of 12 children, one of which was going to school at an early age.

Day after day we sat in a one-room school, until finally we were sent to what I called a "real" school because it had so many rooms.

In July of 1969 my parents received a letter from the board of education announcing that the state of Alabama was required to bus a number of Black students to White schools, and I was selected to be one of those students.

I was a happy and comfortable 15-year-old eleventh grader. My life was very secure. I always had an older sister or brother to be with and friends from my own community. Now I was being sent to an all-White school in an all-White neighborhood. "Why me?"

I asked. My life was just fine as it was.

When I entered that new school in September, all the fearful things I had anticipated never came about. And each day I felt more at home.

I made new friends with students who, like me, made themselves friendly. We must have looked beyond the colors of our skin, because color wasn't the issue whenever we decided whether or not to build friendships. We were attracted by personality and character.

As I look back on those days, I think I understand why I was chosen to be bused to that White community. I needed to learn from that experience. God had a plan for my life in which the color of a person's skin could not be an obstacle or issue. He knew that someday I would marry a minister, and that together we would accept the commission to carry the gospel message to any and all who would listen.

John 3:16 now has a clearer meaning for me: I know without a doubt that God does so love the world (all peoples) that He gave the ultimate gift (His Son), that whosoever (Black, White, Jew, Hispanic, Asian) believes on Him will have eternal life. Thank God, He looks straight through the skin and into the heart and loves us all the same.

NETTIE M. ANDERSON

MARCH 31

Creative Alterations

And the scribes and Pharisees brought unto him a woman taken in adultery. . . . They say unto him, . . . Moses in the law commanded us, that such should be stoned. . . . But Jesus stooped down, and with his finger wrote on the ground. John 8:3-6.

The summer I was 13 we drove from Ohio to California to visit my aunt Ardath and uncle Lansford. I was a professing tomboy at the time and devoted to anything that breathed of strength, savvy, and survival know-how. No matter that the back of the station wagon was packed to the hilt with "survival" gear or that my mother did all the cooking on a propane camp stove as we camped along the way, I was a real pioneer. I could even walk a few feet in the forest without breaking a twig or rustling a leaf.

From the right rear seat of the car I analyzed plants from the farmlands of the Midwest to the deserts of the wild West, fancifully categorizing them for their usefulness to a wagon train blazing a new trail or to myself deserted by my station wagon and unable to follow the sunrise or the moss on tree trunks to the supermarket. I investigated every holster and knife and other piece of gear displayed in souvenir shops and, in general, attempted to disregard the fact that fate had assigned me to the ranks of the gentler sex.

My parents deserve credit for *not* deserting me with the station wagon. If appearance or grooming had anything to do with family connection, they surely should have. When we arrived, Auntie looked me over from head to toe with a skeptical eye.

I immediately sensed something of a kindred spirit and liked her. But her pithy gift of shampoo, toothpaste, and nail clippers would have been completely wasted if my mother hadn't enlightened me about the implications of such a gift.

Then Auntie gave me the bracelet.

I looked at my dad for help, smiled a wan smile at Auntie, mumbled a thank-you, and felt very confused. The confusion was largely because I wasn't supposed to like this thing for a variety of reasons, but I thought it was absolutely beautiful.

"You really should put it on, you know," my father said when we were alone. He looked away from my startled face and continued. "A gift is from the heart, and that's more important than any rule." Put it on? The thought had hardly crossed my mind.

But I did put it on. And I shampooed my hair. And I brushed my teeth and trimmed my nails and voluntarily put on a dress. And I felt beautiful for maybe the first time in my life—even content, for the time being, to be a girl.

When we find that we need for those close to us to change something about themselves, we must not be content with critical words and acts that only alienate. Our God and some loving deliberation will often provide a wise and inventive solution that will be life-changing instead.   SUSAN SCOGGINS

APRIL 1

My Friendship Garden

A friend loveth at all times. Prov. 17:17.

I can't wait to begin work in my garden. Already the tulips and daffodils are up! The primroses and pansies are blooming, and I saw some new shoots on the rosebushes yesterday.

I really must budget time for my garden. There are piles of last fall's leaves to be cleared away. Weeds need to be pulled. But time is not all I need to spend. I'll have to spend money for seed, fertilizer, and new rosebushes. I care about my garden, so I'll find a way to invest the time and money it needs. I'll willingly give of myself so that flowers might bloom in my spring garden.

My spring garden has set me thinking about my Friendship Garden. Caring for it means investing my money, but mostly my time, to help friends grow. I give myself that another might bloom! People are the flowers in my Friendship Garden.

Some are faded flowers, like Grandma Jones. Caring for her could mean picking her up for church, sitting with her, and later sharing a bowl of soup with her in my home.

Lynne is a wilted flower. Divorced, mother of two small children, she often looks a bit droopy. Caring for her might mean giving her a warm hug to let her know I have not rejected her. It could mean including her on our next outing.

There are other flowers in my Friendship Garden—flowers such as Beth, whose husband died not long ago. She feels left out of things. I might make her bloom by sitting with her in church or asking her to work with me on the next potluck.

There are bright, happy flowers who give me pleasure by their performance at church. Caring for them could mean a telephone call or a note to let them know how much I appreciate them. It's easy to bloom when you are appreciated!

Then there are the flowers who no longer bloom in my Friendship Garden. They've moved away, or I have moved. Caring for them might mean a card or a letter to tell them I want to keep the friendship alive.

I think of the new flowers in my Friendship Garden—ones planted since I moved. I must find the time to cultivate the soil around them. Who knows, they just might put down roots and become a permanent addition to my emotional and social landscape!

A host of flowers grow in my Friendship Garden. Will they be there this time next year? A lot depends on the attention I give them now!

DOROTHY EATON WATTS

APRIL 2

The Smoke That Thunders

He also wanted to reveal his abundant glory, which was poured out on us who are the objects of his mercy, those of us whom he has prepared to receive his glory. Rom. 9:23, TEV.

We stood where David Livingstone had been on that November day in 1855, when he and his African followers floated down the mile-wide Zambezi River in a dugout canoe. Suddenly the slow-moving waters vanished. The great river disappeared into a narrow chasm, hiding itself in clouds of drenching spray.

One of the first Europeans to see the falls, this great missionary, explorer, and liberator of slaves exclaimed, "I shall name it after my queen, Victoria Falls!" The locals called it Mosi oa Tunya—the smoke that thunders—because the pouring waters roar into the boiling gorges and rise up in a pillar of mist that can be seen at flood time for 70 miles. You can hear the muffled roar several miles away. From the Rain Forest precipice the terrific thunder of the Main Falls drowns all other sounds, making your own voice inaudible.

Victoria Falls cannot be seen as a whole from any point. Four times we walked the trail along the chasm edge, capturing the majesty of the five separate waterfalls at each of the 15 viewpoints in Zimbabwe. Approximately twice the height of Niagara Falls, it drops about 350 feet. These falls almost become one in the awesome grandeur of the summer flood. Then the Zambezi pours enough water to fill about 350 Olympic-size swimming pools every minute and stretches more than a mile in width.

Watching the white waters of Victoria Falls reminded my husband and me of the never-ending blessings and love of God. We heard His power and strength in the roar of the falling water. As the rays of the morning sun fell on the spray, we counted 11 rainbows arching the waterfalls, some vivid and complete, others faint, all emblems of our Father's gifts of peace and hope. Sometimes the full African moon creates a misty rainbow that spans the entire gorge.

Now you know why this spectacular falls is one of the seven natural wonders of the world, a beautiful demonstration of how God longs to pour His glory on you. Right now He's preparing you to receive His glory. You are the object of His mercy. Are you choosing to let Him reveal His abundant glory in you?

EILEEN E. LANTRY

Created in Love

For you created my inmost being; you knit me together in my mother's womb. I praise you because I am fearfully and wonderfully made; your works are wonderful, I know that full well. Ps. 139:13, 14, NIV.

I remember the day as if it were yesterday when my mother lovingly cupped her hands around my face and said to me, "You're my beautiful Black baby." I loved to hear those words from her, but it wasn't enough. It wasn't enough because I didn't believe those words. I had no self-esteem. I was too tall, too skinny, my hair was too short, and my complexion too dark. "Why did God make me this way? Doesn't He love me and want me to be a beautiful woman?" I asked in tears. Then it happened. Overnight it seemed I began to believe those precious words of my mother. Her words became real to me only because Jesus became real to me. I found in His Word that I was created in His image, and that all He made was good—it was wonderful! He created me in love, He died for me in love, and He will return in love for me.

I began to find value and self-esteem in the fact that Jesus loved me *so* much. So much that He died for me; for God so loved Terrie . . . I have learned to seek and to appreciate God's gift of true beauty: "Beauty is fleeting; but a woman who fears the Lord is to be praised" (Prov. 31:30, NIV). True beauty comes from within and can only be found in Jesus. Once we have Jesus in our hearts, our beauty shines outward from within. I am now able to smile with confidence, knowing that I am fearfully and wonderfully made. Created in love.

Out of this painful growth experience came the beauty of words. I hope through these words you will feel affirmed and valued for the beautiful women you are. TERRIE E. RUFF

In Memory of Her

I tell you the truth, wherever this gospel is preached throughout the world, what she has done will also be told, in memory of her. Matt. 26:13, NIV.

I was lying on the couch, listening to a tape of an evangelistic sermon about the Last Supper. As the preacher explained the foot washing, he observed that the disciples were probably sorry later that they had not washed Jesus' feet but instead let Him wash theirs. I thought to myself, *I'll just bet they were!* Suddenly a thought hit me so hard that I sat right up, knocking over the recorder. The disciples may not have washed Jesus' feet, but a woman did!

You know the story, I'm sure. It was the week before the Crucifixion. Jesus was attending a supper at the home of Simon the leper in Bethany. Somehow the customary foot washing was overlooked. But as Jesus was reclining at the table, Mary quietly broke an alabaster jar and poured perfume on His head and washed His feet with it and her tears. It was very expensive perfume, the best she could buy. Maybe it was her entire retirement fund.

She had not done this to fulfill any customary social ritual. She was doing it as a sign of devotion and gratitude. Jesus had shown her total acceptance and forgiveness, and she wanted to show her love. It was nothing required or forced; it was totally unexpected. She then wiped the excess perfume and her tears with her long hair. Not only did she wash and dry Jesus' feet; she didn't stop kissing them—"she loved much" (Luke 7:47, NIV).

And when she loved much, everyone in the room knew it. It must have smelled wonderful. ARDIS DICK STENBAKKEN

Only a Doll

Also, the Kingdom of heaven is like this. A man is looking for fine pearls, and when he finds one that is unusually fine,

*he goes and sells everything he has, and buys that pearl.
Matt. 13:45, 46, TEV.*

I have many beautiful dolls from all over the world. Some are antiques, but none of them is more valuable to me than Boo-Boo.

Boo-Boo was my first doll. I got her before I was able to speak properly, and I'm not sure what Boo-Boo means in baby talk. I loved her dearly, but her body was made of rubber, and over the years it disintegrated.

My mother recently gave me my childhood dolls, and Boo-Boo was simply a plastic head with a rag sewn over what was left of her body. Her arms were long gone, and her legs were dangling loosely.

I took Boo-Boo and made her a new body out of muslin, washed her grimy face, and put a fresh dress on her. She looked absolutely beautiful!

Sometimes I think I must look like a ragged little doll to Jesus. I come to Him as I am—with my imperfect character and broken spirit—but He bolsters my sagging courage and gives me a new heart.

GINA LEE

APRIL 6

Sometimes All We Can Do Is Pray

Pray without ceasing. In every thing give thanks. 1 Thess. 5:17, 18.

My mother used to knit and crochet beautiful, big, thick, colorful afghans. One year for Christmas she decided to surprise me with a lovely fisherman's afghan edged with fringe. Christmas came and went. Then I received a phone call asking if I had received the afghan. "Why, no!" was my reply.

January passed, then February and March, and to my consternation and wonder, no box arrived in the mail. I felt heartsick at the thought of the hours of labor my mother had put into the afghan, only to be lost. I asked Jesus about the problem. No one else could help, for she had sent it by U.S. mail. There was no way to trace the package.

April arrived, and I had pretty much given up hope that the afghan would ever show up. One day, however, when I arrived home from work, there on my front porch sat a perfectly wrapped box in brown paper, tied with string. The postal label clearly indicated that it was from my mother and was properly addressed to me. Awestruck, I carried the box inside the house and examined it carefully. It was in perfect condition, as if my mother had just wrapped it and handed it to me. There wasn't a mark on it, and there wasn't a single crease in the paper, as one might expect a package to have after traveling through the mail. I took the brown wrapping and string off. Underneath, the box was wrapped in beautiful bright Christmas paper with a big bow, protected so it wouldn't get crushed. I proceeded to take the Christmas wrap off, and as I lifted the lovely afghan out, a pungent aroma of fresh pine needles rushed out to perfume the air.

Where had this box been all of this time? I wondered. *Where did the fragrance of the woods come from?* Somehow, sometime, it had traveled the more than 3,000 miles to reach me. Then I thought, *All those five months the Lord knew every moment where it was, and He ordained that I should finally receive this wonderful gift. Yet all that time, while He was working out His will, there was nothing I could do except pray.* I dropped to my knees!

And so it is. Sometimes as God is working out His will in our lives, all we can do is pray. And more times than we can ever remember or realize, God has delayed answering our prayers for some unknown reason, only to provide a glorious answer at just the right time!

The afghan isn't quite so new looking anymore. But as it graces my bed today, I still thank Jesus. It will always have special meaning to me. DIANE MUSTEN

APRIL 7

God's Prayer Line

He will be very gracious unto thee at the voice of thy cry; when he shall hear it, he will answer thee. Isa. 30:19.

Today I received a letter from a friend telling about an annoying experience she had trying to get past the automatic touch tone answering system of a business to talk to a *real* person.

"Remember when we used to call businesses and talk to *real* people?" she asked. "I'm so glad that I never hear this when I pray: 'If you're praying about a personal need, press 1; if it's about a blessing, press 2; pleas for a loved one, press 3.' Praise God—He's *real*! His line is not automated. He personally hears and answers our prayers."

Our prayers will not be put on the tape of an answering machine to be listened to at a later time or after return from a vacation. (God is never on vacation!) Our prayers will be heard the moment they are prayed. For God has promised, "*I* will answer him." Not the answering machine, not the secretary, not even the vice president, but the "CEO"—God Himself.

How thankful we should be for this amazing promise and the awesome access to our Father through His direct prayer line!

JOAN MINCHIN NEALL

APRIL 8

Pure Gold

The precepts of the Lord are right, giving joy to the heart. . . . They are more precious than gold, than much pure gold; they are sweeter than honey, than honey from the comb. By them is your servant warned; in keeping them there is great reward. Ps. 19:8-11, NIV.

One day over lunch Elder Mikhail Kulakov, former president of the Euro-Asia Division, told my friend Susan and me the following story.

During the 1930s, when the persecution of Christians was at its worst, women carried on the work of the church in the former Soviet Union. At great personal risk, they visited church members to pray with them and encourage them to be faithful to God. Tragically, the majority of our pastors had been imprisoned or sent to die before firing squads.

The Bible was the most prized possession a believer could own, and many lost their lives because they copied God's Word to share with men and women without hope. With 11 sheets of onion skin and 10 sheets of carbon paper they pounded the keys of antiquated typewriters at the risk of losing their lives if they were discovered.

One evening in a cell at a women's prison, several women were talking among themselves. They began to tell each other why they had been sent to prison. As the conversation made its way around the circle of dejected souls, one after another confessed to being there because of gold. Everyone was aware of the government's mandate that demanded citizens to hand over their gold jewelry to the state. It was needed to fuel the machines of war. The majority of the women in this particular cell confessed to being there because they had refused to comply with this law.

In the circle there was a godly older woman, and when it was her turn to speak, she did so with conviction in her voice. "I'm here because of gold too," she said. "The purest kind of gold. The precious gold of God's Word, from which I was unwilling to be separated."

Today many of us purchase Bibles in a variety of translations, sizes, and colors. For women, it can be a difficult choice—like deciding which flavor of ice cream to choose. We ask ourselves, "Should I choose the dusty rose or the cranberry? Or maybe the navy blue would look better with my coat." The next time you're faced with this dilemma, remember that when it comes to Bibles, the gold is on the inside—the color on the outside is of little importance.   ROSE OTIS

APRIL 9

Hospitality

[Lydia] said, . . . "I beg you to come and stay in my house." And she insisted on our going. Acts 16:15, NEB.

One missionary duty in Korea in the sixties was to take turns feeding all the GIs who came to church at the mission. Isolated from families, often hungry for home cooking, and sometimes experiencing trials of faith, these young men needed a home after church. Our turn came every two or three months. We might have between 25 and 35 men—or none, if the Army suddenly announced an alert.

We might buy 20 pounds of potatoes, five pounds of lettuce, and 12 quarts of milk. With six pies and vegetables from the freezer, we'd hope to have enough. These guests always came hungry.

We all have memories of those experiences; they become funnier with time. Mine include the summer week that our new, irreplaceable refrigerator motor burned out right after I had bought 150 ears of corn, six watermelons, and several quarts of milk.

God mandates hospitality: "Practice hospitality" (Rom. 12:13, NEB). "Be hospitable to one another without complaining" (1 Peter 4:9, NEB).

But have you ever noticed how God turns our hospitality to reward us? We gain more than we give—certainly true of feeding GIs in Korea.

No cook could find more appreciative guests. Army fare made a great appetizer. Often someone would say, "That's the best pie I ever ate. Could I get the recipe for my mother?"

Dick always brought us honey or some other PX treat we couldn't buy. Jim quietly took pictures of the children in each home. On his next visit he'd leave 8" x 10" pictures in some inconspicuous place. Whenever Larry got a leave, he'd come and treat car ailments that baffled local mechanics.

We watched men grow. The Army truly "makes 'em or breaks 'em." Some Christian servicemen deliberately avoided church contact, but those who hunted up the mission early in their 13-month tour usually kept coming, and returned home more mature. Need forced them into leadership. Jerry once said, "I never got up in front for anything at home. I just told them I couldn't. And here I am teaching a Bible class."

Some passed out Korean literature. Others helped a struggling school or orphanage. Dave left behind a strong church from evangelistic meetings he and a Korean friend conducted. One church school teacher will never forget Ted, who persuaded his friends to help with her college tuition when she was disowned after her conversion.

These men left Korea with firsthand knowledge of mission. Some later became missionaries. Others, previously unsettled, returned to school. One Marine captain gave up his commission to become a Bible teacher at a Christian school.

Because of these guests, many a small missionary boy thought the ultimate in life would be to reach draft age. Their perspective included John, who romped with them every Saturday night; Frank, the baker who decorated all their birthday cakes; and Byron, who got an afternoon off to help our boys build a tree house.

Sometimes we review the old guest book and ponder these men. Occasionally we see one. Recently one called when he came to Andrews University for his daughter's graduation. We realize again that through hospitality we received much more than we gave.

MADELINE S. JOHNSTON

APRIL 10

Joy in Hope

Be joyful in hope. Rom. 12:12, NIV.

The only thing that makes life really worthwhile is hope. Most of us hope for things and experiences that are different or better than what we have. Some of those things are as simple as hoping the pencil won't break, or as challenging as hoping for recovery for a seriously ill loved one.

Hope. The very word is a nice comforting idea. But what is

hope? *Webster's New World Dictionary* defines hope as "a feeling that what one desires will happen." I appreciate Lloyd Ogilvie's additional explanation in *A Future and a Hope*: "Hope is a gift of God through Christ that produces a confident, unshakable trust in His faithfulness, and a vibrant expectation of His timely interventions in keeping with His gracious promises to us" (p. 50).

But Satan is constantly working to discourage us. And for many people life is, or at least appears to be, hopeless. So when we feel hopeless we can know that it is Satan at work to destroy us.

It isn't always easy to be hopeful. This past year several of my family and friends have experienced serious illness. Some have died leaving children, grandchildren, spouses, parents, and friends. One was a school roommate of one of our sons. He left a wife and three small sons. It is hard to understand.

My husband told me about Nina, whom he had met in Russia. Through her tears she described the sudden death of her 27-year-old son. Although it had been four years earlier, she was reminded every day because she has assumed parenting responsibilities for his little daughter. And she asked, "Why, why?"

I can begin to understand Nina's hurt because I have a son who is the same age that her son would be now. Even though she said she was not a believer, my husband gently explained that God feels what she feels, for He lost a Son too. One of Dan's favorite Bible promises is Isaiah 41:10. He put Nina's name in place of the personal pronouns. "So do not fear, for I am with [Nina]; do not be dismayed, for I am [Nina's] God. I will strengthen [Nina] and help [Nina]; I will uphold [Nina] with my righteous right hand" (NIV).

After quietly sharing her pain and a simple prayer, Dan encouraged Nina to reread the promise and just say, "Thank You, God," each time her burden became too heavy to bear. Nina went out into the cold, dark night. She returned the next evening with a broad smile and her granddaughter. She said she had not slept so well in a long time as she had the previous night.

Christ provides precious promises to inspire us with faith and hope. He also gives us strength to handle whatever challenges may come our way. Even though life appears hopeless, we are promised "joy in hope."

Hebrews 6:19 says: "We have this hope as an anchor" (NIV). With Christ as our anchor, we can cope with, and have hope for, life today and every day.   BETSY MATTHEWS

Trust, Turn, Tally

I will say of the Lord, "He is my refuge and my fortress, my God, in whom I trust." Ps. 91:2, NIV.

Mom, where's Dad?"

The question from my 11-year-old daughter turned the agony of the night into an unbearable cry. Tears are good for you, my grandmother used to say, and I never cried like I did that morning. All night long my husband suffered from excruciating pain. We were new to the campus of Andrews University, strangers in a strange land. We knew no one. We had no phone. We had no car. All night I stayed by my husband, trying to share his pain, but in no way lessening it. Early in the morning I rushed him to a nearby hospital, and I returned home alone.

I joined my daughter, and together we cried. Never before was life so lonely, so helpless. But even as we cried, my son, not yet 6, stood stoic. Head erect, eyes dry, but with a calmness that carried a message of concern, he came near me, gave me a hug, and in a voice that still sounds in my ears, said, "Mom, why don't we pray? Dad will come home all right."

Dad did come home all right after surgery, with a leg that needed a brace for years and with a cross he had to bear for the rest of his life. But it is my little boy's words that keep coming to me every time I face a crisis or an opportunity in my life. His words taught me three things:

Trust God always. Trusting God is not a doctrine to believe, but a reality to experience. He is as real as the water we drink and the stars we see. To trust Him is to taste Him, and to taste Him is to find Him good, even when times are bad.

Turn to God always. God is not emergency equipment to turn to when we have a situation we can't manage. My son taught me that God is a friend, always willing, always ready to listen to us, to give a helping hand, to provide a shoulder to lean on. To turn to Him means to affirm that He is my everlasting strength.

Tally His promises. For every situation we face, there's a reassuring promise in Scripture: "When you pass through the waters, I will be with you; and when you pass through the rivers, they will not sweep over you. When you walk through the fire, you will not be burned; the flames will not set you ablaze" (Isa. 43:2, NIV). Each day as I rely on His promises, I find Him to be my real friend in whom I can trust. "He will never disappoint those who put their trust in Him" (*Testimonies*, vol. 9, p. 213).   MARY FOWLER

If You Could

For God so loved the world, that he gave his only begotten Son, that whosoever believeth in him should not perish, but have everlasting life. John 3:16.

If your child were lost and alone,
    You would trade places—
        IF YOU COULD.
If your child were blind,
    You would trade places—
        IF YOU COULD.
If your child were very sick,
    You would trade places—
        IF YOU COULD.
If your child were drowning,
    You would trade places—
        IF YOU COULD.
If your child were in serious trouble with "the law,"
    You would trade places—
        IF YOU COULD.
We are God's children,
    Jesus traded places—
        BECAUSE HE COULD!

DEBORAH SANDERS

Warning: This Planet May Be Harmful to Your Health

For our light and momentary troubles are achieving for us an eternal glory that far outweighs them all. 2 Cor. 4:17, NIV.

When I was in fourth grade I sat in the third seat from the front, in the row by the windows. I remember particularly one balmy day, listening with my science book open before me as Mrs. Daley expounded on the virtues of asbestos. I was awed by the thought of such a wondrous material. Although I couldn't imagine it or understand it, a substance existed that simply *could not burn*. It made me feel safe, protected. Fire, the worst fear that preyed on my 10-year-old mind, could be held at bay by modern technology.

Other things were added to my mental list of "the good and safe" as I left Mrs. Daley's room and went on to Mrs. Haggerty's and then Mrs. Newberry's. Six glasses of pure water a day, I discovered, cleans out your system. Fresh air and sunshine bring vitality to life; a swim in the ocean is healing; apples and grapes and strawberries promote good health.

I imbibed all this learning with zeal, accepting the knowledge on a practical level for my life. I never felt better than when sitting among the rows of red berries at McDermott's U-Pick, popping the fruit into my mouth straight from the plant, knowing that I had a direct line for vitamins to enter my body.

I am no longer a student at John B. Stanton school, and the intervening years have brought with them some cruel realities.

I cringe at the thought of having sat for so many years in an environment laced with asbestos—a material now known to produce cancer in large numbers of individuals each year.

The pure joy of plucking a sun-warmed fruit from the plant and popping it into my mouth has been marred by the knowledge of pesticides, Alar, and other cancer-producing sprays.

I cannot draw a drink of water from the tap anymore without fearing contaminants, lead pipes, and brain disease in children.

Being out in the sun too long brings to mind the tear in the ozone layer and harmful rays. And I arrived at the beach the other day to find a sign straight out of a futuristic novel: "Seaside Park Closed Because of Unhealthful Swimming Conditions." Even the ocean that at one time seemed so vast and cleansing has succumbed to garbage scows, discarded medical waste, and raw sewage.

Now, I don't mind being told that cigarette smoking causes cancer. I can handle the idea that cirrhosis of the liver springs from overindulgence of alcoholic beverages.

But the fact that drinking tap water and sitting in the sun and eating strawberries and swimming in the ocean are hazardous to my health threatens to make me into something of a cynic. Even the good things are bad—the berry has soured on the bush, and the ocean curdled in the wave.

Amid the erosion of all that is good and decent and pure and fresh, I sense a message from above. Could it be that in these days of scientific advancement and technological wonder God is telling us, "You can do nothing to advance your position on earth; you have but one alternative—trust in Me"?

Often human beings have had the option of *doing*. Follow the rules, and things will come out right. But as our world begins rapidly to consume itself, things have changed. We are left standing on a planet that has been strip-mined of much that was once good.

Yet Paul says: "We do not lose heart. Though outwardly we are wasting away, yet inwardly we are being renewed day by day. For our light and momentary troubles are achieving for us an eternal glory that far outweighs them all" (2 Cor. 4:16, 17, NIV).

Much that was once good is gone. Yet the eye of faith, fastened on a divine Being, holds out the hope of a berry that will once again be sweet, a tree whose leaves will heal nations, and a stream of water that will be clear as crystal. SANDRA DORAN

APRIL 14

The Real Enemy!—1

Have no fear of them. 1 Peter 3:14, NEB.

When my husband and I got married, we moved into an old frame house in Fayetteville, North Carolina. He was a private in the Army, and we were very poor. We didn't have extra money to be feeding mice. Every morning for the first week we found our bread in little pieces scattered all over the floor, inside the kitchen drawers and cabinets, and all over the counters. We couldn't imagine how mice could make such a mess, so we decided that it must be the neighborhood children playing a prank on us. Soon we had a plan to catch them at their game. We set an elaborate trap with rope, buckets, and pots so that anyone opening the door would make so much noise they would wake us and be scared away. Well, all was silent that night, and in the morning the kitchen was a mess again.

After looking over the situation again, we decided it must be a rat. So we bought a *huge* rat trap and set it that night. In the morning we found a rat whose body alone was eight inches long! We found the hole where it had been coming in and repaired it.

Some years later, when my husband was in the ministry, we moved to Oxford, Mississippi, to a subdivision nestled in the woods about seven miles out of town. The utility room was outside the kitchen door and connected to the carport. It was large enough for only a washer, dryer, and the water heater. In fact, it was so small that to unload the dryer I had to open the door and stand on the side and unload it. Now at that time we already had four children, ages 6, 4, 2, and 2 months, and we had a 17-year-old girl and her 13-month-old son living with us also. In those days disposable diapers were considered a luxury, so, you guessed it, I washed a lot of clothing and diapers! One day when I was unloading the dryer I grabbed something that felt funny. It was warm just like the rest of the clothes, but it felt furry. In my mind I took a quick inventory of what I had put into the washload and didn't remember washing any stuffed animals. I grabbed the handful anyway and pulled it out. When I saw that I had a dead mouse, I threw it, screamed, and ran out of the utility room into the house. I was still screaming "A mouse, a mouse!" and crying! It was the only time in my life that I have been totally out of control and hysterical!

As I look back on that experience, I realize how silly it was to be terrified of a dead mouse! What we really need to be terrified of is the real enemy, Satan!   CELIA CRUZ

APRIL 15

The Real Enemy!—2

Awake! be on the alert! Your enemy the devil, like a roaring lion, prowls round looking for someone to devour.
1 Peter 5:8, NEB.

A few years and moves later we unpacked our belongings at a lovely house up on a mountain, with a beautiful view of the town below. The first night we were so tired. We crawled into bed expecting to get a good night's sleep, but instead we were kept awake by the sounds of some creatures in the attic. It sounded like a football game going on up there! In the morning my husband went up to check it out, but found nothing. The second night we had another football game! The third day we bought some mouse-traps.

My husband didn't want to kill the mice, so my son and I set the traps and placed them around the house. In the morning all six traps were full! We bought six more, and the next morning they were all full, so we decided to reuse the traps. Now, I didn't want to be the one to unload the traps, and my husband refused, so I convinced my oldest son to do it for me. We washed the traps, reset them, and caught some more mice.

The mice got into my bags of dry beans, noodles, cereal, and everything else packaged in a box or bag. I got tired of throwing food away and didn't have enough containers to put everything in.

Those mice even tried chewing their way into my Tupperware!

My husband decided that I couldn't kill any more mice, so he contacted a pest control company and got a spring-loaded trap. It was a metal box with an "apartment." It had a swinging door on one side and a "hallway" with a bait gizmo on the other side. We set the trap, put it in the kitchen, and went to bed. In the morning we had 11 mice in the "apartment"! My husband put the full trap in the car and drove off several miles down the road to the woods and set them free.

Through the years we found out that mice can get in through a tiny hole the diameter of a pencil, and that they can eat their way into almost anything. Plastering a hole isn't enough. We found that steel wool and concrete are the only combination that works for us!

Mice are like our greatest enemy, Satan. Just as mice can get in through the tiniest hole, Satan looks for the smallest entrance to our souls. We are told to guard well the avenues to our souls, but we seem to be blinded and blunted to the infiltration of the enemy! We *can* plug up the holes that Satan comes in through with morning and evening worship, Bible study, prayer, and by refusing to allow immorality to come into our homes via the television, magazines, books, and radio. Jesus is coming soon, and we can't take chances! Be on guard against Satan!   CELIA CRUZ

APRIL 16

Reflecting His Beauty and Perfection

Therefore you shall be perfect, just as your Father in heaven is perfect. Matt. 5:48, NKJV.

My husband and I sometimes reminisce about the origin and circumstances of purchase surrounding the Kashmiri carpet that beautifies our home. It was one of several practical items acquired during the first years of our marriage while serving with the U.S. diplomatic corps in Cambodia.

The October sun bathed the Kashmir Valley in peacefulness. Dubbed the "Venice of Asia" because of its numerous waterways, Srinagar's medieval buildings, mosques, and temples sparkled with beauty. Fall splashed its first tinge of color on poplars, willows, and other foliage. Snow-capped Himalayan peaks towering to more than 20,000 feet provided a majestic background. Exquisitely manicured lawns and shrubs of the world-famous Shalimar Gardens contrasted with the cascading chrysanthemums and marigolds. The sweet aroma of jasmine and roses pervaded the air. Yes, the magic of summer lingered tentatively for our enjoyment as we vacationed in this Shangri-la of the East, far removed, it seemed, from the rush and bustle of Western civilization.

From our houseboat we taxied by *shikara* along waterways bordered by creamy, waxlike lotus lilies. In the marketplaces the delicate art of the Kashmiri people captivated us. Exotic birds and flowers typified their work and were replicated in wood carvings, papier-mâché objects, woven cloth, floor rugs, and carpets. We felt the closeness of these people to nature and to nature's God, although their worship of Him was mostly expressed through Islam.

In a carpet factory we observed small children seated behind large weaving looms as they deftly plucked woolen threads through the warp yarn, tying them in minute knots on the back side. Incredulously we watched while the little fingers literally flew from one knot to the next, blurring the movements to our eyes. It was not happenstance that resulted in the intricate beauty of the design formed beneath their petite fingers. The motif had been preplanned, and the children had memorized it, although the written pattern remained at their side for reference. We chose and purchased an exquisitely beautiful carpet of the same size and pattern as one we had observed being made.

Now more than 30 years later we still enjoy the rich colors and design of this plush, velvetlike carpet, and we remember with nostalgic delight from whence it came. Just as our Kashmiri carpet is a perfect expression of the beauty of the natural world in that little Himalayan province of India, so we should perfectly reflect the beauty and character of God. As we daily seek to fashion our lives after the Divine Pattern, we then, as one author put it, "may be perfect in our sphere, even as God is perfect in His" (*Thoughts From the Mount of Blessing*, p. 77) .   YVONNE MINCHIN DYSINGER

APRIL 17

Flames That Would Not Kindle

But now, thus says the Lord, who created you, O Jacob, and He who formed you, O Israel: "Fear not, for I have redeemed you; I have called you by your name; you are Mine. When you pass through the waters, I will be with you; and through the rivers, they shall not overflow you. When you walk through the fire, you shall not be burned, nor shall the flame scorch you. For I am the Lord your God, the Holy One of Israel, your Savior." Isa. 43:1-3, NKJV.

One bright summer day my mother received a telegram from her uncle saying that my grandmother was quite ill and that we should visit her immediately. Seeing the urgency of the situation, my mother and I booked our train tickets from Bombay to Madras and left the very next day.

We had a safe journey and reached my grandma's place the following day. We were glad to see that her health had improved. During our stay, my mother and I shared a double bed, since my grandma lived in her brother's house.

That evening the mosquitoes were very pesky, so I decided to do something about it. I was told that if I kept a lighted incense stick in the room, the smoke would deter them. Taking this advice, I lit an incense stick and stuck it in a small crack in the wooden headboard of our bed and went to sleep. You may think I was crazy to go off to sleep when there was something burning over my head, but before I proceed any further, let me explain about incense sticks. After lighting an incense stick you blow out the flame, and it just glows. As it burns, only cool ashes fall off. At that time it did not occur to me that this might be a fire hazard; apparently it was.

It happened in the middle of the night. I still don't know what woke me, but suddenly I saw this inferno of flames just above our heads. I quickly woke my mother, and of course we woke all the other people in the house. The wooden headboard, both pillows that we slept on, a storybook that I kept under my pillow, a cloth change purse that my mother kept under her pillow, and the mattress made of coconut fibers were all on fire. As you can imagine, these are highly combustible things, and the soaring flames reached to the ceiling.

At that time, there were no fire engines in Madras. It took six men drawing water from a well more than an hour to put out the fire. Afterward we assessed the damage. The headboard, mattress, pillows, and book were destroyed. Even the coins in my mother's change purse were charred. But the small Bible from under my pillow was not burned at all. I am thrilled to say that neither my mother nor I received any burns. The others in the house at the time, and the neighbors who came, could hardly believe it.

I believe that God protected my mother and me from that fire, because it started so close to us. My mother was convinced and so grateful for God's intervention that she often shared our experience as a testimony of God's miraculous care.

To this day I still have the small Bible and the burned pillowcase to remind me of my heavenly Father's promise in today's verse.

STELLA THOMAS

To Receive Graciously, Without Protest

For we hold that a person is justified by faith apart from works prescribed by the law. Rom. 3:28, NRSV.

From the time they were born, raising my three children was largely my responsibility since their preacher-father was not often home. So it was I who washed their bodies, their clothes, and their dishes.

Boarding school and college made renewed demands on my energies. New clothes, bedding, labels, suitcases, etc., had to be provided, but I really enjoyed mothering to my children.

It seemed such a short time before wedding bells summoned me once more to my children's service. I worked with their preacher-dad to provide creative wedding services that I knew they would appreciate. My lovely daughter and I worked together on a thousand and one details to make her wedding a memory to cherish.

Inevitably grandchildren were joined to the family tree, and the plaintive call came, "Mother dear, could you mind the children while we get some business attended to?" or "We have to go overseas to a medical conference; would it be possible for you to stay in our home and mind the babies while we are absent?" or "Would it be convenient to bring your holiday to the U.S.A. forward a little?"

"No problem," we assured them all. "We love to be at your service."

But yesterday all that seemed to change. I was celebrating a high-digit birthday, and my children were all at home.

I recommended that we eat at our table. I was used to serving.

But no! A special lunch in a glorious rain forest restaurant was decreed.

I wanted to help pay for the costly food. But no! This was the children's treat. I was choosing the least expensive food. But no! My plot was discovered, and I was ordered to select the best dishes, irrespective of cost.

Gifts began to flood across the table. I protested. Surely the luncheon was gift enough! But it was then that my daughter uttered a most significant rebuke to her mother.

"Mother dear, today you are *not* a servant. This is the day when you must learn to accept gifts and favors graciously and without protest."

Suddenly I was hearing echoes of similar but very ancient words. Long before, I had struggled to find acceptance with my Lord by *doing* all the right things. I was a compulsive *doer*. I wanted eternal life, I wanted perfection, and working like crazy seemed the only way to attain them.

But perfection eluded me. I became discouraged and ready to quit because my best toiling was not achieving that goal.

And then came ringing the words of Paul. He was speaking primarily to the Romans, but I heard him say, "Edna, a person is justified, declared perfect, and assured of eternal life by *faith* quite apart from 'working like crazy' to keep the law" (my adaptation of Romans 3:28). But Paul had more to say: "God doesn't *pay* eternal life as wages; it is a *gift* that Christ agonized to provide" (see Rom. 6:23). "It is a *gift*, Edna. It is not appropriate to toil and struggle to obtain it. This is the day when you must learn to accept the gift of an endless life graciously by faith."

And because there was no other way, I embraced the *gift* with all my heart, and life has never been the same since that grand day when I accepted heaven's sweetest gift without protest.　　　EDNA HEISE

APRIL 19

My Guardian Angel

The angel of the Lord encampeth round about them that fear him and delivereth them. Ps. 34:7.

How often have we repeated that text without really thinking about it? How often, as we look back over our lives, can we see instances of that protection that only the Lord can provide?

I live in Australia, in a suburb of Sydney, the capital of New South Wales. Not very far from my home is a busy highway. When my husband and I first moved to this suburb, the highway was a two-lane road with dirt shoulders. Now it is a six-lane freeway—busy night and day.

Some years ago while driving home along this highway, I had to stop to make a right turn. It should be realized that here in Australia we drive on the left side of the road, so a right-hand turn is often a major exercise, particularly if the intersection is a wide one without traffic lights, as this one was.

While waiting to turn, I was suddenly hit from behind by another vehicle, which propelled me diagonally across the intersection. Had there been any other cars coming in the opposite direction, there was no way I could have missed them.

Miraculously, the road was empty at that moment. There was damage to the car, of course, but all I sustained was some shock.

There have been other instances when I believe we were protected by angels. Living in a big city, as I do, creates its own particular dangers, not the least of which is burglary.

My husband is a busy doctor with one of his offices at our home. Needless to say, this gives some people the idea that there could be drugs or money there for the taking. Several of our windows bear evidence of marks where someone has tried to break in.

Now, we all take precautions to protect our homes and property, but there is little we can do to keep a determined thief out. One day I walked into my husband's office and surprised a young man trying to break in. I was so angry that without a thought I rushed out and chased him down the road. Fortunately for him, and maybe for me, running is not one of my strong points.

Each day I ask for divine protection for my family, my home, and myself. And as I survey my life I know that the Lord has answered my prayers. I am so much better able now to understand that the angel of the Lord does indeed camp about us and deliver us.

MARIE MUNRO

APRIL 20

A Matter of Trust

Do not be afraid; simply have faith. Mark 5:36, REB.

I wish I could just fast-forward my life so I would know what I'm supposed to do!" I exclaimed to one of my friends. I was wrestling with what career I should pursue, what classes I should take, whether or not I should transfer to another college, and whether or not I should officially change my major—the kinds of issues college students struggle with. I was wishing God would just tell me plain and simple what He wanted me to do.

In Bible times Jesus was walking with Jairus, a synagogue ruler, toward Jairus' home, where his daughter lay dying. The crowds were slowing the process, and before they reached Jairus' house, news reached them that the little girl had died. What Jesus said to Jairus may seem odd. He could have said plainly, "She is dead now, but I will raise her back to life." But He did not. His response was simple: "Don't be afraid. Just believe." What a strange thing to say to a parent who has just lost a child!

Perhaps Jesus says the same thing to us. We may ask for our life's outline. We may want to know what our career will be, whom we will marry, how many children we will have, where we will live, etc. But Jesus does not show us our future. He simply challenges us to not be afraid of the future, whatever it may hold; to trust Him and to believe that He does hold our future in His hands.

"Don't be afraid. Just believe." Easier said than done—for me, anyway. But when we let go of our fears and trust in God, two things happen. We discover that peace that passes all understanding. It comes from trusting God to work in our lives. Second, good things start happening. Jairus trusted in Jesus, and he got his daughter back! God has wonderful things in store for us if we will only allow Him to work in His own good time. Just believe that He will take care of your future, and you will find that your future will be better than you imagined. MINDY RODENBERG

APRIL 21

Outside/Inside

The Lord does not look at the things man looks at. Man looks at the outward appearance, but the Lord looks at the heart. 1 Sam. 16:7, NIV.

During the month my husband and I spent in the former Soviet Union in the summer of 1992, we were intrigued by the T-shirts the local populace sported. Times were hard, and people welcomed the help offered by Western countries.

This help included an abundance of T-shirts from Germany and the United States. The latter displayed the usual American slogans, sometimes quite amusing when found so far from their original context—always in English, unknown to most of the recipients.

One day we were sightseeing in Moscow. I saw a bent little Russian *babushka* (grandma) walking down the sidewalk, looking for some bit of food to buy from a local vendor. Her gray hair was pulled back into a simple knot, and the lines of her face bespoke the years of toil she had experienced. Nevertheless, emblazoned across the front of her T-shirt in bright letters stood the message "I'm the Boss."

Later while walking across a beautiful town square in Kiev with a local seminary student as our guide, we ran into a group of new church members returning from a vesper program at the church. The several young ones among them, about college age, swarmed around our guide, hugged her, and babbled delightedly as they told of their joy and filled her in on events in their lives. She had been at the seminary all summer and had been home only rarely for a weekend.

She explained to us later that these were all new converts who had joined the church the previous year during an evangelistic series conducted by an American team. During the evangelist's meetings she had held meetings for the young people, talking about Christianity and its application to their own concerns of schooling, romance, and family life. This had endeared her to them, and the fondness was obviously mutual. "They are *my* young people," she explained.

As these young people talked with Natasha, their faces and voices bubbling with the joy they had found in the Lord, I noticed a T-shirt on one of the girls. It was a blatant ad for a certain make of brandy. Conspicuously pinned to the front of it and worn with pride was a wide metal button proclaiming "I ♥ Sabbath School." These had just been given out at a conference to train members to work for children, a conference attended by many enthusiastic new converts who know that their church *needs* them. (In the former U.S.S.R. even older members have little idea how to do such work, because work for children was previously forbidden.)

How nice it was to know that the outside message meant nothing.   MADELINE S. JOHNSTON

APRIL 22

The God Who Sings

The Lord your God is with you, he is mighty to save. He will take great delight in you, he will quiet you with his love, he will rejoice over you with singing. Zeph. 3:17, NIV.

What is your favorite picture of God?" the teacher asked. It didn't take long for me to choose. The portrayal I like best of all is God singing over His children. I am drawn to a God who sings to express His delight and rejoicing.

When my children were small, I rocked them to sleep at night, and it seemed natural to sing while rocking. Although much of parenting small children was stressful for me, singing while rocking was a special delight. A pajama-clad child hugging a "blankie" makes a satisfying armful.

Sometimes when we needed a quiet time during the day, the rocking chair was an oasis for me and my child—or both children at the same time. We would rock and sing Jesus songs, songs from *Sesame Street* or *Mister Rogers*, or songs we made up ourselves. Sometimes our songs were quiet and comforting, other times loud and joyful. The music, the creak of the wooden rocking chair, the motion, and the cuddling all blended together—whatever our mood. If things had been stressful, we were soothed. If things had been going well, we were content.

When I get exhausted, jaded, or irritated, I need to remind myself that God will quiet me with His love. He is with me, He is mighty, and He takes great delight in me. He even rejoices over me with singing! What a relief it is to allow the child in me to climb into God's rocking chair to be enveloped in His songs of delight.

My response, like David's, is "Because you are my help, I sing in the shadow of your wings" (Ps. 63:7, NIV).

RITA EISENHOWER DUNCAN

APRIL 23

Bread of Hope

Cast your bread upon the waters, for after many days you will find it again. Eccl. 11:1, NIV.

It was a hot Saturday afternoon in midsummer. After lunch my husband and I went with a group of Christian brothers and sisters toward a public square near a Catholic cathedral in the heart of one of the most populous districts of south São Paulo—Santo Amaro. At that time we were leading an evangelistic work in public parks and squares.

The crowded streets were full of workers, merchants, buyers, and sellers, all marketing their products. Our group stopped to make arrangements for distributing literature and for preparing the sound set for a musical presentation.

While I observed people rushing around I saw a striking scene. A woman had been arrested and put in a small booth—a kind of police post—in the center of the square. She was in despair. I could see her untidy hair, her dirty face, her poor dress. Suddenly, she started shouting incessantly as she furiously beat on the glass window, "Let me out! Let me out! I'm innocent!" Moved by curiosity, some people stopped, but moments later went on their way. The two police officers outside the booth seemed impassible and didn't bother with her cries.

I was touched by the situation. *Oh!* I thought. *God created man and woman in His own image, and here is this woman in that small police booth, looking like a beast in a cage.*

I decided I would talk to her. She needed to know that Jesus loved and died for her. I walked toward the booth and asked the officer, "What happened to her?"

"Well," he responded, "she's a thief. She tried to steal a lady's purse and was almost lynched by the crowd. She was put here to avoid worse things."

"May I talk to her?" I asked. The officer looked at me with a curious expression on his face, wondering why I wanted to talk to that apparently despicable woman, but he unlocked the door and allowed me to go in for a few minutes.

As I drew near I realized she was pregnant. In my heart I loved that poor and hungry woman. I knew she needed food—the material bread—but more than that, she needed spiritual food, "the living bread."

"Why are you here?" I asked.

Tears rolled down her face. "I'm not a thief. I didn't try to steal the lady's purse," she repeated.

I knew she was lying, but I loved her anyway. "Dear," I said, "don't do it anymore. I know you're a good person. You're pregnant. Just think about your child. Jesus loves you and died for you. Did you know that?"

I showed her a picture of Jesus I had in my hand. Immediately she took it and looked at it for a few moments. "Do you believe He can change your life?" I asked her.

"Yes, I do," she replied.

The officer opened the door. My time was up, and I left.

Now there was silence in the booth. No more shouting or striking the window. Just a poor woman inside, looking at Jesus' face printed on the tract I had given her.

Later a police car came and drove her away. Before going, she waved goodbye to me. One day I hope to meet her again, looking clean, neat, and elegant, dressed in the white robe Jesus will give to those whose lives are restored by His unlimited love.

SONIA GAZETA

APRIL 24

Higher Ground

If I take the wings of the morning, and dwell in the uttermost parts of the sea; even there shall thy hand lead me, and thy right hand shall hold me. Ps. 139:9, 10.

I'm pressing on the upward way, new heights I'm gaining every day; still praying as I onward bound, 'Lord, plant my feet on higher ground.' " This was one of the hymns frequently sung at church when I was a child. I had not thought much about that particular hymn until my husband was called to disaster duty when a devastating flood hit Rapid City, South Dakota, several years ago. When we arrived, the crippling results of the flood were evident almost everywhere. It was difficult to imagine that dwellings had once been on the very spot where now only debris was strewn. Twisted trees might hold a lone shoe. Pieces of clothing, scraps of wood, and pieces of metal dotted the landscape. And there was, as it were, a car graveyard, where the skeletons of many cars had reached their final resting place.

Stories of the flood abounded. One rescuer told us about trying to evacuate some homeowners. One woman who had lived in the area a long time would not leave her home. She had seen a great many floods in her day and felt that this one was no threat to her. Despite all the pleadings, she would not leave, and that was the last anyone ever saw of her.

Every day the news reported that day's unearthed bodies. The paper ran a feature on missing pets, and some big rewards were offered for their return or even evidence of their remains. In most cases the fortunate who had left town in time had nothing to return home to. And one family who had survived the rushing waters left a beautiful home and said they would never return to it. If even one window had been broken in their home, the whole house would have been swept away and all would have perished, so it had been a terrifying experience for them.

In subsequent flood warnings no one hesitated to flee to higher ground. The area of the worst flooding was declared unsafe, a place where no homes could be built. In the Christian's life, the only safe ground is higher ground. "If the path is difficult and dangerous, it is God's plan to have us follow in meekness and cry unto Him for strength" (*Testimonies*, vol. 4, p. 442).

"Yes, Lord, plant my feet on higher ground!"   PAT MADSEN

APRIL 25

Long-distance Prayer

Encourage one another—and all the more as you see the Day approaching. Heb. 10:25, NIV.

Three o'clock in the morning. The telephone rang. Startled out of my sleep, I thought perhaps that something had happened to one of my family members or that this was a "crank" call. The voice on the other end of the line asked hesitatingly, "Lorna, are you all right?"

I was stunned. The person calling me from across the country had met me only once and we had spoken only one other time by phone. "I know this is the middle of the night," she continued, "and I have been arguing with the Lord about calling you." For several hours this dear lady had been impressed to make this phone call to me and had been putting it off. "But the Lord demanded 'Call Lorna now!' so I am calling you," she said.

Initially I began to reassure her that all was well, that I was enjoying the new area in which I was living and working. Then I awakened sufficiently to realize that I had spent most of the previous week going to doctors. There had been several medical tests and other procedures to complete because of health concerns.

As I began to relate this to her, my night phone caller broke in with "And you are concerned about your voice, aren't you?" That got to the core issue very quickly and was indeed the fact that had been underlying my anxiety.

"The Lord has something very important for you to do this year and the devil would love to discourage you," the voice continued. "Give your health to the Lord who created your body." We prayed together over the telephone before she hung up.

I lay there quietly in bed marveling about the wonderful gift the Lord had given to me that early morning. I was stunned to realize the implications of her call. As a child of God, did I have a talent that God wanted to use? Something the devil wanted to thwart? I thought about her words. Sometimes overwhelming events drop into our lives, events that can keep us preoccupied with other concerns, events that can keep us off track.

We can use such a jolt to bring us back to center and to remind us that we are about the King's business. God is in control of us, our talents, our health, our very existence.

I picked up the telephone to share my early-morning encouragement with a close friend. We, too, prayed together on the telephone, encouraging each other. We began the day with renewed determination to be about our Father's business, to rebuke our adversary, giving all facets of our life to God's keeping and concern.

LORNA LAWRENCE

Judgments

As Jesus went on from there, he saw a man named Matthew sitting at the tax collector's booth. "Follow me," he told him, and Matthew got up and followed him. While Jesus was having dinner at Matthew's house, many tax collectors and "sinners" came and ate with him and his disciples. When the Pharisees saw this, they asked his disciples, "Why does your Teacher eat with tax collectors and sinners?" On hearing this, Jesus said, "It is not the healthy who need a doctor, but the sick. But go and learn what this means: 'I desire mercy, not sacrifice.' For I have not come to call the righteous, but sinners." Matt. 9:9-13, NIV.

What wisdom among us can expressly reveal
The trials and the triumphs our sister can feel?
We look and we ponder—it's a game as we whittle.
Not a care or concern while our judgments belittle.
If we each would take notice, our own feelings aside,
It's our differences that make us just humans . . . with pride!
So the next time you're tempted to disparage and rage,
Try to tune in to beauty, with the thoughts of a sage.

God uses common people who are willing to work directly with Him. Look at Jacob. Known as a deceiver, he became the father of the Israelite people. Joseph, a slave, was utilized both in the restoration of a nation and in saving his family from starvation. Hannah, a housewife, became the mother of Samuel. Esther was a slave girl who was able to save her people from certain massacre. Matthew, a tax collector, became an apostle and Gospel writer. Luke, a Greek physician, came to be a companion of Paul as well as a Gospel writer. Peter, a lowly fisherman, became an apostle, a leader of the early church, and a writer of two New Testament letters. And finally, Mary, a peasant girl, became the mother of Christ.

How many times have we allowed our concern for what others might think to cause us to refrain from doing a special task? Do we think someone else can do it better, or so-and-so has more time than we do, or we don't want that person to think we're being "uppity" just because we're up in front?

It is so much easier to sit on the sidelines, noting the sharps or the flats, deciding how the job could have been done better or differently.

But you can make a difference! You can be part of the problem, or you can help solve the problem.

Daily polishing of our character is internal, frequently unseen. Only God knows us intimately, knows what we've been through to cause us to be who we now are. We each have our own characteristics, our own aptitudes, our distinctive specialness, that allow us to put our own "spin" on the ball called life.   JUDI WILD BECKER

APRIL 27

Playing "Bible Days"

Look unto me, and be ye saved, all the ends of the earth. Isa. 45:22.

Come on, Mary, we have to go to Bethlehem," 3-year-old Roger says to his older sister, Leslie. They are playing "in Bible days," and acting out the story of Mary and Joseph.

Mom looks on, listening. It is interesting to see them use Ollie, their riding toy, as their donkey. To make the story as true as they can, Leslie stuffs Elizabeth, her favorite dolly, into her robe so she looks the part of pregnant Mary. Then they use backpacks with canned goods and sleeping bags with pillows to complete the scene.

The journey is from one end of the hall to the other, but in that short distance something always falls off Ollie—for he was not meant to be a beast of burden. All too frequently, by the time they arrive in "Bethlehem," Elizabeth, who plays Baby Jesus, has been "born" several times.

Undaunted, Roger and Leslie abandon Ollie, pick up their book, and journey into the living room, where the manger scene is held under the piano.

Leslie delights in the birth process—calling for "Joseph" to hold her hands and recite with her the twenty-third psalm. A cassette tape of this Bible story has Mary doing this, so that is how she envisions the birth of Jesus.

And isn't that how it should be? We welcome the risen and living Jesus into our lives by reciting precious Bible promises. And each time we call upon Him, He is born anew.   ELIZABETH WATSON

Don't Fence Me In!

*All that the Father giveth me shall come to me; and him
that cometh to me I will in no wise cast out. John 6:37.*

A few years ago I was traveling to a far country with my husband
and our son. When we came to the border, it looked formidable. Tall watchtowers loomed about every half mile. Uniformed
guards, each carrying a small arsenal, patrolled the freshly plowed
areas between the high towers. They controlled big fierce-looking
dogs with heavy chains. A couple of the cars ahead of us seemed to
be in the process of dismantling as the rear seats were being hauled
out for inspection underneath.

Our son said to us, "I don't think they want us in their country;
it looks pretty iffy to me." It looked that way to me too.

When our turn came, we presented our passports and visas at
the first station. There was much stamping of papers, scrutinizing
of our records, and comparing our faces with the passport pictures.
The guard gave us one more long look, and the official stamp was
finally entered into our passports. We had passed with flying
colors! So far, so good.

As we reached the second gate, it swung open and we were
waved through. I held my breath as the examination of our rented
car began. We did not have any real contraband, just three Bibles in
the local language and some religious materials. We were asked to
get out of the car, and the rear seat of our car was raised and looked
under. When the glove compartment was searched, the leftovers
from our lunch tumbled out. The trunk was opened and our
suitcases were barely inspected. Then *we* were examined closely, as
were our cameras.

We sighed with relief, but we weren't finished yet. There was
still a third gate to stop at in order to change some of our U.S.
dollars into local currency after presenting our confirmed hotel
reservations. We were asked, by body and sign language, to part
with a couple of cheap pens that were protruding from my
husband's shirt pocket, which we quickly did. At last the big iron
gate swung open, and we were permitted to pass through. We
couldn't believe it—we had passed!

When I remember this fantastic journey, I'm reminded of one of
my favorite Bible texts found in John 6:37, "The one who comes to
Me I will in no way cast out" (my paraphrase). There will be no

inspection or checking of baggage, no scrutinizing of passport or visa, nothing but acceptance.

Friend, if you are afraid to approach God with a murky past or mistakes you made just recently, fear no more. He's been waiting for you with open arms! VIRGINIA CASON

Jesus Meets My Deepest Needs — 1

But my God shall supply all your need according to his riches in glory by Christ Jesus. Phil. 4:19.

As a young pastor's wife and a mother I gave little thought to my needs. But years later, while recuperating from breast cancer surgery, I realized that my pattern of attempting to meet others' needs while neglecting my own was like trying to fill someone's cup from my empty one. As the Lord has patiently led me along in the growth process, I have been learning that Jesus meets my *deepest* needs.

The awesome promise is that God will supply all we lack (not just our physical needs) "from his glorious resources in Christ Jesus" (Phil. 4:19, Phillips). His riches know no limit; therefore, His ability to meet our deficiencies is limitless.

You could make your own list of things you lack that our Lord abundantly provides. My personal list keeps on growing as I learn more about my heavenly Father and more about myself.

His unconditional love meets my need to be fully known and totally loved. Fearing rejection by others, I must have begun early to develop a more acceptable false self. But honesty is essential for intimacy. How beautiful that the One who knows me best loves me most! I can face the reality of who I am, and who He is in His loving presence—a true worship experience. With all my neediness open to the One who gives me absolute acceptance, He heals my shame and low self-worth. How amazing that Deity desires closeness with me. Jesus' prayer to the Father reveals that oneness—"I in them, and thou in me" (John 17:23). This same verse says that God loves us, as He loves Jesus. See John 15:9 for another incredible truth—Jesus loves us, as the Father loves Him. Such oneness meets my need for connectedness and belonging and removes my loneliness and insecurities.

Caught in the trap of trying to be "good enough," I used to long for freedom. "So if the Son liberates you, then you are unquestionably free" (John 8:36, Berkeley). What a paradox! True freedom comes as I surrender to Jesus—allowing Him to possess all the parts of my life: emotional, spiritual, physical, mental, relational.

"Thank You, Jesus, for Your transforming power working deep within." LILA LANE GEORGE

APRIL 30

Jesus Meets My Deepest Needs—2

He did not spare his own Son, but gave him up for us all; and with this gift how can he fail to lavish upon us all he has to give? . . . Then what can separate us from the love of Christ? . . . For I am convinced that there is . . . nothing in all creation that can separate us from the love of God in Christ Jesus our Lord. Rom. 8:32-39, NEB.

When I think of my Christian sisters around the world who have invested so much of themselves in family, church, and community, I am awed. What a beautiful picture of love, devotion, time, energy, and talent graciously and generously shared. But sometimes we give too much and neglect nurturing our own needs, desires, and dreams.

If your life were symbolized in a painting, I wonder what the theme, tone, textures, colors, shades, and shapes would be.

It helps me to visualize Jesus meeting my deepest needs, so I did an abstract painting, symbolizing myself as a dark, empty vessel. Beautiful pastel colors swirl around me, representing His loving, powerful attributes filling me up and enfolding me.

At the bottom of the picture, like faded toppled idols, are the things and people I had used to fill my emptiness.

This painting reminds me of God's transforming work in my life, and praise spontaneously wells up within me: "Thank You for Your presence that takes away my loneliness, healing my fear of abandonment. Thank You for Your mercy and grace that pardon my sins, lifting my heavy load of guilt, providing the gift of salvation. Thank You for Your unconditional love and acceptance that surround me, healing my wounded self-worth. Thank You for the peace of Your Spirit that sets me free from my fears and anxieties. Thank You for Your unlimited power to create and re-create me (from the inside out). Thank You for Your glorious resources that provide everything I lack. I praise Your ability to provide for all my deficiencies from the vast supply of Your glorious resources. Nothing can separate me from my Creator because of Your lavish love." LILA LANE GEORGE

The Woman on the Path

Carry each other's burdens, and in this way you will fulfill the law of Christ. Gal. 6:2, NIV.

She sagged under her burden, a shabby figure in her faded and frayed shatanga-cloth wrapped African-style around her waist. A baby tied on her back swayed to her labored pace under the weight of a metal tub balanced on her head. The hoe gripped in her hand told me she was returning from her fields, where she had probably wrestled with drought-packed earth since the birds first began their morning serenade. Her eyes reflected the hardened landscape—no color, no vitality, no hope. She could have been 18 or 48—I couldn't tell in the few moments it took for her to pass me by.

I did not know her name, but I had seen her before and knew her village. She was going home to a mud hut where grubby children awaited her preparation of the supper's porridge. Like most of her kind, she would be spending the evening hours hauling water, building fires, cooking, cleaning, and tending children. Her bedroom would be shared with two other wives and a well-rested husband, along with the several children curled up on grain sacks lining the dirt floor. What little sleep she could hope for would be relentlessly disturbed by the mosquitoes, and sooner or later she'd be sick again with malaria.

With eyes lowered she neared me, casting her dark cloud of weariness across my path, momentarily blocking out the rays of my blinding self-absorption. In the cold shadow of her world my painful inadequacy and inability to lift her burden stood starkly naked. Hers was another haunted face in a continent of struggling women who daily plod through the tasks of survival until their life forces are sapped from their weary bodies. I could not change her predicament. I could not rescue her. I could not even pretend to understand how she must feel.

I wanted to look the other way for fear she would see my nakedness and despise me for being so insulated from her pain, but I could not. Something more powerful than self-reproach possessed me, and I sought her glance. Our eyes locked for an instant, and I simply smiled and said hello.

A gleam of light sparked in her despondent eyes, and a smile shyly stole over her. Sensing I had flattered her by my greeting, I quickly followed with "How are you?" Her gaze strengthened with my attention, and pulling herself a little higher, she bashfully replied with a heavy accent, "Fine, thank you. How are you?" Smiling, I answered that I was fine too, thank you. She nodded gratefully, and then was gone down the path.

I pass her now and then, and whenever she sees me coming she seems to walk a little stronger, and a smile lights her face as we exchange our greetings. I sense that for her, I am an important person who gives her a little self-esteem by noticing and greeting her. I still feel terribly inadequate to soften the rugged path she treads, but I have had a glimpse of how powerful the gift of influence is to strengthen her spirit along the way.   DEBORAH AHO

MAY 2

A Prayer Come Winter

And we know that all things work together for good to them that love God, to them who are the called according to his purpose. Rom. 8:28.

Sitting at my desk where I work as an advertising copywriter, I smile as I look down at my list of seemingly endless assignments. It seems kind of funny that at one time I longed to use my writing talent in God's work and was afraid I wouldn't find my way. But in 1986, I thought it would take a miracle.

Winter had painted a picturesque scene in my small New England town, and as I stepped out into the brisk air I was enveloped in swirling snow. I walked along an old dirt road, intent on setting a steady pace, but the beauty of the rolling fields and soft purple hills made me pause. The words of Robert Frost's "Snowy Evening" crept into my mind. *It was probably a scene just like this that inspired the well-loved poem*, I thought.

The New England landscape had inspired a lot in me, too, over the years. But little good it was doing. Instead of the exciting opportunities I had anticipated upon graduating from college, I found myself facing intense loneliness and frustration. I couldn't find work anywhere. My college friends had moved away. My neighbors looked the other way when I smiled and said hello. And my husband, Michael, exhausted from his long day's work, fell asleep at the table most nights beside his half-eaten dinner.

Reaching toward the gray sky, I caught a large fluffy snowflake as it drifted on the gentle wind. For a moment it lay like a jewel on my hand—unique and intricate, yet so very fragile. For unable to withstand its inhospitable environment, it was lost in the warmth of my glove. *Just like my dreams, Lord*, I thought.

Suddenly my eyes flooded with tears and the pain of the past few months found its way to God. "I've believed since I was a child that You made me to write for You, Lord," I cried. "I've tried everything—and it's no good. If You want me, God," I challenged, "please, get me out of here!" I didn't really want to leave behind family and the place I'd grown up in. But something inside me was beginning to die, and I knew I couldn't take any more. And I believe God knew, too. Because He was already changing things as I made my way home.

When I received a letter from the Review and Herald Publishing Association several weeks later, I knew it contained God's answer. (They had seen my brief résumé in Atlantic Union College's placement book.) Within two months from my prayer that snowy day, Michael and I were settled in Hagerstown, Maryland!

I would never want to relive those awful seven months. But somehow in the darkness God gave me a treasure that will always light my path. I learned from personal experience that all things really do work together for good to them that love Him. That there is no burden He will ever let me carry too long. What assurance that gives me!

What about you? Is there something in your life that robs you of happiness, peace, or fulfillment? His promise in Romans 8:28 is for you, too.

LAURIE R. GUST

MAY 3

I Will Give You Rest

Come to Me, all you who labor and are heavy laden, and I will give you rest. Matt. 11:28, NKJV.

I was seated in the prayer and counseling room that was provided for those who attended camp meeting. I prayed, "Dear Lord, help me to give comfort and encouragement to any who may come in."

"We moved to this area to be close to my husband's aging parents," the first woman confided. "We had to leave our own grown children in Chicago, and they need us, too. Am I doing the right thing? I miss my sons so much. Yet my husband's parents need us. Is there something better we could do?" The tears in her eyes revealed the burden of her heart.

"My son-in-law has cancer," the next visitor revealed. "Could we pray for him?"

After prayer, as she was about to leave, she suddenly blurted out an old hurt. "My son died a homosexual. I've never told this to anyone, even my pastor. Each time this subject is mentioned, it feels like a knife is turning inside me. I fear my son will be lost." There was anguish in her voice and tears in her eyes.

An elderly, distressed woman entered later and came quickly to the problem. "I'm lost," she anguished. "My husband passed away last year, and I'm lost without him. I don't know which way to turn. We had 40 years together, and we were very close. We had no children. I'm torn between remaining in our retirement home in the state where he is buried and moving to be close to my relatives."

"I'm living in hell," the last person to enter the room said abruptly. "My husband, whom I still love, is trying to kill me. I've moved out of his bedroom and keep my door locked.

"I'm seeing a doctor for health problems," she added, "and have talked with him about it. I've talked to the pastor, but I don't think the doctor or the pastor believes me."

I listened with sympathy to each one and tried to ease their pain or help them solve their problem. We prayed together. One said as she left, "Could I give you a hug?" Another said, "It's so good to talk to a woman."

People, who on the campgrounds looked calm and peaceful, had opened their hearts and revealed problems that are common in the world today. While most of these problems could not be humanly solved, the hurt was eased through sympathetic listening and prayer.

Much of Jesus' ministry was to "heal the brokenhearted" (Luke 4:18). Today He is saying to those with similar problems: "Come unto me, all ye that labour and are heavy laden, and I will give you rest" (Matt. 11:28). BEATRICE HARRIS

MAY 4

Fret Not Thyself

Train up a child in the way [s]he should go . . . Prov. 22:6.

Mom, do we have to learn all these memory verses?" inquired Beverly, my middle child, as we reviewed the little memory verse picture card booklet a thoughtful children's leader had provided. Her sister Shirley nodded in agreement with the question.

"Someday, girls, you will be glad you did," I responded in my "Mother-knows-best" voice. "These verses will come back to you later and will help you face life with courage and the assurance of God's love for you."

The review completed, I reached for the binoculars, and our family headed for a nearby country lane to look for birds—a favorite activity. The two older girls ran ahead, while the younger clung to Daddy's hand as we strolled at a more leisurely pace. Soon Shirley came running back. "I see a black bird with red on its wings, Mom. Let me look through the binoculars."

I handed them over, reminding her, as mothers will, "Be careful, now." She turned and rushed back to Beverly. Daddy, Paula Jo, and I hurried to join them. Before we arrived, Beverly snatched the binoculars from Shirley's hands and turned toward the woods.

"Mom, Daddy," Shirley turned to us, "see what she did? I had them first! Make her give them back!"

Beverly turned away. I reached for the glasses. "Girls," I began to preach, "remember those memory verses we just reviewed?" I was about to quote one that seemed appropriate for the moment.

Shirley interrupted, "But Mom, I had the glasses first! You gave them to *me!* And she grabbed them before I could look. And now the bird is gone."

"Well, Beverly," I began as I turned in her direction, "what do you have to say to your sister?"

With a twinkle in her eye and a mile-wide grin, Beverly turned to her older sister and said, "Fret not thyself because of evildoers" (Ps. 37:1).

Not exactly the memory verse I had in mind, but it broke the tension and we all laughed. I thought of scolding her for using Scripture as she had, but thought better of it. After all, she had fulfilled my prophecy! And it was a text I would often use myself in later years.   PATRICIA A. HABADA

MAY 5

The Lord Is My Strength

The Lord is my light and my salvation; whom shall I fear? the Lord is the strength of my life; of whom shall I be afraid? Ps. 27:1.

It was late at night on June 15, 1976, and I was lying in a hospital bed in Brasília, Brazil. The next morning I was scheduled to have surgery on one of two broken legs. How could things have gone so wrong? Just 10 months before, I had arrived in South America eager to begin a four-year term as a missionary secretary. And now this! A head-on collision between the church's Volkswagen van and a smaller car that crossed the median had caused the death of the two individuals in the car. Three other church secretaries and I were now in the hospital with various injuries. My mind raced as I wondered if this was the end of my mission service, and I worried about when I would be able to walk again. I wished my parents were with me, but I was all alone except for a woman from the local church who had offered to keep me company during the long night. And she didn't even speak English! My own Portuguese was so poor it was clear that we would never be able to have a conversation. I felt so alone and so afraid.

And then through words and sign language she indicated that we would read Scripture verses aloud to each other from our English and Portuguese Bibles. I do not remember who found Psalm 27:1 first, but as soon as I read the words peace came into my heart. I knew God was in that room by His Spirit, comforting and strengthening me. A lovely song based upon that passage, "The Lord Is My Light," came into my mind. The next morning as I was rolled into the operating room, I was humming the melody of that beautiful hymn. Somehow I knew that if I could just remember God's promise of strength, I would be fine and my future would be secure. Apparently the text and song made an impression on my subconscious, because I was later told I serenaded the surgical staff with the song during the operation.

During the 18 months before I was able to walk and work again, I frequently read and thought about this text. It has sustained me through more than a dozen operations on my legs, and comforted me when despair has begun to crowd in because of pain and uncertainty. These wonderful words remind me that my Lord and Strength has been with me in the past and will be with me in the future. With Him beside me, guiding and comforting me, "whom shall I fear? . . . of whom shall I be afraid?" ROWENA MOORE

MAY 6

Happy Mother's Day

I have been reminded of your sincere faith, which first lived in your grandmother Lois and in your mother Eunice and, I am persuaded, now lives in you also. 2 Tim. 1:5, NIV.

Dear Mom:
   I thought it was time to tell you how much you have meant to me since I came into the family. It was a new way of life for me to be married to a minister, especially since I hadn't been born or

reared in the church all my life. But thank goodness you were also a minister's wife, and a good teacher, who had faith in me. You took me in and made me part of your family right from the start. Yours was a loving, caring, and sharing (sharing with us when you didn't have all that much to share) family. Your mind and source of energy has always been switched to "go." In fact, sometimes I would tire just trying to keep up with you and would wonder to myself, *What's wrong with me?* You are really something else, Mom!

I'll never forget you encouraging me to sew. One day the church-owned moving van was going through our little town. The driver stopped at our front door and delivered an old treadle sewing machine from the Dorcas Society down your way. I nearly fainted! Your encouraging words were, "*You* can learn to sew now." At first I thought, *This has gone too far!* With two babies 19 months apart and being head over heels in evangelism and every phase of church work there was, when was I going to learn to sew? I did try to teach myself, but at first I couldn't even read the patterns. I didn't even know how to buy fabric let alone which side had a nap! I'd cry, fuss, try again, pray a little, and say, "I'll never learn to sew anything I'd be seen in!" Sometimes I'd stay up late or get up early in the morning to sew when the babies were sleeping. I guess I just kept trying because you said I would learn and you seemed so positive about it. Well, with your encouragement and the good Lord's help I did learn to sew, and it was a blessing to our bank account! You are the most positive-thinking person I've ever known, Mom, and I admire and love you for these qualities.

Your positive attitude pushed me to meet new people—thought I'd go bananas! But I really did learn how to do it—from your example. You were friendly to everyone. Your enthusiasm just runs over. I know you probably thought I'd never catch on, and I remember balking at times. But I knew you were right, and I wanted to be warm and friendly like you.

I could go on and on pointing out your good qualities and the many things you've taught me, but you might tire of it and think I'm insincere, and I wouldn't want that to happen. Mom, although we are different individuals, we respect each other's views and differences, and I love you for granting me that freedom. You had faith in me, you encouraged me, but you let me do things my way. I've never known you to be upset with me. I'm sure you must have been at times, but it never showed. That's why I think you are the best, most wonderful mom anywhere.

Love,
Frances

FRANCES McCLURE

Miracles Still Happen!

*I will send you Elijah the prophet before the coming of the
great and dreadful day of the Lord. . . . He will turn the
hearts of the fathers to the children, and the hearts of the
children to their fathers. Mal. 4:5, 6, NKJV.*

For almost 12 years my only child, Keith, and I had been
estranged. He had allowed various circumstances to separate
him from his family. Even when his father had suddenly died, there
was no response. Five years slipped by at one point before I even
discovered that he had moved East with his family. Continually I
prayed for a reconciliation, but nothing happened. And I did not
know how to break the stalemate.

One spring, while recovering from an illness, I listened to a tape
by Gary Smalley entitled *Keys to the Human Heart*. A message just
for me! It provided me with some deep insights concerning my role
as a parent and how I had failed in some ways to meet the needs of
my sensitive, musical child. Oh, how that realization hurt! But with
that realization came an idea.

It was as if my guardian angel spoke loud and clear—urging me
to write a letter to my family. Through a flood of tears I wrote, and
now when I read that letter I feel certain that an angel held my pen
and guided my thinking. I asked for forgiveness and understanding,
and sent off the letter by registered mail.

That same day my housemate, Enola, called friends ("prayer
warriors") to ask for prayer support. What an anxious time! Finally
on Mother's Day 1991, a beautiful floral arrangement was delivered to the house. The card accompanying it read, "All my love,
Keith." What a thrill, and once again the tears flowed—from
grateful hearts.

My son also made arrangements with Aunt Pinkie (as he calls
Enola) for us to fly back East where he and his family were living.
I still had not spoken to Keith directly and did not know if the
family would meet us at the airport, but there they were—
granddaughters as tall as I; granddaughters I had not seen since
they were infants. What a delight.

Our first day in church was a thrill. The pipes of the organ rang
with praise as Keith opened the crescendo pedal and played to the
glory of God. Misty-eyed Mom was most grateful—twice grateful!

The Lord had truly answered our prayers and performed a
miracle. That letter marked the beginning of a new, warm relation-

ship between my son and me. Each day that has passed since has been a joy. God is alive, cares, and reigns—and I have learned firsthand the value of James's admonition to confess our sins to each other and to pray for each other so that we may be healed (see James 5:16, NIV). NELL B. THOMPSON

Happy Mother's Day

When Jesus therefore saw her weeping . . . , he groaned in the spirit, and was troubled. John 11:33.

This is the day when humanity honors mothers, whether single, married, widowed, alive, deceased, foster, surrogate, or whatever. Today motherhood is remembered and women are honored.

On this great occasion I would draw your attention to Jesus and cause you to remember our Saviour, who also honored and blessed the women of His time.

Remember how He honored His mother and blessed the new bride by replenishing the wine supply at the wedding feast. Remember how He healed the woman suffering from an 18-year affliction. See His great and tender mercies as He allows His virtue to flow through and heal the woman plagued with bleeding for 12 years. Take another look at His compassion as He heals the Syrophoenician woman's daughter. Feel His gentle strength as He raises Peter's mother-in-law from her sickbed. Catch the shout of joy from the widow of Nain as her son is raised to life again. Hear our Saviour groan as He beholds Mary weeping over her brother's death. Run with the woman at the well as she returns to the city carrying Jesus' message of love to others. Marvel with the woman taken in adultery as she hears the gentle words "Woman, where are thine accusers?"

Then ere breathing His last breath, call to mind our Saviour's concern for His own mother as He places her in the care of another. "Woman, behold thy son," and to His disciple, "Behold thy mother."

On this Mother's Day remember this same Jesus still reaches out in love with concern and tenderest compassion for the women of today. JUNELL VANCE

She Saw Beyond the Sour Notes

So we fix our eyes not on what is seen, but on what is unseen. For what is seen is temporary, but what is unseen is eternal. 2 Cor. 4:18, NIV.

Many memories have washed over me since my mother's death three years ago. They seep into my mind without the slightest provocation. Sometimes they bring tears to my eyes, but more often they bring joy to my heart. For you see, I was blessed with a mother who loved me unconditionally! Just last week, while driving home from work, I remembered an experience Mom and I shared at an academy Mother's Day brunch.

When we arrived, the stage was a wall of pink Kleenex roses tucked into a backdrop of chicken wire. Beaming mothers and tittering teenagers filed into the dining room. For us the event was larger than life. Looking back, I have to smile, but at the time I was a bundle of nerves. When Mom and I were seated, I reached for the pink program beside my plate, and opening it I read, "M-O-T-H-E-R, by the Sophomore Girls Trio." This was my reason for being rattled.

We'd practiced the song a number of times, and I could have sung the melody in my sleep, but that was the problem. In a weak moment I had agreed to sing the second soprano's part, when I knew all along that I was born hearing only the melody. When I stood close to the piano at practice, Mrs. Leftrook accentuated my notes. But now the piano was some 20 feet from the podium, and as I made my way to the front of the room I had serious doubts about my ability to stay on key.

After a flawless introduction we began to sing a musical tribute that spelled out M-O-T-H-E-R. I struggled desperately to find my notes, but halfway through I gave up and timidly joined the first soprano singing the melody. In a few brief moments the Sophomore Girls Trio had become a duet!

When it was over I wanted to vanish from the campus, and I may have been tempted to do just that, except that my mother was waiting for me back at our table. I was sure she was embarrassed. More than anything else I had wanted her to be proud of me. Instead, I had botched the song! But before I could apologize, she reached over, pulled me close, and whispered, "Honey, I'm so proud of you!"

I couldn't believe my ears, but the look in her eyes told me that she spoke the truth. In spite of my "sour notes," she was proud of me! I couldn't understand it, but somehow her "mother eyes" didn't see a frightened 15-year-old singing off-key. Instead, she saw a child she had given over to God singing a tribute to her.

I've heard some great preachers in my life, but the sermon my mother preached at the Sunday brunch is one I'll never forget. She may never have known it, but that Mother's Day she gave me a priceless gift. She taught me that my heavenly Father doesn't focus on my failures, the "sour notes" in my life, but instead measures my value by the price He paid for me.   ROSE OTIS

MAY 10

Mothers-in-law

Then Orpah kissed her mother-in-law good-by, but Ruth clung to her. Ruth 1:14, NIV.

I am a new, first-time mother-in-law. And I want to be a good one. I want my daughter-in-law, Gelerie, always to feel comfortable—a part of the family. I already have a wonderful daughter, but I like the idea of having two. We had met and been with Gelerie several times before the wedding. But because we then lived in Alaska, she had never been in our home before this recent holiday season. Although this was her first time to visit, Gelerie was welcomed as family, not a guest. She could read the Christmas cards, look at the books and albums, and use the sewing or washing machine. She was clued in on family eccentricities. Why? Because Erik had chosen her. He loves her, and she loves him. We trust his judgment and know Gelerie makes him happier. We want this relationship to last and flourish.

I like to think of God as a sort of in-law (maybe mother-in-law—see Isaiah 66:13). Some picture God as some ogre trying to catch us doing something wrong, even trying to kill us. But I think God is joyful about my relationship with the Son, knowing that it makes both of us much happier. God has given me the privileges of family, open access to its blessings, and invited me to know the other family members well.

I've known cases in which marriages didn't work out and the in-laws were considered outlaws. Great unhappiness results. But with God as my in-law I never have to worry about that unless I myself sever the relationship with Jesus. I don't want that to happen. I want to be a good mother-in-law to Gelerie and a good daughter-in-law of God's. Only happiness can result.

ARDIS DICK STENBAKKEN

From Dependence to Delight

One thing I ask of the Lord . . . that I may dwell in the house of the Lord all the days of my life, to gaze upon the beauty of the Lord and to seek him in his temple. Ps. 27:4, NIV.

When I was about 17 years old, I watched a pastor diagram a chart of relationships for people at different stages of development. He said that the way we relate to people defines our concept of God. His comparisons started with the age of 2, when the child begins to say "I love you, Mommy." S/he would then also begin to say "I love You, Jesus!" When the child reaches kindergarten, everybody becomes a "best friend." Now Jesus becomes his or her "best friend," too. When a teenage girl wants to wear her boyfriend's watch, it is to symbolize their commitment; sometimes teens also carry a Bible to show they belong to Jesus.

Consistent with this theory, I have found that being a parent has certainly redefined my concept of God. My 3-year-old son has taught me insights into our Father that I never knew before. My first awe-inspiring lesson came when Joshua was only 11 weeks and 2 days old.

A church member was holding him one day as he was fussing and crying. But then she turned him so he could see my face, and the most wonderful thing happened. His crying stopped, his eyes opened wide, and he smiled the biggest smile at me! I thought my heart had stopped. It was the very first act of recognition he had shown. For the first time he was able to distinguish his mommy from a stranger. I wanted to laugh; I wanted to cry; I wanted to shout—all at the same time! It was as if I knew in a flash why my husband and I conceived him.

Imagine for a minute what it must be like for our heavenly Father when one of His children recognizes Him for the first time. He loves and cares for each of us as we go about our life. But all too often we take for granted the unfailing loving kindness with which He cares for us. Then one day we know His face!

Surely He must want to laugh, to cry, and to shout, all at the same time. Surely He wants to tell everybody, "My child just realized who I am!" And as we acknowledge Him as our Father, our Creator, and our Saviour, maybe He is reminded of why He created us.

David says that "the Lord takes delight in his people" (Ps. 149:4, NIV). If I as a human mother can take so much delight in the simple smile of my child, imagine God's joy when we enter into a relationship with Him.

"Dear Father, I want to see Your face today. I will worship and praise and exalt You, so that You will remember why You made me. Amen."
Teresa Gay Hoover Krueger

MAY 12

Mom as Hero

Honor your . . . mother. Ex. 20:12, NKJV.

The following appeared in the "Mother's Day Letters" section of the Hartford *Courant* on May 10, 1992. Aside from the beautiful sentiment it expresses, it is uniquely special because it was written by a 16-year-old daughter to her mother:

"I must be the luckiest person in this world to have actually met my hero. I know that some people never get to actually meet the person they admire the most. I not only admire this person, but love her also. She has shown me the true definitions of courage, love, respect, and fun. She is my mother. In the 16 years that I've known her, no matter what happens, she has always been there for me.

"The past two years have been the most trying for us. My brother was diagnosed with lymphatic cancer, and my stepfather was in a car accident. My mother has had to work to support all of us, including my older brother who goes to college—and a very expensive one at that. Even I had to have minor surgery this year. To me it was nothing, but my mother stayed with me the whole time, and I'm glad she did. And I was amazed at the way she handled a horrendous divorce.

"After all that our family has gone through, my mother still manages to keep us happy. There are some bad times, but there are always bad times in every family in the world. That is to be expected.

"What I admire most about my mother is that even when it seems like the world is going to cave in on me, or the family, she finds something or some way to put a smile on our faces. And even if we are not at home or together, Rebeca (Misorski), my mother, never fails to say the three words we all love to hear: 'I love you.'—Evelyn B. Muriente, Glastonbury, Connecticut."

What I find interesting about this tribute to this mother is that her daughter is able to appreciate not only the sacrifices, but the mother's capacity to keep her sense of humor through difficulties. We need to maintain a sense of balance and perspective when a trial strikes the family, a sense that life will continue after this crisis. What better way to achieve this equilibrium than to be able to smile and even laugh!

Another dimension to this beautiful tribute to a heroic mother is her ability to keep the other members of the family in the forefront of her affections, even as she is forced to give the lion's share of her attention to the hurting one. Oftentimes, the only one to receive a mother's love in such circumstances is the ailing child.

If we take the time to think about what a miracle this kind of mother is, one can begin to understand the character of God. It takes commitment to duty, courage to face reality, a willingness to sacrifice one's own comfort, and a heart submitted to the working of the Holy Spirit to see a child safely and healthfully into adulthood. We can each be this kind of mother by entrusting our lives to God. We can do all things through Him who strengthens us (see Phil. 4:13).

LOURDES E. MORALES-GUDMUNDSSON

MAY 13

Not Without My Daughter

The Lord shall preserve thy going out and thy coming in from this time forth, and even for evermore. Ps. 121:8.

She walks with head held high, this woman of God. And she is my daughter. My heart rejoices because her heart sings and her mind is focused on sharing her gifts with her brothers and sisters in Calcutta, India. I watch as the plane carrying my flesh and blood races by the airport window that serves as my vantage point, and climbs into the clouds, heading for a place too far. And I wonder, *Where have the years gone?* She's gone from the four walls of our home, and the dynamics of our precious foursome will never be the same again. Seems like roots are so easy to give, wings so difficult. I miss her so much, this child of my womb, this beautiful woman of God, who not so long ago gave me reason to carry burp rags, who filled the dirty diapers, got me up in the middle of the night for feedings, and gave me so many memories of laughter and joy. There will be reunions to anticipate and yet more memories to be made. But home is not the same—not without my daughter. I asked God for a promise. And He said, "Be strong and courageous; do not be frightened or dismayed, for the Lord your God is with you wherever you go" (Joshua 1:9, NRSV).   JOYCE HANSCOM LORNTZ

MAY 14

Put "in Christ"

Through him everyone who believes is justified from everything you could not be justified from by the law of Moses. Acts 13:39, NIV.

Broken" is a well-worn word in my vocabulary. It's not that I break a lot of things; it's just a word that presents itself often in my mind in reflective moments about who I am. It's helpful to be identifying the sources of my brokenness—the all-pervasive sinful condition I inherited as a child of Adam and to which I contribute by my own action, the fragmentation that has come in the wake of painful life experiences not of my own making, the devastating effects of a toxic faith that I thought demanded human striving and perfection in exchange for the assurance of God's love and acceptance.

I have found peace and full assurance in a new understanding of what it means to be "in Christ." Last night at prayer meeting I marked my Bible so I would be able to share the good news. No one should live another day without it! It's simply this: God sent His Son, not because we are doing our best, but because He loves us unconditionally (see Titus 3:4, 5). He saved us by taking the initiative Himself to put us "in Christ," in whose life and death all the requirements of the law for justice and perfect obedience are met (see 1 Cor. 1:30; 2 Cor. 5:14). God put us "in Christ" at the Incarnation when He joined our common human life to divinity. Though we are born into a condemned family, God gave the whole human race a new history by joining us to His Son (see Rom. 5:18; Eph. 2:1-6). "In Christ" the law no longer condemns us. We stand perfectly holy before God (see Rom. 10:4). "In Him" we are once again God's children, in whom He is well pleased (see *The Desire of Ages*, p. 113).

All this God did out of love while we were still sinners, before we were born (see Rom. 5:6-10; Eph. 1:4). We are "in Christ" by an act of God, not because we believe or do anything. There's only one "but," and that is God will not force His good will on us. It's hard to imagine anyone who could be foolish enough to reject so great salvation, but it remains our prerogative. As for me, I have never been so happy to believe!   KAREN FLOWERS

Candle Power

Let your light shine before others, so that they may see your good works, and give glory to your Father in heaven. Matt. 5:16, NRSV.

Dear Lord, make me a beacon strong
to shine for You;
But if a beacon's not Your choice,
a lamp will do.
Still, if a candle's all You need
to shed the light,
Give me a corner where a beam
would be too bright.

Connect me to Your power, charge
my battery,
Replace my bulb, or trim my wick
to burn for Thee.
Then draw me to some precious souls
who've gone astray,
That by Your light that shines through me
they'll find the way.

LORRAINE HUDGINS

Always, Continually, and in All Circumstances

Be joyful always; pray continually; give thanks in all circumstances, for this is God's will for you in Christ Jesus. 1 Thess. 5:16-18, NIV.

The words "always," "continually," and "in all circumstances" seem so comprehensive and inclusive. It is easy for me to accept that God has an overall plan for my life—but in "all circumstances" is so all-encompassing. Over the years, however, God has given me many experiences that have strengthened my belief that it is His will for us to be joyful, to pray continually, and give thanks in all circumstances. Here are just two of them.

One year while I was in the Philippines, the membership of the Pasay church increased to where the overflow had to sit outside during the services. We feared the rainy season with its typhoons and knew that the expansion program would not be completed before the rains came. We talked to our heavenly Father about our concerns.

It rained before and after the services, but only once in all of that time did it rain during the services. By the time the next rainy season rolled around, the church had been enlarged and we said a heartfelt "Thank You, heavenly Father." It was very reassuring to know that God was so aware of our needs.

After retirement I cared for my mother, who was housebound. She was a people person who had enjoyed visitors all her life, but I wondered (at our age) whether we should be so ready to invite all our friends and relatives to visit us. Once again I talked it over with my heavenly Father and believed He would work it out. Indeed, many people came to see her over that eight-year period but never more than I could handle comfortably. It was evident to me that God cared about my mother's need to visit with loved ones as well as for the welfare of our visitors and myself!

When I talk over the details of my life (minor as well as major) with my heavenly Father, I find I have so much more for which to be thankful. God is continually available to us, and it pleases Him very much—under all circumstances—to give us reason to rejoice. With Paul, let us sing and make music in our hearts to the Lord, "always giving thanks to God the Father for everything, in the name of our Lord Jesus Christ"! (Eph. 5:20, NIV).   ENOLA DAVIS

MAY 17

Persistent Growth

But to you who fear My name The Sun of Righteousness shall arise with healing in His wings; and you shall go out and grow fat like stall-fed calves. Mal. 4:2, NKJV.

Spring is just around the corner here. I can see the tips of my spring bulbs cautiously peeking out above the sod. A few unusually warm days may have caused them to be overly optimistic, but growth is in process. As I watch the green coming through the brown earth, I feel happy knowing that sometime in the not-too-distant future, blossoms will appear and reward every passerby with their beauty.

Watching this process of growth brings me to examine my own spiritual growth. I want so much to grow quickly and bloom profusely. Sometimes progress seems so slow. Just when I think I'm making good progressive growth a cold spell hits, and like the tips of the emerging bulbs, I halt and end up with some dark frozen parts.

It's so easy to become discouraged with one's Christian growth. We expect it to be like the "Jack and the Beanstalk" fairy tale—just throw a few magic beans out the window and climb to heaven the next day.

Flower growth requires many days of basking in the sun's warmth. Spiritual growth requires steady, everyday warming from time spent with God's Son. Be patient but persistent in His presence. Gradually you will grow and one day bloom in the fullness of His beauty. ELLEN BRESEE

MAY 18

Thoughts From a Window

For I am the Lord, I change not. Mal. 3:6.

It is early morning as I sit at my bay window looking through an arch of trees to the distant lake. The early-morning mists rise gently from the waters as the first faint rays of the sun filter through the trees and dispel the predawn grayness. A lone duck silently moves across my pictured view. Dewdrops poise on the windowsill as the first soft rays of the sun touch my African violets.

Here, morning by morning, I come for inspiration and a talk with God. This special place—the chair, the window—becomes a sacred spot where God and I meet. It is here that God speaks to me in whispers as I tune my soul to His. It is here that I can bare my burdens, which dissipate like the dew, and I find courage for the day.

My life seems so full of change. My children have grown. I am no longer the very much needed mother of four active little children. My youngest daughter is at home planning her wedding, and we are facing a move from this Georgia home that has been so loved, so lived in, and so full of memories. There is a deep gnawing in the pit of my stomach, and an uneasiness that disturbs my mind. Why, oh why, must things change so? The kaleidoscope of this earthly life is ever moving before my eyes.

Taking my diary, I write, "Dear God, I feel so disturbed this morning. I thank You that You are always there though things around us change. Thank You for the promise that 'I am the Lord, I change not' (Mal. 3:6). Thank You for the things of nature that speak of Your presence—the quietness of this morning hour and a time to 'Be still, and know . . .' (Ps. 46:10). Thank You for Your promise: 'Jesus Christ the same yesterday, and to day, and for ever' (Heb. 13:8)."

As I leave my window to take up the duties of the day, I am reassured of stability. My heart pours out its plea in the Serenity Prayer:

> God, give us grace to accept with
> serenity the things that cannot be changed,
> courage to change the things which should be changed,
> and the wisdom to distinguish the one from the other.
> —Reinhold Niebuhr

JOAN MINCHIN NEALL

MAY 19

Justin: The Miracle of a Tragedy

"But didn't I tell you that you will see a wonderful miracle from God if you believe?" Jesus asked her. John 11:40, TLB.

There's so much tragedy in the world," the old man mused as he watched Justin working with his physical therapist. *Tragedy?* I thought. His words kept echoing in my mind.

In the 13 months of Justin's life, the word "tragedy" had never entered my thoughts. If I had not been so taken back by his words, I could have shouted, "He's not a tragedy—he's a miracle." There was such a flood of mixed feelings in my heart—anger, sadness, and forgiveness. Anger at the possibility that this is what everyone really thought of Justin. That this is what he would have to face as he grew—people thinking of him as one of life's tragedies. Sadness that this man was looking only at what Justin could not do, instead of seeing how much he was accomplishing. And finally, forgiveness—because how could the old man know that there was a time in Justin's first hours and days of life when he had fought to live, and that God had given him the strength to beat the odds?

Webster defines *tragedy* as "a disastrous event; calamity; misfortune." Tragedy to me is hunger, child abuse, battered women, and death. When I think of tragedy, I think of the homeless derelict sleeping on the sidewalks and streets. The tragedy being that some of these seemingly helpless people have chosen not to help themselves. That somewhere along the way someone may have considered them to be one of life's tragedies when they were struggling, and because of their low self-esteem they believed what people said and thought about them. I think the ultimate tragedy is sin. It is because of sin that there is so much suffering in the world. I pray for the day when there is no more tragedy.

Miracle is defined as "an extraordinary event manifesting the supernatural work of God." Why is it that we as a society give medals and awards to those who save the life of another human being or animal, yet we consider those who are not "normal" to be a tragedy when, perhaps, they have fought so desperately to live?

I wanted to tell the old man that every day I celebrate Justin's very existence and that I thank God for this precious little baby. No, Justin is not a tragedy, but a miracle with the most wonderful smile in the world. CHERYL LINN

MAY 20

A Child's Wisdom

For by grace you have been saved through faith, and that not of yourselves; it is the gift of God, not of works, lest anyone should boast. For we are His workmanship, created in Christ Jesus for good works, which God prepared beforehand that we should walk in them. Eph. 2:8-10, NKJV.

Walking along hand in hand with someone, especially someone bigger and stronger than oneself, feels warm and secure. We feel safer beside somebody, holding on tight. When we are walking on a marked trail beside a rushing river, the walk is beautiful and peaceful. However, if we stray off the trail, we may slip on the mossy rocks by the riverbank. One could call these rocks cheating, lying, overeating, stealing, jealousy, anger, selfishness, etc. Even if we hold on to someone's hand, these rocks may be so slippery that the hand we're holding on to cannot keep us from sliding into the river below.

If you've ever been to a national park, you've walked on marked trails. These trails are guidelines. They are meant to keep us safe from the edges of cliffs, from slippery rocks above the water's edge, or maybe from the whirlpools in a rushing river below a beautiful waterfall.

The Ten Commandments are like the trails—the law that keeps us safe if we'll but follow. It is impossible to stay on this trail without holding on to God's hand.

This reminds me of a story my mother told me once. She was vacationing in Yellowstone National Park. As she walked down the trail to Yellowstone Lower Falls she overhead a little girl talking to her father. There was a sign beside the path, and the little girl wanted her father to read it to her. He said, "The sign says, 'Stay on trail.' " To which she responded, "The sign *should* say, 'Hold on to hand.' "

What a perfect balance of law and love there is in Christ. The ten-commandment trail to keep us going in the right direction, and the grace of God to empower us for the walk.   SHONNA DALUSONG

MAY 21

Creation

And God saw every thing that he had made, and, behold, it was very good. Gen. 1:31.

Creation glistened in the morning light of the newly created sun—the ripple of the lakes, the breeze in the treetops, the rustle of the grass as a brand-new deer explored its new domain. All was ready! All awaited the crowning act of Creation. God looked and it was "good." Everything He had called into being was "good." But it was not yet complete. It lacked the most important element that would fulfill it and make it "very good."

For this most important event, God not only took time to speak; He took time out of His universal itinerary to be physically present and physically involved in the creation of man and woman. God wanted to be right there when man took his first step, his first look at his new surroundings, his first look at his new bride. God wanted to be there when Eve opened her lovely bright eyes to behold the garden of roses, daffodils, and lilies. When she felt the brush of a furry kitten, saw the wonder of a playful hummingbird, and experienced the blush of innocence as her eyes met the loving gaze of her husband, Adam. Those were moments that God could not miss—would not miss. Other things in the universe must wait! Of all His creation, man and woman, at that moment, were the most precious.

"Lord, of all my world that I have created around me—house, furnishings, cars, job, clothes—my family is the most precious. In my heart I know this. But unlike You, sometimes my 'itinerary' doesn't seem to include sufficient time for them. I don't know why my earthly matters are that much more urgent than Your universal concerns.

"You showed Your concern and Your consideration of our importance by Your presence and Your time. I know I should and can do no less. The opportunity to spend time with my children is so fleeting. When they are small, it seems so expendable. But all too soon they are grown and gone, and so are the opportunities to talk and interact, to fellowship and pass on values. The elementary school programs, the beginning piano recitals, the science fairs, and parent-teacher conferences—all these seemed insignificant compared to my busy schedule.

"But in retrospect, they were little indicators to my children of my interest in them. Where did I put my preference? Did I give them enough time? I hope so.

"The nest that once was full is now almost empty. My precious little 'chickadees' are now ready to fly. What course will they take? What influence have I had? What values have I managed to pass on? Will they decide to fly in the heavenly atmosphere of Your love or in the deadly malaise of the earth?

"When my 'creation' is finished, will I be able to say it is 'very good'? Or more important, Lord, will You?"

NANCY CACHERO VASQUEZ

MAY 22

New Growth

All the days of my hard service I will wait for my renewal to come. You will call and I will answer you; you will long for the creature your hands have made. Surely then you will count my steps but not keep track of my sin. My offenses will be sealed up in a bag; you will cover over my sin. Job 14:14-17, NIV.

Job's intense expressions in these verses explain a valuable fact: having correct theories is not adequate. Understanding our own theology doesn't complete the necessary formula to gratify God. Belief untried by encountering daily living might miss entirely, becoming passive. As roots of the oak are driven to great depths in the earth by lack of rainfall, so encountering pain can propel us past merely sufficient adoption of reality assumed to be truth to an understanding reliance on God for security and our very existence.

The pain of rejection experienced in a divorce may cause that person to become bitter or promote a dependence on God, who will always be there.

The parents whose child is taken from them in death can choose to blame God. But through trust in God, they can come to realize the true experience of parenting. God also lost a child, but through Christ's death there is hope in a coming resurrection.

> Someday this disaster now near to your heart,
> Will be just a sad memory, as new life you'll start!
> Fond dreams of adventure, great hopes to aspire,
> Will grant for your future a creative desire!
> You'll glance back at aches now seen with despair.
> The distance will numb as you learn how to care.
> Friends you have shunned for fear they're too rare
> Will warmheartedly aid you. You'll be caught by the glare
> Of a glittering garden, newly washed by the rain.
> So lushly enchanting, you'll forget prior pain.

Visualize with me a storm. Black clouds gather in the sky. Darkness overtakes day. Harsh winter winds begin to blow. A blaze on the cabin hearth strains furiously to overcome bone-chilling cold. With a woolen blanket wrapped tightly around you, eventually you find comfort in front of the fireplace. Next morning you are awakened by a glimmer of light coming through a window. A vision of white loveliness in the pale light covers bushes and fence posts you know to be there.

Several things have happened. You treasure the friendly warmth of the fireplace more, having felt grave discomfort in the extreme cold. And you observe an altered view, a velvet carpet is covering angles and ridges that are still a component of the scene—they have only been concealed.

We now see from the viewpoint of Job, who states, "My offenses will be sealed up in a bag; you will cover over my sin." Our new growth is made possible because we can depend on God for hope and for life!   JUDI WILD BECKER

MAY 23

The Opposite of Love

My command is this: Love each other as I have loved you. Greater love has no one than this, that he lay down his life for his friends. John 15:12, 13, NIV.

The opposite of love is not hate, it is indifference." The reminder hangs above my desk, jolting me a dozen times a day.

Peggy's nagging back pain is still hanging on today, I overhear her say as I walk by. I wonder if Pam's unsmiling face is a mark of suffering inside. Cynthia's adored and only granddaughter won't be out of the hospital for her first Christmas, the doctors have just announced to the agonizing family. Neighbor Lynne is going through a very painful divorce and now has two small children to parent and support on her own. Someone mentions that Lillian is unhappy in her new job.

"They will know you are Christians by your love." Having grown up in church, I've sung those words over a thousand times. But they never cease to haunt me, to make me feel uneasy, somehow negligent, inadequate, uncomfortable. Of course I love the world out there, I rationalize; I accepted Christ as my Saviour when I was only 10 years old and I've never wandered since. Surely through all these years the world has seen that I love it. Or has it?

Walking into Linda's kitchen one day, I was stopped short by something new on her refrigerator door. "Love is something you do." Immediately my mind protested. Something you do? I had always thought love was something you felt. Mulling that over for days afterward, I realized finally that it made sense, that it was indeed the gospel. In fact, this must be what Jesus meant when He commanded those first Christians, "Love each other as I have loved you," and in the same breath added, "Greater love has no one than this, that he lay down his life for his friends."

The words hang on, coming back each time my gaze falls on that scrap of paper above my desk. "The opposite of love is not hate; it is indifference." "Love is something you do." "Love as I have loved." The inner voice pushes at my complacency, my satisfaction with my life, and my level of Christlikeness. If you love Peggy, Pam, Cynthia, Lynne, and Lillian, I hear it say, *do something*. Show them you care about the hurts in their lives, the problems that seem too big to climb over, the pain that hangs on and on and on. Of course you are busy; so is everyone else, but doing needn't take much time. Maybe just a card, a deserved compliment, or a gentle hug will lift a tiny part of those clouds that hang over their worlds. Maybe you can do more. But do something, for doing nothing is the opposite of love.

Those words still hang above my desk and will for many months to come, I am sure. Each and every day I need to be reminded again that love may not always involve feeling, but it always involves action. If I love, I will do.

CAROLE SPALDING COLBURN

The Circle of Prayer

And we know that all things work together for good to them that love God, to them who are the called according to his purpose. Rom. 8:28.

The little girl cried out in fear. Her mother held the child's long, skinny body close. The child, although tall for a 12-year-old, weighed only 53 pounds, the victim of an intractable illness that had wasted her body for more than a year.

Gathered around the pair were the child's father and several tall, somber men in dark suits. The men knelt in a circle on the polished wooden floor. One of them smiled and took the child's hand. Another touched her on the forehead. In a voice that was deep and gentle, he asked God for her healing. The child wasn't soothed by the prayer. She felt only helplessness and fear.

I can remember so vividly what it felt like to be small, sick, and frightened. Strangely enough, what I can't remember is getting better. There was no miraculous strengthening of weakened arms and legs. There was no immediate cessation of the pain that came with every breath. But slowly, following that anointing service, good health returned. I went away to academy, and later to college, and the memory of that long illness faded.

Gradually, as I matured, I came to realize that the Lord had truly healed me. "God must have something very special in mind for you," well-meaning friends would say. It worried me. What was it? What was the big thing God wanted me to do? I prayed that He would reveal His plan, but no revelation came.

As a bride I wondered, *Is this it, Lord?* Then when I looked down at the baby in my arms, I wondered, *Is he the reason, Lord? Is this child the reason you saved my life?*

The years have passed. My life has been and continues to be full—filled with making a home, raising children, returning to school, launching a career, and changing career directions a time or two. God has taught me to give everything I have to each endeavor. Sometimes He uses me to bless others, and many more times He uses others to enrich my life. Through the years, however, I have still questioned the Lord about the big plan, but no direct revelation has come.

Now, I think I know. Just as the healing came slowly, the knowledge came gradually too. The answer is in the living of each day to its fullest, in giving my best, and in growing ever closer to my heavenly Father. And I am thankful for each new morning. Aren't you? SUSAN HARVEY

A Good Name

A good name is rather to be chosen than great riches. Prov. 22:1.

What does your name mean? My name is Elizabeth, and it means "devoted one." I suppose I was given that name because my parents wanted to use a Bible name—and there was a favorite aunt in the family who had that name, too.

When I was quite little, I was given all kinds of nicknames. There are so many versions of Elizabeth, I am sure that at some time or other I have been called every variation, including Bea, Beth, Betty, Betti-Betts, Liz, Liza, Lizzo. Some lasted only a few years; a few did not stick at all. Several I absolutely hated, and some are still being used.

The names I am called by my family and friends indicate which period of my life they knew me. So I cannot seem to shake the nicknames.

Now just what do I want my name to mean? When others see me, what will they think? When they encounter me, what will they expect? When I leave their presence, what impression will they have of me? What will others connect with my name?

I think of myself as a Christian teacher. I am an associate professor of social work. I also direct a program to enable single parents to complete their college education at Andrews University, so I think I am a leader. I am a parent of three teenage youth, which qualifies me to have some parenting skills. Hopefully, my young folk, who think of me as "Mother," cherish that name. And as I am endeavoring to write these devotional thoughts, I would like you to think of me as a spiritual author. Most of all, however, when you hear or read the name Elizabeth Watson, I want you to instantly think of someone who has positively directed your mind toward God and encouraged you to choose Him each day as you prepare for heaven! ELIZABETH WATSON

Women's Gifts

But the greatest of these is love. 1 Cor. 13:13, NASB.

Have you ever wondered about the gift(s) God has given you? What does God expect you to do with the gift(s) He has bestowed on you? In your mind, how does the gospel commission and your gift(s) as a woman fit together?

As Christians we know that "global mission" means "finishing the work"! Ponder a moment on what that may mean for you personally. "Finishing the work," as I see it, means allowing the Holy Spirit to empower *all* to work for Him. It means the church following the Holy Spirit's leading in doing for God.

While this is true, an equally important thing to remember is that our mission is more than just what we *do*. It is also what we *are* with one another. It is how we are with each other as we walk through life's experiences. It is how we treat each other. It is, in fact, treating people as Jesus treated them. It is treating the different groups of people as Jesus did (the Jesus model of ministry).

I think of the disabled, and the paralytic man comes to mind. Jesus touched him. He healed him. He talked to him. Jesus made room for him. And the poor and the rich: Jesus ate at the tables of the wealthy and the poor. The ethnic groups: the Jews and the other groups of Jesus' day—all were of equal worth.

And women: how did Jesus treat women? Think for a moment about our society. How does the media depict women? Television advertisements and magazines often show them as sexual objects, vain, and interested only in shopping; or they are portrayed in commercials as ecstatic over a clean, sparkling sink! In this way women are pictured as having unimportant agendas, and as helpless, passive, and unable to manage.

It's easy to see that the cultural stereotypes represent themselves as the wisdom of the world. In fact, they are myths. I believe we must not let the world set the woman's agenda.

Jesus rejected the teachings of the world about women. The "weak woman" myth prevails, but it is not in God's design. Jesus invited women to follow Him. He allowed them to touch Him. He healed women and spoke to them. Women are part of Jesus' miracles and parables. Women were the last to be with Him when He died and the first to discover His resurrection.

Global Mission is the "people" we bring in: their diverse needs, their diverse ways. The book *Evangelism* states it beautifully: "If, like the diverse branches of the vine, they were centered in the vine stock, all would bear the rich clusters of precious fruit. There would be perfect harmony in their diversity" (p. 101). Mutual support, respecting one another's diversity, and working together are basic scriptural principles.

In and of ourselves, we are powerless to love, to care, to share. It is God alone, and His Word, that is power! May you choose to spend time with Him each day, that your life may show the greatest "gifts" of love—kindness, warmth, and gentleness—that others may surely know that you have been with Him.

RAMONA PEREZ-GREEK

MAY 27

Of Slugs, Snails, and Butterflies' Tales

Therefore, if anyone is in Christ, he is a new creation; the old has gone, the new has come! 2 Cor. 5:17, NIV.

My 2-year-old son loves to collect creepy-crawlies. Caterpillars are the most exciting for him. He collects them and feeds them on leaves until they turn into chrysalises. Together we watched a red admiral butterfly emerge from its dull-looking cocoon, its blood pumping through to the tips of its new wings. We put the butterfly on a sunny flower to dry out, and then saw it suddenly flutter and dance through the summer sky, elated at this taste of freedom after days of cramped confinement.

Nathan has such a love for God's little creatures that we even have to be kind to the slugs and snails in our garden! We collect all the snails he finds and keep them in a special container until we can go out to the lanes nearby and let them go in a safe place, away from humans and prize chrysanthemums.

Once he found a dead slug and made a nest for it in an old plastic container. We tried to tell him it was dead, but he wouldn't believe us. "No," he said, "it's only asleep. I'm sure I saw it move." After a couple days we had to bury it.

One day I entered the kitchen to find a particularly ugly specimen of a snail on the worktop. It was large, muddy, and coated in cobwebs. I had to look at it hard for a while to figure out what it was, but I knew immediately how it had gotten there.

"Nathan!" I called. It was one thing having to run an emigration service for snails, but they definitely weren't welcome in my home! Nathan came running. "What's the matter, Mommy?" he said. "*This* is the matter," I said, pointing at the offending beast.

"What is it doing in the kitchen?"

"But it's my pet!" Nathan was finding it difficult to appreciate my distaste for his latest acquisition. "But why do we have to keep *this* snail?" I demanded. His next statement was a memorable one. "Because it might turn into a butterfly, of course!"

It can be so easy to write people off because they don't seem to be able to offer anything positive. Maybe they look ugly and dirty. Maybe their habits aren't too pleasant. Maybe we just don't know how to get along with them. We decide we don't want them in our homes, but we try to do what we can for them, in the same way that we helped the snails emigrate. We may offer them help programs, or soup kitchens, or even a dutiful smile as we pass by.

But do we see them as Jesus sees them? Jesus specialized in collecting friends that no one else wanted. He saw their potential. He knew that every slug, snail, spider, or worm could turn into a beautiful butterfly. He had that much faith, that much love, for each one of His creatures, whoever they were. Do we?

KAREN HOLFORD

MAY 28

The Phone Call

And forgive us our sins; for we also forgive every one that is indebted to us. And lead us not into temptation; but deliver us from evil. Luke 11:4.

Hello," I said cheerily as I interrupted my work to catch the ringing telephone. "And how are you doing today?" I asked when I recognized the voice of the caller. I was stunned as I heard that something I had recently done had deeply upset this person. In fact, the caller said that absolutely nothing I could ever say or do, or any excuse I could ever make, would be enough for the caller to forgive me. Before I could get my thoughts together, an abrupt *clunk* pierced my heart. My first thought was that I wished the caller had held on long enough for me to say I was sorry. It had never entered my mind that what I had done would be hurtful to anyone—in fact, it had cost me dearly in time, energy, and money. I could scarcely believe my own ears because my every motive had only been to bless and comfort. *Have my efforts displeased God?* I wondered. What could I possibly do?

I've always found that when I face anything I don't know how to handle, I have a "best" Friend who can take care of the situation. So I sent up a silent, anguished prayer for help. I had truly thought

178

I would be told how much my action was appreciated. Now events had taken a very different turn.

Although it was a painful experience, I have always felt that everything that comes to us should be used as stepping-stones—not stumbling blocks. I thought about our dear, forgiving Saviour. How, while going through the cruelest of treatment, He murmured not—He even asked for His cruel revilers to be forgiven. What a wonderful Saviour we have! Even though we fail Him again and again, He forgives and never breaks the line of communication with us. But we, too, need to be forgiving.

"He who is unforgiving cuts off the very channel through which alone he can receive mercy from God. We should not think that unless those who have injured us confess the wrong we are justified in withholding from them our forgiveness. It is their part, no doubt, to humble their hearts by repentance and confession; but we are to have a spirit of compassion toward those who have trespassed against us, whether or not they confess their faults. However sorely they may have wounded us, we are not to cherish our grievances and sympathize with ourselves over our injuries; but as we hope to be pardoned for our offenses against God we are to pardon all who have done evil to us" (*Thoughts From the Mount of Blessing*, p. 113).   PAT MADSEN

MAY 29

A Small Transfiguration

The Lord is my strength and song. Ex. 15:2, NKJV.

This trip to town was like so many I had experienced before with Mother. My brother, Leslie, was in the driver's seat with his wife beside him; Mother and I sat in the back.

The almost constant nonsensical chatter from Mom was characteristic of the past two and a half years when I had moved closer home in order to assist with her care. Physically well for a woman approaching her eighty-eighth birthday, Alzheimer's had made its characteristic inroads on a once energetic and active mind.

My mind, blocking the input from my ears, scanned back over the years this woman had been such an integral part of my life. Small, energetic, hospitable, and always as dependable as a rock in crisis, her perseverance in times of adversity had been the inspiration helping me manage the difficult trials in my life.

Now as I gazed at the kaleidoscopic scenery flitting by the car window, a deep sadness filled me. Scenes of my mother singing as she worked about the house or in the garden intertwined with the warmth of sun, scent of flowers, songs of birds, and aroma of fresh-baked bread that pervaded my memory.

I was startled from my reverie by a sound that caused me to turn abruptly toward Mother. She was singing! The quavering, and at first hesitant, words came clear and distinct:

> "At the cross, at the cross
> Where I first saw the light,
> And the burden of my heart rolled away,
> It was there by faith I received my sight,
> And now I am happy all the day."

Finished, Mother turned to me, and with blue eyes shining, said, "There, I didn't think I could sing again." Then she sat back and very quietly gazed out the window.　　CHRISTENE PERKINS

MAY 30

Puppy Sins

Bow down Your ear to me, deliver me speedily; be my rock of refuge, a fortress of defense to save me. Ps. 31:2, NKJV.

Leaving our subdivision for my morning errands, I got stuck behind a school bus with its flashing red lights. Impatient to go on with my day, I twiddled my thumbs on the steering wheel of the car. That was when I noticed the reason for the extended delay. An adorable little puppy had been playing with the children waiting at the bus stop, and it insisted on going to school on the bus with the kids.

A little girl put her backpack and lunch down on the bus steps and picked up the puppy, carrying it back to the curb. Then she ran as fast as her little legs would carry her onto the bus. But right behind her was that stubborn little puppy. Again she picked up the puppy, carried it away from the bus, set it down, and hurriedly scrambled on board. But the little puppy was as fast as she was, and once again she picked it up to place it outside the school bus. This happened over and over—the girl setting the puppy on the curb, then running onto the bus with the puppy right on her tail.

Assuming this might take all day without some sort of intervention, I jumped out of my car and held the puppy until the bus with its flashing red lights had moved on down the road. I found the puppy's home and deposited it there before going into town.

180

As I drove off, errand list in mind, foot making up for lost time on the accelerator, God spoke. He compared the puppy on the curb to the pet sins in my life that follow me around. He reminded me that I need Someone bigger than myself to hold the sins back so I can continue on my spiritual journey. Not only does He give me power over those pet sins; He deposits them right where they belong, in the depths of the sea. Are there any pet sins in your life that you'd like to turn over to Him?

RONNA WITZEL AND SHONNA DALUSONG

MAY 31

Through the Eyes of a Child

The wolf will live with the lamb, the leopard will lie down with the goat, the calf and the lion and the yearling together; and a little child will lead them. Isa. 11:6, NIV.

The church service was over, and my 2-year-old daughter, Heather, and I were walking the two blocks to our home. After having been indoors for several hours, our eyes were having to adjust to the bright sunshine. Before long Heather said, "Mommy, the sun is tickling my eyes!" I smiled with joy at her description. That was the beginning of a journey that has been taking place as we, a family, have opened our eyes to what children can show us. They marvel at the tiny things: the beautiful rocks that they collect and stuff in their pockets, the dainty wildflowers they pick and hand to us with love, the trips we take to the zoo because of their fascination with animals. And we as adults are usually eager to show them the squirrel that scampered up a tree or the cardinal that sits on the branch. We take them to watch the ducks on the pond and feed them the pieces of bread we have saved for that purpose.

God knew what we needed in this world: children who would innocently and purely show us God. I know so much more about God because I have looked through the eyes of my children at the incredibleness of the universe. I have seen God's reflection in the speckled rocks and the dainty flowers, in the mighty lion and the fascinating pond. I have seen God's reflection in the delight of the child and in the joy of discovery. I have seen God's reflection because the child slowed me down and gently tugged at my heart saying, "This is God's world. Rejoice and be glad in it." I have come to know God because a little child asked me to slow down, to "be still, and know that I am God." Truly a little child will lead us.

NORMA OSBORN

181

Prescription for a New Day

Then Jesus told his disciples a parable to show them that they should always pray and not give up. Luke 18:1, NIV.

The other morning, my errands completed earlier than expected, I stopped in at the local library. It's my favorite place in our small city, but I seldom have time to spend there. Thus a leisurely hour was a rare treat.

In my purse I keep a list of books that I'm hoping to read, so my first priority was to track down *The Search for Significance*, by Robert McGee. With that volume safely tucked under my arm, I proceeded to the new book section. Because most of my reading is either work-related or for my own spiritual edification, I seldom select one of the new titles, but I do browse among them and occasionally succumb to a biography or some other tantalizing topic.

Once I have exhausted the new books, I head for the gardening shelves. The best for last! Unfortunately, I have read nearly every book there, but I run my finger along the spines, hoping for a new title. Aha! A nice big coffee-table glossy by Penelope Hobhouse, full-color illustrations on every page. And with Penelope behind the pen, the text will be as glorious as the photography. As I've come to be more knowledgeable about plants, I enjoy going through such a book and attempting to identify all the flowers in those famous old British gardens. What I usually discover is that I still have much to learn, but it's a lovely game. So I tuck *Country Gardener* under my arm, along with *The Search for Significance*, and head for the check-out desk.

On rare occasions, maybe once each winter, my daughter, Amy, and I spend an afternoon at the library. We don't waste time searching through the stacks for elusive titles, but head, instead, straight for the reading room. There, on winter days, a fire blazes on the hearth and we wander along the racks selecting choice specialty magazines to which we'd never subscribe, but which we fully enjoy. Sinking onto a soft leather couch, we settle in for a totally luxurious afternoon.

There's something about that dark-paneled, fire-lit room—so cozy, so serene, so removed from the hurly-burly of life—that projects an aura of timelessness, of some bygone leisurely age. Beyond its stone walls, of course, traffic ebbs and flows, and all the duties I'm neglecting crouch like predators, but we relax and read and share whispered discoveries, my daughter and I. And when we leave, something good has ended. We both know it, and tuck it away like a choice treasure in a memory box.

One morning when I completed my devotions, it occurred to me that those moments with God that I'd just spent were a lot like our winter afternoons at the library. There was the same entering into warmth and peace and seclusion from a demanding, raucous world. The same awareness that the golden moment must be hugged to one's heart and carried out into life like a glowing coal. But there the comparison ends, for the healing in one's rendezvous with God cannot be found in any reading room. And there's a "foreverness" about it that contrasts sharply with life's secular experiences.

Come into the presence of the Lord. Be healed, nurtured, and taught. Rest in the quiet. Only then open the doors of the new morning.   JUNE STRONG

JUNE 2

My God Is Like the Ocean

Mightier than the thunders of many waters, mightier than the waves of the sea, the Lord on high is mighty! Ps. 93:4, RSV.

God is like the ocean . . .
    eternal . . . awesome . . . never-ending . . . deep . . . mysterious . . .
God is like the ocean . . .
    full of hidden treasures . . . teeming with life . . .
Who can fathom all the beauty hidden in His depths?
    Who can fully explore all the grandeur of His shore?
God's love is like the tide . . . a continuous miracle . . . always dependable,
    Yet with each new wave, His love is exciting and new.
My God is like the ocean . . . powerful . . . strong . . . mighty . . .
    Yet little children run laughing on His shores.
God is like the many moods of the ocean . . . sunny, warm, bright . . .
    Roaring with majestic splendor . . . calm, restful, peaceful,
        Breathtakingly beautiful.
God is like the ocean.
    He spreads to all shores and touches all people.
All life revolves around Him and is sustained by Him.

Men plan their lives around the changing of His tide.
God is like the ocean . . .

Thousands travel His shore searching . . .

for love, for rest, for excitement, for a light in the darkness.
God is all of these things, and He says to all those who earnestly
seek Him . . .

"Come unto Me all who are weary and discouraged and tired,
listen to My waves and find rest. View My splendor and
power and learn of Me. You will find rest for your soul."

MELODIE GAGE GUSTAVSEN

JUNE 3

Nests for Wounded Birds

*The Spirit of the Lord God is upon me; because the Lord
hath anointed me to preach good tidings unto the meek; he
hath sent me to bind up the brokenhearted, to proclaim
liberty to the captives, and the opening of the prison to
them that are bound. Isa. 61:1.*

She came into my office one February morning of 1992. A
good-looking young woman about 27 years old with a radiant
smile on her face, she said, "I'm going to work with you. I've
learned you need an assistant, and the administrator sent me to
your department."

"Good!" I replied. "So sit down and let's talk about you.
Where are you from?"

When she started talking about her life the bright smile faded,
an anxious expression appeared, and tears flowed down her face.
Taken by emotion, she could hardly speak.

I realized that seated in front of me was a broken heart. She was
a wounded bird who could not fly anymore, bound by the suffering
of a recent divorce. I silently prayed, asking the Lord for wisdom,
love, and care, knowing that we are the Lord's agents and many
times His voice, His hands, His feet, and His face.

She had come to college to try to find a shield against the storm,
a nest where she could heal. From that day we shared moments of
prayer, visits, and counseling, and had good times together.

Wounded birds require time, patience, caring, and love to heal.
Time passed. Now she feels completely different from when she
arrived on our campus. She has regained her enthusiasm and she's
a spiritual leader among the young women. An active participant,
she is one of the best students in our education program. In my

department, she's efficient, and a good and loyal friend. She often demonstrates her gratitude for receiving love and care at the most difficult time in her life.

My wounded bird is almost healed. I know that one day soon I will walk to the open window, stretch out my arm, and from my hand she will fly higher and higher into the blue sky of freedom.

SONIA GAZETA

JUNE 4

Making Papa Proud

He does not punish us as we deserve or repay us for our sins and wrongs. Ps. 103:10, TEV.

For nearly 20 years I deceived my father. I can admit it now and even laugh at myself for thinking the deception necessary. You see, I pretended to love spinach, when in truth I could barely gag it down even when disguised with butter or lemon juice. But Papa liked spinach, and I was determined to be like him. I was happiest at those times when my mother said that I was just like my father—usually, alas, just before I got in trouble for something!

Spinach was not the only thing I pretended to like—it was only my most successful attempt to be like Papa. After his offhand remarks during a softball game that I both ran and threw "like a girl," I strove mightily to swagger like the guys in the neighborhood and spent hours throwing a softball against the garage door to improve my aim. It didn't help. To this day I still run and throw like a girl!

I talked to my father about softball when I was an adult. To be more accurate, I apologized for my lack of skill and all my other wimpy traits, like collecting dolls. Basically, I apologized for not being the son I was sure he always wanted.

I used to spend a lot of time apologizing to God, too. Seeing Him as a father figure, I often tried the same tactics to earn His love. I performed good deeds whether or not my heart was in them, simply because I wanted to make Him proud. Like my earthly father, I saw Him as someone to be copied, so I tried to accomplish things I obviously wasn't suited for. I was so busy trying to be perfect that I had little time left for fun. Every childhood mistake was worried over as I begged forgiveness from the Father I was trying to emulate.

Then came the revelation, not in a celestial vision, but in the simple acceptance that no matter how hard I tried I could never be

185

more than a pale imitation of my Creator. All the while I thought I was trying to make Him proud, when I was really too full of my own pride to accept His gifts. I was too proud to accept someone else's help. I believed that I had to pay my way to heaven. It took me a long time to realize that Jesus Christ had already paid for my soul with His life and that, like Papa's love, it was not something I had to eat spinach for. I still try to make Him proud of me, but the guilt and the fear of failure are gone.

Even after my confession, Papa never admitted to wanting a son. He insisted that daughters were far superior, and that he never cared much for sports anyway. Of course, maybe by telling me that, he was just paying me back for all that spinach I ate.   GINA LEE

JUNE 5

God's Cleaning Solution

Is anything too difficult for the Lord? Gen. 18:14, NASB.

One wall of our bedroom is floor-to-ceiling windows. A few days ago I was taking a midday breather in the prone position and noticed how dirty those windows were. Finger marks, nose prints from the dog, paint spots not scraped off when we painted, a spider's golden web across the upper corner . . . and I became exhausted just thinking about those dirty windows. Furthermore, I detest washing windows.

What's the point in washing windows anyway? The next person going outside will leave fingerprints. When the window is clean the dog sees the stray cat better. There are more nose prints. What's the point in expending all that energy to get dirty windows clean!

I contemplated where on my to-do list I would place window washing. Or better yet, how could I cajole my husband into washing them? (Miracles sometimes do happen!)

How like our lives are dirty windows. We let material gains and everyday life cloud the glass of our souls. How about the inner attitudes we develop from our external surroundings? Or the frantic web we weave in the hustle and bustle of life? Do our lives get so cloudy we can't see things clearly?

Can God make use of the dirty window that each of us is? In order to wash the windows in my house I use a bucket of warm water, some ammonia, a drop of vinegar, a rag, a squeegee, and a towel, and, oh yes, some elbow grease. I thank God that He doesn't use that concoction to get me clean. Instead, He uses a simple solution of G-R-A-C-E.

All we need to do is contemplate our need and desire for His grace and He washes us sparkling clean. Because of His grace we can attain what before seemed impossible—God's eternal reward.

Abraham had his windows cleaned a number of times. He really had a knack for getting them dirty. But Abimelech told him, "God is with you in all that you do" (Gen. 21:22, NASB). He could see into Abraham's window. God could shine through him.

Abraham was no more special in God's sight than each one of us is. He accomplished some pretty remarkable things during his life. He also knew the voice of God. He had been cleaned and polished so often by God's grace that there was no question in his life where God fit in.

We have the same opportunities today as did Abraham. He was no better, or worse, than any of us in God's sight. He was ordinary, just like us. One who had feelings and emotions as we do. God shined and polished him so that others could see through him. Why not let God clean you right now?   SUSAN CLARK

JUNE 6

Life at Its Best

I have come that they may have life, and that they may have it more abundantly. John 10:10, NKJV.

Yes, they were *white* this morning! I know they were *white!*" I emphatically affirmed.

"Come now," chided a friend who had joined me for lunch, "you are lonely for your husband, and you are not seeing clearly. Those flowers are *pink.*"

True, I missed my husband, for we recently had settled in Singapore and he was on his first mission itinerary in Southeast Asia. But I was sure his absence had not affected my mind to that extent. Had something happened to my eyesight? Could I really become that confused? There was no denying it, the flowers on the bush were definitely pink. Since I had nothing to support me but my fallible memory, the flowers were presently forgotten.

At suppertime I glanced out the window. Startled, I looked again. Oh no! Could it be? The flowers were *red*. Completely bewildered, I dared not say a word, for surely I was losing my mind.

Early the next morning, while I was eating breakfast, my eyes again fell on the flowering bush—the flowers were *white!*

187

I soon learned that the rose of Sharon grows on a large sprawling bush with pointed leaves. With blossoms resembling a large double hibiscus, but more delicate, the petals are white in the morning, turn to pink by noon, to red by evening, and during the night the shriveled blossom falls to the ground.

How like life! In this short life there is the white beauty of youth, the mellow pink of middle age, the rich, deeper hue of old age, and then death. "Man that is born of woman is of few days, and full of trouble. He comes forth like a flower, and withers; he flees like a shadow, and continues not" (Job 14:1, 2, RSV).

Since life is so short, how can we get the most out of it? How can we live the abundant life that Jesus promises?

In His short life on this earth Jesus set a perfect example. The Son of man came "to serve, and to give his life to set many others free" (Matt. 20:28, Phillips).

Through a friendly word, a visit to a shut-in, a letter to a lonely friend, we are following Jesus' example. And bringing happiness to others is the key to living life at its best.

> "Oh life, so short, so soon to pass,
>   What counts most I ask?
>   Make others happy, be this thy task;
>   Only what's done for Christ will last."
>   —*Author Unknown*

LILLIAN R. GUILD

JUNE 7

Precious Promises

Do not let your hearts be troubled. Trust in God; trust also in me. In my Father's house are many rooms; if it were not so, I would have told you. I am going there to prepare a place for you. And if I go and prepare a place for you, I will come back and take you to be with me that you also may be where I am. John 14:1-3, NIV.

In the weeks before our baby daughter was born I was very nervous about the birth process and becoming a parent. Since this was our first child, everything was so new to me, and I was full of questions. *What should I do to get ready for the baby's arrival?* I wondered. *When will she come? What will the labor and birth be like? How will I cope with the pain?* At times these anxious thoughts crowded out the anticipation of cradling in my arms a new baby—so tiny and soft.

As I sewed curtains for her room and attended childbirth classes, I could have been reveling in the expectation of her birth . . . the tender moments her father and I would share as we touched her little hands for the first time and brushed kisses onto her petal-soft cheeks. I could have delighted in the fact that the two of us would soon be three, that we were participating in the joy and wonder of creation. But I dreaded the pain of childbirth, and I was afraid of the unknown. What would our lives be like after the baby came? Would it really be as wonderful as people said?

As Christians we often experience the same types of conflicting emotions about events in our future—like the return of Christ and going to heaven. We know that life before Christ's return will be hard, just as I knew childbirth would be painful. But we also know that God will be with us and the reward will be greater than we can ever imagine. And while I couldn't fully know the answers to my questions before our baby was born, we can read every day the beautiful and precious promises in God's Word that will help us to be ready for Christ's coming and to realize how wonderful eternity in heaven will be. Looking forward to the rewards of heaven will get us through the troublesome times! BRENDA DICKERSON

JUNE 8

Impassable Rivers

When thou passest through the waters, I will be with thee; and through the rivers, they shall not overflow thee. Isa. 43:2.

A favorite Bible story of mine is the story of Moses and how he led the children of Israel through the wilderness to the Promised Land. Specifically, my heart thrills when I think of how God opened the Red Sea and they passed safely to the other side (see Ex. 14). Metaphorically, there have been many such impassable—but not impossible—rivers in my life. God has promised that with Him "all things are possible" (Matt. 19:26).

There was a real river in my own life. Playful, placid, green, gurgling, and flowing. As a child I lived in the area of the giant redwoods, a portion of northern California filled with grandeur and wonderment, and it was there that I became acquainted with this river. But this same river took on an entirely different character with the arrival of winter.

Then the river, which was normally a 10-minute walk from our back doorstep, would inch its way slowly but steadily toward our home. I can remember those nights when, with the wind howling, the rain beating down, the lightning flashing, and thunder crashing, my cousin Jeanne and I would steal out the back door to check on its progress. Reassured that it was still within a few inches from the top of the bank, we would return to the house and fall asleep feeling we were safe for yet another night.

How many winters we carried out our little regime I cannot remember, but during our stay in our cozy hideaway home the river stayed below the bank and we were safe from its devastating effects.

We moved from this peaceful, playful place in 1953. Years later, the empty homestead faced an early winter that arrived with full force and fury. Jeanne and I were no longer there to check the progress of the river. This time it would not stop below the embankment. It came in around the back of the cabins, filling them, and turning them over. The full force of the river ran through the entire area leaving only destruction in its path. Would we, after many winters of checking this river, have become numb to its rising and falling pattern? Would we have been aware of the sudden shift of the river's pattern and made the necessary preparation to evacuate?

As I contemplate this, I wonder if our relationship to the Holy Spirit is not similar to this experience. Are we prepared to heed the call needed for our evacuation from this world? Do we callous ourselves to the gentle calling of the Holy Spirit and simply assume that we can go back to sleep? This is not the day, or the night, or the hour, that we can just sleep on.   DORIS KENNEMER LANGHAM

JUNE 9

God's Care

Consider the ravens: for they neither sow nor reap; which neither have storehouse nor barn; and God feedeth them: how much more are ye better than the fowls? Luke 12:24.

In January of 1991 war in the Persian Gulf began, and the United States sent thousands of American men and women to the area. I had never seen my country in a major conflict; war was something from a history class—events with dates and places to memorize. So I followed the news diligently, read newspaper clippings, and engaged in lively discussions with friends over dinner.

Then, with a phone call in the wee hours of the morning, the word "war," and the horror and pain it causes, took on new meaning for me: my sister was leaving for Saudi, leaving her husband and 3-year-old daughter behind. Suddenly I followed the updates with more intensity, straining to hear if there had been any casualties. I wrote postcards with texts on them every day. And I prayed for her safety like never before.

I imagined my sister with scud missiles whizzing overhead, dust stinging her nose and eyes, and homesickness hanging over her like a shroud.

One day I listened with fear as the radio announcer stated that three American personnel had been killed in practice drills. I shivered at the thought that one of them could be my sister. I quickly shared this news with a friend and was shocked at her response. "It's only three," she shrugged. "That's not that many." When I imagined my sister fighting in the desert, and how the families of the three who were killed must be feeling, I whispered, "If it's someone you love, it's one too many."

Later I thought about that statement, and realized anew how special each one of us is to God. There are so many people on earth, it's hard to imagine that God really knows us individually and cares what happens to us. Yet God says that He knows how many hairs are on our heads, and that our names are written on the palms of Jesus' hands. He will never force us to know Him; yet He yearns for each one of us to choose Him and share His friendship. God longs for us to find the peace and joy that can be ours by following Him, and gently woos our hearts to choose eternity in heaven with Him. Though the world may consider one or two lives a small loss, when God considers losing us, He says, "Even one of My precious children lost is one too many." KATHRYN M. GORDON

JUNE 10

My Bodyguard

The angel of the Lord encampeth round about them that fear him, and delivereth them. Ps. 34:7.

While I was working at a summer camp a few years ago, the director, knowing how much we all needed to get away for a day to relax and have fun with the entire staff together, planned a well-kept surprise "field trip" for us.

When the day came we boarded a big, yellow school bus, asked God to send our angels to watch over us, and proceeded down the mountain with the surprise destination still unknown to us.

Someone read us a story, "Alexander and the Terrible, Horrible, No-good, Very Bad Day." We were laughing, and filled with excitement. As the bus continued down the narrow, winding road, I noticed a smell of heated rubber, and clenched my boyfriend's hand in fear. He too began to worry as he realized we were going much faster than we should have been. The bus driver tried to downshift the gearing on the bus to slow it down, but instead his efforts only produced the sound of grinding metal. We all prayed silently as he maneuvered turn after turn, continually gaining speed, until the speed increased so much that it became impossible to make the next turn successfully. Instead, we headed straight for the edge of the mountain with only two feet of bushes as a barrier between the asphalt and the steep drop off the side. Amazingly, the bus turned gently on its side and stopped inches from the edge.

We safely emerged from the bus with a few bruises and scratches. A tow truck took the damaged bus back to the camp, and we went back in smaller vehicles. As I looked at the bus, chills went through my body as I realized again what could have happened to us if it were not for our angels.

The local townspeople were stunned and could not understand why the bus didn't go over the edge of the mountain. Some of them said it was pure luck, but we all knew the real answer! God had answered our prayers and had sent His angels to be with us and protect us. And when that happens, the devil doesn't have a chance!

"Thank You, Lord, for my bodyguard!" SHERYL GARRISON

JUNE 11

My Earthly Father

Honour thy father and thy mother: that thy days may be long upon the land which the Lord thy God giveth thee. Ex. 20:12.

He looks so weak and helpless, this shell of a man who is my father. There he lies, semi-paralyzed, unable to turn over, talk, feed himself, or even eat by mouth. The results of three strokes have taken their toll.

As I enter his nursing home room to visit him this evening, he opens his eyes, acknowledging my presence. But I do not know if he even recognizes me. I suspect that he understands very little. Already diagnosed with Alzheimer's disease, he now has, less than 100 days later, debilitating dementia. It has reduced this once active, intelligent, educated man to being essentially helpless. Oh, how cruel this life can be—the sometimes inevitable consequences of our earthly existence.

I approach his bed. After giving a cheery greeting—sounding brighter than I actually feel—I hold his hand and begin my chatter. I talk to him as though he understands and wants to hear of the events of my day. I share news about classes and students, my meetings and errands, my three young people and their activities. I stroke his brow, rub his hands, cover him with a blanket.

He reacts by tracking me with his eyes and periodically making moaning sounds, appearing to try to respond with nods or grunts. He can reach for and squeeze my hand, perhaps his only form of communication.

Sometimes I stand in silence, wondering what this charade of a visit means. What does it mean to him? What does it mean to me? I rehearse my memories of this man—my father. I think of our lifelong strained relationship—of my hurt feelings, of his broken promises, of the longing in my heart for his denied approval. Perhaps this is a final chance for me to forgive and accept. A chance to forgive his distance and harshness. A chance to accept him as a child of God and love him for that. I believe it is. I appreciate these moments, for in fact the change is coming.

I can look at him with compassion and love. I can cry tears of sadness for the state he is in, while offering tender comfort and sympathetic support. Although he cannot be the father I once envisioned, I can still be the daughter I imagine I should be, and I am grateful for this opportunity.

Sometimes I sing a song, read a scripture, and say a prayer. And somehow I feel we both are being blessed. A gentle kiss good night, and I am on my way. I become updated with his "progress" at the nurses' station before I leave—and my visit is over.

"God bless aging parents—and bless us in finding love for them because of You. Amen." ELIZABETH WATSON

JUNE 12

Do You Bend Your Back?

And be kind to one another, tender-hearted, forgiving one another, just as God in Christ also forgave you. Eph. 4:32, NKJV.

We were obviously tourists as we sauntered slowly down the sidewalk looking around carefully in order to see as much as we could. It was the first time we had been in this city, and it would probably be the last, so we did not want to miss anything of interest.

Pausing in our ambling, my husband lifted the video camera to his eye and began panning the sites of the city. It was a beautiful day, and this would be a good record of where we had been and what we had seen. I was standing nearby hardly noticing the people passing when all of a sudden my attention was drawn to a man who walked by right in front of the camera. He walked on tiptoes to be sure his head, within a few inches from the lens, completely blocked out the picture.

What an ugly fellow, I thought. *Why did he have to do that? He has nothing against Jim, because he does not even know him. He must be very miserable inside and just angry at the whole world.*

With that I became aware of the people around us and observed their reactions to a man taking a picture. A slight step to the right or left in their measured beat easily took them around the photographer. One man halted just slightly, then bent low as he passed in front of Jim, well below the camera lens.

More thoughts flashed through my mind. *Now look at the difference. That man is a gentleman. He must be happy and contented to be so considerate of a stranger.*

I doubt that either of those two men ever thought about the photographer on the street and what they did, but I have often thought about the experience. Let me share my musings.

I would like to think kindly of the "ugly" man who spoiled the picture, because he might have had an extremely hard life and might enjoy the fleeting satisfaction of revenge whenever he can get it. Maybe he grew up an orphan; if he did have parents maybe his father, or mother, was a drunkard and cruel to the family. Maybe he is out of work, or maybe his boss just gave him notice to quit at the end of the month. Maybe he is going through a divorce. Maybe his wife is dying the slow death of an incurable disease. Maybe one of his children has to be kept in a mental institution. Maybe he thinks God has let him down, if he thinks of God at all. Maybe . . . Maybe . . . Maybe . . . I will never know why he blotted out the picture.

But what about the gentleman who bent his back? He must be happy with life. He probably grew up in a comfortable home with kind and loving parents who taught him how to be courteous and polite. He probably has a good job, or his own business, with plenty of money. His wife probably kissed him goodbye as he left the house in the morning. His children are probably doing very well in school and are a credit to the family name. He is probably a good Christian man and appreciates God's bountiful blessings every day. Probably . . . Probably . . . Probably . . . I will never know why he bent his back to save the picture.

Wait a minute. Is it possible that the maybe's and the probably's could be reversed? Could the "ugly" man have the blessings of life and not appreciate them? Could the "gentleman" have the hardships of life and live above them? Yes, it is possible. Do you "bend your back" as you pass another along life's way? I hope so.

CAROL BRADFIELD

Never a Flower Girl

The Lord does not look at the things man looks at. Man looks at the outward appearance, but the Lord looks at the heart. 1 Sam. 16:7, NIV.

As a spindly, speckled child I was often told by my grandma Gracie, "Pretty *is* as pretty *does*." The full meaning of this riddle escaped me, but from the sympathetic expression on Grandma's face as she looked me over, I deduced that prettiness was not one of my strong suits. This was reinforced by my big brothers, who convinced me that I was a family blemish, an eyesore of doubtful ancestry.

Indeed, I often heard my mother speak of how strikingly handsome the boys had been from birth, with creamy skin, big blue eyes, and curly hair. I, on the other hand, was freckled, with straight, dull brown hair. Mom's fitful attempts (via home perms) to transform me into a Shirley Temple came to naught but a stiff, shapeless mound of frizz. This was not a good omen.

I was scrawny, too, a starveling for whom Dr. Coopersmith recommended a "tonic" unless immediate weight gain were achieved. To steer clear of this ill-defined substance, I wore to my next doctor's appointment my heaviest corduroy jumper, its pockets surreptitiously filled with rocks camouflaged with Kleenex.

By the time I was around 11, my obsession with being pretty was full-blown. I knew what "pretty" looked like—it looked like my best friend Marla, who was the perennial flower girl in every wedding at our church. I prayed nightly to be chosen just once to drop rose petals in the path of some beautiful bride; it was never to be.

Disappointment besieged me. *Perhaps,* I thought, *I'm not doing enough of what "pretty" is supposed to do. But what is that?* I racked my brain. *Maybe if I could be kinder, funnier, smarter— would that do the trick?* I resolved to practice my piano hymns more faithfully, share my crayons (even the coveted red-violet), and let myself be caught by the slow runners when we played tag at recess. My list grew longer as time went on.

Beginning my freshman year in boarding school, I weighed 87 pounds soaking wet, and my chest was as flat as a flounder. I had long since abandoned hope of some latent gene seizing control of my mutant DNA and transfiguring me into Annette Funicello. Yet my circle of friends expanded, and academy seemed to me to be the most cordial and exciting place on earth. Maybe being pretty wasn't going to be absolutely necessary.

I don't recall ever wishing harm upon the beautiful, but I did harbor a suspicion that for some reason charm, wit, and altruism were required only of the flawed. Life seemed so much easier for the gorgeous.

Over the years as my understanding grew, I realized that there were far more of "us" than there were of "them." And, strange as it may seem, many of us plain folks even got married! Even more astonishing, some of the loveliest ladies I met didn't think of themselves as pretty at all.

No longer do I steal a look in the mirror to see if beauty has arrived. In fact, I'm not so sure anymore what "pretty" looks like. I know who "pretty" is, though. It's Fannie Mae, the ageless silver-haired beauty who hugged me and giggled with me at church each Sabbath. She made me feel like I was special to her, even at my gawkiest.

"Pretty" is my German teacher, Wilfriede. Having lost almost everything, she still has more to give than anyone I know. Or how about Gayle, whose infectious joy can drag you from the slough of despond and make you try, try again.

To me they are all beautiful, but there the similarity ends. Those on my long list of "Most Lovely" are not birds of a feather. All sizes, colors, and shapes are here. You would probably never give any of my beauties a second look if you met them on the street. Not until you knew them.

They all have at least one thing in common, however. All have consulted with the same Plastic Surgeon. His creative genius in trimming, implanting, and lifting gives birth to creatures of unsurpassed beauty. I've begun consultation visits with this Surgeon. He promises that, although His procedures may not be painless, He can turn me into a princess, "polished after the similitude of a palace" (Ps. 144:12). That's even better than being a flower girl.

SHARON HOLMES

Fragrance of Life

But thanks be to God, who always leads us in triumphal procession in Christ and through us spreads everywhere the fragrance of the knowledge of him. For we are to God the aroma of Christ among those who are being saved and those who are perishing. To the one we are the smell of death; to the other, the fragrance of life. 2 Cor. 2:14-16, NIV.

The pungency of the first whiff confuses even the keenest nose. The aromas wafting in the still air of a humid New Orleans perfumery display room entice customers from the sidewalk outside. Curious connoisseurs sniff their way along the dissimilar bottles scattered on the glass countertops, searching for the tantalizing scent they detected among the initial aromatic confusion.

Few have the chance to select the name of an acclaimed perfume. However, in this perfumery the personnel not only give you the chance to name but to blend your own personal fragrance. A drop of the essential oils is placed on the inner arm and the oils combine with the skin's own chemicals. The best-smelling essences are then blended in a variety of ways to create the scent desired by the customer. We frequently recognize the popular fragrances by just a trail of scent as someone walks by. But when you wear a distinctly new fragrance all your own, you may be asked, "What is that unusual perfume? I don't think I've smelled that fragrance before."

A brand-new fragrance ascended to the courts of heaven 2,000 years ago. The Father smiled contentedly as He savored the impact of what this new aroma guaranteed for His kingdom throughout eternity. "Christ loved us and gave himself up for us as a fragrant offering and sacrifice to God" (Eph. 5:2). Christ became the personal fragrance that preceded the final resolution of the great conflict that had absorbed heaven's energies. The substitution of Christ's death for our death and His resurrection assuring ours became the focal point of eternity. Christ's sacrifice was at immeasurable cost to the Godhead. The eternal redemption of Their offspring was worth every painful moment.

We will never comprehend the full impact of the "fragrant sacrifice" until eternity sharpens our perceptions. To help us understand with all our senses, God revealed His plan to us in ways we could comprehend: through smell (frankincense and myrrh), sight (a heavenly star), sound (a carpenter's hammer), taste (the Last Supper), and touch (Pilate's scourging whips).

Each human child reclaimed from the prince of darkness is a scent Christ adds to the final aroma of His bride adorned for her heavenly wedding. In his triumphant fragrance each individual essence is crucial, given a unique name, paid for by the priceless blood of the Son of God, and preserved for eternity.

May the heavenly fragrance of your life spill out like the box of costly ointment Mary poured over Christ's feet at the feast before His death—unmistakable to all around.   LINDA HYDER FERRY

JUNE 15

Have You Ever Kissed a Frog?

Kind words bring life. Prov. 15:4, TEV.

Some time ago I read an article with the heading "Kissing Frogs." In the article the following questions were asked of some very young children. "Do you know any stories about frogs? What makes some frogs different from other frogs?" After a pause one of the children answered, "When they are really handsome princes." "Have you ever kissed a frog?" was the next question, and the answer came immediately. "No, eeeuuccchhhh." After the children had made it clear how they felt about kissing frogs, they were asked one more question: "But if you don't kiss it, how will you ever know if it really is a handsome prince?" They had no answer.

Kissing frogs comes from fairy tales, not from the Bible, but the article still made me think of an episode found in Acts 15:36-40. Paul and Barnabas were ready to depart on their second missionary journey, and Barnabas wanted to take John Mark with them. Paul did not think it was right to take him, because John Mark had not stayed with them to the end of their other mission but had left them in Pamphylia. In Paul's eyes John Mark was a failure, "a frog" not worth a second chance. Barnabas, however, saw behind John Mark's failure and saw the "handsome prince." He saw the missionary John Mark could become given the necessary support and encouragement, and he was ready to give John Mark another opportunity. The argument between Paul and Barnabas became so sharp that they parted. Barnabas and John Mark sailed off for Cyprus, while Paul chose Silas as his new coworker. Surrounded by Barnabas' love and support, John Mark matured in his Christian experience and became a valuable missionary for the Lord, and also later for Paul (see 2 Tim. 4:9, 11).

In the article the children were asked, "But if you do not kiss the frog, how will you ever know if it really is a handsome prince?" I would like to rephrase the question and ask: "Would John Mark have stayed a frog in Paul's mind had there not been a Barnabas?" Maybe.

When Jesus lived on earth He went around finding the handsome prince hidden in those whom others thought of as frogs—in the lepers, in Mary of Magdela, and in the rough fishermen who became His disciples. His way to bring out the prince in each one was by acts of love and kindness, and He wants us to do the same. In Hebrews 13:8 we have the assurance that Jesus is the "same yesterday, and to day, and for ever." He has not changed. He sees a handsome prince in the people we disagree with, in the people we do not like to associate with, and in you and me. If it had not been so, there would have been no Christmas message, no cross, and no resurrection. If Jesus can see a handsome prince in everyone, do we have the right to look at the same people and see a frog?

God wants us to be a Barnabas. To see in each human being not so much what he or she is at the moment, but rather what this person can become by the grace of the Holy Spirit. When we learn to do that, we begin to see others the same way Jesus sees us.

BIRTHE KENDEL

JUNE 16

Amazing Grace

But God has shown us how much he loves us—it was while we were still sinners that Christ died for us! Rom. 5:8, TEV.

Speaking to a group of young women, I shared an experience from my childhood during which my father had supported me through a difficult time. Afterward, several ladies came to me and said things like "You are so lucky to have a father like that" and "I wish my dad were like yours." I stood in numb silence and stared at these people as ugly, painful memories flooded back over me. I wanted to scream at them, "You don't know what you're saying. One little incident doesn't make a good relationship." I even regretted telling the story. It was supposed to point them to God, not make them covet my dad.

Years later I was working on my graduate degree when I got *the call* from my sister. It had finally been discovered by others that Daddy had sexually mishandled all four of his daughters. Everyone was in therapy and maybe I should consider getting help also.

I was married three years later. At the time of my sixth anniversary I discovered a letter in my attic. I didn't remember it, and I was shocked that it would show up five days before I would be going home to see my parents. My father had written it while he was in therapy, asking me to come home. He concluded with "Love you very much and need you as a daughter, Daddy." I don't think I ever acknowledged it.

I guess it was because of the timing of the letter that I let my mother lead me into a conversation about the incest for the first time. A child never wants to hear one parent speak badly about the other. But this time I had to listen. It was part of the process of acknowledging the existence of evil in someone I still needed to love and longed to be accepted by. And yet as I listened to my mother tell of her experience of coping with a dysfunctional family, through all the bitterness and anger, I actually heard her loving my dad. She was facing the same dilemma that I was.

We both are struggling to be able to actualize that he is valuable because he is my father, and that the bad things do not negate his value. And yes, I have come to believe that God put that letter back in my hands because I needed it to reach this difficult conclusion. The letter tells me that he loves me even though he otherwise can't express it by word or action.

My dad's sin does not negate his value; he is valuable because of who he is in Christ. Isn't that what grace is? Can there be anything about us for the heavenly Father to love? Yet we are valuable because of whose we are. As Paul said: "You are not your own; you were bought at a price" (1 Cor. 6:19, 20, NIV).

TESSIE HATFIELD

JUNE 17

Getting Better

Those who wait on the Lord shall renew their strength; they shall mount up with wings like eagles, they shall run and not be weary, they shall walk and not faint. Isa. 40:31, NKJV.

I had lunch last week with three workmates, all young enough to be my sons. The subject was cryogenics, the science of reducing body temperature and thereby possibly retarding the chemical changes of aging. The theory was immensely more attractive to me, the middle-ager, than it was to the three twentysomethings, who view wrinkles and stiff joints as alien by-products of another generation.

You say, "I'm not getting older, I'm getting better"? Prove it. What have you learned in the past five years? Do you have a better sense of humor? More tolerance for diverse viewpoints? Do you lead a more balanced life?

How old will you be in five years? What, if any, baggage do you want to lose by then? What goals do you want to have reached?

What do you like least about your life right now? What can you do to modify/change it? God is in the life-changing business. You might consult with Him. Check out His Best-seller, which is chockablock full of ageless advice on goal-setting, problem-solving, and people skills.

Deep-freezing is cold comfort and temporary respite from inevitable aging. In Hebrew, "renew their strength" is "change their strength." As we age, God is willing and ready to help us adapt our abilities and objectives to fit His unique plan for our lives.   CAROLE BRECKENRIDGE

JUNE 18

"Did Not Our Heart Burn Within Us?"

And they said one to another, Did not our heart burn within us, while he talked with us by the way, and while he opened to us the scriptures? Luke 24:32.

While I was visiting a member of one of our churches recently, she confided how alone she felt. She has no family, and had been so ill during the past few months that she had spent more time in the hospital than at home. She felt that God had forgotten her. My heart went out to her, and I reminded her of God's promise that He would never leave us nor forsake us. We have shared some happy moments together since then, and it is thrilling to see her rejoice in the knowledge that when she is at her lowest Jesus is especially near.

How like the experience of the two men on the road to Emmaus. The events of the past weekend had left them depressed and dejected. They had expected so much of Jesus. They expected Him to redeem Israel, but instead He had been crucified. We are told in Luke 24:10 that Jesus appeared to Mary Magdalene, and together with the other women she had told the apostles of His resurrection. But verse 11 tells us that they did not believe. How much pain could have been avoided. The journey to Emmaus should have been a joyful experience, but their hearts were sad because they were unaware that the stranger who walked and talked with them was their risen Lord. I wonder how many times we have felt depressed, dejected, and alone when Jesus is right there with us.

Sometimes an experience is so painful that we feel that Jesus must have deserted us, but it is then that He is closest to us. As the men looked back on their encounter with Jesus they had to exclaim, "Did not our heart burn within us?" How often during trying times we get up from our knees feeling a peace that only Jesus can give! With confidence we can sing:

> A wonderful Saviour is Jesus my Lord,
> A wonderful Saviour to me,
> He hideth my soul in the cleft of the rock,
> Where rivers of pleasure I see.

Thank God for Jesus! CHELCIE STERLINE-ANIM

JUNE 19

The Fonz

He that giveth, let him do it with simplicity. Rom. 12:8.

You've probably all seen the television program called *Happy Days*. It's set in the late fifties, and one of the main characters is nicknamed the Fonz. He's the ultimate in "cooooool"!

I watched an episode a few weeks ago that was almost a parable. An unknown seaman turns up and gives Fonzie a present from his father. This would have been fine, except that his father had run away when Fonzie was only 3, and he hadn't seen him since. Fonzie gives the seaman an earful about a present not making up for the absence of a father.

The Fonz's friend, Richie Cunningham, tries to get him to open the parcel. Fonzie is anything but cool!

The next day, however, Richie brings up the subject again. "Have you opened the present from your father yet?" he asks. The look on Fonzie's face tells Richie that it's time to beat a hasty retreat.

The parcel ends up under the Christmas tree of Richie's family, with whom the Fonz spends a lot of his time. It's Christmas Eve, and Joanie (Richie's sister) chooses one present for each of them to open. At her brother's suggestion she puts the parcel in front of Fonzie.

After a tussle they get him to open it. Inside is a note:

"Son, I'm writing this letter in case I don't have the guts to tell you it was me who delivered the parcel."

Fonzie, who has always believed his father hates him, can't believe it. "I didn't even get to see his face real good!" he cries out in torment. The note continues: "When I met your mother I really thought I could settle down. But the truth is, I just can't stay in one place for long . . ."

Fonzie stops reading and slumps in a chair. The family watches him worriedly. Suddenly he leaps up.

"Do you know how good it feels not to hate anymore?" he shouts. "I always thought it was my fault—like because I was born or something!"

At last the parcel is opened, and Fonzie puts on the beautiful bathrobe from Singapore. "That's in the Orient, you know!" he tells the family. Then proudly fingering the silky robe, he adds, "It's from my dad!"

That story made an impression on me for several reasons. One is the way the family decided that Fonzie would be happier if he opened the present and the way they went about it. Even though it caused some members of the family embarrassment and the possibility existed that Fonzie would show the uncool side of his nature, they persisted because they loved him. It made me think of the present (the good news about God) that we have for people who are often not all that eager to receive it. Do we ever hesitate to tell our friends, our neighbors, and our children about what God has done for us?

Notice that the family didn't unwrap Fonzie's present for him. They simply put it in his hands. Really, that's all we have to do. The same as Andrew, Peter, Philip, and Nathanael did when they said, "We have found the Messiah." We can safely let Jesus reveal Himself, and when He does (when they get to see His face "real good") they can't help loving Him. But they won't ever get the present if we don't give it to them.

The second point is that once Fonzie knew that his father really did love him, he was able to stop worrying about how his father really felt about the gift, or about him. Suddenly it wasn't his fault for "being born." His father loved him! And because his father loved him, his father's present was acceptable.

One last thought. What did the Fonz do once this had all been sorted out? "It's from my dad," he said proudly. The first thing he did with this wonderful information was pass it on.

ANITA MARSHALL

The Edited Life

Yet I am always with you; you hold me by my right hand.
You guide me with your counsel, and afterward you will
take me into glory. Whom have I in heaven but you? And
earth has nothing I desire besides you. My flesh and my
heart may fail, but God is the strength of my heart and my
portion forever. Ps. 73:23-26, NIV.

Writers are a varied and interesting lot. They express theory. They produce journals or write speeches. Perhaps they delight in orchestrating thought, developing story lines, styling subtle plots, treating distinctive characterizations, or embellishing fact. Their liberation of intelligence might be caught up as a child's kite floating on a breeze, held aloft by a mere thread, stirring fantasy, causing diffusion of beliefs that in any other medium might seem stilted or critical, but here allowed to soar free—almost phosphorescent in uplifted thrust toward a brilliant sky, luminescent with dreams and wished-its! They are inventive—discovering original thought through fabrication of new words, or frolicking with an unfamiliar twist to bring fresh light to old ways of saying things. They resort to the life of a recluse, bemused by what they deem to be noble reflection and grand devotion. Influencing current opinion carries a return far beyond monetary reward.

But when the result of their craft is distilled, frequently brought to a level of exasperation through energies known only to a consummate editor; when revisions, rearrangements, corrections, adaptations, and subjective improvements are handed down, mandated to accomplish the hoped-for publication—that is the moment of truth—when fledgling author is either borne aloft or kindly freed from her slavery, never to return to the addictive bondage of her art.

A child's capacity to learn, to walk, to talk, to commune with the universe, is limited only by her desire or her environment. Without direction, there is a nonconformist within each of us, allowing our innate ability to question, to search the unlimited knowledge that is out there just for the grasping! It is an easy thing to head into the melee, secure in an inner knowledge of empathy in the hearts of most people. Our fantasies are to be cherished, to be allowed to roam free.

But we have a holy Editor. He understands all things. He sees the end and the beginning. He recognizes character traits, aptitudes, distinctions between individuals that may allow one person to grow within a style that works for her, but which would cause another person to fall into difficulty in using precisely that same style.

When we honor God—allowing Him to bring us into compliance, correct our path, revise our direction, replace our "dangling participle" with a clear connection to Him—the hoped-for possibility of producing a publishable work becomes real. We can conduct our lives within an editorial partnership with Christ. What a wonderful existence, what a generous reward! JUDI WILD BECKER

JUNE 21

Retype!

And ye are complete in him. Col. 2:10.

If she had written that hated word on my sheets of typing once, she must have written it a hundred times in her efforts to turn me into an efficient and accurate typist!

I had so cleverly erased my errors, in those precomputer days, and I felt certain that even she could not detect my erasures. But she did. And upon her discovery she circled the indiscretions in red and wrote that dreaded word *retype* across the bottom of the page.

I recoiled from discussing my frustration with my fellow typists for two reasons. 1. If they had not suffered the indignity of having the dread word penned across their typed sheets, my humiliation would be unbearable. 2. If they should turn the question back on me, I would have to confess that painful verb in the imperative mood was *often* scrawled across mine. I could not face either option, so I bore my agony alone.

But when for the ninety-ninth time (I think it was) I saw that word in red on my page, my humiliation had reached its limit. I tearfully approached my teacher.

"Miss Thorpe," I began quaveringly, "it's really no use my going on with this typing class. I can't type. I can't do a single page without having *retype* written across it. I'm just wasting your time and I want to leave the class."

But Miss Thorpe seemed neither angered by my outburst nor moved by my tears.

"Edna, my dear," she gently replied, "you are showing real promise as a typist. And it is my job to help you to strengthen your weaknesses and to guide you to a greater degree of efficiency and accuracy. Practice is what you and every other member of the class need. They all see that word that you dread so much on their pages, and they hate it as much as I dislike writing it there. So you just gather up your courage and keep practicing until errors are swallowed up in accuracy."

When at the end of my graduating year, I was presented with the Incorporated Phonographic Society's certificate for speed and accuracy—with distinction—I knew what Miss Thorpe's smile said: "My congratulations are for sticking to it: the success was simply a by-product."

Last night I talked with my Lord, like I did to Miss Thorpe so long ago. "Lord," I said, "I can't hide my failures and mistakes from You. And I wish I could quit when I think of the ungenerous judgments, self-centered choices, and unfair criticisms I have made. Lord, if only You would write 'Retype' across today's page and let me start over again."

Patiently my wonderful Lord reminded me: "You can't retype it, even though it is a sorry mess. But you confessed your foolishness. Your repentance was sincere, and do you know what happened?"

"I just hope I have been forgiven," I answered uncertainly. "But, oh the mess! Lord, I can still see it all."

"But that's the difference between you and Me," my heavenly Father said reassuringly. "I don't see as you do because the perfection of My Son, your older Brother, now covers your page. All I can see is a perfectly clean page as I view it through Him. And I see what you call 'a mess' no more.

"Edna," He concluded, "if you can believe what I have just said, your future life pages will always receive the same treatment. Needing to be retyped they may be, but your plea for forgiveness puts those pages under the perfection of My Son, and that's how I, your loving Father, will always view them—perfect and complete in Him."

EDNA HEISE

JUNE 22

Vitality

But they that wait upon the Lord shall renew their strength; they shall mount up with wings as eagles; they shall run, and not be weary; and they shall walk, and not faint. Isa. 40:31.

Before dialing the number for Florida Hospital, I paused to ask the Lord for a verse to share. Isaiah 40:31 came to mind. A beautiful text, but I didn't realize how perfectly suited it was until talking with my friend.

Sheila had undergone open-heart surgery a few days before to repair a congenital heart defect. Although I had prayed for a successful surgery and speedy recovery, I was amazed at how strong she sounded on the phone.

Sheila has always had difficulty in building up or maintaining stamina while exercising, yet never knew why until the recent discovery of her septal defect. Even on walks of only a mile or two she would feel faint. It was as we talked about exercise fatigue that Isaiah 40:31 popped into my mind again. *You will run and not grow weary; you will walk and not faint.* "Sheila," I exclaimed, "this verse has your name on it. It fits your situation perfectly. Now you can walk and not be faint!"

I thought more about this passage after hanging up the phone. "Even the youths shall faint and be weary, and the young men shall utterly fall: but they that wait upon the Lord shall renew their strength; they shall mount up with wings as eagles; they shall run, and not be weary; and they shall walk, and not faint" (verses 30, 31).

Strength and energy—what coveted possessions these days. But what is the key for acquiring physical, emotional, and especially spiritual vitality?

Vitality and power are promised only to the weary, the weak, and those who stumble and fall. If Sheila had been too proud to admit she felt weary and faint, too proud to accept the fact that she had a heart defect, she would never have gotten a fuller lease on life. Strength comes only to those who admit weakness.

Then there is the wait. Not the kind of weight we generally have excess of, but the patient waiting we have in short supply. Wait—a hopeful expectancy, a patient looking to, tarrying.

I chuckle to myself as I imagine what would have happened if Sheila had been too impatient to wait until she woke up in the recovery room to find out how her surgery went. What if she had decided to bypass anesthesia so she could be in on the surgery? Maybe even give a little advice or caution. "Oh, don't spread my rib cage that wide—just think how sore I'm going to be." "Hurry, cauterize that bleeder!" "Easy does it with the heart—it's the only one I have." Too many quips like these and the surgeons might have said, "If you know so much, do it yourself."

Wait upon the Lord. How hard it is to wait when we don't first give up. How easy to wait once we give 100 percent control to the Doctor in charge of anesthesia. Then He, with the surgeons, can perform the major heart surgery. Actually it is God who does the real waiting. He's always on call. He's just waiting for us to submit to the Great Anesthesiologist.   HEIDE FORD

Too Busy Serving?

But Martha was distracted with much serving, and she approached Him and said, "Lord, do You not care that my sister has left me to serve alone? Therefore tell her to help me." Luke 10:40, NKJV.

My parents tell of an amusement ride in a small park that we sometimes visited when we lived in Miami, Florida. My sister, Audrey, was about 3 and I was about 18 months when we were put into a small car (on a track) and sent off for a wonderful ride. Audrey, probably because she was older, happened to be sitting at the steering wheel and instinctively felt it her duty to steer. When she saw the curves approaching, she desperately tried to steer in the right direction, but the car followed its own path! After several attempts, my brave sister gave up and laid her head down on her hands in despair. Then, suddenly, she jerked up her head, looked at me sitting beside her, and began steering again for all she was worth! More than once during that ride, Audrey was tempted to give up until she remembered that I was in the car too. Evidently I was oblivious to the possibility of danger that Audrey saw, and I enjoyed the ride completely. Poor Audrey must have been exhausted from her self-imposed responsibility and her burst of emotional energy!

Can you see Martha taking care of Mary that same way? Poor Martha—so intent on the busy work, using up her energy "doing things" when she could have been enjoying time with Jesus. It seems that Martha was frustrated that Mary wasn't pulling her share of the load. Mary seemed oblivious to the necessary work, but she was truly busy—busy listening.

Audrey's driving didn't make the car go any better or faster. In fact, it only wore her out. Yet she felt her choice would keep us both safe. Today, I am less oblivious than when I was 18 months, sometimes driving my own vehicle when it should be steered by Another. I am learning that the Mary attitudes about life are important, valuable. "Oh, rest in the Lord. Wait patiently for him."

Thanks, Audrey, for wanting to keep me safe in that little car in Miami. You're a great sister! Life does have many dangerous twists and turns. I'm indebted to you. But how much more to my heavenly

Father. I'm planning to spend more time sitting at His feet, learning to love and serve others in His way. Distractions will always be a part of life. I want it said that I have "chosen that good part, which will not be taken away" when the Lord returns to take His children home.   IRIS SHULL

The Lord Yearns to Gather Us Together

Oh Jerusalem, Jerusalem, you who kill the prophets and stone those sent to you, how often I have longed to gather your children together, as a hen gathers her chicks under her wings, but you were not willing. Look, your house is left to you desolate. Matt. 23:37, 38.

When we lived in Ghana, family members were always close by. Our house was always full with relatives, friends, neighbors, and the neighbors' children. It was normal to have a neighbor's child live with us for a period of time—it was impossible to feel lonely in our house. Then my husband and I traveled to Berrien Springs, Michigan, to study at Andrews University. Work and studies did not allow much time for socializing there and gradually, being alone became the normal way of life for me until Esta came.

Esta, my sister's daughter, and her 4-year-old daughter came to visit. Esta and I have always been very close. From the time she was 3 months old I was made responsible for her. Her visit was therefore very pleasing to both my husband and me. Furthermore, Esta gave birth to a son while she was with us. Our house bubbled with new life, becoming the kind of house I had known before.

But then came the day when she had to go back home. As my husband prayed for God's protection, Esta began to cry and I could no longer contain myself either. We were both in tears. When I returned home from the airport, I felt unusually lonely. And then it hit me in the face—I had become comfortable with loneliness without realizing it.

It dawned on me that one could have the same experience spiritually. The insidious slipping into spiritual desolation can happen when one gets used to staying apart from God.

In Matthew 23:38, Jesus finally declared the end of the efficacy of the ceremonies of the Temple in Jerusalem. Nevertheless, the priests had been so used to living apart from Him that they continued their daily rounds of sacrifices, not realizing the sacrifices were empty and meaningless—spiritually desolate.

We start slipping into spiritual emptiness and isolation when we begin to neglect our Bible study and prayer. Jesus wants us to open our hearts to Him, to spend more time with Him, and not become comfortable without Him. Let us allow Him to gather us together the way a hen gathers her chicks under her wings. He is yearning to do so.

MABEL OWUSU-ANTWI

JUNE 25

Spiritual Instruction

Love the Lord your God with all your heart and with all your soul and with all your strength. These commandments that I give you today are to be upon your hearts. Impress them on your children. Deut. 6:5, 7, NIV.

Mom! Watch me!" shouts Hans before he jumps into the water and glides quietly under its surface. Is this the same boy who used to huddle on the pool's edge, afraid to get wet?

Lisa, who first swam the crawl with flailing arms and gasping breath, now smoothly covers a lap, then does another.

Their achievements surprise me, though I've been watching their progress since toddlerhood.

As much as I love to swim, they had to learn for themselves. I showed them that water play is fun, and I faithfully took them to swim classes. I did not force them into the pool, but neither would I let them shiver on the sidelines.

As they gained strength and coordination, I minimized their errors and applauded their successes. I trusted others to teach and guide them. I had to be willing to stay at the poolside—not directly involved, but always alert—when they first tried the deep end or jumped from the diving board into an instructor's arms.

This approach applies to spiritual training as well. As enthusiastic Christians, Dick and I did not wait until our children would discover God on their own. We tried to make worship as pleasant as possible and regularly attended church. We could not make them believe, but it was our responsibility to coax Lisa, Hans, and Raymond into participation and appropriate attitudes.

Now they know the Bible stories. They sing hymns and pray as naturally as they walk and talk. They enter the worship experience. A relationship with God, though girded by habit, has become personal.

My prayer for my children is that they will be vigorous in their pursuit of God and disciplined in their search for truth. As they internalize spiritual values, I want them to be strong. As religion becomes individual, I pray they'll have full assurance of salvation. I want them to be brave risk-takers but not foolhardy thrill-seekers. And when they must enter "deep water," I trust God to help them to the other side. —Cherry B. Habenicht

JUNE 26

A Moving Experience

A friend loves at all times. Prov. 17:17, NIV.

Moving is not one of my favorite pastimes, but being married to a pastor gives me many opportunities to remember that this world is not my home.

The disruption of moving is always hard on me emotionally, so I try to think about the happy times spent with our congregation. Knowing that there will be new sisters in Christ for me to learn to love whenever we get settled into another home helps ease the pain.

When I look back at the many moves our family has made, I always recall one especially "moving" experience. Our home had sold very quickly to a neighbor's mother who wanted to be near her grandchildren. Praise the Lord for good neighbors!

Now there was the sorting and packing to do. After a few weeks the boxes were numbered and labeled. The house began to have that empty feeling.

The next task was that huge chore of "spring cleaning." It was going to be a busy week before that dreaded day arrived and we could finally leave. I had no idea about the surprise that was in store for us.

The doorbell rang constantly as families trooped in with their buckets, vacuum cleaners, dusters, ladders, and smiling faces. I couldn't believe my eyes!

Someone must have carefully organized the schedule, as everyone knew his or her task, which was accomplished with love. The day flew by so quickly. Never did the proverb "Many hands make light work" mean so much to me.

But the climax of the day came when the new owners of the house paid a surprise visit. They went from room to room meeting all kinds of nice people. Their look of amazement led them to ask, "Who are all these people?"

Joy, mingled with pride, filled my heart as I happily told them that they were my family, my church family, who had come to show their love at a very difficult time.

Do you know a family planning to move? Why not give them the surprise of their life? Make theirs "a moving experience" they will never forget. JEAN SEQUEIRA

JUNE 27

Living in the Real World

As a father has compassion on his children, so the Lord has compassion on those who fear him; for he knows how we are formed, he remembers that we are dust. Ps. 103:13, 14, NIV.

The world I grew up in
was flat, two-dimensional,
a world of either/or:
either good or bad,
either right or wrong,
either lost or saved.

It was a safe, simple world
with inflexible boundaries,
a world of absolutes, but also
a world of intolerance
and prejudice.

The world I see today
has a thousand shades of gray
between black and white;
I see a world that is
infinitely complex,
where things are seldom
what they seem.

In this real world
only God can see the heart
and know the circumstances
of each life.
Only He can judge with
mercy and compassion.

He asks us,
with our fallible wisdom,
not to judge,
but to show love
and forbearance
for one another.

CARROL GRADY

JUNE 28

The Gift

The King will reply, "I tell you the truth, whatever you did for one of the least of these brothers of mine, you did for me." Matt. 25:40, NIV.

Her voice seemed small and very far away. It was easy to reach her because she worked the college switchboard, and I'd called to find out what she planned for spring break. She had no plans. Nothing was working out as she'd thought it would.

She sounded so lonely that my mind raced, wondering how I could help her. At the same time I was acutely aware of the cost of a daytime international call and felt anxious that the conversation not drag on forever with no solution.

"Would you like to come home for a week?" (This was a stab in the dark, as I couldn't think how we'd manage to pay for it.)

"No-o-o." The word seemed drawn out in sadness.

I paused. This was impossible. There was no way I could do it, this wild thing that had flown into my mind.

"What are you going to do, then?" I asked.

"I don't know. Just stay in the dorm, I guess."

Again, the impossible thought. "Robyn," I asked, "would you like for me to come visit?"

A pause. "Would you?"

Now that I'd said it, it seemed simple. "Listen, I don't know if it's remotely possible. I have no idea if I can find a flight I can afford, and even if I can, I don't know if I can get off work or get the money together to come. But you be by the dorm phone at 10:00 tonight, and I'll call and let you know."

This time I heard her tears. "OK."

Thirty hours later I was on a plane heading to London. And even though I have the reputation of not being able to drive across town without directions, I made it through two train changes to a cab and pulled up in front of the dormitory before 10:00 a.m.

213

Robyn ran down the steps to meet me.

The week I spent at Newbold College with her was a gift that no one can take away. I'd been there before, but this time it was just the two of us. She confidently led me through the London subway system. She recommended Indian "fast food" from street vendors. We went through the National Gallery and British Museum. She studied train and bus schedules, and we found the magnificent ruins of Tintern Abbey in Wales.

In the two years since my visit I have pondered what made it so very special. It wasn't that I got a quick, inexpensive trip to England. It wasn't the sightseeing or even the fun I had with my eldest daughter.

This trip is a memory to cherish because Robyn gave me the most beautiful gift a person can give to someone who loves him or her. She had been in school overseas for three years. She had grown up into a competent, self-assured young woman. But I hardly knew her anymore. She didn't need me.

And then in one moment she gave me a gift beyond price—the gift of needing me.

God, who has the universe at His fingertips, has given us the same gift. The gift of needing our love, and asking for our help in sharing His love with others. PENNY ESTES WHEELER

JUNE 29

God Prepared the Way

The Lord is the one who goes ahead of you; He will be with you. He will not fail you or forsake you. Do not fear, or be dismayed. Deut. 31:8, NASB.

For 12 years I had worked for the same company, and I had just received a promotion that would require me to move near the home office. It would mean uprooting from the area where I had lived most of my life, but I decided to accept it. Then four months after I moved, I received devastating news: the company had just filed for bankruptcy!

I was a single mother with two adult children, one of them just beginning college far away from home. It was the first time in my life that I didn't have a job! What was I to do 1,500 miles away from my family and longtime friends? I didn't have any emotional support in this new town. "Should I move back 'home,' look for a job in this already depressed employment area, or look elsewhere?"

I wondered. How would this all affect my daughter in college? It was so hard for me to decide what to do!

Within a week I had explored the local job market, which wasn't very promising. After a few more phone calls I had two job offers that would both require a move. One job was farther west and the other was completely across the nation in the Mid-Atlantic region. Both areas were strange and scary to me. I didn't really want either job, and I didn't want to move! Why couldn't I just have my job back? I would have to make a quick decision if I was going to take the first job offer, but I wasn't ready to decide. The second job offer would remain open a bit longer.

I spent a lot of time reading my Bible and praying, wrestling with my problem. The promise in Psalm 32:8, "I will instruct you and teach you in the way you should go; I will counsel you with My eye upon you," kept popping up in my mind. How was God going to show me the way to go? In my fear of the unknown, He pointed me to today's scripture in Deuteronomy 31:8.

Even though I kept my resistance up, God still led me. I was given a position that I'm sure I enjoy more than I would have the first job I was offered. As I look back I can truly say that God was definitely looking out for and directing me. This experience has reaffirmed for me that if we could see the end from the beginning, we wouldn't choose any other way than the way God leads us.

NORMA McKELLIP

JUNE 30

Finding Him

And you will seek Me and find Me, when you search for Me with all your heart. Jer. 29:13, NASB.

Doctrine is meaningless without a personal relationship with Jesus Christ. When I use the words "personal relationship" it may seem like a cliché. Perhaps you've already tried praying today but you got up from your knees feeling like your prayer hadn't gone beyond the ceiling of your bedroom. Perhaps you even went to prayer meeting this week, but while the preacher preached, your mind wandered to "more important" things that you needed to be doing. And even when you left the church, you didn't have the desire to share what you had experienced. Even when the preacher said "Jesus died for you!" it was like old news that had lost its punch!

Has this ever happened to you? My spiritual connection was

215

broken. And the most frightening thing about this fracture was that I didn't have a desire to fix it!

Then one day the thought came to me that even when I didn't sense His nearness, He was standing by me. "Admit it! Admit it! You can't even begin to know Him without His help!" my inner being shouted! It was then that I discovered that by admitting this basic inability on my part, I took the most important step in seeking Him. I've learned that if I invite Him—if I give Him permission—He'll plant a desire to know Him within me. The exciting truth of the matter is that He'll do this for you too, and for everyone else who sincerely seeks to know Him—without exception. It has nothing to do with who we are. It has everything to do with who He is!

SABINE VATEL

JULY 1

Broken but Loved

For God so loved the world, that he gave his only begotten Son, that whosoever believeth in him should not perish, but have everlasting life. John 3:16.

Twelve-year-old Nadia Marie Neuman stood on the tiptoes of her high-topped leather shoes trying to see the row of dolls at the Boston store. "Which one?" she said to herself, struggling to make a decision. She felt enchanted by their real hair, sparkling brown eyes, and tiny pearllike teeth.

A nearby sign read "$.50 per doll." The year was 1907, and 50 cents was a lot of money. But Nadia wanted one of the dolls more than anything in the world. At last she handed the prettiest one to the clerk.

The woman put her money into a box, fastening the box to a conveyor track that sent it clanking up to the second-floor cashier. The doll was hers to take home!

Soon Little Doll had a wardrobe of party dresses, nightgowns, and a little rain cape with a button on the shoulder. Nadia's only sister, Elsie, had died of whooping cough the year before. Nadia was lonely without her sister, and Little Doll became her best friend. She loved sewing for her.

The years passed. At last Nadia tucked Little Doll into a Brach's candy box with a purple orchid on the box top. Now and then she took her out to show to her own little girls, Adora and Mary Louise. They loved to hear the story of how their mother had gone to the Boston store to buy Little Doll. "And that is how I learned to sew for all of us," Nadia would say as she carefully put Little Doll away again.

One day she called to me, her oldest granddaughter. "Karen, you're 12, so you're old enough now. I want you to have Little Doll."

I was thrilled beyond words. Little Doll had always been part of my memory and now she would be my own.

Mother and I went together to get Little Doll. But as Grandma reached down from the attic to put the doll into my outstretched hand, something terrible happened. The doll slipped out of my hand and crashed to the floor. We looked at her shattered face and body and wept together. How could she ever be fixed?

My mother tried to glue Little Doll back together, but that only compounded the doll's problems. So she put her back in the candy box, and we all felt sad. Little Doll needed an expert, a redeemer!

In 1992, after a long search, I found a porcelain antique restorationist. After examining Little Doll she said, "Yes, I can fix her, but I will need to keep her for several months. And the cost of my time may reach $500." Five hundred dollars! For a 50-cent doll!

"Can you fix her by my grandmother's ninety-fifth birthday in October?" I asked her.

She considered a moment. "Yes, if all goes well."

A week before Grandma's birthday Little Doll was ready for the celebration. She looked almost like new, and I was ecstatic. The whole family was excited and gathered around as Grandma unwrapped her special gift. It was difficult not to be disappointed when at first she didn't remember the doll. But it had been several years since she'd seen it—then broken with no hope of repair—and Grandma's memory wasn't quite the same as it once was. But eventually the memories came flooding back, and she gasped, "Oh! I didn't know she was so pretty." Once more she told me about the trip to the Boston store. Her happiness in seeing Little Doll's restoration was worth every penny spent.

As I sit here today looking at Little Doll I think of how infinitely greater was the sacrifice Christ made to restore us to rightness with Him. What an incomprehensible price He paid to make us whole in His sight. Broken but loved! Restored in spite of the price.

KAREN KOTOSKE

Turned Around

For we are God's workmanship, created in Christ Jesus to do good works. Eph. 2:10, NIV.

Betty Jean is a beginning quilter. One day in sharing "shop talk" she said, "I spend so much time trying to get every little piece to line up. I want my quilt to be just perfect."

I could appreciate what Betty Jean was saying. Even with carefully measured templates and exacting seams, I don't always come out *exactly* right. However, the fact that I am enjoying the overall design instead of worrying about minute details is encouragement for me. My tendencies toward perfection and idealism have, at times, caused me to be driven and worn. It has been a measure of growth that I have learned to enjoy my best efforts just as they are.

Betty Jean continued her thought. "Someone told me that when the Amish ladies make quilts, they always leave one little mistake because they say that God alone is perfect. I don't know if it's true or not, but when I have a mistake I just can't fix I remind myself of that idea."

We both laughed. And I remembered a mistake that even I couldn't leave. I had placed my carefully constructed quilt blocks out in perfect order and sewed them together. I thought all had gone well until I looked at the finished top. Much to my chagrin, I discovered that somehow I had turned a block. The symmetry of design was ruined. It had to be changed.

Now, this block was not on a corner or edge with easy access. It was surrounded on all sides. Laboriously I ripped out stitches and turned the offending piece to proper position. Next I pinned and basted and sewed. I pressed and stretched.

Perhaps that quilt block has a lesson for us in our spiritual journeys. There are times when God's plan for us gets out of balance. And it is only with God's help that we get turned around.

So even if you feel like a quilt block that had to be turned around, you are a very important part of God's design. If you let Him, He can use you to minister to others whose lives have gotten out of balance, and you can help them get turned around too.

BEULAH FERN STEVENS

JULY 3

Reckless Love

I have loved you with an everlasting love. Jer. 31:3, NIV.

I'm in the middle of a good book. I have to admit, however, that I've already read the last chapter. (I always read the end before I decide if a book is worth my time.) It gives a fairly real picture of life in a parish, probably because the cleric who wrote it also has a doctorate in sociology. I can identify with the middle-aged pastor who's afraid he's losing the exuberance and optimism of youth and who wrestles hard with disillusionment and cynicism betimes. His confessions may be a little stark for some, but there's enough right to keep me reading. Besides, my son, who's away most of the year at college, seemed impressed that I checked a book out of the library.

I knew I was going to like the author's bottom line the minute I read the next-to-the-last page. He wrote about a sermon he preached one Easter Sunday about a God who, despite all good taste and hard reason, even plain sanity, had fallen in love with His creatures. He used terms like *reckless* and *passionate* to speak of God's love for us. He said it was like a man and woman falling head over heels in love with each other. Only God's passion for us is stronger and more vigorous than the most powerful of human passions. Easter, the author said, is an invitation to renew our romance with God and then, at the altar of His love, to renew our romances with one another.

I'm only beginning to get used to thinking about God's love in terms of reckless passion and romance. I don't know why it's taking me so long. The imagery is as old as Solomon and the Hebrew prophets. But it's imagery that keeps Him enticing in my mind all day. Somehow I think God wants it that way. It's bound to spill over into my relationships.   KAREN FLOWERS

JULY 4

Love Gifts From Friends

I will not let you go unless you bless me. . . . Then he blessed him there. Gen. 32:26, 29, NIV.

Some time ago a friend came calling with several freshly dug plants packed neatly in a cardboard box. Among them were two that have brought me great pleasure. Shirley and I had a mutual friend, Eunie, who grew lovely patches of old-fashioned pale yellow primroses. When Eunie died, it left a terrible hole in our hearts. Shirley was fortunate enough to have a small patch of primroses in her garden that Eunie had given her. So this day Shirley had generously dug a little clump of the primroses so that I, too, might have a bit of Eunie's garden in my own.

I have tended them with care, and each spring the clump gets a wee bit bigger. Sometimes I cut a few and put them in a tiny glass vase, as Eunie used to do. It's sad and comforting at the same time.

The other plant I've treasured from that cardboard box is a primrose too, but a very different one. (It's amazing how many varieties of primroses there are.) This one is an evening primrose. In the daytime it's a very ordinary plant, just a little clump of saw-toothed leaves with thin, floppy stems supporting tight, elongated buds. But when dusk settles over the garden a miracle takes place. The ever-so-ordinary plant becomes a star. Those tight buds begin to unfurl right before one's eyes like a time-lapse nature film. The only experience to which I can liken it is waiting for Old Faithful to spout. Both events are breathtaking. Each pale yellow petal gradually unfolds in the near-darkness until finally there's a lovely gleaming cup. People who watch inevitably let out little sighs of delight. It's somewhat hard to observe it all, for there may be as many as six or eight blossoms opening up at once. Guests become so fascinated that they often bring lawn chairs to the edge of the garden to observe the event close-up.

There's nothing funnier than watching a little group leaning forward on their chairs in the gathering night, completely bewitched by a tiny patch of performing flowers.

Jesus comes to you this morning. He has a little box for you full of comfort, wisdom, strength, and much, much more. It will carry you through the hard places, give you miracles to share and a new appreciation for His love. Take care that you don't leave Him standing there offering His gift as you whirl into the day.

JUNE STRONG

A Resting Place

He makes me lie down. Ps. 23:2, NIV.

I walked slowly up to the towering giant. Spreading my arms wide I let my body lean against its rugged bark, making a tiny arc on its vast circumference.

Resting on this California redwood, sunlight dimmed by the tree's distant canopy, I listened to the quiet. Nothing at first. Then sounds of wind and small forest creatures. I breathed in the peace and strength around me, content to be in this awesome place. It had not been simple getting there.

Only my strong need eventually drowned out my endless excuses for not taking care of myself. After healing rest among the redwoods and a few extra days to care for my own neglected home, I found renewed energy. I began to see problems in perspective once more. I took new interest in family and friends. My sense of humor revived. Rest has restored me to a more abundant life.

In our society, rest has taken a ridiculous rap. We confuse it with laziness, apathy, and inability. In an inhumane, treacherous view of life, we brag about our incessant activity; we prove ourselves by our overtime hours; and we feel guilty when we aren't at least scheming about our many tasks and activities. Our headaches increase, while our creativity and efficiency decrease.

Did the devil convince us rest is wasteful and useless? Or is it just our frantic tendency to always do and seldom to be?

Before my own delayed acknowledgment of the need for rest, a cancer patient had gifted me with warning flashes of insight: "I have learned to adjust my priorities. With less life to live, I've had to think about how to live it. I plan to spend a lot more time with people I love, with beauty in nature, with beautiful music, and just having fun. I regret my 'Type A' living. I thought the thrill of working and worrying and rushing was all there was."

A deep and ancient reality echoed in the patient's words. Although long ignored, God's call to weekly rest rolls down the ages from the creation of the world: "And God blessed the seventh day and made it holy, because on it he rested from all the work of creating that he had done" (Gen. 2:3, NIV).

The healing begun for me among the Redwoods is now continued by the Sabbath's rhythmic cycle of rest. Weekly, I can choose God's required rest, which prevents repeated burnout.

It wasn't easy to get to the redwoods. It isn't easy to keep the

Sabbath that keeps me. But when I do, I understand what David meant when he said that "[God] makes me lie down in green pastures [and] . . . restores my soul" (Ps. 23:2, 3, NIV).

PENNY SHELL

JULY 6

When Your World Collapses

Simon Peter answered him, "Lord, to whom shall we go? You have the words of eternal life." John 6:68, NIV.

For most of us, life has its share of disappointments and frustrations, problems, and stress, but we learn to cope. We make adjustments, and we usually find many opportunities for satisfaction, fulfillment, and happiness.

But what do we do when suddenly, unexpectedly, our safe, comfortable little world comes crashing down around us and we are plunged into a black pit of pain and despair?

If you have never experienced this, try to imagine yourself in one of the following scenarios: During a routine physical exam your doctor discovers advanced cancer and tells you that you have only a few months to live. Two years before retirement your husband, who has served the church faithfully and well all his life, is told that he is being laid off because of budgetary constraints. Your precious daughter, a talented academy senior with a promising future, comes to you in tears and confesses that she's pregnant. As a young mother you are enjoying a good visit with your neighbor when, in a moment of inattention, your toddler chases a ball into the street and is struck by a passing car and killed. Your beloved son calls from across the country and haltingly, painfully, breaks the news that he is gay and HIV-positive.

Yes, we know how a Christian *should* respond in such situations. But as weak and sinful human beings, a crisis like this—or even one of less dire consequences—is much more likely to reveal to us the superficiality of our faith. Struggling with questions, doubts, and fears, we are forced to face our utter inability to handle the situation by ourselves, and our urgent need for God's sustaining love and wisdom.

When we can see no way out, no possible solution to our problem, we turn at last to God and exclaim, like Peter, "Lord, to whom shall we go? You have the words of eternal life!" In the midst of our anguish, we sense a new awareness of God's nearness and comfort. As we cling to His promises in our desperate need, our

222

faith stretches and grows. Our pain awakens in us an increased sensitivity to the suffering of others and makes us more understanding and sympathetic to their needs. In wrestling with the grim realities of our sinful world we gain a new perspective on what is really important in life. And the promise that "all things work together for good to them that love God" (Rom. 8:28) takes on a new and personal meaning.   CARROL GRADY

Reach Out and Touch Someone

Get rid of all bitterness, rage and anger, brawling and slander, along with every form of malice. Be kind and compassionate to one another, forgiving each other, just as in Christ God forgave you. Eph. 4:31, 32, NIV.

The adult need for touching is more basic than the need for sex. This need begins at birth and is the infant's first reassurance of nurturing. The cuddling and stroking the newborn receives is critical to his future development. It is so important that infants who lack this kind of affectionate care grow up to be emotionally disturbed adults. Touching is essential for physical well-being.

Adults are very little different from children when it comes to the need for physical closeness. We all have deep needs for touching and the intimacy it creates.

Another word for touch is caress. Webster defines caress as "an act of endearment; as tender or loving embrace, touch, to touch, stroke, pat tenderly, lovingly, or softly." Nurturing is involved in each word of the definition. If you trace the origin of *caress* to the Latin word *caress*, from which it was derived, you will find it was a term for "dear," which implies caring and nurturing.

Someone has said that three hugs a day keep depression away. And according to new medical evidence, touching can also stabilize the heart rate of the intensive-care patient, improve movement for cerebral palsy victims, heal the sick by the "laying on of hands" as evidenced both in Bible and present times, raise children's grade-point averages, and activate hemoglobin and brain wave activity.

When healthy habits of touching are regularly followed, feelings of warmth, psychological satisfaction, and emotional security will be built. Touching can do more to heal the wounds of bickering and hostility than any treatment modality.

A married couple can experience a dramatic change in their marriage simply by touching each other in affectionate ways. For instance, a couple can join hands during prayer. They may hold hands while going for a walk or cuddle at night with no demands for sex. They can sit close at church or while watching TV and greet each other with a hug and kiss after being separated.

Harry frequently follows me to the kitchen (especially when he smells something good), slips his arms around me, and holds me close. I need his hug. It reassures me of his love and makes me feel secure in his affection.

There's someone out there today who needs a healing touch from you. Ask God to place in your path on this day someone who needs your personal caring. Reach out and touch someone near you today. NANCY VAN PELT

JULY 8

The Love Gift

Let all that you do be done with love. 1 Cor. 16:14, NKJV.

Camp meeting Sabbath school had already begun as I stood in the entrance looking for a seat. None—except in the very back. *Not there*, I thought. *I won't get anything out of the service with all the noise and moving around in the back.* So I kept looking, hoping a seat would miraculously show up. Ah! Half a bench was empty about 10 rows from the front, behind one of the posts. Quietly I moved to the unoccupied spot, happy with my good fortune.

In less than a minute I realized why the bench was empty. Discreetly I looked around to see where that terrible odor was coming from. I could hardly resist plugging my nose. To my right, in the middle of a huge empty space on the bench, sat an elderly gentleman. He looked my direction and smiled. I smiled back. His clothes were mismatched, rumpled, and torn. His wrinkled face was covered with stubble. Clearly he hadn't used water and soap recently. What was *he* doing at camp meeting?

My choices were limited—stay where I was or sit in the back. I chose to stay. The smell became a little more tolerable as my nose grew accustomed to the assault. Every now and then I stole a brief glance his way. He didn't seem to notice my curiosity, for he was engrossed in the service, hanging on to every word and song.

Soon the offering was announced. The speaker made a strong missions appeal, and I responded by looking in my wallet for an appropriate bill. I noticed my new friend—yes, I was beginning to think of him as my friend!—searching all his pockets. Nothing. He looked so disappointed that I wondered if I should give him an offering. *No. He might be offended. Adults give offering money only to little children. But . . . maybe he's one of God's little children.* Impulsively I reached over, touched his arm, and offered him a dollar bill.

His face crinkled into a huge smile. He knew what the dollar bill was for! He looked positively ecstatic. When the paper carton for the offering came down our row, a wrinkled, trembling hand proudly placed "his" dollar bill in the container. Satisfaction wreathed his face and entire body. *He* had given an offering to the Lord! *He* could give—just like everyone else. He seemed to sit more proudly, head and shoulders erect, his whole demeanor changed.

I felt ecstatic too. My giving had been accepted in the spirit in which I had offered it. In some small corner of my mind I wondered, *How often have I hesitated to give, afraid to offend, afraid my gift might be rejected or misunderstood, afraid it wouldn't be "just right"?* And then I heard the gentle voice of the Spirit. *God gave. His gift was rejected and misunderstood. But He gave anyway. Give with love. God will take care of the outcome.*

DONNA J. HABENICHT

JULY 9

The Miracle Dish

And my God will supply all your needs out of the magnificence of his riches in Christ Jesus. Phil. 4:19, REB.

The week was just beginning, and I knew that I wouldn't be getting paid for almost two weeks. I had no other income, for my husband and I had separated and I didn't want to ask him for money.

I had sifted through all my options but one. I really needed to sell something. That evening I had just put the children to bed and was relaxing in front of the TV with my knitting in hand when the idea hit me. Why couldn't I sell the hand-knitted dishcloths I was making? Someone had interested me in making them a few short weeks before, and I had been wildly knitting ever since.

The idea seemed good, but I didn't really know exactly who would be in the market to buy them. I knew that I didn't have much talent in selling anything, so this venture had to be on a small scale. I quickly bowed my head and stopped my needles from clicking and asked the Lord to help me sell my dishcloths the following day at the business college where I was currently teaching.

I felt sure that God would have to give me a miracle because of my lack of finesse in selling anything, plus the place where I would be inviting people to buy. I'd be selling to people who were probably in more financial difficulty than even I was. Even so, I spent the rest of the evening knitting feverishly—turning out 10 freshly knitted dishcloths. In the morning I tucked them in my briefcase and said another little prayer.

I arrived at school at my usual time—15 to 20 minutes before class and sheepishly went into the student lounge with my dishcloths. It was hard to set them out, but before the first bell rang for class I had made $20 and even had orders for more.

What a wonderful miracle! I had the needed money for milk and other food staples. But more important, I had the rich experience of seeing my faith grow—reminding me that it is in the small symbols of faith and prayer that great things are accomplished.   PEGGY JANELLE SMITH

JULY 10

Trust God When You Can't Trace Him

We are troubled on every side, yet not distressed; we are perplexed, but not in despair. 2 Cor. 4:8.

During our early marriage my husband worked for the navy yard in Brooklyn. Once he was out with the flu for three days. Upon his return the following Monday he had to be examined and cleared for work by the infirmary. The time it took for a checkup delayed his getting aboard the ship on which he worked as a shipfitter (one of the only Black shipfitters in that navy yard at the time).

He joined his helper, who was waiting for some instructions, because the hose for welding a job they last worked on was too short for their purpose. They climbed the stairs up to the main deck to retrace it and left a carpenter below deck working on a job.

To their surprise, a lot of excitement was taking place on the top deck. Small fires were not uncommon on deck, as sparks from acetylene torches would ignite from workers overhead, but they were quickly extinguished. This was no ordinary fire, however. Despite the fire department's boats that were hosing the deck, the fire was spreading rapidly, igniting the paint that was spilled from a paint drum accidentally punctured by a forklift.

My husband noticed cranes taking people off the ship on gangplanks, and as he looked around he realized that he and his helper were among the last to be rescued. They hurriedly boarded

226

the next gangplank. As they were being transferred to the dock they could see workers waving their hard hats out of portholes so they would be seen and rescued. Others were shimmying down thick cables that tied the ship to the dock, trying to escape the fire.

Meanwhile, I was back at home with my two young sons. One was sick in bed, while the other was watching his favorite television program, *Romper Room*. Suddenly the program was interrupted by a report and pictures of a terrible fire burning on board the *Constellation*.

I immediately tried calling the navy yard to see if I could ascertain the condition and safety of my husband, but all circuits were busy.

Friends and relatives from far and near began calling my home to see if my husband was safe. I explained that I couldn't get through to find out but asked them to pray for his safety. I felt helpless. All I could do was sit and watch the snow falling outside my window and pray.

The phone kept ringing as the television continued to show the burning ship. One after another of my church family members called to see if I had any word about my husband.

Finally I couldn't stand it any longer. I knelt down in my bathroom to petition the Lord concerning my husband's safety. Feeling desperate, I asked Him to keep the phone from ringing again unless it was my husband.

About 20 minutes passed, and the telephone remained quiet. Suddenly its ring broke the silence. It was my husband on the line. I almost jumped though the telephone with joy. I then knelt down and thanked the all-hearing God of heaven for a direct answer to my prayers.

My husband told me that after he was rescued he immediately ran to a telephone but had to wait his turn in line, as his fellow employees were doing the same. Every time he found the line busy because of all the well-wishers calling me, he stepped out of line to permit others to call, then waited to try again.

Fifty men lost their lives below deck, including the carpenter who stayed behind when my husband went on deck.

This near tragedy brought me closer to God, increasing my faith in Him and in prayer. The experience changed my husband, too. He became a minister of the gospel and has dedicated his life to saving souls who are bound in darkness, trapped by the sins of this world.

RUBY E. FOSTER

God's Timing—Part 1

Now glory be to God who by his mighty power at work within us is able to do far more than we would ever dare to ask or even dream of—infinitely beyond our highest prayers, desires, thoughts, or hopes. Eph. 3:20, TLB.

Driving back home from the airport, I let the tears flow freely. I didn't have to be brave. No one could see me now. I'd just sent my husband off for another five-week evangelistic series, and my heart was heavy with loneliness. We were living in Singapore, where our youngest was in the academy. I spent my days working in the accounting office.

It hadn't always been that way. For our first two years of mission service I had been able to travel with my husband. We both enjoyed the meetings held in different countries and the experience of learning to appreciate various cultures, living conditions, and foods. It was exciting to watch God open the hearts of those who came to listen and learn of Jesus' love for them.

What is the matter with me now? I asked myself. *How can I be so unhappy when I have the opportunity to live on this compound with so many lovely people? Everyone else always seems so cheerful. Why do I feel so sad?*

As I entered the gate and drove up to our house my thoughts became a prayer. "Lord, I know I'm not handling this very well. It's selfish for me to dwell on myself, but right now I'm just not able to cope. Lord, You are going to have to help me. Please lift this burden of sadness and depression and show me this is Your plan for our lives at this time, and You are going to see us through."

I didn't want to go back into the house to face the duties there, so I walked around to the opposite yard. Suddenly, I couldn't believe my eyes. Our six-foot gardenia bush—which usually had one or two blossoms each week—was covered with flowers! A grand display of perhaps 30 of the creamy white blossoms. The air was heavy with their fragrance, and I closed my eyes and drank in the sweet scent. It took me back to the first corsage my husband had given me, early in our friendship. I've loved the fragrance ever since.

After standing amazed for several minutes, I had to praise the Lord for showing me His love in such a special way. I realized that He had been preparing these blossoms for my enjoyment long before I called for His help. Tears of joy filled my eyes as I gathered flowers for every room in the house. More flowers remained on the bush, so I took a basket to each home on the compound. By the time I finished delivering the bouquets and telling others the beautiful thing the Lord had done for me, my heart was truly singing.

If I'm ever tempted to doubt the Lord, I just think back to this experience and know He has something planned for me far better than I can even imagine. MARIANETTE JOHNSTON

JULY 12

God's Timing—Part 2

Because your love is better than life, my lips will glorify you. Ps. 63:3, NIV.

My surgery was scheduled for the next morning. The nurses had finished the necessary evening care and visitors had gone their way. Just before turning off the light, I took my Bible and opened it to the place where I'd stopped the day before. It happened that I was reading through Psalms using *The New English Bible*.

Before I began to read, I closed my eyes. "Lord, I know this surgery is somewhat routine," I prayed, "but I need Your assurance tonight. Thank You for Your care."

My marker was at Psalm 63 and I read, "O God, thou art my God, I seek thee early with a heart that thirsts for thee and a body wasted with longing for thee, like a dry and thirsty land that has no water." *(Wow! I'd just read the orders for nothing by mouth after a certain hour.)* "So longing, I come before thee in the sanctuary to look upon thy power and glory. Thy true love is better than life; therefore I will sing thy praises. And so I bless thee all my life and in thy name lift my hands in prayer. I am satisfied as with a rich and sumptuous feast and wake the echoes with thy praise. When I call thee to mind upon my bed and think on thee in the watches of the night, remembering how thou hast been my help and that I am safe in the shadow of thy wings, then I humbly follow thee with all my heart, and thy right hand is my support" (Psalm 63:1-8).

It was so comforting to realize that the Lord had directed me to that particular passage that I felt overwhelmed with His love. Before I went to sleep, I memorized the verses, repeating them over and over. They spoke directly to my circumstances and to my heart. I began telling the surgeon my experience when he came to pray with me before surgery, but the medication took effect and I faded off into sleep. Though I couldn't finish telling my story that morning, I have never forgotten God's perfect timing! MARIANETTE JOHNSTON

He Understands

My dear children, I write this to you so that you will not sin. But if anybody does sin, we have one who speaks to the Father in our defense—Jesus Christ, the Righteous One. 1 John 2:1, NIV.

How often I have agonized about my failure as a mother! Though I did what I thought was best in rearing my children to know and love God, as they reached maturity one by one they chose to live their lives apart from Him. This despair I feel is not mine alone. Many other Christian mothers, some of whom are the most godly women I know, express the same turmoil of spirit. "If only" they cry. "If only I had done things differently." If only! But even as I cry out to God in my deepest pain, I remember that He understands. He has been there! He was perfect, yet one third of His angels chose to live apart from Him. Even Adam and Eve had a son who chose not to follow God, though he had been to the gate of the Garden of Eden and knew the story of his parents' fall. I do not suggest that I have been a perfect mother. Yet my heavenly Father knows that I did my best, and He understands and weeps with me. It gives me courage and hope to know that the One who gave His only begotten Son to redeem me knows my pain.

As I daily lay my children on the altar of God in heartfelt prayer, I am comforted by such promises as Philippians 1:6, "He who began a good work in you will carry it on to completion until the day of Christ Jesus" (NIV). I know that as much as I love my children, God loves them infinitely more. He will continue to draw them to Him. He will never give up.

"The love of God still yearns over the one who has chosen to separate from Him, and He sets in operation influences to bring him back to the Father's house. . . . A golden chain, the mercy and compassion of divine love, is passed around every imperiled soul" (*Christ's Object Lessons*, p. 202).

Keep loving your children and praying for them. As long as there is life there is hope. PAM CARUSO

The Making of a Poem

There will always be poor people in the land. Therefore I command you to be openhanded toward your brothers and sisters and toward the poor and needy in your land. Deut. 15:11, NIV.

Some poems are born through hard work, struggle, and determination. Others flow freely from the heart, mind, and hand of the poet. In this instance, the latter was the case.

"Indian summer" is a term that Americans use to describe that period of unexpected contrasts in the weather just prior to the cooler nights of autumn. "My Indian Summer" describes the unexpected contrasts experienced on an unforgettable family visit to that ancient land of India.

The form chosen is that of the English sonnet because I wanted to make use of the two final lines, which clinch the soul of the sonnet. While this is not primarily a religious poem, it was inspired by the faces of the poor, those whom Jesus loves so much.

The lavishness of gold-embroidered saris conflicted with the simple cotton clothes of the people in the street. The exquisite furnishings found in our hotel seemed out of place. We could not eat the banquet laid out before us in the hotel dining room, knowing that others outside were hungry. Their needs touched my heart with indelible ink, etching themselves in my mind forever, inspiring the following words:

In Bombay's streets lay people, tired and worn,
Their homes mere sheets of plastic, nothing more.
The hotel where I slept held only scorn
For those outside its marble-inlaid door.
And then, on through the heat and dust to see
The tomb that love had built for a dear wife.
The Taj, famed sight, too beautiful to be,
Loomed like a dream, an image true to life.
A northbound flight transported me away
To Himalayan meadows, grassy green.
On Sunset Lake my Kashmir houseboat lay,
While I bought rugs and shawls, the finest seen.
An Indian summer ran its natural course—
A patchwork quilt of beauty and remorse.

Insert the name of the largest city near you. Add some local color. The poem will fit any inner city in any country of the world today. The nameless, the faceless, the homeless. Jesus knew what He was talking about when He said, "The poor you will always have with you" (Matt. 26:11, NIV).

Will today be the day when you make a difference in the lives of the poor, those whom Jesus loves so much?　　　JEAN SEQUEIRA

God Likes Keeping in Touch

I remember you . . . because you have always been my help. In the shadow of your wings I sing for joy. Ps. 63:7, TEV.

Singing has always been one of my favorite pastimes, but as a timid child I didn't feel comfortable singing unless hidden in a secluded place. My favorite spot was in the woods near my home. On this particular morning I couldn't wait to get to my "retreat" as April showers had kept me from the woods for days. The air smelled springtime fresh, and bright views of nature filled my eyes no matter where I looked. I knew I'd remember this day forever!

I hiked up inclines, around underbrush, and over stone walls, finally reaching the familiar log where I could rest and sing. As soon as I sat down I noticed the strange silence. I scanned the hovering trees and the leaf-covered ground for the usual animals, but none were around. I began singing quietly in the peaceful air, and soon I felt comfortable singing out loud.

Soon I saw a number of birds flying nearby and perching on the branches above me. Within seconds these birds were "singing" along with me! I was so astonished that I stopped singing, but the birds continued. As tears filled my eyes, inexpressible joy filled my heart, and I thanked God for this momentous experience.

I continued to sit there, lost in the melody of birdsong that surrounded my peaceful nook. Somehow I felt God's delight in this experience as if He had brought about the harmony of sound and spirit, and I became even more aware of God's desire to communicate with us.

Scripture verifies the importance of expressing ourselves to God, be it through thoughts, speech, song, or action. God wants to hear from us and speak to us—perhaps in even unconventional ways. I appreciate the profound words of David that I find throughout the Psalms. He sang to God from the depths of his despair to the heavenly heights of his life. The Psalms are filled with prayers and promises that directly relate to our lives today. One of my favorite themes developed in Psalms is God's love. His love helps us up when we fall, and enables us to put the past behind us. This unconditional love strengthens our spirits and faith to meet the trials before us, enabling us to reach out in love to others.

When we acknowledge God's unfailing love and endless blessings, and lift our hearts to Him in gratitude, I believe we present "music to His ears."   NORANN CUBBERLY WALLER

JULY 16

They Shall Walk

Those who wait on the Lord shall renew their strength: They shall mount up with wings like eagles, they shall run and not be weary, They shall walk and not faint. Isa. 40:31, NKJV.

"How could I, who have always been healthy, suddenly become so helpless and full of pain?" I anguished. "Will I ever be without this pain? Will I walk again?"

Just weeks before, I had retired after a busy, fulfilling life as a Bible instructor. My husband, Earl, and I immediately left cold Ohio for a winter in the sunshine state of Florida. But without warning I was reduced to pain and dependency by a herniated disk in my back.

I recovered sufficiently that we made a quick return to the security of our home and friends in the frigid North. Soon after our return, the problem returned with a vengeance.

I was in pain whether lying down or sitting up and could barely walk—even to the bathroom. For the first time in my life I had the dubious privilege of being served my meals in bed. I was dependent on Earl for my every need.

One evening we decided that in order for Earl to get some rest, he would sleep in the guest bedroom. From my large collection of bells, he randomly picked one for me to ring if I needed him. As he handed it to me I was startled as I read the promise engraved on the bell: "They shall run and not be weary, they shall walk and not faint."

Where did this bell come from? I had forgotten that I had it. How did Earl pick up this bell from among the many that were there? I believe the Lord guided his hand to bring this message just when I needed it.

When I looked up Isaiah 40:31 and the verses preceding it I

found further encouragement. The everlasting Creator-God does not faint or become weary. From His great storehouse He gives "power to the faint, and to him who has no might he increases strength" (verse 29, RSV).

I thanked God for these precious promises that were gradually fulfilled in me as I slowly returned to my active, healthy self.

Thank You, dear God, for the assurance and comfort that You give. Help me to always realize that whether or not You choose to heal or to direct my life the way I would want, Your guiding presence is always with me. Amen. — BEATRICE HARRIS

JULY 17

Why Not Ask for More?

Until now you have not asked for anything in my name. Ask and you will receive, and your joy will be complete. John 16:24, NIV.

He was a modern prodigal, so the story goes. Like the prodigal of the New Testament (Luke 15), he too had spent the fortune his father had given to him—and was now one of the homeless, finding his food wherever he could. One day he received word that his father had died. As he walked along the street, thinking about it, he wondered if his father's will would permit him to have just $5 so he could have one good meal. The thought made him quicken his steps, and he hitchhiked back to his hometown.

Arriving in town, the son located the address of the legal firm that had taken care of his father's business and went to the attorney's office. Two of the lawyers were visiting as he entered. When they offered their help the son said, "Is there anything in my father's will that would permit you to give me $5 so I can have one good meal?" One attorney gave an affirmative answer and handed him $5. The man happily left the office, anticipating all of the good things he was going to eat.

After the door to the office closed, the attorney who had answered said to the other, "What a pity! His father's will reads, 'Give my son any amount that he asks for.'"

Whenever I think about this story, I always wonder if this is why so many of us go through life with so little of God's love in our hearts; why we have so few answers to prayer; why we claim so few of God's promises.

We must learn to ask! There is no need to go through each day of life metaphorically with just $5, when we could have $5 million.

Are we not the children of God (1 John 3:1, NIV)? God tells His sons and daughters to "ask"!

Remember that our Father's will reads: "Give My child any amount that he or she asks for." Oh, let us ask—and receive.

ALICE SMITH

Finding God in Mother's Garden

Fix these words of mine in your hearts and minds . . . Teach them to your children, talking about them when you sit at home and when you walk along the road, when you lie down and when you get up. Deut. 11:18, 19, NIV.

Mother loved to work in the garden, especially with her flowers. Together we staked drooping carnations so they would grow straight and tall, and while we twisted the ties we enjoyed their spicy fragrance. We laughed at the faces we found in the yellow and purple pansies as we removed the faded flowers. Chrysanthemums were grown in the lathe house. All summer the plants were lovingly watered and weeded. Weak side shoots and buds were carefully pinched from each plant, leaving one large bud at the top. During the cool autumn days of sunshine and showers, each bud developed into a magnificent bloom of rust and gold.

The long row of roses along the front lawn also required our attention. Mother would prune, spray, and fertilize, and I would water with the water wand, being careful not to break down the sides of the basins of soil she had built so precisely around each rosebush. Once, when I tired of watering, I helped by digging up lots of little white potatoes, which I presented to her with great pride. Then came my fall. Mother firmly instructed me that those were the bulbs for her favorite bluebells. Together we replanted them. Months later we enjoyed the carpet of blue and green that grew from the ground, a carpet that sparkled with spring raindrops.

At night we would sit together on the side of my chenille-covered bed, Mother would read to me the lesson from *Our Little Friend,* and I would repeat the memory verse. Afterward, we would kneel together beside the bed, with our eyes closed and our hands folded, and I would echo after her, "Dear Jesus, thank You for the beautiful day . . ."

Thank you, Mother, for encouraging me to grow straight and tall, for helping me to discover laughter in the unexpected. I am continuing to learn how to prune out the weak, unwanted areas in my life, and try to not break down the boundaries that are there to protect and nourish me. Thank you, Mother, for helping me recognize my mistakes, innocent or not so innocent, and then to correct them. Thank you for showing me how to study and to learn, and how to talk with God as a friend.

"So if you faithfully obey the commands I am giving you today—to love the Lord your God and to serve him with all your heart and with all your soul—then I will send rain on your land in its season, both autumn and spring rains" (Deut. 11:13, 14, 15).

Thank you, Mother, for fixing these words in your mind and in your heart, and teaching them to me.   P. DEIRDRE MAXWELL

JULY 19

The Key

Judge not, that ye be not judged. Matt. 7:1.

I struggled with a document in my computer. There seemed to be no rhyme or reason why the words on that page would not line up or move to the position where I wanted them. Keystrokes and commands that normally would have resulted in predictable behavior now only produced chaos. Computers may not have "real" brains, but at times they do seem to have minds of their own.

I was at the point of exasperation when I remembered a neat little command in my machine called "reveal codes." This wonderful little key opens up a window on the screen that reveals all the codes that have been placed in a document. Understanding what behavior each code produces, you are enabled to reason from cause to effect and subsequently remedy the situation. After searching through my document, I discovered a misplaced and unwanted code to be the culprit, and its removal through my "delete" key solved all my problems.

Have you ever known people who were obstinate or unpredictable? Were you ever exasperated because they would not act or react the way you thought they should? Most of us have "codes" in our brains that cause us to act in certain ways. And most likely we are not even aware of the presence of those codes. Maybe their entrance into our subconscious stems back to a childhood situation. Perhaps they were implanted through the subtlety of the media. Or we may have even consciously implanted an obnoxious code or two in our minds on purpose.

So we must realize that people react to situations according to how they have been "coded" or programmed. Wouldn't it be nice if we had access to a "reveal codes" key so that we could peek into their brains and see what makes them tick? Reasoning from cause to effect, perhaps we would be more understanding and tolerant. Perhaps we would express more love and understanding instead of criticism.

But because we don't have a "reveal codes" key, we don't have access to all the facts, and that's exactly the reason that God tells us to "judge not." Only God has access to that key. Only He knows why we act the way we do, and therefore only He can be a true Judge.

So whenever we're tempted to judge the actions of our husband or children or that obnoxious coworker, let's remember "the key." Then we can ask God for help to look beyond the obvious and see the person the way God sees him or her, and loves them anyway!

NANCY CACHERO VASQUEZ

JULY 20

One Woman's Personalized Witness

But you will receive power when the Holy Spirit comes on you; and you will be my witnesses . . . to the ends of the earth. Acts 1:8, NIV.

The late afternoon southern California sun filtered through the pines and oaks along the mountain trail behind our home that day in early July 1987. Several members of our family were hiking with our longtime dear friend, Hulda Crooks. Seeking to acclimatize herself to the higher altitude, 91-year-old Hulda accepted our invitation to stay in our home situated at 5,000-feet elevation in the San Bernardino mountains. Two great challenges faced her during the following weeks—a proposed climb up Japan's Mount Fuji, and another planned ascent of Mount Whitney in California.

As we rounded a point overlooking the vast San Bernardino Valley, we met another group of hikers. Recognizing Hulda from newspaper publicity, one of them began plying her with questions. Instinctively, she responded with her vibrant witness to the value of exercise, proper diet, and healthful living, giving God the glory. She declared, "Climbing is a great inspiration. When I come down from the mountain, I feel like I can battle in the valley again."

Hulda Crooks knew many personal battles. While in her 40s her own health was deteriorating. Mostly because of her late husband's encouragement, Hulda developed an intimate relationship with nature. She studied trees, plants, and wildflowers. She began climbing mountains at age 66. "It's never too late to change your lifestyle if you realize it's not appropriate," she affirms. Personal vindication of this statement comes from the fact that Hulda climbed 14,494-foot Mt. Whitney, highest peak in the continental United States, 24 times from age 66 to 91. Also since age 81 she conquered dozens of other peaks and high ridges of southern California.

On Friday morning, July 24, 1987, not long after our hike together, Hulda Crooks became the oldest woman ever to scale 12,388-foot Mount Fuji, Japan's highest mountain. "Grandma Whitney," the nickname given Hulda because of her frequent record-breaking climbs of California's highest peak, didn't hesitate to witness on this trip also. She took every opportunity at rest stops with the various reporters and camera crews to express her personal faith in God and her gratefulness for His goodness. Hulda, a vegetarian and a Seventh-day Adventist, declared, "I don't try to make people believe everything I believe. . . . The Lord gave us all a very fine body design, and if we use it properly we can enjoy His wonderful creation. But it's foolish the way we use ourselves up. Life is so precious, and so many people squander it on things that aren't good—things that don't even make sense."

Hulda's witness has spread far beyond the mountainsides of Fuji and Whitney. Public honor has been hers on numerous occasions, including many interviews on TV, write-ups in national and international magazines, and an invitation to the White House. In 1991 at the age of 95, a rare honor dubbed by the Los Angeles *Times* as "A Real High Point" was given Hulda. After a helicopter ride into the mountains near Whitney, a surprise crowd of family, friends, and dignitaries participated in a ceremony honoring her achievements and naming a nearby mountain peak "Crooks Peak."

Yes, Hulda Crooks long ago discovered her own personal blueprint for sharing God's love. And He has provided her the strength to do it with every muscle and fiber of her body. His love through her has surely gone out to the "ends of the earth."

YVONNE MINCHIN DYSINGER

JULY 21

Family Reunion

After this I saw a vast crowd, too great to count, from all nations and provinces and languages, standing in front of the throne and before the Lamb, clothed in white, with palm branches in their hands. Rev. 7:9, TLB.

I love family reunions. There is something very special about meeting with relatives, sharing family news, and just feeling that you belong. In most Latin American countries the night of December 24 is a big night for family reunions and families eating together. Christmas is the day for presents, but Christmas Eve is the time to share love, to experience family togetherness anew. And when Latin Americans say "family," they include all their big extended family: brothers, sisters, aunts, uncles, cousins, grandparents, and anybody who "belongs."

We work at Montemorelos University in Mexico. Not being Mexicans, we are very far from both our families. Therefore, this year (1992) when I saw most of the students and many of the teachers leaving for home my heart grew heavy, knowing that we would not be able to be with any of our family. And it didn't get any better when families started gathering with loved ones on campus and I could see the joy of family reunions all around me.

Since I am an action person by nature, I started thinking about what could be done to give us some semblance of "family reunion" on December 24. As a result, we spent a very happy Christmas Eve together with five other families who like us, did not have relatives close by. It was a truly international "family."

Two of the families were Americans, one was from the Dominican Republic, one from Jamaica, one from Mexico, and our family—from Costa Rica. Because we love the same God and because we work together here in Mexico, we had become one big happy "family" of 19. Our group included a couple who are close to retirement age. They could well represent the grandparents. We had families with young adults, teenagers, and small children too. Our meal was a blend of favorite things from very different countries.

After this happy time, I began recounting the different years and places in which I grew to love different people as much as I do my own family, and how hard it has been to say goodbye. I truly long to have a "family reunion" with them too.

Then I remembered that we do have an appointment for the best "family reunion" ever. It will be a reunion "from all nations and provinces and languages." And I can picture God, as the patriarch of that great big family, and the joy we will all share in being together at long last. As in all big family gatherings, there will be joy and shouts, hugs and questions. But the best part of the reunion is that we will not need to part again but will be able to share fellowship for all eternity.

I long to be in that great "family reunion"! Don't you?

ADA GONZALEZ DE GARCIA

JULY 22

The Balloon

May the God of peace . . . equip you with everything good for doing his will. Heb. 13:20, 21.

It was a perfect sun-drenched day touched by a spring breeze, ordered by moms and 5-year-olds. It was just Jez and me, and the bright-green balloon tied securely to his wrist. It was one of our rare and special "no rules" days, a day for 5-year-olds to express freedom of choice, and moms to exercise patience.

The park? The bookstore? The ice cream parlor? Where do we go first? The choice was difficult! Time ticked away, inconsiderate of my son's need to make monumental decisions. The light at the crosswalk turned red, amber, green, and back to red.

"Hurry up, Jez," I said, concealing impatience with motherly overtones.

"An ice cream. I want an ice cream first!" he finally yelled with excitement, pulling me in the ice cream direction.

"Chocolate, chocolate-chip, strawberry, vanilla, fudge?" asked the woman at the counter. Jez's big black eyes looked at me for help, but I shook my head no, encouraging him to choose for himself. He slowly scanned the choices, then decided, "Chocolate!"

We walked toward the park, licking our cones faster than the sun could melt them, discussing major issues such as the difficulty of eating spaghetti and the advantage of zippers over buttons. Now and then the breeze blew Jez's balloon over our ice cream, spicing serious talk with laughter. A perfect day!

Skipping his way through sun-basking window-shoppers, Jez forged ahead of me. Less than a moment later, I heard a sobbing "Mommy, Mommy, Mommy!" I looked ahead, expecting the worst, and saw him. There he was, my little boy, arms reaching up as high as they could toward the big green balloon that rose farther and farther away from him.

I ran to hold him as he silently cried over his lost balloon. Between sniffles, he pointed to the store across the street, saying, "They sell bigger and better balloons. Can I have one? Please?" But my quarters were gone with the ice cream. I just couldn't get him one of those fancy $3 balloons. So I gently told him, "I can't today, son. Maybe another day."

Would he fuss, throw a temper tantrum, and cry some more? I waited for his reaction. I didn't want to spoil the "no rules" day with discipline.

Moments later Jez slowly looked up at me, clutched my hand, glued a fourth of a smile on his face, and said, "All right, Mom. Let's go to the park." No "whys," "buts," or "right nows," just quiet resignation. Unexpected behavior for *my* son, especially on "no rules day."

We tickled and played, tried out everything—the swing, the slide, the seesaw, and the sandbox, too. When it was almost time to go home, an elderly gentleman came up to us. "Excuse me, ma'am," he said. "I've been looking all over for you. Could you walk with me to the store? There's a balloon waiting for your little boy." Then taking Jez aside, he said, "Some of us on the street were watching you when you lost your balloon. These days it's hard to find little boys who don't throw a fit. We're proud you're part of our community."

Jez treasures the remains of his neon-colored Mickey Mouse balloon. When he is older, being bruised by life, I hope the memory of the special "no rules" day will be a balm of assurance. An assurance of the strength within him (and every Christian)—a Godlike strength that overcomes all.

How often we are satisfied with a purely random choice, reveling in the knowledge that we have done well. But it is when the balloon slips away and we smile through the tears and say, "Thy will be done," that we are truly sons and daughters of God.

FYLVIA FOWLER KLINE

JULY 23

Quietness

Be still, and know that I am God. Ps. 46:10.

After two hectic weeks of camp pitch, camp meeting, and pastors' meetings I needed quietness, so I drove to a sparkling blue lake edged by snowcapped mountains where I could be alone. In the stillness I sketched the scene in my journal, then recorded what I saw, felt, smelled, and heard in the two brief hours I spent there. The following is what I wrote on that lazy August afternoon.

"It's so quiet. As I listen, I hear the far-off drone of an airplane engine, then the hum of dragonfly wings. There is an occasional splash of fish jumping out of the still water, the faint rustle of aspen leaves and grasses at the water's edge. Ducks call from the far right side of the lake; a chickadee chirps to my left. A fly buzzes near my head. A family of 14 mallards make only an occasional splash as they search for food not far away in the grass growing out of the shallow water.

"I feel the warmth of the sun, even though I am sheltered in the shadow of the trees along the bank. I feel it more on the front of my body facing the lake and wonder if it is a sort of radiant heat reflected from the surface of the water. A breath of air stirs the pages of my journal and causes the fireweed nearby to sway and shimmer.

"The smell of fall is in the air. It is a ripe smell, a pungent, earthy smell.

"A small airplane roars across the lake from the mountains toward where I sit, skimming the tops of the trees, circling to the right. From some hidden spot in the grasses, a frog scolds the pilot for disturbing the peace of the August afternoon.

"Three fishermen, decked out in orange lifejackets, come across the lake in a low-slung motorboat. They disappear far to my right.

"Marsh grasses have gone to seed already, turning gold and bronze in the sun. The fireweed blooms are almost to the end of the stalk. Here and there fireweed seedpods have split open, releasing their soft white cotton. Rose leaves have turned yellow and rust. Wine-red rose hips dangle among them. Birches and alders are splotched with bright yellow.

"The strange, haunting call of a loon sounds to my right.

"Far across the lake the breeze has ruffled the water enough to catch the sunlight. It looks like a flock of a thousand silver-winged birds dancing on the surface of the blue lake."

Lord, thank You for this beauty. Let the calmness of the scene seep into my soul, taking away the stress and worry of my life, helping me to trust completely in You. I want to be as sensitive to Your voice as the aspen leaves are to the whisper of the wind.

DOROTHY EATON WATTS

JULY 24

You've Got Talent

For the kingdom of heaven is like a man traveling to a far country, who called his own servants and delivered his goods to them. And to one he gave five talents, to another two, and to another one, to each according to his own ability; and immediately he went on a journey. Matt. 25:14, 15, NKJV.

Perhaps you could say that I was born that way. I know for a fact that my parents pointed me in that direction. They took every opportunity to tell me and the rest of the family that we were born to serve others. The older I got, the more I wanted to reach out, touch others, and make their lives better. It only seemed right that as a child of God I should be a blessing to the people around me—friends and strangers alike.

Yet most of the time the feelings hidden deep inside of me pointed to the fact that my goals were mostly unmet. Why, I could not think of even one person I'd led to baptism. I couldn't recall one person whose life had been changed significantly because he or she knew me. What difference had I really made? Days blurred into endless days, and more often than not, I'd be on a survival course, just staying alive myself.

The path to discouragement is wide, well-traveled, and seemingly endless. Try as I might to avoid it, often the devil would whisper to me, "I've got you. You're selfish and a good-for-nothing. God can't use you! Aha! What do you say to that?"

I'd fidget and fuss at friends and family in my frustration. How could life be full of joy or service if I had to keep muddling on without knowing if I walked in the right direction?

How long the trap of misery would have held me prisoner I cannot say. But one day I learned about how God in His love had made each one of us with talents to be used for Him. Every man, woman, and child has at least one. The talent of *time* cannot be denied. With such precision it comes—in 24-hour segments—daily.

Then other talents came into my mind: money (whether I had little or much), my hands and feet, a voice I could use for good or evil—to build or tear down. Now I see the list is unending. Perhaps you will start your own list or add to mine. Whatever you do, remember, you've got talent! Yes, you. Use it for good. Don't bury it.   GINGER MOSTERT CHURCH

JULY 25

Unlimited Possibilities

Ah, Sovereign Lord, you have made the heaven and the earth by your great power and outstretched arm. Nothing is too hard for you. Jer. 32:17, NIV.

I was paging through my now 14-year-old daughter's baby book when I came across the following conversation that had been recorded when she was 3 years old.

"Mommy, will we go to heaven in a car?"

"No, darling, we won't need to, because we will be able to fly."

"But I don't want to fly, Mommy."

"Why not, sweetheart? Are you afraid of falling?"

"No, but how will I put my clothes on if I have wings?"

Obviously, her concept of heaven and of God was extremely limited to her short-lived experience, her inability of abstract conceptualization, and the difficulty of imagining anything different than she had previously experienced or seen in pictures.

As I was meditating on this conversation, scenes flashed through my mind of occasions when even I, as an adult, experiencing a personal relationship with God, had had a very limited perception of what God is and what He can do in my life and the lives of others. How many times had I said, like my daughter, "No, I don't want to do that!" Not necessarily because I was afraid to, but because it may have seemed ridiculous, absurd, unrealistic, or humanly impossible. Now I realize that on those occasions I had tried to limit God, to place Him within my own framework, my private conceptual model. I had limited God, who created substance from nothing!

When the pieces don't seem to fit just right in your life, when you feel that God is asking you to do something that doesn't seem logical and you are resistant to follow through, ask yourself if you are limiting God's possibilities to work miracles in your life.

Although we intellectually know it, in practical, everyday, down-to-earth life God sometimes has to remind us, like He did Jeremiah. "I am the Lord, the God of all mankind. Is there anything too hard for me?" (Jer. 32:27, TLB).

Let us tear down the walls that place restraints upon God's unlimited power and allow Him to change our narrow, restricted, shallow concept of what He can do in our lives today.

EDELWEISS RAMAL

JULY 26

Trust in Him

He that dwelleth in the secret place of the most High shall abide under the shadow of the Almighty. I will say of the Lord, He is my refuge and my fortress: my God; in him will I trust. Ps. 91:1, 2.

The sky was midnight black, though it was early evening. Time for me to leave for the airport. I had to pick up my husband and the division secretary.

Getting in my little red Volkswagen "beetle," I thought about taking our Rhodesian Ridgeback dog with me. But I quickly decided that wasn't feasible. She was so big there wouldn't be room for Ken and Pastor Ndhlovu and their luggage. But I felt uneasy, wondering what I could take for protection. I hurriedly ran back into the house and picked up a can of insect repellent.

Back in the car my knees began to shake. I'd heard of knees smiting themselves, but this was the first time I had experienced it. Until now I hadn't realized how traumatized I'd been by a recent tragedy that affected our division office.

Just a few days earlier one of the office secretaries had been murdered, and her body found in a culvert on the main highway. The road I was to travel to the airport went right by the spot where they'd found her. Since the murder, security precautions had been in force for all division office workers and especially for those of us who were home alone a great deal. This was my first trip to the airport since the day we'd discovered her missing.

I repeated various verses of Psalm 91 and prayed as I started the car. An immediate sense of calmness and peace came over me as I pulled out into traffic and drove to the airport.

I continue to marvel at the power of prayer. What a comfort to know we can go to the Lord with our concerns and leave them with Him. With the same peace and trust that God gave me that dark night, you too can trust in Him and His love. BARBARA MITTLEIDER

JULY 27

His Touch of Love

Be kindly affectioned one to another with brotherly love; in honour preferring one another. Rom. 12:10.

I love to touch people—to reach out to others. I must have been born with a desire for touching, because it comes naturally to me. Many psychologists suggest that we need 10 to 15 hugs a day to maintain emotional health. I believe we can reach out to others no matter what our circumstances in life may be—whether single, divorced, married, or widowed. Not only will we feel human warmth, but we can help to fill another's touching needs as well! Thinking of others instead of ourselves is really the happiest frame of mind. Isn't that what Romans 12:10 means?

I love to see others hug and touch. It makes me feel warm inside. How I enjoy walking into church and being greeted with a warm, sincere handshake or a heartfelt hug from a dear friend. I became especially aware of the importance of these gestures during a particularly traumatic period in my own life. I held on to these signs of Christian loving as I would a lifeline. In fact, I can still name one by one the people who were instrumental in my life through their loving, comforting words of affirmation or gentle touches, showing me they cared. These words and deeds are forever etched in my memory—still bringing warmth to my inner soul.

I'm certain that if I were to relate to others the impact they had on my life, they would not even remember what they said, the encouragement they offered, or the love they gave. The kindness of each may have taken but a moment, but it made *all* the difference to me.

Their special caring—still fresh in my memory—has taught me a valuable lesson. It is this: You may never realize how that warm smile, compassionate word, or loving gesture will impact a life. Jesus wasn't afraid to offer words of hope and to touch those around Him. He felt the healing go from His body and acknowledged a timid woman who touched His garment.

Let's be challenged to go out of our way to be warm and friendly. Let's make a place in our churches, our homes, and our hearts for hurting, lonely people, to enable them to experience God's all-encompassing love.

By showing love, you may give someone else a reason to live—and find true happiness in the process.

I love to touch people. How about you? Karen Kinney Shockey

JULY 28

Never Alone

I will never leave thee, nor forsake thee. Heb. 13:5.

Alone. I did not care whether I lived or died. Earlier that day I had wished to die, feeling too tired to fight any longer. Life had become too hard, too complicated. I seemed to have more problems than anyone else.

The hot, muggy air matched my withered spirit. Temperatures had soared into the 90s for days with no relief. I ached physically and mentally. I had failed in my set goals, nothing worked, everything had gone wrong. But on Wednesdays I always attended prayer meeting, and tonight would be no exception. After arriving at church, I had a few spare minutes to visit a friend in the adjoining hospital. I would stay only a minute. Following the visit, I felt more dreary than ever.

I walked to the church with heavy steps and heavier heart. Barely able to keep back the tears, I felt like a failure—and nobody cared! As I sat down in the pew alone the song service began. Even that seemed slow and meaningless. However, the enthusiastic singing of one member perked me up a little.

The sermonette began with the question "What doest thou here, Elijah?" I couldn't believe my ears—that question was just what I needed! I too had contemplated running away from my problems and antagonists. Like the prophet, I had no more energy with which to fight. The story described how Elijah became discouraged and afraid. A woman had threatened him and he ran 90 miles to get away, then ran some more.

The minister explained that Elijah needed to stop looking at his problems and look to God. As he did so, his problems became manageable because they no longer looked so terrifying.

I had looked only at my problems, without seeing God. Feeling alone in the world, I couldn't sense the presence of my heavenly Father. As I drank in the minister's message, my spirit revived. I felt alive, ready to let God have my problems. I needed only to look up.

Feelings follow thoughts. The Bible explains that as a man "thinketh in his heart, so is he" (Prov. 23:7). I see now how this is so. For the realization of God's presence made me feel secure. He did not wait for me to call for Him to come and help me. He came to me. Before I called, He had answered. As I sat there I knew the Lord would always meet my every need. He had let me know that the promise had my name on it: "Before they call, I will answer; and while they are yet speaking, I will hear" (Isa. 65:24).

My heavenly Father assured me that I would never be alone. No matter how "down" I might feel, He would always be there, ready to pick me up. I need not feel afraid, for He would not leave me any more than He abandoned Elijah when he felt down, when he focused on his problems instead of on his Saviour.

I left the church and got into my car, randomly inserting a tape to listen to as I drove home. What a pleasant surprise to hear the words ring out over the speakers, "Never alone . . ." The words seemed to caress my soul, bathing me in the oil of God's loving care. He was concerned about me. He loved me.

No longer alone, I experienced His promise, "I will never leave thee, nor forsake thee."   AUDRE B. TAYLOR

JULY 29

Unity in Diversity

How good and pleasant it is when [brothers and sisters]
live together in unity . . . For then the Lord bestows his
blessing, even life forevermore. Ps. 133:1, 3, NIV.

It's just a little wicker doll buggy. Some paint is chipped, and there are signs of wear. This carriage clearly has had its tumbles. But for having survived 50 years, it is in comparatively good condition. It no longer carries dolls to tea parties or a make-believe market. It now occupies an honored space in the corner of my sewing room as well as in my heart. This special little buggy was a Christmas present from Mother and Daddy when I was only 4.

In the buggy is another prized possession, a doll-sized quilt lovingly stitched for me by Grandma. Even today I can look at the bits and pieces of color and say, "I remember when Grandma wore that dress," or "Mother had an apron like that," or "My sister and I had dresses . . ."

Dark pieces, light prints, plaids, stripes, and polka dots make up the precious little coverlet. Diverse pieces stitched together, made into a whole. A lovely little quilt that has now become a beautiful piece of family heritage.

Have you looked around your home, church, or community lately? Do you see evidence of diverse personalities, gifts, needs, and interests? Can you find yourself appreciating the contributions each person makes to the whole? Separately we may tend to be fragmented—only bits and pieces. But together we can bring comfort, happiness, and lasting joy. May God bless as each of us seeks to appreciate unity in diversity. BEULAH FERN STEVENS

JULY 30

Made From Scratch

Train up a child in the way [she] should go: and when [she]
is old, [she] will not depart from it. Prov. 22:6.

Earth mother—that's what my daughters call me. As a young mother of the seventies, I baked my own bread, washed my own gluten, and grew my own vegetables. Like many women of my generation, I assumed that my destiny in life was to be a Proverbs 31 wife and mother. However, the financial realities and opportunities of the seventies forced me to expand my thinking and cut back on my doing. With reluctance, I went back to college to complete my bachelor's degree in English. On the way to graduation I threw in an extra major—home economics. Why not? I certainly had the experience for it.

Once in my new job, I resolved never to let my busy teaching career interfere with my desire to "train up my daughters in the way they should go." My little darlings would become proficient at the same delightful skills of homemaking I enjoyed. I tried, I really did. And at least once every spring I declared that this would be the summer we as a family got "back to basics." My eyes would glaze over as I described the quilt we would stitch and the garden we would grow. I could almost smell the aroma of homemade soup wafting from my kitchen once more. Summer would arrive, and before I knew it, it was the middle of August and we were back into another school year.

In spite of my enthusiasm and instruction, Rhonda and Kelli shied away from the very domestic skills I believed to be indispensable to any woman. I was horrified to discover that the girls ambitioned to become attaché case-bearing, cellular phone-wielding career women of the eighties. They placed cookery, stitchery, and other domestic skills with bell-bottoms and double-knit polyester suits.

"If at first," I reasoned. Abandoning my sublime arguments for domesticity for the practical, I reminded them that whether or not they married, whether or not they developed high-powered corporate portfolios, sooner or later they'd have to come home to an empty kitchen and a bathroom-in-distress.

Their naive replies ran from "I'll have a maid" to "I'll marry a man who likes to cook."

"Yeah, right!"

Somewhere during their late teens, I gave up. While I still required them to do their share of the household chores, I stopped harassing and accepted the inevitable—I'd failed.

"Face it, Mom. We'll never become happy little homemakers like your generation."

So you can imagine my surprise one Friday night in June, a few years later, when we were in the middle of a three-way conference call between Rhonda's place in Portland, Kelli's apartment in Walla Walla, and our home in Santa Cruz, and Rhonda mentioned that she and her husband, David, had enjoyed fresh strawberries with homemade shortcake for supper.

Before I could recover from my surprise, Kelli replied, her voice ringing with excitement, "Hey, Mark and I did too. I picked up a pint on my way from classes this afternoon." Her voice filled with enthusiasm. "What recipe did you use for your shortcake? I used *Betty Crocker's*."

"I got mine out of my *Better Homes and Gardens Cookbook*. I thought about buying those mushy little cupcakes from the store, but I like the ones made from scratch so much better."

"I know what you mean. It takes no time at all to whip up the batter and pop them in the oven. And you know they have to be much better for you." Richard and I listened in stunned silence as my two undomesticated daughters chatted on about the benefits of baking from scratch.

Betty Crocker lives! I thought. The words "by precept and example" popped into my mind. *More by example than precept,* I thought. I'm afraid Rhonda's and Kelli's perspectives had changed with maturity. I was relieved that neither had espoused the super-woman syndrome of the eighties, but had found a way, as women of the nineties, to combine their career goals with the values they'd inherited from the "earth mother" generation.

As I reread today's text, I'm sure Solomon was thinking more of growing strong mature Christians than of making strawberry shortcake. Perhaps, though, the process is the same. Trust in God is learned through example. Obedience to God is learned by imitation. Faith in God is learned at the knee of the faithful. And service to God is learned by seeing and doing.

While sometimes, as parents, it seems our lessons dissolve in a sinkful of dirty dishes, or our wise counsel is tossed in with yesterday's trash, Solomon reminds us that our efforts are not wasted. It's not always easy to remember that the proverb talks about the beginning and the end but makes no mention of the time in between.

Perhaps he knew from his own experience that children occasionally detour around fool's hill. Parents' knees may develop calluses from long hours of praying and their tongues scars from biting back uninvited counsel during those years. It is the happy parent who enjoys the fruits of her efforts, which just may include homemade strawberry shortcake.   KAY D. RIZZO

The Fragrance of Christ Within Us

As far as God is concerned there is a sweet, wholesome fragrance in our lives. It is the fragrance of Christ within us, an aroma to both the saved and the unsaved all around us. 2 Cor. 2:15, TLB.

I love my garden. I love the beauty of its many and varied plants and flowers, and I see God at work in each, with its own individual shape and growth pattern.

One plant that has always been my favorite is the "daphne." It is a rounded, bushy, evergreen shrub, grown for its very fragrant clusters of small waxy-white to wine-red flowers. Their delightful perfume pervades a wide area.

Over the years, I had nurtured this shrub in varied environments and situations, but when I came to our present home there did not seem to be any suitable spot to plant one, until my husband made some alterations and additions to our front entrance. Then there was a new space for a small garden—the ideal spot for a daphne—and all who came to my door would be blessed by its perfume.

I visited the local plant nursery, and a small daphne was soon installed in its new home. The shrub grew vigorously. Each year it produced more flowers and gave off more perfume.

Then one day I noticed some abnormal growth on a few of the lower branches. I removed it, hoping to prevent the condition from spreading, but without success. Gradually the disease spread to much of the bush and affected the flowers.

"Fungal disease," the nursery diagnosed. "Can't give you any assurance that your daphne will ever be healthy again. Better pull it out."

This saddened my heart. I was loath to lose the plant that had given so much pleasure, so for some time I let it remain and watched its gradual deterioration. The leaves yellowed and fell. The flowers became small, stunted, and only partly opened. Yet the delicate perfume still pervaded the area. Though diseased and sick, the shrub was still a blessing.

One day I made the momentous decision. My precious daphne had to come out. Even as I cut away its diseased branches, its lovely perfume filled the air. What a lesson it was teaching me that day!

When I'm not feeling well, what kind of atmosphere surrounds me? Is it a fragrant aroma or an unpleasant odor? Am I grumpy and irritable, or am I like the daphne bush, though diseased and dying, still pervading the area with its perfume?

I thought of my Lord and Master, bruised, broken, and dying, shedding His blood, giving His life that I might have more abundant life. Yet in all His agony and suffering, He breathed the prayer "Father, forgive them, for they know not what they do." The beauty and fragrance of that love still lingers in this sad old world and gladdens the hearts of all who accept Him.

Let us each determine by His grace to be more like the daphne bush, to have the fragrance of Christ pervading our lives, so that in whatever condition we may find ourselves, we spread peace, contentment, and thoughtfulness to all who enter the circle of our influence. VEYRL WERE

AUGUST 1

Something Valuable

Accept one another, then, just as Christ accepted you, in order to bring praise to God. Rom. 15:7, NIV.

Do you remember those childhood atolls, places, and times when you first tried on hearts with a variety of friends? The secret-keeping days. Sneakers and snickering. Best friends dressed in look-alike clothes—down to the shoelaces! Loyalty to the nth degree.

And do you recall how a group of three seldom made it? It seemed that the even-numbered bevies felt more comfortable (so that no one grumbled at being left out in case of whispering?). Fortunately, you matured and outgrew such nonsense. Or did you? Are you sure that you aren't excluding other friendships in your adulthood because you're simply too comfortable with the ones you already cherish?

Samuel Johnson offered sage advice about the awareness of heart-printing: "If a man does not make new acquaintances as he advances through life, he will soon find himself alone. A man should keep his friendship in constant repair." Naturally, this counsel goes for women, too.

Several years ago I found a way to keep my friendship garden expanding. I start praying for my new friends long before I know their names or meet them. My simple request goes something like this: "Lord, bless that stranger who is soon to become my friend." After all, God is the friendship designer. Thus, I've already prayed for them in advance and the borders of my heart welcome them immediately—and I gladly accept them. I know this is the new friend God sent me. And I know there's a corner of that person's heart already reserved for me.

Friendship, of course, is never a one-way experience, else it wouldn't be friendship. Friendship's artistry, provided by the brush strokes of acceptance, presents a picture to the world of something valuable.

To take on the responsibility of trendsetting via the art of friendship presents you with the opportunity to leave a legacy of love. Friendship-making and friendship-keeping allows you to enlarge your heart without limits, to flex the borders of your heart.

When the new friend comes into your life, not only do you delight in the discovery of each other but this gift gives you another reason to thank Jesus for His blessings.

There's a lovely poem written by an unknown author, certainly as wonderful a Christian friend as the one who shared it with me a few years ago. Now, let me share it with you—and by the way, let's be friends!

A Friend

I never knew God loved me in so sweet a way before.
'Tis He alone who can such blessings send.
And when His love would new expression find,
He sent thee to me and said,"Behold a friend."

BETTY KOSSICK

AUGUST 2

Self-Sabotaging Self-esteem

Are not two sparrows sold for a penny? Yet not one of them will fall to the ground apart from the will of your Father. And even the very hairs of your head are all numbered. So don't be afraid; you are worth more than many sparrows. Matt. 10:29-31, NIV.

A dear friend of mine married, birthed a beautiful daughter, and divorced—all without logical reason to me and with clearly observable distress. At times I have had difficulty remaining quietly on the sidelines, observing her suffering, watching her struggle with the many tiny catch-up steps dissonant choices required. Her life became an abysmal game, never quite partaking in individual success. To me, it appears she questions her right to succeed. Little does it matter that she is highly prosperous in the business world! Thinking about her private life of pain, I wrote:

Whodunit? . . . Sweet Saboteur

You appear in such quand'ry; is there something to fear?
Ugly secrets you honor, great pain you hold dear?

Has distress so enfolded, your reason's been banished?
Past effort to live life . . . all energies have vanished?

Could be I can hazard an unholy guess,
That what you've been feeling is self-sabotage at its best!

To perceive it, one must have done it oneself.
It's just watching you hurt recalls from my shelf,

We load ourselves up with "Shouldn'ts" and "Wouldn'ts"
If only belief would remove all the "Couldn'ts"!

Accepting ourselves with great admiration,
As wonderful beings—a goodly Creation,

Removing the power of the saboteur within me
Will give freedom to see the best "me" I can be!

Many times as I've reread these words, I have realized this message is also directed at me. Self-expectation can be quite stress-laden. We can either take responsibility to make change by visualizing ourselves as capable of learning to do or handle anything within our aptitudes or interests, or we can grieve that we are not as good as so-and-so, so we just do not deserve success.

Instead, being reminded that I am worthy, that I have great value—beyond that of many sparrows—has helped me maintain a positive response, where in the past, life's difficulties easily became insurmountable negatives. Awareness of having a loving, friendly hand hovering over me is truly a comfort.   JUDI WILD BECKER

Moving Vans

Trust in the Lord with all your heart, And lean not on your own understanding; In all your ways acknowledge Him, And He shall direct your paths. Prov. 3:5, 6, NKJV.

Mom bustled around the house that morning before we left for church. She placed the casseroles in the oven on time bake, gave my sister and me a quick inspection, and then pushed us out the front door.

On the way to join Dad at church we asked Mom, "What's going on here?"

"The conference president will be here today," she announced.

Growing up in a pastor's family, we got periodic visits from conference presidents, and we knew what they meant—soon a moving van would pull into our driveway and carry all our furniture away. We would follow, of course. Away from our friends. Away from our home. Away from everything familiar.

That day the conference president had come all the way from California. He wanted Dad to pastor a church on the other side of the United States.

My sister and I ran out of the house and sat by the creek. We cried and vowed to stay behind and live with our friends. But somehow we ended up in the car heading for California.

When we got to our destination, I dreaded starting a new school. But once I'd settled in, I discovered that my new teacher actually liked me. Evidently my teacher back east hadn't sent word of how I'd always been in trouble. I'd spent half of fourth grade sitting out in the hall, where my teacher would ban me with my desk.

Now suddenly my new teacher thought I had some writing ability and encouraged me to write. She even sent some of my poems to a local newspaper competition, and one got printed. Suddenly I began to love school.

When I'd seen that moving van pull into our driveway, my heart had sunk. But I hadn't counted on God's principle of "something better."

Since grade school I've made other moves. And although moves are always painful and involve loss, God inevitably brings us something better. A new experience to help us grow. A new friend. A new understanding of His presence.

I'm not as afraid of moving vans anymore.   LORI PECKHAM

AUGUST 4

A Lesson in a Margin Shell

He who is faithful in a very little thing is faithful also in much; and he who is unrighteous in a very little thing is unrighteous also in much. Luke 16:10, NASB.

One evening while collecting shells in some eel grass at low tide, an expert collector friend of mine commented to me about the uncommon margin shell I'd just found. "But it looks almost like the common species," I told her. But as I looked closely, I noticed it didn't have any little dots. Such a small detail, yet that small detail made the difference between the common and the rare.

As I contemplated this seemingly small detail in nature, I thought about many other small details that God created that do make a difference. This tells me that God is even more interested in the small aspects of my life. It tells me that how I attend to the seemingly small routine duties is important.

Also, the small joys we can bring to others are important—a smile, a few words of encouragement, a touch, a helping hand, a short note. These small things are little exercises in our faith and trust in God, ways that we express our hope to others.

It has been said that the secret of life's success is in a careful and conscientious attention to the little things. God took as much care to make a simple leaf and tiny flower as He did to create the world. Likewise, the symmetrical structure of a strong, beautiful character is built up by each act of duty. We need to be faithful in the little things as well as in the greatest responsibilities. Our work cannot bear the inspection of God unless it is found to include a faithful, diligent, economical care for the little things.

We cannot doubt the importance God puts on the little things in our lives when we consider the detail in nature such as the dots on the tiny margin shell.   MARILEE MCNEILUS

AUGUST 5

Encounter With God

Be still and know that I am God. Ps. 46:10.

Another hectic Friday afternoon. No matter how well I plan, Fridays often become too busy. This day was no exception.

Impatiently I turned the key in the church door and dashed into the cool, empty sanctuary. I walked quickly down the darkened side aisle, glancing along each pew to be sure everything was in place for the Sabbath services. Into the children's rooms I hurried, putting away stray hymnbooks and papers. Through the pastor's study, the kitchen, and the restrooms, eyeing the walls for unwanted fingerprints. Mechanically—from months of experience—I straightened pictures, closed cupboard doors, and changed the towels. Tomorrow the rooms would be filled with chattering children and happy adults, but at this hour all was quiet except for my footsteps echoing on silent walls.

Still racing, I took three or four hasty steps into the cathedral-ceilinged sanctuary, unaware of anything unusual. I glanced at the hymnal racks and the ferns standing on each side of the pulpit. Suddenly I stopped. I don't know what stopped me. Maybe it was the sanctuary stillness contrasting so sharply with my rushed hurriedness. Or was it God's presence that awed and overwhelmed me? Before I realized what I was doing, I was on my knees in the center aisle speaking aloud to a God I could not see, yet whose presence I could not deny.

"O Lord, this is Your house. You live here. Yet I've not even taken the time to greet You. Week after week, for nearly two years, I've run in and out of Your house—Your presence—thinking only of my duties, my responsibility to keep Your house neat and tidy. But I've not spoken to You before today. I've not even said, 'Hello.' Forgive me, Lord. I've been very impolite. But more than just politeness, Lord, I've missed the opportunity of talking with You—alone—here in this quiet place. O God, have You been here all the time, waiting, hoping, longing for me to stop for just a moment and talk with You? Have You been waiting here every other Friday afternoon? When You heard the metallic sound of my key turn in the lock, did You hope I'd stop to talk?"

I paused, half expecting Him to answer audibly. In the silence I knew what He would say, what any friend would say. I responded, "Forgive me, Lord, for the many times I've disappointed You. I'm glad You didn't give up on me. You've been here again and again. Hoping. Waiting. My concern has been that the tablecloth is neat and hanging straight, that the flowers are in place, or that the carpet is clean. All those things are important, but slow me down, Lord. I long to be filled with Your love."

I remained kneeling in the silence for a long moment, overwhelmed with His nearness.

Slowly I rose from my knees, reluctant to leave the warmth of God's presence, reluctant to leave my patient Friend. A renewing peace enveloped me. "I'll return, Lord. I'll stop next time. I want to meet You here again." My voice was small in the large, silent room.

But the sanctuary had changed since my encounter with God. No longer was the room empty and dark. Sunlight streamed through the stained-glass windows, flooding the room around me with a golden glow. I basked in its warmth. As I turned to leave I imagined God surrounded with the sunlight, a smile of joy flooding His face. I had stopped and talked with God!

HEATHER GUTTSCHUSS

The Self-rising Christian Woman

The kingdom of heaven is like unto leaven, which a woman took, and hid in three measures of meal, till the whole was leavened. Matt. 13:33.

During a visit to my mother's home, I decided to make a sweet potato pie even though the only flour Mom had in the cabinet was self-rising. Hoping to counteract the self-rising effect, I rolled the piecrust as thin as possible before pouring in the filling. But even though I'd thoroughly pressed down the crust, when I took the baked pie out of the oven it was easy to see that the crust had risen.

That experience made me think. No matter what I did to the crust, I couldn't stop the self-rising quality of the flour. A Christian woman is like self-rising flour, I pondered. She is often pressed down with the rolling pin of family illnesses, problems with child rearing, endless household duties, employment responsibilities outside of the home, church responsibilities, and personal problems. Yet she has the tenacity to rise above it all and face each day joyfully, knowing that Christ is by her side walking with her each step of the way.

However, this self-rising quality can be accomplished only when God is daily given first place in her life. He is the only one who can help her meet and conquer daily trials. The rolling pin of adversity may press ever so hard, but the self-rising quality of the Holy Spirit will help the Christian woman rise with singing in her heart as she praises her Saviour for His many blessings.

God's Word will comfort the Christian woman and give her peace in the midst of the storm. The promise of 1 Peter 5:7 will remind her of God's love for her: "Casting all your care upon him; for he careth for you." With this and other beautiful passages from His Word, she can face the myriads of problems that inevitably confront her in both the home and community. Victory will be hers, and she will be successful—like my self-rising piecrust.

RUTH F. DAVIS

As a Little Child

Except ye be converted, and become as little children, ye shall not enter into the kingdom of heaven. Matt. 18:3.

My older children were born in the 1930s while we still suffered the effects of the Great Depression. Our farm life provided food, but money for clothes and other "extras" was practically nonexistent. And little boys grow! With springtime they could discard their winter coats but still needed a light wrap. Mickey's one sweater barely covered his elbows or his tummy. Worn for play, it became stained and torn.

The Saturday night trip to town was an important event for most farmers. Mickey liked to walk through the stores and look at all the pretty things. But on this particular night, he stayed in the car with Daddy and baby brother while I searched for a sweater in the few stores our small town provided. I found a pile of them, but the $1.10 they cost was more than our strained budget would stand. Sadly, I returned to the car and told Mickey that we'd have to wait until next week. His patient acceptance hurt me more than a violent protest would have.

The next week proved to be financially more stringent yet. Again I had to tell him we must wait. Bravely he swallowed his disappointment, saying that Jesus would help us.

As I listened to his confident prayers, I inwardly determined he would get his sweater if we didn't eat next week. But as we started for town the next Saturday night my husband told me, "You'll have to cut the groceries to the bone tonight. I had to buy a part for the car."

All the way into town Mickey chattered about the sweater Jesus would give him. I tried to bolster my faith by his, but there was no way I could squeeze $1.10 from our small grocery allotment. "Please, Lord," I prayed. "I don't know how, but honor this little boy's faith. He trusts You."

With not the slightest idea of what my procedure would be, I strode purposefully to the department store. I found the same pile of sweaters. But lying on top was a pretty, fuzzy blue one marked 29 cents. All the rest were $1.10.

I could hardly believe it. Shakily I asked a clerk, "Is there some mistake?"

She smiled brightly. "That sweater was left over from last year, found in the stockroom yesterday. These others are part wool. This one is brushed cotton, but it is very warm."

I carefully counted out the coins and hurried to the car.

Naturally, it fit perfectly. It was made by angels. Mickey happily wore it as he looked at the pretty things in the store. Some folks smiled at the boy in the fuzzy, blue sweater—just the color of his shining eyes. A few may have noticed that his mother's eyes were shining too.   LILLIAN LAWRENCE

AUGUST 8

Lights Are Gone?

But ye . . . are not in darkness, that that day should overtake you as a thief. Ye are all children of the light and the children of the day: we are not of the night, nor of darkness. 1 Thess. 5:4, 5.

The day was passing. It was about 2:30 p.m. when I opened the refrigerator for a cool drink and the light did not come on. *No problem*, I thought. I guessed that the current must be off for a reason and assumed that no one else on the mission compound had lights either. This happens every so often. After a few minutes my mind traveled to the load of unwashed clothing. So I went to the washing machine to begin the wash only to find that the water didn't flow in. No crisis; the wash can wait. My husband was in Cameroon. If he'd been home, I would have taken a different approach.

About an hour later I went to listen to my French tapes. I do this every weekday morning and afternoon (my understanding far exceeds my speaking at this point). But there was no current! I'd forgotten again. No matter. I decided to settle down and finish reading a book I'd begun and a recent much appreciated letter from our daughter Gayle.

Five-thirty. It was growing dark and almost time to close the shutters. My attitude of not wanting to trouble anyone was slipping away. Reconciling myself to the fact that a problem really existed, and wondering if my nearest neighbors had electricity, I ran across the compound and discovered bright lights all over their house. *What a pity*, I thought. *Why did it take me so long to realize that just because my house lights were out, it didn't mean the whole compound was without electricity?*

Fred and his son came with flashlights and checked our fuse box. No problem there. He then summoned another neighbor, who came immediately. After working for a while, the man told me,

"I'm sorry, but you need an electrician. We'll get one tomorrow."

My evening was short, for candles don't provide enough light for eyes already a bit dim. In bed, in quietness, in darkness, I had time to reflect on my "uneventful" day. My much-too-late conclusion: I was foolish to spend hours of uncertainty concerning my lighting situation when the same help called at night was available all day!

Then I began to ponder, Do I sometimes go along thinking all is well when darkness is lurking nigh? Do I ignore a serious problem by pretending it doesn't exist? Do we need to contact our "heavenly Electrician"?

One of my favorite authors beautifully writes: "Light comes to the soul through God's Word, through His servants, or by the direct agency of His Spirit; but when one ray of light is disregarded, there is a partial benumbing of the spiritual perceptions, and the second revealing of light is less clearly discerned. So the darkness increases, until it is night in the soul" (*The Desire of Ages*, p. 322).

It is imperative that we receive and adhere to the light God sends our way, keeping our minds open to its leading. It usually happens that one finds himself gradually slipping and waning in interest—until darkness overcomes.

May our walk with our Saviour be so constant and our joy in the knowledge of a soon-coming Lord so melt and subdue our souls that we stay aware of creeping situations that could alter our relationship with Him or weaken our witness. This awareness will keep us ever watchful, enabling us to care for each indication that might lead to the moment when the lights are gone and it is "night in the soul."

ORA NEWTON

AUGUST 9

Who's Afraid of New Things?

Because of the Lord's great love we are not consumed, for his compassions never fail. They are new every morning. Lam. 3:22, 23, NIV.

Ba-cho, a Chinese wise man, declared on one occasion, "Put two wings in a red pepper and you will have a butterfly. Take out the wings and you will have a red pepper."

When I study this statement I think how creative Ba-cho was in making such a comparison. In fact, it was not only the external shape he referred to. He was teaching the principle of how to see things better, or how to be innovative with common things.

Thousands of people around the world are used to doing the same things day after day without changing anything. A housewife, for instance, knows that when she wakes up every morning there is an endless list waiting for her—preparing breakfast, washing dishes, driving children to school, cleaning house, going shopping. It's easy to become tired and discouraged doing the same things over and over. But homemakers aren't the only people who face what can be boring routine. Whether one is a teacher, a manager, a salesperson, a gardener, a physician, a secretary—no matter the profession, all jobs can and often do contain monotony. The endless list of must-do tasks that must be done to keep things running smoothly.

It's important to consider how creative and innovative God is, and that He wants us to be like Him. He gave us special gifts and talents so we could use them to renew our surroundings. Nature has its own cycle, but renewal is always present in the new leaves of a tree, in the new feathers of a small bird, in the blossoms of a flower, in the seasons of the year.

Renewal means to develop yourself, to search for a fresh start daily, for God's mercies are new every morning—He gives us the power of renewal every day.

Why don't you try it today? Try something innovating in your relationship with God. In earnest prayer, tell Him how you would like to renew your life before Him.

Try something new in the relationship with your husband and children that will show how much you really love them. Try something different in the decor of your home, in a special dish, in the family worship, in your professional environment, and you will see that a "red pepper" can be changed into a colorful butterfly.

SONIA GAZETA

AUGUST 10

Light at Work

In the same way, let your light shine before men, that they may see your good deeds and praise your Father in heaven. Matt. 5:16, NIV.

Broken ribs, crushed teeth, a smashed leg, a coma. A skiing accident. Five days of darkness, silence. Terry, 14 years old, is in mortal danger. The darkness of fear surrounds her parents. They cannot see light. But suddenly people come who comfort, who help, and light pierces the darkness of their sorrow.

People who care are a light, giving strength to hope and courage to trust. Jesus used the imagery of light, referring to Himself as the Light of the world. And where there is light darkness cannot exist.

The light—Jesus—changed everyone He touched. The guilty felt the load of shame lift from their souls. Swindlers turned into honest men. Cowards became leaders. Adulterers understood faithfulness and pure love. Misers distributed their wealth. The super self-confident said, "Lord, I want to serve You."

And Jesus—the light—saw the oppressed, people who had never known self-confidence. He looked at them and warmth came into their souls. Something inside them became wider; something grew. They felt taller, stronger. A glance from Jesus changed their souls, held them tight, flooded them completely. His love said: "You are very, very precious. Let's be friends." He met people wherever they were and invited them into His presence. He unconditionally accepted those living in darkness. His eyes expressed acceptance, friendship, light. And yet today, through His eternal light Jesus can transform you and me into little lights, enabling us to comfort others with a warm touch, a helping hand.

Light shines when you cry with me because I am sad, when you laugh with me because I am happy. Light shines when, through the ashes of this life, you clear a way for me to your heart. When you have time to hear my sigh or to celebrate my deliverance from fear.

Like a warming light, kindness fell on Terry's parents. They in turn, formed a group that decided to encourage others weighted down with sorrow, to help them in practical ways as they had experienced helpfulness when they were worried about their daughter. Terry has recovered from her injuries, and out of the fear, worry, and anguish that Terry's parents experienced immediately after her accident grew a support organization without a name for families experiencing the trauma of injury, illness, death, and divorce. People want to simply carry "light" to others and lift the darkness in the lives of other people through the "weapons of light."

Ursula Strasdowsky

AUGUST 11

My Reality

For we do not have a high priest who is unable to sympathize with our weaknesses, but we have one who has been tempted in every way, just as we are—yet was without sin. Heb. 4:15, NIV.

It was one of those days! If something could go wrong, it did go wrong. I was one-and-one-half hours late to the women's Bible study, so I made a quick change of plans. I decided to stay in town, do some errands, and enjoy some time with my 3-year-old son, Joshua.

We stopped at a pet store, where I dropped three pounds of bird seed on the floor. Our next stop was the library only to discover that it didn't open for another two hours—by then Joshua would be in day care. Next I went to the automatic teller, but my bank card was at home on my desk. We went to the grocery store, but guess what? No check-cashing card. Joshua's hat was missing, so back to the pet store. After much searching, we found it in an empty fish tank. I stopped at the church to do some duplicating but was locked out of the office. We did get to the baby-sitter 15 minutes early, but she wasn't there. Thirty minutes later I left a note saying I'd be late to an appointment if I waited any longer, and took my son with me. As I finally sat down at my typewriter, I discovered I was out of typing paper!

Some time ago I attended the concert of a well-known Christian musician and listened to her tell a similar story of such a horrible day. I left the concert in "righteous indignation." Why, that person had no idea what problems really were! Her husband didn't beat her, her 13-year-old daughter wasn't pregnant, her son wasn't carrying a gun, and she had formula to feed her baby. Obviously, her testimony was only for upwardly mobile, middle-class Americans.

Now I faced my own reality. My difficulties hadn't come close to my fictional list of "real" problems either, but it certainly had been a stressful day. I felt weary and worn. Exhausted.

My mind turned to Jesus. He too grew tired. He was hassled by the 101 little things that interrupt our plans and purposes. He *understands*. He actually understands me.

Thank You, Lord, for Emmanuel, God with us. No matter what life's problems are to us, the reality is that Christ lived for us and died for us—for me. We draw strength from His experience. He loves me. He loves you.

"Beloved, do not think it strange concerning the fiery trial which is to try you, . . . but rejoice to the extent that you partake of Christ's sufferings, that when His glory is revealed, you may also be glad with exceeding joy" (1 Peter 4:12, 13, NKJV).

TERESA GAY HOOVER KRUEGER

The Blessed Woman

She selects wool and flax and works with eager hands.
Prov. 31:13, NIV.

Before you begin, you may want to read Proverbs 31:10-31.)
We had moved into one of our church's missionary homes, in Uruguay. Two American missionaries, with their families, were our new neighbors. Both the ladies were very friendly and pleasant.

Dorothy was tall and elegant, but above all she glowed with the happiness and kindness of a true Christian. She was the treasurer's wife and the mother of three lovely teenagers. Capable and diligent, she kept more than busy with her many responsibilities. However, she often found the time to reach out in friendship to me, a newcomer and mother of two young children.

Dorothy was extra busy during those first months we became acquainted. She was helping their daughter get ready to move to the United States to continue her studies in nursing. Dorothy was an excellent seamstress and sewed beautiful dresses, skirts, and blouses for Anita. She used good material, saving quite a bit of money by doing the work herself. The money would come in handy, since the trip—as well as college costs—was expensive, especially on a missionary's salary.

Naturally, Dorothy wanted to do the very best for her daughter. One day she showed me several of the garments she had made. They were professionally done and in excellent taste. I remember she told me, "The only thing left that I'd still like to do is make a linen summer suit for her trip," (in those days one wore hat and gloves on an airplane trip!) "but I guess that won't happen. I shouldn't spend any more money. But I know Anita would feel so happy if I could make her a suit."

The next afternoon I was out in the garden with my little ones when she called me over. There in her sewing room, on a mannequin, was a beautiful light-brown linen suit. It was almost finished, and was adorned with a lovely silk handkerchief. Anita would have her suit, and it was a classic! How much had it cost?

"Last night as I was going to bed," Dorothy told me, "I remembered that when we first came as missionaries we were given a tablecloth of fine material, big enough for a large table. The color didn't match our plates, though, so I'd never used it."

She'd risen very early that morning and with her experienced hands transformed a piece of cloth into a lovely, elegant suit. It had taken her less than a day.

"She selects wool and flax and works with eager hands." Dorothy Emmerson was not just a kind, pleasant Christian neighbor. She was also a modern "ideal woman," as described in Proverbs 31. She was an inspiration for her young neighbor, who together with her husband was just beginning the missionary life.

May God bless women like Dorothy, who not only teach the Word of God, but also work with their hands, teaching by their example.   EUNICE PEVERINI

AUGUST 13

A Living Temple-Garden

And the temple of the living God is what we are. 2 Cor. 6:16, NEB.

Many Christians have grown up with the concept that they are God's temple and have learned to avoid destroying their bodies with tobacco, alcohol, and other toxic or unclean substances. A quick look through the Bible tells us that "we are God's fellow-workers; and you are God's garden . . . You are God's building" (1 Cor. 3:9, 10, NEB) and "surely you know that you are God's temple, where the Spirit of God dwells. Anyone who destroys God's temple will himself be destroyed by God, because the temple of God is holy; and that temple you are" (verses 16, 17, NEB).

But it is a lovely new idea to me that we are God's garden. I love gardens! Now, a building and a garden seem different. A building is a place that occupies space, and a temple is a very special building to be sure. We associate ideas of spiritual activity like prayer and communion with heavenly beings that we cannot see with a temple. But a garden? A garden has flowers and beauty, life, aromas, and perfume! Who wouldn't want to keep a garden tended and cared for?

While cigarettes, liquor, and street drugs may not be a problem for some of us, we may have a greater problem with stress and abuse in other ways. It's easy to abuse our bodies by not getting enough sleep and rest, always pushing our limits for time. Some of us fight a continual battle with bad thoughts, depression, and despair. Still others allow people in the family or at work to abuse body and spirit by agreeing to do too many chores and assignments. They work too late, either at a job or in the home. And still others feel they must endure actual physical or mental abuse because of marriage vows or economical situations. Does God intend that this go on?

If we truly are God's temple or God's garden, we must take every precaution to tend and care for that temple and garden. Not only in diet and sleep but in mental and spiritual care. Some of us indeed need to look at diet and snacks and weight control in the light of obligation to God's garden. Others need to seriously consider how to adjust work and home schedules. And those who are in situations of actual abuse will probably need the help of others to reclaim God's temple.

God put us here on earth to help one another, and we must be serious in our attempts to learn how best to care for ourselves and to help others. Educational seminars on subjects dealing with health and wellness, support groups for a healthful diet, and support groups for those in abusive situations are all options to consider. We must look out for each other and be willing to change our own patterns as well.

Our bodies are a shrine for the Holy Spirit; the Spirit is God's gift to us. The Bible tells us, "You do not belong to yourselves; you were bought at a price. Then honour God in your body" (1 Cor. 6:19, 20).   JULIA L. PEARCE

Invincible

The angel of the Lord encamps around those who fear him, and he delivers them. Ps. 34:19, NIV.

It was my last day selling books. Tomorrow I was going home. Selling Christian literature had been profitable. I'd earned my college fees and learned a lot about myself, but now it was time to go home.

The sun was shining and I felt good. The pressure that I'd felt all summer had been lifted. I was determined to enjoy selling on this last day. I felt invincible, and nothing could change that.

I knocked at a door. A slightly unkempt man opened it. I explained who I was and what I was selling. He invited me in.

I sat down and started to take out my books. Then I noticed the empty bottles littering the floor and the stale smell of alcohol. All of a sudden I did not feel so invincible. It didn't take long to realize that he was not interested in my books. I felt panic rising in my throat as he sat down beside me, and I realized we were alone.

Silently I began to pray and, packing my books away, told him

267

it was time for me to leave. "No," he said. "Stay and keep me company." Again I said that I was leaving. He got up and stood between me and the door, telling me again that he wanted me to stay. I walked toward the door, and three times he tried to grab me. Three times he fell back as if someone had pushed him away.

I opened the door to find a neighbor just about to ring the bell. "Are you OK?" the man asked. "You just sold my wife a book, and when she saw you coming in here she was worried and asked me to come and make sure you were all right. The man who lives here has been in trouble many times and is an alcoholic."

As I went on my way saying a prayer of thanks, I realized that I was not invincible. But I had a God who was.   AUDREY E. BOYLE

A Light in the Night

You are all [daughters of the light] and [daughters] of the day. We do not belong to the night or to the darkness. So then, let us not be like others who are asleep, but let us be alert and self-controlled. 1 Thess. 5:5, 6, NIV.

John tossed his notebook and the hotel credit card room key he'd been issued on the bureau. It had been a long day. His brain swirled with all the new and exciting things he'd learned during the first day of meetings at the ministerial seminar. He glanced at the television and video menu card and shook his head. All he wanted was a hot shower and a good night's sleep.

The young pastor finished his shower. Wrapped in a hotel towel, he placed a call to the desk clerk asking to be awakened by 6:00. He took out his Bible and read a few favorite verses, then tossed the towel onto an easy chair and reached for the light switch beside the bed. But before turning off the light, he decided to leave on the bathroom light and close the door. Then if he awakened in the night, he wouldn't be quite so disoriented in a strange room.

Some time later John awakened with a terrible thirst. Drugged with sleep, he climbed out of bed. *Where am I?* he wondered. He scratched his beard. Then spotting the light shining beneath the door, he remembered. "Seminar, San Francisco, hotel . . ."

John groped his way toward the strip of light, opened the door, and stepped into the light. Before his eyes could adjust to the blinding glare, he heard the firm, gentle click of a lock. He glanced about in horror—suddenly wide awake. He was standing, towelless, in the empty hallway of the elegant San Francisco hotel. John had followed the wrong light.

Hearing the "bing" of the elevator and the sound of laughing female voices, he ripped the tablecloth from a nearby occasional table and wrapped it around himself before three middle-aged women turned the corner and walked toward him.

Wearing only his best smile and the purloined cloth, the preacher asked one of the women if she would please call down to the front desk on her room phone and ask that someone from room service be sent upstairs to unlock his door. He didn't try to explain his condition, nor did anyone ask. During the rest of the convention, the mortified man dodged meeting the three women face-to-face again.

Embarrassing? Yes, but hardly life-threatening. However, when it comes to spiritual light, the damage can be eternal. Ministries abound, each claiming to have new light. Cassettes, videos, films, books, pamphlets, and lecture series promote new discoveries on everything from the origin of man to the apocalypse and beyond. How can I know which light to follow?

Like John, the beams of light seeping under the closed doors can be confusing. It can send me in the wrong direction. Like John, the darkness can lull me to sleep. And when I awake, I will be disoriented. One stream of light can look much like any other until the end of our journey and the "door" clicks shut. Then it could be too late to retrace my steps back to the place where I first lost sight of the true light. Chilling, isn't it?

It would be except that I serve a loving Saviour, the source of true light. He does not leave me to wander after every foolish fable that comes along. He's given me all the light I need in order to reach my destination of life eternal with Him. By keeping my eyes focused on Jesus and by claiming the promises of His Word, I will not stumble in darkness. With the guidance of Jesus' equal, the Holy Spirit, I will not become disoriented from sleep. I will discern the light of truth from error.

Jesus Himself said, "I am the light of the world. Whoever follows me will never walk in darkness, but will have the light of life" (John 8:12, NIV).   KAY D. RIZZO

A Friend in Jesus

Casting all your care upon him; for he careth for you.
1 Peter 5:7.

When the song leader announced the opening song, it took an effort to keep the groan to myself. Of all the songs in the hymnal, did it have to be "What a Friend We Have in Jesus"? I first learned that song in our local language 30 years back. We sang it in English in academy and in college. Translated into Amharic, it was a favorite in Ethiopia. In the French hymnal, it had the same page number as in *The SDA Church Hymnal*. I thought it was sung far too often and decided not to join in the singing, to keep my sanity.

As the song progressed, I couldn't keep my eyes off one participant on the platform. I couldn't hear her voice above the rest, but her face glowed and her eyes shone as she sang.

"We should never be discouraged." She shook her head slightly, almost imperceptibly. "Can we find a friend so faithful?" Her look showed a challenge. By now I was humming. At the third stanza I was singing as loudly as the brother next to me, full heart and close to full volume, eyes still glued to this lady whose face and gestures had revived the message of the song for me.

"Precious Savior, still our refuge." The words burst alive with meaning. Hadn't He been our refuge just the night before? We were then going to Lusaka, Zambia, from Lubumbashi, Zaire, when my husband found the headlights of an oncoming truck too bright. Rather than undercalculate distance from it, he moved to the edge, bringing us off the asphalt road. The truck roared by. That was close!

We stopped to check our tires. "Oh, no!" The way our son Paul's voice sounded, I knew it wasn't just a flat tire. The sharp edge of the asphalt road had cut into the two left tires.

"Lord, if it were one tire, we could solve the problem. But two at this time and in this place . . . This is Your problem, for we can't solve it," I whispered.

Of all the vehicles that were rushing to their destination, and of all that we tried to stop for help, only one stopped. And its driver was a godsend. No, it wasn't as easy as lending us his spare, for his tires didn't match ours. But just a short distance ahead he had a friend who could help. He drove my husband to and from there, and helped us get back on the road. At almost midnight we reached the union office compound in Lusaka. Waiting for the gatekeeper to unlock the gate, we heard a hissing sound from a rear wheel.

"Is there trouble anywhere?" Yes, there was some here, too. But there was nothing we couldn't take to the Lord in prayer, no trouble that He had not made provision for.

"What a friend . . ."! When pressures and trials abound, I sing or hum this song to keep my sanity. BIENVISA LADION-NEBRES

Gratitude

And Jesus answering said, Were there not ten cleansed? but where are the nine? Luke 17:17.

"If we cannot be grateful for something bad that
has happened to us, we can be grateful for what
did not happen." Anonymous.

Any fall is bad, especially when you're injured in it. I recently had a bad fall down a flight of carpeted stairs going to the basement of my office. At the bottom of the stairs was a vault with heavy steel doors and a refrigerator. I had gone down those stairs hundreds of times over the years, and was always cautious as the staircase did not have a railing.

As I started down the stairs to get something on that fateful day, I lost my balance and fell headfirst with nothing to grasp to stop me. The carpeting cushioned my fall as I tumbled, repeatedly hitting my ribs and shins. It happened so quickly, and as I landed on the mat at the bottom of the stairs and lifted my head, I realized my glasses were broken and my nose was bleeding. The mat and the linoleum floor were stained with my blood.

By the next day my ribs were so sore I could hardly turn the steering wheel of my car to drive to work, my whole body ached from my bruises, and my nose was so tender I couldn't touch it.

Since my fall renovations have been made and we now have a handrail on the staircase.

My injuries could have been worse—much worse. I am not one that can give thanks for bad things, but I am truly grateful that:

1. A piece of glass did not go into my eye or cut me.
2. There were no broken bones—hip, ankle, ribs, or neck.
3. That the vault door was not open. The edge of the heavy steel door barely misses the rubber mat.

Thank You, Lord,
That You know where I live.
Thank You, Lord,
For what You always give.
Thank You, Lord,
For the Son that was given,
Thank You, Lord,
That my goal is heaven.

PHYLLIS DALGLEISH

Loyalty

Many women were there, watching from a distance. They had followed Jesus from Galilee to care for his needs. Among them were Mary Magdalene, Mary the mother of James and Joseph, and the mother of Zebedee's sons. Matt. 27:55.

How much of the Crucifixion proceedings did these devoted women observe? Had their valiant protests been drowned out by the shouting mob before Pilate? Did they also weep with the daughters of Jerusalem as Jesus struggled under the heavy crossbeam? Were they close enough to hear the mallet's thud as nails were pounded into Jesus' wrists?

Golgotha was no place for a woman. Who wouldn't recoil from ranting thieves, hardened soldiers, and mocking priests? Yet, they were there.

Had they been able, they would have stormed that cross to rescue the Man they loved. I'm sure they longed to offer Him water, to fan away the flies, to shield Him from the merciless sun.

Instead, they waited. I see them wincing as Jesus tried to raise His chest for a breath. I hear them crying when they looked at His face. I feel their indignation when scoffers taunted.

They listened for a word, watched for a nod, prayed for a miracle.

Three hours of darkness did not appall them. The violent earthquake did not scatter them. A bloody, bruised body did not repel them. They stayed by.

And when Joseph of Arimathea had taken down the body, washed and wrapped it, and placed it in his own tomb, Mary Magdalene and the other Mary were sitting there across from the tomb.

I am in awe of these godly women whose love would not let them forsake Jesus at Calvary or at the grave. Through the years I have met many women with this persistence and strength. By God's grace we can be firm under pressure, compassionate under injustice, and courageous under opposition! CHERRY B. HABENICHT

Time Is Your Friend

But I am trusting you, O Lord. I said, "You alone are my
God; my times are in your hands." Ps. 31:14, 15, TLB.

One of the ladies attending a newly formed support group for "women alone" shared with the group how she had gained strength from the Lord's assurances that time can be your friend. She indicated that many times she'd prayed, "Patience, Father in heaven. Please help me to be patient. I want to be saved, truly I do. Whatever is necessary for my salvation—I surrender all."

She prayed that often, she told the group, sincerely seeking God's direction. But many times she felt as if the Lord's hand in her life was more than shaping a diamond in the rough, as it were. It felt more like having a wisdom tooth extracted without anesthesia. There were the times she shared feelings with selected friends, only to be severely betrayed. The hurt went to her heart, stomach, and even to her toes. The pain was almost unbearable and unexplainable.

There were times when she cried out, "Father, is this necessary? I want out!" And then, reading the Bible, she saw in words that seemed neon-bright that "the peace of God, which transcends all understanding, will guard your hearts and your minds in Christ Jesus" (Phil. 4:7, NIV). She gained peace from this promise and felt her stress immediately calmed.

New crises occurred and the stress mounted again. Her heavenly Father whispered, "But those who hope in the Lord will renew their strength" (Isa. 40:31, NIV). Miraculously she received strength for the trial she faced then. God had intervened in all her affairs, and she discovered that time was indeed her friend. The clouds of bewilderment and the pain lifted. She had a new realization that given time, all pain would pass away.

God patiently works through our lives. He heard our sister and He hears us, too. When we wait for the Lord without fretting, ever knowing that He cares, God weighs our trials and gives us strength to assure victory in His own time.

We all live through periods of distress and hurts. In such tests let's allow time to be our friend. With God's help we will pass through the water and the fire without harm (see Isa. 43:2). "The Lord is good to those whose hope is in him, to the one who seeks him" (Lam. 3:25, NIV). CAROL BOOTH

Fire!

But whoever trusts in the Lord is kept safe. Prov. 29:25, NIV.

The sun shone brightly upon the fields of ripened grain. Harvest time was here! A time of joy and anticipation for every farmer. The big red machines had left the yard hours ago to go to the fields and gather in the bounty. Trucks filled with grain had been coming in regularly to unload and return for more.

I spent the morning fixing dinner for my husband, Darrell, our son Rod, and the hired men, Craig and Neil. To make the best use of time, I took dinner out to them. Since the men were working in three different locations, I'd stop at each field to serve the noon meal to the men working there. Standard procedure for busy days when it is necessary to make every minute count.

At 12:00 I set out with my car loaded with food. Stopping first to give Neil his dinner, I noted a pickup truck coming. As I drove on down the country road, I met Craig driving much too fast. Mentally I made a note to tell Darrell to remind the men that they must be careful and not drive so fast on rural roads.

Going on to where Rod was working, I saw immediately the reason that Craig was driving so fast. We had an emergency and Darrell had to know—now! Flames and smoke were boiling from the top of the combine. Pushing down on the accelerator, my thoughts were for the safety of our son. As I drew closer, I saw Rod digging up dirt with his hands and throwing it up on the engine to put out the fire. Fear and anguish were mirrored on his teenage face. When we arrived, he dropped to the ground in sheer exhaustion, knowing he had done all he could. The other men took over and extinguished the fire.

As Rod told us of his struggle with the fire our nephew, who'd been working a couple miles away, arrived. He had seen the flames shoot up from the combine as Rod was driving it down the field. "I was sure it was going to blow!" he told us. "It reminded me of 'Nam!"

Noting the position of the just-filled fuel tank in relation to the source of the fire, we marveled that it did not "blow." The financial loss was substantial and the timing of the loss of the combine was a very real concern. To be without a combine in the middle of harvest was devastating. But though the loss was great, our joy over the watchcare of our heavenly Father was greater.

Once again we knew that God has a special care and concern for each one of our family members. We lifted our hearts in praise and thanksgiving.   EVELYN GLASS

Come to the Fair

Thou art fairer than the children of men: grace is poured into thy lips: therefore God hath blessed thee for ever. Ps. 45:2.

When they were little my nieces were convinced they couldn't enjoy the fair unless in the company of Auntie Nita. Many's the time I watched their little faces, blue in the cold March wind, whizzing around on various contraptions as my hand waved loyally while the rest of me wished I were sitting cozily at home!

Why are we fascinated by fairs? Maybe you're not, but as a child I loved them and I've sometimes pondered the reason.

Why do children—and adults—enjoy fairs? Is it the hundreds of bright lights? The freedom to make as much noise as we like because we are surrounded by noise? The expectation of seeing the unusual—the world's smallest woman, the snake man, the rat woman, the five-legged sheep, and even a two-headed giant!

Or is it the sheer abandonment of being whizzed through the air as you scream your head off—half with delight and half from naked fear?

Is it the surrealistic food? Pink, green, or yellow candy floss (cotton candy); hot dogs with lashings of onions; doughnuts, soft and straight from the sugar bowl; coconuts; and brandy snaps?

Is it the doll you lovingly carry home, all decked out in a mass of white net and sparkly bits?

Or is it the thrill of winning for a change—even if the prize is only a half-dead goldfish?

I've come to the conclusion that it is all of these things and more. It is being out in the normally forbidden dark. Fact is, I hardly remember ever seeing anyone misbehaving at the fair. Everyone was too busy having fun.

The fair means seeing the unusual. And not, for once, turning away embarrassed, because you expect the unusual, the dazzling, even the bizarre, at the fair.

And it is simply letting go. That was my biggest thrill of all. Being taken off terra firma and shooting through the dark and dazzling night air. Something different. Something wonderful. Something magical.

The sense of fun, adventure, of really letting yourself go, was put in us by a God who is not afraid of fun, laughter, and sheer joy. Maybe these things are misplaced at the fairground, though I can't believe so. If nothing else, the fair gives us unemotional British a bit of practice at letting go for a change! Let's face it, it isn't until we "let go and let God" that we begin to enjoy the fun, the adventure, the wonder, the absolute difference of life as a Christian. Because He has made it fun. He has made it different. He has made it desirable. He has made it everlastingly exciting!

And, ultimately, one day we'll experience a real extraterrestrial tug as He pulls us through the air to be at His side. And then the meteoric rides we knew as children will fade with that earthly neon-lit fairground, and we'll be on our way to a God-lit heaven with experiences more dazzling and wonderful than we could ever imagine.

I shall always be thankful that someone said to me as a child, "Come to the fair," because it gave me a taste for experiencing the excitement of the unusual, a momentary but magical loss of self-consciousness, a sense of wonder.

And I shall always be glad someone said to me as an adult, "Come to the Fairest," because from the moment I did, I've had the wonder of enjoying His often surrealistic creations. I've felt the safety in letting go and letting God. Within me there has been growing the marvelous, exciting anticipation of a real space ride with my Saviour and a deep longing for the brighter lights of heaven.   ANITA MARSHALL

AUGUST 22

Take It to the Lord

Praise be to the Lord, to God our Savior, who daily bears our burdens. Ps. 68:19, NIV.

Do you ever get weighed down with the problems that others lay upon you? I used to, but not anymore! No, I haven't stopped listening, but I've changed my method of handling the cares and woes of others.

People often ask why I studied English instead of social work. They seem to believe that since my husband is a pastor, I should also be a social worker of some type. My answer always used to be the same.

I am the kind of person who feels deeply the hurts of others, and there is only so much that one can handle on their behalf. I was sharing this with Betty Rayl, from Baker, Oregon, not too long ago. We met at a women's retreat in Idaho and were chatting together. Betty serves on the North Pacific Union Committee representing women, so she has some deep insights into the problems that women face.

Betty's response was so simple. "What do you do with your own problems?"

"Well, I talk them over with the Lord and trust that He will take care of them for me," I replied.

"So why don't you do the same with the problems of other people?" Betty asked.

Somehow it had always seemed my duty in life to carry the burdens of others. But that burden was taking its toll. Why hadn't I found out Betty's way sooner? I think it had something to do with pride.

Well, I tried it and it works. Now whenever others feel like unburdening themselves on me, I listen. Then I pray with them and pass the problem on to the Lord. His shoulders are much bigger than mine.

If you are facing a difficult day because someone else's problems are weighing heavily on your heart, point this person to the Lord, then remember that "The eternal God is your refuge, and underneath are the everlasting arms" (Deut. 33:27, NIV).

JEAN SEQUEIRA

AUGUST 23

The Good Samaritan

Do not judge, or you too will be judged. For in the same way you judge others, you will be judged, and with the measure you use, it will be measured to you. Matt. 7:1, 2, NIV.

Clunk. Bang. Something was frightfully wrong under my car. It sounded as if I were dragging along a garbage can. Had I run over something? I pulled off the road and stopped, trying to recall the rudimentary auto mechanics to which I had long ago been exposed. My knees settled into hot, sticky asphalt as I peered under the Toyota. The axles seemed to be intact, but what were all those pipes hanging down in the roadside clover?

"Please, God, You've got to do something. I've got 400 miles to go, and home is 400 miles behind me. You shouldn't have let this happen in northern Minnesota—hardly anyone even *lives* up here. I've seen only a few cars in the last 50 miles. I'm alone and defenseless, so could You send me the highway patrol?"

Almost immediately a car pulled in behind me. It was old and rather battered, with a brown body and red fenders. A thin, wiry man walked toward me, his twitchy smile framing discolored and broken front teeth. "I'm Carl," he said. "Do you need some help?"

Oh no, God, couldn't You send someone better than this? I need someone to help me, not some drifter. And this guy's car looks worse than mine—he probably couldn't even get me to the next town!

Perhaps Carl sensed my skepticism. "Come see what's in my trunk," he offered. I could not imagine anything of any interest whatsoever being in this fellow's trunk, but I was afraid to be rude so I followed him. His hair was long and straggly, matted on the back of his neck, and his Grateful Dead T-shirt was frayed and stained. What sort of man was this? I tried to be brave.

He lifted his trunk lid to reveal a vast array of tools, neatly organized in metal trays. From a wrinkled Kroger grocery bag he pulled out a denim coverall and proceeded to zip himself into it. "Let me take a look under that baby—I do a little tinkering now and then."

For the next hour Carl went back and forth from my disabled Toyota to his trunk toolbox. He seldom spoke, except to apologize for not having any muffler clamps with him. When he was finally finished he approached me, his thin shoulders drooping in the heat. "I cobbled stuff back in place the best I could," he said, "but I ain't sure how long it will hold."

All I needed was 400 miles. I thanked Carl profusely and tried to give him some money, but he refused. When I asked for his address he responded that he was "on the move" and had none. We shook hands, and as Carl headed for his old Chevy he turned back and said, "It's sure hot today; d'you want something to drink?"

Before I could refuse, he reached into his back seat and brought out a small ice chest, from which he took two cartons of milk, an apple, and some chocolate-chip cookies. We shared them in silence—he was evidently not a talker. I noticed a bit of clover blossom stuck to his ear. Finally I said, "Carl, I think God sent you here to help me."

He looked at me long and hard, then spoke slowly, in almost a whisper, "Ain't nobody ever said that to me before."

After that I could not trust my voice to say anything except a small "Thank you." We parted with a wave, and I never saw Carl again.

My exhaust system held together until I was three miles from my destination, but the lessons I learned from my kindhearted good

Samaritan will be with me forever.

Thank You, Lord, for sending me just the right person.

SHARON HOLMES

AUGUST 18

Scars Remind Us

I know whom I have believed, and am persuaded that he is able to keep that which I have committed unto him against that day. 2 Tim. 1:12.

Early one morning I awakened to the singing of birds outside my window. They were attracted to a tree that was in full bloom. They seemed to be chirping a chorus of praise—high tones and low tones, a chorus of jubilation and thanks.

I rolled out of bed and fell on my knees. It was my turn for prayer, praise, and thanks to my God for His love and care. The Lord came so near to me that morning that it seemed as if I could reach up and touch Him. I felt a new beginning for me and I committed my life to Him for keeping that day.

What could go wrong on such a perfect morning? I'd dressed and hastily started down the stairs to the garage, attaché case in one hand, books and purse in the other. One misstep and I tumbled halfway down the flight of stairs. It was a terrible, jarring fall, but thank God I had no broken bones. I was badly bruised and had a serious abrasion that left an ugly scar on my leg after it healed.

One morning while looking at the scar, it occurred to me that scars remind us of events, circumstances, and consequences. They remind us of injuries from falls, burns, briers, moments of distraction, unexpected occurrences, close encounters, stumbling blocks, unguarded affections, or misguided trusts. These are also testimonies that we survived! Scars remind us of the pain, and the healing process; the lessons learned, and situations to avoid. They also remind us of victories we have gained over sin and besetments.

Although we may bear scars for a lifetime, they serve as a positive reminder of God's divine presence and protection. Then on a seemingly perfect day, when the unexpected event occurs and new scars appear, we can be assured that He is able to keep that which we commit to His care.

ELLEN ANDERSON

Jesus, Is It You?

She turned around and saw Jesus standing there, but she did not realize that it was Jesus. John 20:14, NIV.

Mary Magdalene and I have a lot in common. Our times and lifestyles are light-years apart, our choices differ vastly, and our personal views on family, religion, politics, and the role of women would no doubt cause each other great consternation. But we definitely would agree on our deep need of Jesus' tender acceptance of our brokenness, and our indebtedness for His proffered healing.

Mary has been gently (and not so gently) chided in sermons and articles for mistaking Jesus for the gardener outside the tomb. Instead of being oblivious to the unmistakable, critics say, she should have paid closer attention. We are in danger of making the same mistake, they warn. We must *know* Jesus' voice, or we will be led astray or lose our salvation. All of which has a grain of truth in it.

On the other hand, Mary paid more attention than anyone during the last hours of Christ's life, and the first hours past His resurrection. Her heart told her He really was going to die, when the disciples remained in denial. She alone tuned in to Jesus' words, saw the darkness ahead, and poured out her deepest self to minister to Him. She was the last to leave the grave and the first to return Sunday morning.

Intense pain blurs all other senses, and as Mary wept over her intense loss outside the tomb that morning, it isn't so surprising that she confronted the gardener. She looked straight at Jesus, heard Him speak, and in a fog still mistook Him for a stranger.

He didn't leave her guessing. He spoke her name in that familiar way, and she *knew*. He didn't shame her, either. In spite of her preoccupation and pain and lack of immediate discernment, He gently sent her with the most astounding announcement to the disciples. He entrusted this first post-Resurrection mission to a woman who simply loved Him.

In my pain and confusion, I don't always recognize His voice either. He waits, speaks my name as only He does, and sparks recognition. And then, despite my fragile faith and lack of confidence, He entrusts a special fragment of His work to me. What a wonderful risk-taker He is!

DARLYNN MELLO

Serendipity

Then Mary took about a pint of pure nard, an expensive
perfume; she poured it on Jesus' feet and wiped his feet
with her hair. And the house was filled with the fragrance
of the perfume. John 12:3, NIV.

Serendipity" is the name given a little surprise that suddenly
pleases you. It is not a full-blown miracle or anything that
important. It's not even something you have to have. It's just an
unexpected joy. It can happen when a friend does something
special, or it may be a delightful moment shared with a total
stranger. It may be such a little event that only you are aware of it,
but I thank God for these little surprises.

Let me tell you about one of my favorite ones. Several years ago
I had a job that frequently required me to walk a ways to another
building in the complex to get photocopies made for my office. It
was not a long walk, but in the summer, after coming out of an air
conditioned building, it could be extremely warm. At one particular
place—it never failed—a slight and surprisingly cool breeze would
waft across my face. It was such a welcome relief. Sometimes I
would be so pressured with deadlines and work problems I would
forget to watch for it. But all at once there it would be, and it
always made me smile and relax just a little. And it always made me
think of the goodness of God.

Sometimes when I listen to world news and local news, I think
how gloomy it must be for God when He looks down on our small
shadowed planet. He sees and hears endless trouble, endless
tragedy, night and day without end. When we get weary of bad
news we can change channels and look for a happier show, or put
down the newspaper and read a good book. Sometimes I think I
would like to give God a change of scenery. I like to think that in
the midst of all the sad and dismal scenes, He finds a bright spot in
the world. A Bethany-type of place that He wants to return to as
often as possible.

The Bible says there is rejoicing in heaven when even one sinner
repents. Naturally we want to bring joy in heaven by repenting of
our sins and by helping others find assurance in God's love as well.
But I'm not talking about such serious miracles as changed lives.
For no particular reason I just want to say, "I love You, God. I'm
so glad You are there." And then I hope that the sweet perfume of
my thankful heart is wafted, gentle as a breeze, across the face of

281

my Lord and that He smiles and thinks about the soon-coming reunion in heaven.

No trumpets have sounded, no great victory has been achieved, and there is still much work to be done before sin will be destroyed forever. But I hope the loving heart of God has been cheered by just a little serendipity, not unlike the perfume Mary poured out on His feet.   RACHEL PATTERSON

Surprise!

Suppose a woman has ten silver coins and loses one. Does she not light a lamp, sweep the house and search carefully until she finds it? Luke 15:8, NIV.

I don't know how often you lose your car keys, or credit card, or payroll check. It happens to me all too frequently. One of the few good things about the experience is that it is a call for me to remember this anecdote that Jesus told.

The stage was set when the "good" people of Jesus' day came to Him and accused Him of giving too much attention to those low in status.

Jesus loved to surprise and shake people up enough to start them thinking. I imagine that in those days almost no one believed that God would be compared to a woman. For at the time of Christ mothers and other women were considered completely inferior to men. Women were first their fathers' and then their husbands' property. They couldn't attend the synagogue schools. In most court cases their witness had no value. They were considered to be inherently more sinful than men. Yet in this story Jesus compares God to a woman who is looking for a lost coin. She finally finds it and then celebrates with her friends.

And there's more. The comparison is with a woman who drops everything to hunt for something she has lost. Lighting a lamp, she takes her broom and sweeps every nook and cranny of her shadowy house, listening for the tinkle of a coin on the stone floor. The woman's search is urgent, her effort unflagging, her attentions painstaking.

Remember now that the story is Jesus' way of answering His critics. They believed you shouldn't associate with riffraff—as Luke says, to eat with sinners. The critics want His whole ministry written off as a sham. "Look!" Jesus says, "God is *interested* in people like that. You don't have to overcome your problems before

God will pay attention to you. You don't have to be perfect before God befriends you. And because God is that way," Jesus says, "I'm that way too. You bet I eat with sinners and tax collectors—it's no scandal."

Again, surprise! It's natural to think that God's favor is something you earn. It's not. God's favor is a gift. A gift offered to flawed people, double-dealing people, despised people, people in general who don't get things right in their lives.

You know, when I think about it I realize that in a way I am like a coin lost in the dusty corners of this earth. Have you ever felt that you are too? There's nothing I can do in my own power to be found. Again, surprise! Even when I don't know my true worth God values me enough to search for me. There is hope for me even in the most lost periods of my life. I praise my God, who goes to extremes to claim me. SHARI CHAMBERLAIN

AUGUST 28

Prisoners of Hope

Turn you to the strong hold, ye prisoners of hope. Zech. 9:12.

A visit to any institution of incarceration, recovery, or confinement will find the occupants hoping for immediate or early release. Many claim that they're held through some error of justice, some misunderstanding of their innocence, or against their will. Some believe that their illness is not as serious as the diagnosis reveals. They become impatient and irritable because their confinement is for longer periods than they can or will accept.

Children in pediatric wards anxiously look forward to visits from their parents. They know Mom and Dad will bring a surprise—a favorite toy or a new one; an hour reading or playing games; maybe cookies or candy. Often, their hope is rewarded.

Through sin, every person on earth has been held prisoner by Satan. Those who have accepted Jesus as their personal Saviour and look forward to His eminent return are now prisoners of *hope*.

But in the midst of our captivity—above and beyond the strength and grip of the evil one—is hope. We look forward to deliverance by the Great Emancipator, our King of kings, our Lord of lords. We cherish this hope, our expectation of deliverance. Christ is coming to claim us as His own. Then we, the hopeful captives, will be set free from the bonds of sin.

We have God's assurance that there is hope for deliverance, if we are diligent in obeying His voice (see Zech. 6:15; Matt. 7:24-27). We are creatures of hope. Our world is now a place of hope. Though the night is dark, hope knows that every night is followed by morning. Hope enables us to face today, for it anticipates a better tomorrow.

"And thou shalt be secure, because there is hope" (Job 11:18).

Have hope, though clouds environ now,
And gladness hide her face in scorn
Put thou the shadow from thy brow
No night but hath its morn.
—Johann Cristoph Friedrich von Schiller   CAROLYN T. HINSON

AUGUST 29

Lost!

So do not fear, for I am with you; do not be dismayed, for I am your God. I will strengthen you and help you; I will uphold you with my righteous right hand . . . For I am the Lord, your God, who takes hold of your right hand and says to you, Do not fear; I will help you. Isa. 41:10, 13, NIV.

It happened so quickly that no one realized it except 2-year-old Chelsea. With the sudden shock of fear, she found herself in the middle of a hundred hurrying strangers. She was lost. As one of many children leaving their classes to meet their parents, no one saw anything unusual about the little girl who went along with the crowd as if she knew where she was going. She knew she was lost, however, and felt a desperate need to find her father. Without a sound, she ran down the hall to the staircase she remembered climbing on other weeks. The pupils in her large blue eyes were dilated with fright. But no other sign was visible to the many people hurrying to the sanctuary of this 2,000-member church, and no one noticed.

Meanwhile, Chelsea's father was sitting in a parent group discussion in another room, confident that the children were being supervised. He was unaware that quick little Chelsea had slipped away, innocently expecting to leave with Daddy as soon as her class was over. But not finding him, she had gotten lost.

As Chelsea started to climb the staircase, her grandparents decided to go downstairs to the children's classes.

"Chelsea, what are you doing alone?" cried Grandpa as he

quickly picked her up in his strong arms. Her little heart was pounding so hard that he could feel it right through his coat.

Normally chatty, Chelsea couldn't speak. She just clung to Grandpa as Grandma stroked her and spoke soothing and reassuring words.

"Did Daddy get lost? That's scary, isn't it?"

Chelsea could only nod her head.

"Don't worry; we'll find Daddy," Grandma told her as the little group headed back to the classroom.

There was Daddy. Even after Chelsea saw him sitting with the other parents, she didn't want to get down and walk to him. After the terror of separation and aloneness, she needed to feel the safety of comforting arms holding her. As Grandpa held her, Chelsea gradually began to enjoy some of the pictures and toys in the room—but only from the security of Grandpa's arms.

Later that day Chelsea told all who would listen, "I crying. Daddy not there." Even though she had not shed a single tear, inside her little 2-year-old self she was crying piteously. No one heard her for she hadn't uttered a sound.

Sometimes we too are crying inside, but no one can see or hear our pain. We may feel abandoned and uncared for. But we are neither, for the Lord Himself will find us, restore and help us.

SELMA CHAIJ MASTRAPA

AUGUST 30

Eve's Beauty Becomes Mine

Charm is deceptive, and beauty is fleeting; but a woman who fears the Lord is to be praised. Prov. 31:30, NIV.

One morning a few months before my fiftieth birthday I was standing before the mirror preparing for work. As I combed my hair I thought, *Say, I look pretty good for someone in her late 40s!* (To even *think* "nearly 50" seemed to be beyond my mind's capacity.)

As I was admiring myself in the mirror I felt a tap on my shoulder, and a pitying voice said, "Oh, my dear, you should have seen Eve!"

Startled, I looked past my face in the mirror and met God's longsuffering eyes.

"Have you any idea," He continued, "of the beauty that Eve possessed? The most beautiful creature alive today cannot even begin to compare with Eve. Oh, the loveliness of Eve!" God remembered sadly.

I dropped my eyes in shame before God's penetrating gaze. My own face no longer interested me.

"Eve's outward beauty cannot be equaled today; sin has continued for so many years," God told me. "But you may have her inward beauty. That can be as much yours today as it was Eve's in the long ago. I have made that possible. Physical beauty is a temporal thing and can never last on this sinful earth. The flowers bloom and fade and die. But beauty of character is eternal. What begins now in your heart can be the beginning of eternity for you. A lovely character will last forever."

I mused upon that morning's experience as the days progressed and my fiftieth birthday drew closer. Oh, I knew that God hadn't actually—physically, that is—tapped me on the shoulder. Yet the encounter was as real as if He had done that very thing. It startled my mind into beginning to accept the effects of aging upon my body.

Another decade and a half have passed since that morning when God countered me in the mirror. Yet the impact of that experience affects me still. Although aging is a natural process of our bodies and happens to all of us, yet I found it to be a strange road. Somehow I had counted on having eternal youth. But as I journeyed from 50 to 60 and on to 65, God walked with me.

"Gray hair," He pointed out one day, "is a crown of splendor; it is attained by a righteous life" (Prov. 16:31, NIV). And so, I quit coloring my hair and discovered that God was right! I loved the softness of the gray around my face. Why had I ever bothered to color it in the first place?

"The righteous will flourish like a palm tree," God reminded me. "They will grow like a cedar of Lebanon; planted in the house of the Lord, they will flourish in the courts of our God. *They will still bear fruit in old age,* they will stay fresh and green, proclaiming, 'The Lord is upright; He is my Rock, and there is no wickedness in Him' " (Ps. 92:13-15, NIV).

And that promise came true in my life! For now in my older years God has given me experiences that I had never dreamed possible. He is keeping me "fresh and green" in my personal relationship with Him, plus giving me unexpected opportunities to share this joy with hundreds of other people through writing and speaking.

One of my favorite praise portions of the Bible, Psalm 103:1-5, concludes with He "satisfies [my] desires with good things so that [my] youth is renewed like the eagle's" (NIV). As Christians we don't need to dread growing older. Though we may lose strength and energy and perhaps what is called physical beauty, those things will be replaced by a greater joy in the Lord and an even wider usefulness in His kingdom than we ever anticipated.

CARROL JOHNSON SHEWMAKE

For the Birds

Are not two sparrows sold for a penny? Yet not one of them will fall to the ground apart from the will of your Father. And even the very hairs of your head are all numbered. So don't be afraid; you are worth more than many sparrows. Matt. 10:29-31, NIV.

Awakening this morning, I heard a bird singing its heart out. It must have been very close to my window for its voice seemed to fill the room. Listening to it, I thought of the many different birds that had made an impression on me over the years. There was the mockingbird who sat atop our chimney when I was still a young girl at home—singing in the middle of the night! I remembered it when another mockingbird sang me a serenade years later—from my own chimney in the wee hours of the morning.

I remembered the beautiful kingfisher who fished our creek when I lived in Oregon. Very early in the morning, when the rest of my family still slept, I sat looking out our picture window as I fed our newest baby her breakfast. In its brilliant "morning suit," the kingfisher swooped down below the creek bank to catch its early snack.

Then there was the mother robin who made her nest in my plum tree near the kitchen door when we lived in southern California. I watched as she cared for those little chirpy ones each day. Then I watched in amazement when she tore her nest apart and those lazy little learners finally *flew*!

I thought of the many lovely birds I enjoy here in the Napa Valley, especially the little brown sparrows. They are common and ordinary like me. They pick and they peck and chip and chirp and try their little tunes without letup, until their short lives are over.

Those tiny sparrows have their troubles too, I've noticed. Adversity haunts them as well as it does me, but they keep right on singing. They sing, not because they have found an answer, but because they have a song. And not one of them falls without the Father's notice. The sparrow's Father—and mine.

I will keep on singing my little tune for I am worth far more than many sparrows! God *said* so!   VIRGINIA CASON

School Days

Being confident of this very thing, that He who has begun a good work in you will complete it until the day of Jesus Christ. Phil. 1:6, NKJV.

Back to school! The words conjure up so many memories . . . deciding which dress to wear on that important first day, choosing my desk, curious looks at new classmates, that brand-new look of bulletin boards and yet unscuffed hallways, bottled-up excitement regarding projects we'd do and books we'd read. Yes, I have very positive memories of "back to school" tucked away in my mind.

In my not yet three decades of living I have spent more autumns "back to school" than at home. Last fall marked the first year that I didn't return to the climates of learning and/or teaching in several years. And it wasn't without some melancholy feelings that I watched the yellow-trimmed-in-black buses stop beside leaf-laden corners to pick up students.

I'm finding, however, that I have embarked on a lifelong education, which will continue forever. Ellen White has said that "we are granted the privileges of school life in this world that we may obtain a fitness for the higher life—the highest grade in the highest school," where our studies will continue throughout eternity (*Selected Messages*, book 1, p. 245). And although I'm far from "the highest grade in the highest school," I am being taught some important lessons here and now. Here are a few of the lessons I'm learning:

• Only He who said, "You must be born again," can do so within me.

• There aren't many pats on the back for stay-at-home moms, but I love being one anyway.

• God is not glorified when I overcommit myself to even worthy projects.

• There are always more chores to do, so I must daily take time to play and read with my family anyway.

• Laundry is never truly done.

• A good night's rest does wonders to change my perspective.

• When I spend myself for God, He takes care of my needs.

When I step back and look at the lessons God is using to instruct me, I'm encouraged. How truly amazing that the God of the universe stoops to teach me! As you take a few minutes to think back on what God is teaching you, I hope you'll find new strength too. Welcome back to school!   COLLENE KELLY

That Missing "J" Key

I have come that they may have life, and that they may have it more abundantly. John 10:10, NKJV.

The *j* key on my typewriter doesn't work. It hasn't for three or four years. At first it was difficult. I would press the *j* key as I typed along, forgetting that it didn't work, and only later, as I proofread the page, would I discover the blank spots where the *j*'s should have been. It was something of a strain to think of synonyms for all words with a *j* I was unable to use because of the broken key. But with time I learned to compensate quite well. "Envious" for "jealous," happiness instead of "joy," "trip" for "journey," etc. It really wasn't too difficult. In fact, after some time had passed I forgot there was a *j* key. I had trained myself to avoid the use of *j* words for so long that I would automatically use their synonyms. The *j* words just weren't part of my vocabulary any longer. I didn't need them. I had substitutes that worked quite well, and I doubt that anyone even noticed.

As I look at how I've replaced the *j* key on my typewriter by using similar words for the ones I'd really like to use but can't, I wonder if I've done the same thing with the most important *j* word of all—Jesus? Do I find perfectly acceptable substitutes to take the place of a relationship with Him? Do I get so busy with my job, family obligations, and church involvement that I don't even notice that the place "J"esus wants to occupy in my life has been filled with a substitute? "Lord, make me always mindful of my *j* key—the only real key to an abundant life."   JONI BELL

Vision

Where there is no vision, the people perish. Prov. 29:18.

Vision! What is *vision*? Vision means knowing where you are with the Lord, where your ministry is going, and how you are going to get there. It is a divinely inspired insight into how you can minister effectively in your world.

Vision is a picture held in your mind's eye of the way things could or should be in the days ahead. It is personal. It's not somebody else's view of the future, but one that belongs uniquely to you. Vision for ministry is a reflection of what God wants to accomplish through you to build His kingdom.

It is the difference between "watching it happen" and "making it happen"; between "floundering in uncertainty" and "moving ahead in the assurance of God's leading and purpose." Women with a vision are Christian women who are making a difference for Him.

Let's think for a moment about Esther, a biblical figure who was moved by God's vision for her life and ministry. When Esther was queen a law was made in her country that all of God's people would be killed. The message to her was that she must go before the king and ask that God's people be saved. Esther was afraid. Why? Because a person who went uninvited to the king could be executed. But Esther had a vision of God's mission for her. She responded, "Appoint three days of prayer before I go see the king, and if I perish, I perish." Esther went to see the king. He accepted her request, and God's people were saved.

Esther was a woman who had grasped God's vision for her life. A woman who was devoted to carrying out the special task He had ordained for her. A woman whose service exemplified the spirit and commitment of a person in a deep relationship with God.

What about you today? Do you have a clear sense of God's vision for your ministry, for your life?

Without a vision, your life—your ministry—will fail to realize its full potential. I believe that every Christian woman is expected to live each waking moment in light of the special calling God has placed on her life. That special ministry He has designed for you is His vision for your personal ministry.

As I see it, we have only two choices: we either control our own destiny or let outside forces control and choose it for us.

The importance of vision is that it gives you that choice, that control. God expects us to take command over our lives and use them for His glory.

Are you serious about pursuing your life's purpose? of knowing God's vision for your ministry? Pray that God will teach you the value of knowing His vision for your life! This will provide you with strength, direction, motivation, and, most important, His abiding peace!

And remember:

A task without a vision becomes meaningless and mere drudgery.

A vision without a task is simply a dream.

A task with a vision is victory . . . in Christ, where life becomes clearly defined, with distinct purpose and direction.

RAMONA PEREZ-GREEK

SEPTEMBER 4

The Horse That Followed

If any want to become my followers, let them deny themselves and take up their cross and follow me. For those who want to save their life will lose it, and those who lose their life for my sake will find it. Matt. 16:24, 25, NRSV.

Grandpa said that the whole problem was psychological, that the Shetland pony thought he was a cow. After all, cows were the only other four-legged creatures Prince knew. He ate with cows and slept with cows; therefore, he must have thought he was a cow. Tom didn't buy into that philosophy at all. He said it was much simpler: the horse was retarded. That's it, period. After one encounter Tom had nothing more to do with Prince.

The whole family remembers the day Grandma bought Prince at the auction. Each has his or her own version of the noises and smells at the sale barn. It was exciting to sit in the bleachers and watch the animals sell, and the gobbledygook lingo of the auctioneer added to the children's fascination.

The summer that Prince joined the family he was just Terril's size. But she grew and he didn't. In a couple years her feet nearly dragged the ground, but that didn't keep her from riding him. The neighbor boy had a real horse, and Prince would follow him down the road. But with no leader, Prince would go nowhere. However, if the neighbor boy and his horse weren't available to lead Prince, Terril would try to get me to lead him! I did try, once. I coaxed

291

Prince out to the driveway, and then I walked all the way out to the mailbox. But whenever I stopped, he stopped. Terril persuaded me to run down the road "just a little way to get him going." Confident that no one would see my silly venture on the quiet country road, I started running ahead of the horse. And Prince did run and follow me—until I ran out of breath and stopped.

Yes, Prince would only follow. He had no initiative of his own.

Thinking of that silly pony, it occurs to me that Jesus accepts us just as we are. But His salvation isn't ours until we act—until we accept it. And following Jesus takes some initiative. We must lose our own life and accept His life. We aren't just blobs of matter. God created us as active, breathing, thinking, choosing, individuals. God will give us the power to deny ourselves, to lose our life and accept His life. But we have to make the decision to follow Him.

BARBARA HUFF

SEPTEMBER 5

What Can I Wear?

I delight greatly in the Lord; my soul rejoices in my God. For he has clothed me with garments of salvation and arrayed me in a robe of righteousness. Isa. 61:10, NIV.

The amount of time that I spend standing in front of my closet surveying the scene before me must be substantial. Hanging blouses, jackets, skirts, dresses, and jeans piled above are a very familiar sight. The content really changes very little, but I'm always searching for that new combination, considering what color I feel like wearing, and taking into consideration just what the weather might be. The element of surprise is more likely to be the error of omission that allowed something to be hung up that should have gone to the laundry or to the sewing machine.

It was one of those mornings when getting out of bed would not have been my first choice, had there been an option. I scanned my closet as usual, but nothing seemed appropriate—all the same old stuff. It didn't help that rain was pouring down, and I knew what I'd hear at the breakfast table. Today was the seventh-grade end-of-school class picnic. They'd planned a day of outdoor swimming and other fun. Having twin boys in the class, I faced two disappointed class members. The rain had ruined it all. They were vigorous in their dismay, and it was good to finally get them out the door and off to school. I hoped that some other adult or their friends could brighten their day. What would brighten mine?

I flipped on the radio to a Christian station, and instantly one of the radio ministers told me exactly what I should be wearing, and just what would brighten my day. His words came from Isaiah 61:3: ". . . a garment of praise instead of a spirit of despair."

Oh, how I desperately need and desire that kind of clothing. I have experienced a praise attitude just enough to know that I love "wearing" it. I look my very best in it—it flatters my facial features, and my friends like me when they see me in it. My family blossoms in its atmosphere.

I really must redo my closet. Get rid of some of the attitudes that have been there, pushed to the very back, that do not complement me. I don't want to use them again. Instead, I must carefully choose contentment. I must find the best in others. I must be an encourager and a helper. I must preserve those mementoes, build those altars, that will always remind me of how God has led me in the past. As I realize all this, looking ahead I will see a wonderful master plan for my life that unfolds into eternity. How awesome! How exciting! And how very lovely I will look as I praise Him forever. — EVANGELINE LUNDSTROM

SEPTEMBER 6

I'm Alive!

You have granted me life and favor, And Your care has preserved my spirit. Job 10:12, NKJV.

I'm alive!" I shouted as I returned to the scene of the accident near my home in southern Tennessee. I smelled the crisp air and heard the rustle of fallen leaves. I stood still, staring at the official red markings on the pavement where just a few weeks ago I'd huddled beside my mother on the cold, rough, country road. We were broken and bleeding, waiting for someone to help us—and praying for a miracle! At that time we had no idea that just being alive was a miracle.

My husband had told me, "Don't take Red Hill Valley Road south. It's too dangerous." But I loved that little country road. I knew it well—every turn and hill. About two miles from home on a little straightaway, I accelerated to a comfortable 40 miles per hour, climbed the hill, and sped down the dip. Then—directly in my path as I crested the next rise—came a speeding van.

"Get out of my lane!" I screamed as though he could hear me, and slammed on the brakes. But the impact was instantaneous. I've shut my eyes hundreds of times in the past few weeks and rerun that crushing of steel against steel—and shuddered.

Momentarily I gasped for air, then pushed my body back from the steering wheel and yelled, "Mother, say something! Mom, talk to me!" She lay crumpled in the passenger seat but didn't answer. I tried to reach her but couldn't turn. The mangled car stopped my movement. Then I glanced down to where my right foot should have been. My leg bone was empty. My foot dangled helplessly to the side. I reached down to straighten it, but only bloodied my hand.

I had one thought—to get to my mother. "Help me get my door open!" I screamed to the young woman who'd stumbled out of the van. The evidence of her momentary mistake of looking back at her children instead of watching the road was painfully evident. With her pulling and my pushing we managed to move the crushed and crumpled car door.

I struggled to release my seat belt as she ran for help. At last I stumbled out, and with one foot dangling, hopped around and threw open my mother's door. Mom moved! She was alive!

Being age 77 with osteoporosis is no time to be in a head-on collision. With chest and abdomen crushed, a severely damaged diaphragm, collapsed lung, broken left shoulder and arm, and only God knows how many broken ribs, Mom lived only three weeks. I wanted a miracle for my mother. I prayed that God would fuse her broken ribs in place so she could breathe. But that miracle was not to be.

I don't understand why I lived and Mom didn't, when my side of the car sustained more damage. Why did I escape with only a severely dislocated foot but no scratches or broken bones when Mom had so many? There are many things I don't understand. But one thing I do know—life is a miracle.

I look differently at the leaves now—and the flowers, the birds, all the little things I used to take for granted. I smell more intensely. I feel. I should have been dead. That's what everyone says who looked at our mangled car. But instead I'm alive. Oh, I might have a little pain and the inconvenience of having to learn to walk again, but I've been given a second chance at living—and I want to make sure this incredible miracle of life isn't wasted!   KAY KUZMA

SEPTEMBER 7

Drowning!

When you go through deep waters and great trouble, I will be with you. When you go through rivers of difficulty, you

will not drown! When you walk through the fire of oppression, you will not be burned up, the flames will not consume you. Isa. 43:2, TLB.

The first time I saw the Snake River as a little girl, I was filled with the desire to tame those rapids someday. It wasn't until nearly 30 years later that I finally had the opportunity. And it wasn't the Snake River, but the nearby middle fork of the Salmon River. By then the Snake had been nearly tamed by a series of dams.

I went on the rafting trip with a group of teachers from Auburn Academy, where my husband and I both worked. The huge Mae West life jackets required by the Drury's Drifters made us look like a string of large orange pumpkins as we made our way to the rafts. Outwardly I was excited, but inside I was scared; very scared.

For the first hour or so I held on tightly to the rope that encircled the side of the raft. But after going through several rapids I began to feel like a pro. I let go of the rope and began to breathe more or less normally. Just then we went around a bend and into the largest and roughest rapids on the river. As our raft entered the rough water the young guide lost control and our raft turned up on its side. It was standing almost vertical. In fact, Dr. Drury later said he had never seen a raft stand up so straight without flipping over. I was sitting with my youngest son on the downward side of the raft, and we were washed completely out of the boat. Both of us grabbed the rope encircling the raft, and that's how we went through the rapids.

I was so scared all I could think of was that if I let go of that rope I would surely be sucked under the water and drowned. If that didn't happen then I would hit my head on the rocks and drown. The best of all the worst-case scenarios that rapidly passed before my eyes was that the rafts would leave me behind and I would have to walk out of the canyon on my own, and I didn't know how I could do that.

Suddenly I became aware that the people in my raft were shouting at me, "Hang on, Ginny! Hang on!" I remember thinking, *Why do they think I would let go?* My whole life was clinging to that raft! At that moment I became aware that my young son had his arm around me and was saying over and over, "You're OK, Mom! You're OK! I have you! I'm holding you and I'm not going to let you go."

In every church, every community, every town, there are women who have fallen out of the raft and are hanging on because they don't know what else to do. They're afraid that if they let go they'll surely be sucked into the rough waters. They feel like they're drowning in their own tears. Or perhaps they fear they'll have to walk through the rapids alone and they know they can't survive that.

God doesn't say you won't go through difficult times, but He offers encouragement that you will survive because He will be with you. How does He offer that encouragement? Through His Word and through His people. In every church and community there should be women who will cry out, "Hang on! I have you. I'm holding you and I won't let you go!"　　　　GINNY ALLEN

Truth Securely Lodged

I seek you with all my heart; do not let me stray from your commands. I have hidden your word in my heart that I might not sin against you. Ps. 119:10, 11, NIV.

It's fun to travel with Lou. He gets more mileage out of a trip than anyone else I know. He documents everything with his video camera. Then at the end of the day he reviews it all, satisfied that the record is complete with living color, motion, and sound.

Now I'm not a camera person. But I take notes—lots of them—often poorly written. At the end of the day I review them, reliving the best of that day's experiences. But we travel well together.

Recently we visited Rome. We'd been reminded of the street thieves. "Hold on to everything," we were warned. "Don't relax your guard for a minute." Lou had his wallet in an inside coat pocket. His wristwatch was protected in my purse and his video camera was securely zipped inside his camera case. We were ready for the thugs of Rome!

Our subway car had come to a stop. I was standing closest to the door, so was first out. Other passengers, anxious to exit, pressed against Lou as he followed me out. But in that split second his camera was gone, the case left unzipped.

Yes, we were angry! We had taken precautions, but it was not enough. Blaming ourselves didn't help our dilemma either. For the rest of the trip we'd have to recall what we could and rely on my sketchy notes. Not a happy thought.

Then we began thinking about depending on a mechanical device for recalling detail and for capturing beauty. We wondered what people did for memories before video cameras came into use. Then we thought of the treasure we have in the Bible and the urgency of hiding its truths in our hearts. The time may come when God's people are without His Word. But with God's promises and messages securely lodged in our hearts, we will have strength and comfort.　　　　LORABEL HERSCH

Rainbows

I have set my rainbow in the clouds, and it will be the sign of the covenant between me and the earth. Gen. 9:13, NIV.

There is something mystical, almost magical, about rainbows. Perhaps it's the conditions under which they form, the way they appear, change, disappear, or the attention they capture. Little children jump up and down with excitement. Even busy adults stop to admire (and even photograph) a rainbow.

I like to think how Noah and his family must have felt as they gazed upon the first recorded rainbow. How wonderful of God to give them such a breathtaking symbol of His presence and His promise!

Sometimes on sunny days I hang a prism from a curtain rod in my kitchen just to watch the dancing mass of rainbows—red, blue, green, purple, yellow. The light patterns run back and forth across the room, creating surprises of beauty in every corner. And as I watch, I wonder: If the Son of God put light through me, could I somehow create such beauty? Could I show love, happiness, courage, peacefulness, kindness? Could I make pretty patterns in all the corners of my world? BRENDA DICKERSON

Employed by Grace

For it is by grace you have been saved . . . not the result of works, so that no one may boast. For we are what he has made us, created in Christ Jesus to do good works, which God prepared beforehand to be our way of life. Eph. 2:8-10, NRSV.

Growing up attending church, I had the impression that missionaries were a breed apart from struggling church members, sort of super-Christians following David Livingstone's footsteps across Africa. They were men and women of exceptional caliber;

these people never questioned their faith in God or the answers to the world's problems. In confidence they presented the gospel and converted heathen to a better life.

Today I find myself crisscrossing landmarks left by David Livingstone. Several meters from my home is a baobab tree under which he is reported to have slept. According to my earlier notions I should be a super-Christian, but if the mission field is a place for graduates of Christianity, then I feel like an illiterate who ended up with a diploma.

I'm not an exceptional Christian. In facing the challenges here in Africa, I am conscious of sometimes doubting God. I believe the Bible has the answers to the world's problems, but I'm not so sure my understanding of its principles and their application to other's lives and circumstances is always correct. I have had to examine what is biblical Christianity and what is my American culture, and I find myself getting the two mixed up now and then. Even my concept of the gospel hasn't fully matured. I'm growing in my understanding of the good news—that God gave His Son for the whole world and we may truly be righteous through faith in Him, but by nature I am a creature under law. I still find myself approaching God as if I were applying for a loan with bad credit, hoping He'll extend me forgiveness but knowing I'm not worthy and can't be trusted. I still find myself wasting time trying to accumulate a little good behavior in order to boost my credit rating.

Yet I am considered a missionary in Africa. And I am convicted beyond any shadow of a doubt that God loves every hurting soul, and that He wants to use His children to touch the world's pain. I am surrounded by other Christian missionaries all struggling with the concepts of God and their inadequacies. Our circle of spiritual associates includes Catholic priests and nuns, Methodists, Lutherans, and Salvation Army ministers—all seeking to be an avenue of blessing despite being struggling Christians. Theology is rarely debated in our association; most often we discuss the challenge of bringing God's love in contact with the needs of common people. We confess our failures, the times we couldn't see beyond ourselves to serve others. We share our joys, the unexpected blessings that buoy us up as evidence that God is working. Each of us feels in some way that we don't belong here. But when we stop to think about where we do belong, we praise God He didn't leave us there, but is giving us the opportunity to enter into the joy of working with Him.
DEBORAH AHO

Shooting the Saints

Those who say, "I love God," and hate their brothers or sisters, are liars; for those who do not love a brother or sister whom they have seen, cannot love God whom they have not seen. 1 John 4:20, TEV.

Being a history buff, I often run across little-known humorous events history teachers fail to tell their students. However, the one I wish to share with you did more than just tickle my fancy. Perhaps it will do the same for you.

British general Sir William Phips's orders were to load the ammunition in his fleet of boats at the mouth of the St. Lawrence River and to proceed inland to the city of Quebec, where he and his small force of soldiers were to wait until the foot soldiers from the south could arrive in order to attack the French stronghold, thus claiming it for the Crown. That was the plan.

The fleet carrying the precious ammunition inched its way through the wilderness waterways to the walled city, where, under the cover of night, they strategically hid their ammunition-laden boats and waited.

All would have gone without incident except that General Phips, a strict Protestant, hated Catholics. As Phips viewed the walled city from his hiding place, the stone statues of saints mounted strategically along the crest of the city's walls irritated him so much that despite his orders, he commanded his men to shoot the statues off the walls.

The English sailors set up the cannons, loaded their muskets, and fired on the stone saints. Round after round of ammunition was fired, toppling the saints to the ground. Poor General Phips got so caught up with his project that he failed to notice just how much ammunition he was using.

The shooting alerted the French Army to his position, and they began shelling the fleet. In his zeal to take potshots at the saints, Phips exhausted the entire supply of ammunition. The first battalion of English foot soldiers arrived just in time to rescue General Phips and his crew.

General Phips had been commissioned to guard the treasured ammunition that would have given his country and his king a sure victory over the enemy. Instead, he lost his opportunity. He'd been too busy blowing away defenseless stone saints.

Like General Phips, I've seen brothers and sisters in Christ waste valuable energy and time taking potshots at one another. No matter how sincere we may be, gossiping, criticizing, judging, and passing sentence weakens our defenses. We find that when it's time to do serious battle against our real enemy, Satan, we fail, not because God didn't send in His army of heavenly foot soldiers, but because we have used up our supply of moral strength and spiritual firepower. And the accuser of the brethren wins without firing a shot. KAY D. RIZZO

Do Good to Them That Hate You

But I say unto you, Love your enemies, bless them that curse you, do good to them that hate you, and pray for them which despitefully use you, and persecute you. Matt. 5:44.

Moving to a new neighborhood a few years ago we were looking forward to making new friends, so one evening we went out to introduce ourselves to our neighbors. To our surprise and shock, when we got to one house the wife and the children were very happy to meet us, but the husband would not even shake hands. We learned later that this man had protested against our moving to the neighborhood.

Not only would he not speak or respond to our greetings, but he let loose his fearsome dog to roam about his yard. On two occasions, one of our daughters was almost bitten by the dog. All our neighbors advised us to be very careful of this neighbor, because he had openly said he did not like us.

There were times we were tempted to stand up to him and let him know that we also had the right to hate him too, but we were reminded of the text "Love your enemies." We made it a subject of prayer and asked God to help us be able to love this man.

One day we heard that one of his sons had been admitted to the hospital. We sent a get-well card to him, but that did not change the attitude of his father. A year later the same son had surgery. This time we decided to visit him at the hospital.

When we got to the hospital, we found the son's parents in the room with him. We felt uneasy, uncertain of what might happen, and I said a little prayer, asking God to change the father's attitude. We stayed for about 20 minutes sharing words of encouragement with the young man and his mother. Soon the father drew his chair closer and joined the discussion. After this we subscribed to a Christian journal for the family.

Our text says we should love our enemies and pray for them. We are to love those who dislike us or malign our reputation. This is not an easy command to obey. But as disciples of Jesus Christ, we do well to listen when He says, "I say unto you, love your enemies."

Jesus' last prayer was "Father, forgive them." Yes, humanly speaking it's very difficult. In fact, some may insist that it's impossible to love some people. Yet with divine help we can crucify the carnal nature and become empowered to love even our worst enemy.

It is for our own good that we love our enemies. Our own spiritual walk with God depends on it. The forgiveness we all need is dependent on our willingness to forgive others. "But if you do not forgive others, neither will your Father forgive you" (Matt. 6:15, NRSV).

A few days after our hospital visit we heard a knock at our door. We opened it to find that the hitherto-unfriendly man had brought us our mail. With God nothing is impossible. "Do good to them that hate you."

ELIZABETH BEDIAKO

SEPTEMBER 13

The Master's Portrait

Come now, and let us reason together, saith the Lord: though your sins be as scarlet, they shall be as white as snow; though they be red like crimson, they shall be as wool. Isa. 1:18.

Within my deepest heart was placed a canvas white and clean
On which to paint a portrait of my Friend—the Nazarene.
His lips, with tints of hope I'd form; His brow with wisdom shade;
And in His eyes, brushstrokes of caring that would never fade.

Upon His heart the crimson hues of love would rest supreme;
And from His nail-scarred hands, bright rays of saving grace would
    stream.
But selfish pride began to grasp those brushes of my will—
I'd paint my own rich, glorious work with stubborn, human skill.

I spurned His loving voice; I was determined to control
The strokes that guided by my Lord could beautify my soul.
But sad my plight—I soiled and marred that canvas of my heart,

And realized—too late—I have no skill from Him apart.

With surface spoiled, this helpless soul in anguish knelt to pray;
I wept for Calvary's cleansing blood to wash the stains away.
Christ heard my plea and answered, for He'd never left my side;
He beckoned me to yield my will to Him—the Crucified.

I cast the brushes at His feet—old brushes, worn and dried;
The blurred and faded colors of my selfishness and pride.
He took those brushes—made them pliant with His nurturing care,
Then purified the colors I'd rejected in despair.

And then my precious Saviour washed away those guilty stains
By cov'ring my heart canvas with blood flowing from His veins.
So now, because His matchless love has given me life anew,
He holds the brushes of my will and paints in colors true.

Day after day His image is becoming clearer now,
As day by day He walks with me so long as I allow.
Unceasingly I pray that God His Spirit will impart,
For Christ sits for His portrait on the canvas of my heart.

LORRAINE HUDGINS

SEPTEMBER 14

Time and Chance

*Whatever your hand finds to do, do it with all your might
. . . But time and chance happen to them all. Eccl. 9:10, 11,
NIV.*

As I went up the steps to my house the sweet scent of peaches
told me that my husband, Jerry, had picked up some bushels of
peaches while I was at work. With my arms loaded, I couldn't open
the door, so I rang the doorbell. As I waited I could see and hear
Melody, 6, and Julie, 4, racing to the door. Julie, coming ahead,
shouted back, "Let me! Let me!" She grabbed the knob of our
stubborn door and with both hands turned and pulled with all her
might. But the door wouldn't budge.

"I'll do it. I can do it," Melody stated, as she took over. Taller
and stronger, she firmly grasped the doorknob with both of her
hands, then with a push, a twist, and a pull the door flew open. Size
and skill had won out. I could clearly see the triumph and the loss
on each face.

After hugs, greetings, and supper the four of us formed a short assembly line to can the peaches. Julie washed them in a sinkful of water (a 4-year-old's delight). I dipped them in hot water to loosen the skins, then dumped them into Melody's bowl of ice water, where her rubber-gloved hands rubbed off the skins. From there I picked them out and sliced them in half before arranging them by hand in the widemouthed jars. Jerry added the boiling-hot syrup, closed the jars, and put them in the boiling canning kettle. Soon we had dozens of jars cooling on the table and counter. The big, golden half moons layered in each jar looked like works of art.

Then we ran out of widemouthed jars. The smaller peaches could still be cut in half and dropped into regular jars, but my hand wouldn't fit in to arrange them, and doing it with a long-handled spoon took too long. We were discussing cutting them up when again we heard the familiar "Let me! Let me!" Julie pulled her chair over to the counter, stood on it, then reaching down into the jar with her little hand, she arranged the slippery peaches. Once again size and skill had accomplished the task. Her big eyes sparkled, and you could almost touch her pride.

Regardless of our size or skill, looks or education, money or hang-ups, God has promised "time" and "chance." Our prayer is that His Spirit will open our eyes to see the moment and grasp the chance with all the energy, strength, and joy that God supplies.

EVILYN GILKESON

SEPTEMBER 15

Your Children

Thus saith the Lord, Even the captives of the mighty shall be taken away, and the prey of the terrible shall be delivered: for I will contend with [those] that contendeth with thee, and I will save thy children. Isa. 49:25.

We sat waiting in Timber Lodge for the worship service to begin. Suddenly my heart filled with excitement. I nudged Lawrence.

"Ann is here!" I exclaimed. "Right over there across the lodge. See, she seems to be with that young man!"

My husband saw her then, speaking animatedly, with a group of young people around her. We watched, spellbound. It had been many weeks since our daughter had flown off to Mexico for an adventure in learning Spanish. All by herself. As days turned into weeks, we'd watched the mail for some word that she was safe and well. But we hadn't heard from her. When had she returned? Why hadn't she called to let us know she was back? What was she doing here at our church retreat at Sunset Lake? She had declared herself estranged from God—and nearly so from us. Fascinated, we watched her, waiting for her to spot us across the room.

"Carl," we heard her say to her companion.

"Yes, Denise?" he responded.

Amazed, we studied the girl. Surely it must be our little Ann! Slowly we admitted our foolish hopes. Reason told us that our daughter remained far away in a foreign land—that this look-alike knew neither us nor her "twin." Still, compulsion kept our eyes riveted on her. The girl would have been embarrassed, had she noticed two strangers watching her so closely, so as soon as we could, we introduced ourselves and told Denise of her striking similarity to our daughter.

The afternoon's activities included a hike to the waterfall high up above the camp, led by Denise and Pastor Carl Jorgenson, her friend and fiancé. Lawrence and I immediately chose to take the hike. We felt helpless to do otherwise. We seemed to have a deep need to be near Denise. How like our Ann she was! An outdoor person, she loved to challenge nature—climbing mountains, daring river rapids, risking life and limb. I had the privilege of talking with her at some length as we climbed. She and Carl planned to be married at the close of next week's worship hour. I appreciated her willingness to spend time with me, talking as friend to friend, though separated agewise by many years.

I thrilled to hear her voice as she rehearsed her experiences—so similar and familiar, yet strangely unknown to us. Repeatedly I had to remind myself that this was not Ann.

That day proved indescribably exciting to me, so close to that dear familiar face. Perhaps I could not help pretending, for a few hours, that Ann really was with us—worshiping with us, enjoying fellowship with us. Somehow, Denise brought comfort and hope to my heart.

We arrived at last, at the beautiful, thundering waterfall, and I was reminded of God's almighty power. Ann was safe in God's care.

ROBERTA SHARLEY

The Velvet Chairs

When He comes, He will convict the world of guilt in regard to sin, and righteousness and judgment. John 16:8, NIV.

Midway in my professional career, I found that I had outgrown Melmac, Formica, and Naugahyde. One day my husband brought home a lovely new coffee table and set it up in our living room. We immediately became aware of how ill-matched the rest of our furniture appeared in contrast. This led us to buy several pieces of fine maple furniture, and eventually we ordered two winged-back chairs. We special-ordered them in blue velvet, and were told it would be about four months before they'd be delivered.

From then on, all I could do was think about those chairs. Despite a busy career, the preparation and taking of a challenging certification exam, and a Canadian vacation, the possible arrangement of the chairs and how nice they'd look took first place in my spare-time thoughts.

Shortly after my vacation, my morning study included the Parable of the Sower in Matthew 13. When I read the words of verse 22, about the seed that fell among thorns, conviction came to me. Somehow, when I read about the thorns representing the worries of this life and the deceitfulness of wealth, I actually read that "the love of nice things" chokes out the Word of God. I had allowed my mind to be taken over with trivia instead of using my precious thoughtful moments to dwell on matters of eternal weight. With tears of repentance I prayed then and there. I felt sorrow for my sin—that those two chairs had almost taken over my life. At the same time I was joyful that God cares so much for us that He sends His Holy Spirit to continue to lead us in the way that leads to everlasting life.

After this experience I gave no further thought to the chairs. When in due time a call came from the furniture store that they'd be delivered, I had to force myself to decide on their placement.

A number of years have passed since then, and the chairs, now rather faded and shabby, have been relegated to our downstairs recreation room. While I never lost my appreciation for "nice things," they've never since had such prominence in my thinking. I praise God for His love and His Spirit, and that He keeps us in the way, in the little things of this life as well as the big, as we respond to His leading.   MARILYN KING

Forgive, but Don't Die

*I am come that they might have life, and that they might
have it more abundantly. John 10:10.*

Most people withhold their forgiveness because they harbor the
mistaken idea that if they forgive, they must now put up with
everything and anything that the "forgiven" person throws at them.
They envision a nightmare of becoming the doormat of the offender
through guilt like this:

"Give me my slippers!" screams the offender.

"They're right next to you, and stop yelling," the forgiver
calmly replies.

"I thought you forgave me for yelling," retorts the offender.

What should the forgiver say? "I retract!" or "You didn't
deserve my forgiveness" or "Stop manipulating me" or, worse yet,
"Yes, dear"? To capitulate to this kind of emotional bullying is to
misunderstand the purpose of forgiveness. Forgiveness releases the
offender from our justified hurt or anger, but it does not require
that the forgiver lie down and die, as it were. An unrepentant
offender can use your forgiveness against you as a kind of guilt trip,
if given the opportunity. Why? Because forgiveness is generally
misinterpreted as moral weakness. And yet there is an enormous
storehouse of strength from which the forgiver as well as the
offender may continue to draw.

Going back to our pending response, what can a forgiver say to
a manipulating offender? It needs to be a response that acknowl-
edges that the person continues to be forgiven, but that your
forgiveness is an opportunity that you have given him or her to let
go of anger or contempt rather than continuing to cultivate it.
Answers such as the following can be helpful: "I love you and
myself too much to let you do this to either of us" or "Since neither
you nor I need this yelling, can't we just dismiss it from our lives?"

Keeping silent will send the resentment (on the forgiver's side)
and contempt (on the offender's side) into hiding, only to later
resurface in some other ugly form. It is always better to *respond* to
the angry word with a healing word rather than with silence (see
Prov. 15:1).

What we are hoping to achieve with forgiveness is not silent
torment, but an open door to change and growth in relationships.
We want answers that will open the door to that new and more
abundant life that Jesus promises to bring to the life of every

Christian believer. Too many Christians believe they should have life *miserably* because that is what wretched sinners deserve. Like all damaging "truths," this one is partially true. The sinner not only deserves a bad life, he/she deserves death. But the forgiven sinner deserves eternal life, beginning now! In Christ, we all deserve the abundant life because our Creator *wants* us to have it. To close the door on what our Redeemer wants is to close the door on life.

LOURDES E. MORALES-GUDMUNDSSON

SEPTEMBER 18

What to Say?

When three of Job's friends heard of all the tragedy that had befallen him, they got in touch with each other and traveled from their homes to comfort and console him. Job 2:11, TLB.

It was Sunday morning, and I had to get myself ready to perform at a wedding. Just two weeks earlier I had given birth prematurely to our first child—a little baby girl who was born dead. I was fortunate to have survived and spent a week in the hospital recovering from a near-fatal infection. And although I was in no mood for a celebration, I'd promised my friends that I would play at their wedding and was determined to follow through on that promise.

The service was beautiful. It was nice to have an excuse for my tears—everyone cries at weddings. Still, I was glad when it was over, and I looked forward to getting back home. But everyone wanted to hear what had happened with the baby. I recited the story many times and was warmed by the thoughtful condolences for my baby and the concern about my health. These were my friends. I could count on them for strength.

Every now and then, however, well-meaning individuals would innocently say the "wrong" thing. "All things work together for good, you know. It was for the best." "God took your baby because He knew that it was going to have a hard life." Those comments stung my heart, though I tried to remember that these people were just trying to help.

It is hard to know what to say to someone who has suffered a loss. The unfairness of sin is an impossible situation to explain logically. This is not a new dilemma. Job's friends, who honestly wanted to comfort him, turned out to be a most insensitive crew. They started out OK. "Wailing loudly in despair, they . . . put earth on their heads to demonstrate their sorrow. Then they sat upon the ground with him silently for seven days and nights . . . for they saw that his suffering was too great for words" (Job 2:12-13, TLB).

They should have left it at that. Unfortunately they felt compelled to say something. Eliphaz, Bildad, and Zophar took turns blaming Job for his misfortune. "You claim you are pure in the eyes of God! . . . Listen! God is doubtless punishing you far less than you deserve!" (Job 11:4-6).

Thanks, fellows, but no thanks! In Job's hour of greatest need, his friends were unable to encourage him. A potted plant would have been so much more appropriate!

God reprimands sharply this "friendly" trio for their discouraging words to Job. "I am angry with you . . . for you have not been right in what you have said about me" (Job 42:7).

Wow! Did you realize that God would hold you accountable for the incorrect and insensitive things you may have said to someone who needed your encouragement? Have you considered what image of God your comments might reflect?

So, you don't know what to say? Maybe you just need to sit silently for seven days and nights and throw earth on your head. As the song says: "You're never alone, never alone. That's all I know to say." That simple sentiment of friendship is often the best encouragement of all.

CYNTHIA PATTERSON COSTON

SEPTEMBER 19

The Gift of Song

The Lord is my strength and song, and he is become my salvation. Ex. 15:2.

I'll never forget the day my husband and I arrived in Bulgaria. Freezing rain blasted us in the face as we stepped off the plane and headed down the ramp. We had just spent 13 hours in the air, and we were exhausted.

Our job was to distribute Bulgarian Bibles and conduct the first series of evangelistic meetings in the city of Blagoevgrad since the fall of Communism. This city had been the former showcase of Communism. We were told that there had been no religious classes for children in 40 years. For months I had been preparing visual teaching aids for them and raising funds for felts, projectors, and other equipment.

The officer in customs frowned at our boxes and began spitting out questions we couldn't understand. A local pastor tried to explain our mission but was pushed aside. Finally we were told that we could collect our belongings in two days.

He might as well have said two years, for at that moment horror stories of other missionaries whose belongings were confiscated by greedy inspectors flashed through my mind. Our host hurried us out of the airport and shoved us into a rickety orange van. A rather heavyset woman with a big smile plopped down beside me and kept up a steady stream of conversation. I'll never know what she said.

Up until now I was sort of dazed by the newness of the situation. For the first time in my life I couldn't communicate. I didn't know where we were going and I was totally dependant on complete strangers. I faced these people empty-handed when I had planned to give them so much!

A tear fought its way out of the corner of my eye. I brushed it aside, hoping that no one noticed, but I was too late. My Bulgarian sister exclaimed something or other in pity and threw her big arms around me. I could see the helplessness in her eyes as she tried to think of some way to comfort me.

It must have dawned on her suddenly, for without warning she crushed my head to her breast and began singing. Her voice was tender and sweet and she sang with conviction as if the song were her life story! I couldn't understand the words but I recognized the melody of an old hymn.

"Jesus, loving Jesus, sweetest name I know. Fills my every longing, keeps me singing as I go."

It was as if the words had been dropped right out of heaven by God Himself! I was struck by the thought that if I couldn't trust the Almighty with our lives and luggage, then what was I doing here? What could I possibly teach these people who had lived through so many hardships?

May God bless that Bulgarian sister wherever she is, and may each one of us keep a song in her heart. CRYSTAL EARNHARDT

Our Extremity, God's Opportunity

Comfort ye, comfort ye my people, saith your God. Isa. 40:1.

It was a wonderful balmy summer's eve when my young friend Luis and I walked out of the church following an inspiring message. I'd been discipling Luis, a brilliant man from Guatemala, since his baptism. I was attending as many church meetings with him in his native language of Spanish as possible, as a point of encouragement.

As we joyfully rounded the corner of the church heading toward the well-lighted parking lot that night, I gasped in disbelief. I'd locked my car and left it in the church lot. Now it was gone—stolen! Luis was as shocked as I! He'd seen my car just 20 minutes before, parking next to it when he stopped by the church to talk to me. We hurried back into the church office and called the police. Suddenly an idea hit me, and I said, "Let's pray right now for the robbers!" So we knelt and prayed. That car was not just a mode of transportation. As a nutritionist, it was mandatory for my work—and for discipling!

Later, after the police officer finished taking the stolen vehicle report and was leaving, I looked into his eyes and tenderly but earnestly said, "There are two things I want you to remember for the rest of your life: Jesus really loves you. And in heaven, we'll never ever again have trouble with cars!" He sat there, visibly stunned, as if in a daze. I could see by his expression that no one who had just had the deep frustration of a car stolen had ever said those words to him. He couldn't speak as he fought back the tears. It was as if those words touched the deepest chords of his soul, as if spoken directly to him by someone else.

The telephone follow-up with this police officer has taken on a rewarding spiritual dimension. You too can have a telephone ministry, sowing seeds of comfort and truth into the hearts and lives of others.

Oh, how I pray for that police officer and his son who lives with him. I think he got the surprise of his life to learn that God gave me perfect love for the car thief. Yes, there are times when God calls upon us to comfort one another—and He may use the most dire circumstances to accomplish His purpose. So the next time a crisis hits you, transcend the moment and ask, "Lord, whom do You want me to comfort right now with a message from You?"

JUDY COULSTON

Withered Fruit

Say not ye, There are yet four months, and then cometh harvest? Behold, I say unto you, Lift up your eyes, and look on the fields; for they are white already to harvest. And he that reapeth receiveth wages, and gathereth fruit unto life eternal. John 4:35, 36.

It was a cold, damp day in January. Outside our sliding-glass door a few withered apricots clung to dripping branches. They must have been observed by our guests.

Longtime friends from an era gone by, this couple, now in their golden years, made annual trips from Canada to southern California to soak up the winter sun. They had stopped again to see us. As always, we savored the time spent together.

Having reared eight children of their own, these friends of ours could draw wisdom from a wealth of life's experiences. And my husband and I drank it in.

Our talk had turned to allergies, then to the environment and to how we should govern its care. Then came this meaningful gardening gem: "Ungathered fruit, whether fallen or left on the tree, will make the next crops sour."

"Oh, really?" I rejoined. "We have read that we should cut back shrubbery, rake up dead leaves, and bury all sorts of rotting garbage, if these are close to our house; but we have never heard that ungathered fruit can spoil the rest of the tree!"

My mind turned to the fig tree that Christ had cursed; but that tree was cursed because it did not bring forth any fruit. This case was different.

"There must be a parable in that," I mused. "If we don't use the fruit of the Spirit, we will soon turn sour."

"That's right," said the husband, "and if the church doesn't gather in souls when they are ripe, the whole tree will be affected."

How important it is that we make haste to gather in the fruit!

DOLLY ALEXANDER-JOHNSON

In Need of Repair

He heals the brokenhearted and binds up their wounds. Ps. 147:3, NIV.

Excited about the new music my teacher gave me, I opened my violin case, took out my instrument, and prepared to go over the material.

I was learning to play the violin again after years of not owning or playing the instrument. So when I decided to take lessons again, I was filled with enthusiasm. Like many would-be musicians, I'd rather have played a Bach sonata than to practice, practice, practice.

But with great determination I planned to spend time learning to play the notes on the music sheet before me. In the midst of warming up the instrument and adjusting the strings, it happened. Applying a little too much pressure to the string caused it to break—and my bubble of enthusiasm with it.

I had no extra violin strings on hand so sat down on my sofa in defeat. Then I thought, *I know what to do. I'll take the violin to my friend, the man who made it. He'll replace the broken string and tune the violin perfectly, and it'll be good as new.*

Life is oftentimes filled with pressure. Meeting the demands of living in the nineties takes its toll on millions of people. No one seems to be exempt from stressful situations presented almost daily.

It's been nearly 2,000 years since Jesus stood in the synagogue and said, "The Spirit of the Lord is upon me . . . he hath sent me to heal the brokenhearted, to preach deliverance to the captives . . . to set at liberty them that are bruised" (Luke 4:18). God can fix us whether our need is for mental, physical, or emotional repair.

Mary Magdalene was in desperate need of mending when she made her way to Simon's house that unforgettable day. Boldly and unashamedly, she knelt before Christ—washed His feet with her tears and dried them with her hair. Jesus, in His mercy, took her broken heart in His hands, and made it brand-new.

Jesus is our Creator. He made us, and knows us inside out. More important, He's the only one who can restore us perfectly when we're broken.

IRMA R. LEE

Tricky Tracks

*Thus says the Lord to you: "Do not be afraid nor dismayed
. . . for the battle is not yours, but God's." 2 Chron. 20:15,
NKJV.*

Leaving town one day, I was stopped by a line of cars before
some railroad tracks. I figured on a bit of a wait, so I put the car
into park and began to look around. I noticed, up ahead, not a train
holding up the cars, but a family crossing the street between the
railroad tracks. I saw a mother and three small children and three
shopping carts.

At this particular intersection two sets of railroad tracks cross
the road, and ruts in the pavement between the tracks are just the
right size to catch the shopping cart wheels.

As I watched the family, the mother, holding the hand of the
smallest child, made it across the tracks with one shopping cart.
The oldest child followed close behind with her cart, but the middle
child, barely big enough to push the grocery cart, got stuck in the
tracks in the middle of the street. She pushed and tugged, but the
cart wouldn't budge. Then, looking at the long line of cars waiting
just for her to cross, she began to cry.

The oldest child, noticing her sister's difficulty, ran back, lifted
the wheels of the cart, and assisted the little girl safely across to the
other side.

I put the car back in gear and slowly headed home, contemplating how often in my own life I react to difficult situations by
pushing, tugging, straining, and pulling—doing everything in my
power I can think of to mend the problems by myself without
asking my heavenly Father for help. When I finally give up and ask,
He is immediately there to answer. Wouldn't it be so much easier
just to start by crying out to Him?   RONNA WITZEL

The Two Worshipers

For everyone who makes self great will be humbled, and everyone who humbles self will be made great. Luke 18:14, TEV.

There were two women who went into the church to worship and pray. Ms. Self-Righteous prayed thus: "I thank You, God, that I am not like most others who come here to worship. I have given many hours of labor and much funds to Your work. I help in the church and with fellowship dinners as I have time. Of course, You understand that with my important work there are many demands on my time. My children are upright and do what is right without questioning. We are well-known in the community, always looking out to save as much as we can on any business deals so that our money will not be wasted. Our record of church attendance is perfect. I come in my very best clothes to worship You so You do not have to be ashamed of me. I am always concerned about rightdoing and do my best to make sure others do right also."

Ms. Defenseless also prayed, "Oh, merciful God, it has been such a struggle to get here. It seems that when I need You the most something always comes along to distract me in reaching out to You. You know how hard it has been since Mr. Defenseless lost his job. It is taking so long to get things straightened out, and I feel so weary. The children weigh heavy on my heart. Some of the decisions they are making are leading them further from You, dear Father, and I am afraid they will not discover it until it is too late. Please send Your sweet Spirit to keep close to them and woo them back to You. There seems to be no one to hear my cry. The pastors are so busy and burdened with so many more urgent problems that I don't like to bother them with mine. I do thank You for sending my sister to talk to me. It was a great comfort to just share with her.

"Dear Lord, there are so many suffering that I see around here in the church, hungry for Your comfort and love. My heart is filled with tenderness for them because I know what it is like to be comfortless. Please give me strength to know best how to help them. Somehow make up for my feeble efforts so that You may be glorified. I have nothing to give You other than myself. There are many questions in my mind, and You have shown me such great tenderness and patience that I am lifted to greater heights of service than I ever thought were possible."

The two worshipers left church that morning. One was filled

with her own self-worth, and the other with the Holy Spirit.

I looked on in astonishment at these two women, and as they came toward me I recognized their faces. There was some of me in each of them. PEGGY HARRIS

Living Not by Bread Alone

I am the Bread of Life. John 6:48.

Sometimes, even in the mission field, one loses a sense of mission accomplished. As a teacher, in my routine classroom duties—much the same as in homeland classrooms—it was easy to forget I was a witness, in "the uttermost parts of the earth" at that. I needed an occasional jolt from above to jar me to remembrance—as, for example, when we had an official visit from a government Ministry of Education team.

We weren't supposed to know they were coming to inspect us for the possible accreditation of our teacher training program. Such appraisals happen unannounced. But a secretary at the Education office, with whom my husband's effective diplomatic dealings had stood him in good stead, let him in on the secret inspection date: the very next day.

Cancelling out his long list of errands in the capital of that African nation, he made the return trip home as fast as the potholed, mud-slick, mountain roads allowed. Out went his message to staff and faculty: "Everything en ordre, lecons bien preparees and documentes, le jour de gloire (we hoped) est arrive."

I groaned. "How many will I have to feed?"

"None. The secretary said they'd bring their *pique-niques* ["franglais" for brown-bag lunches]." This relieved me of the anxiety of entertaining these dignitaries, if not of the other stress of the anticipation of inspection of my own teaching.

I went to school the next morning at 7:00. At 9:00, my husband caught me between classes. "They're here, seven of them, but only one with his *pique-nique*."

A quick note to my faithful right-hand helper at home flew by messenger down the hill: "Make fresh *pain* [bread] and soup for nine. I'll be there at noon to prepare *omelettes aux champignons*."

That she got everything done in time—the house cleaned, the table set, and a huge pot of steaming vegetable soup prepared, besides crusty brown bread baked—testifies to the level of this dear helper's competence. And Monsieur Trog, the Belgian head of the

Pedaqoqie Department, found the bread in particular so delectable that he ate nine slices of it. (*I* was counting, that's who.)

After the meal Monsieur Trog had two requests, which he humbly presented. Could he possibly have a loaf of that bread extraordinaire—"What is its special taste?" ("Whole grain, free molasses from the Chinese sugar factory, monsieur," I could have told him if I hadn't wanted the idea of a "secret recipe" to mystify him.) And how could he get hold of a copy of the fascinating book *La Traqedie des Siecles (The Great Controversy)* he had begun to read while proctoring a test he was administering to some students?

As casually as possible we conceded we could possibly arrange for both. The grateful Monsieur Trog expressed his deep appreciation by searching out a gift in return—a magnificent unabridged *dictionnaire*. But a better gift, announced later—whether influenced by the bread and the book, I don't know—was the granting of full accreditation for our teacher training program. More important still, the Belgian educator got an exposure to our lifestyle and end-time truth.

"There's a lot of religion in a loaf of good bread," I commented to my husband.

"And 'the cross of Calvary is stamped on every loaf,' " he added. JEANNE JORDAN

SEPTEMBER 26

My God and I

For every animal of the forest is Mine and the cattle on a thousand hills. I know every bird in the mountains and the creatures of the field are Mine. Ps. 50:10, NIV.

It was a particularly difficult and troubled time in my life. Living on the beautiful Oregon coast, I frequently had occasion to drive from my coastal home to Portland. Sometimes the trip was for business; sometimes to visit with members of my family. The drive usually took about two hours, and I spent much of the time in conversation with my Best Friend. I would argue and agonize with God, searching for a reason for my life having taken such a particularly painful direction. Sometimes as we drove along together, God and I, the tears ran down my cheeks and I would be unable to say a word. Usually, however, I talked a lot—and my Friend listened.

That particular drive was beautiful, and there were many pastoral scenes that brought me comfort. I recall one special area where cattle roamed the green, grassy hills, birds sang in the trees, and I knew that little creatures called the pasture home—even if I could not see them. Each time I passed that particular spot, it was as if my Friend reminded me that all the cattle on these hills—and many other hills—were His.

Somehow that thought always brought comfort to me. My crying would quiet. A song would return to my heart. My soul would realize anew that my life was just where it was meant to be at that moment. Invariably, as soon as my eyes would light on that particular scene, I could sing again in peace and understanding.

In retrospect I realize that although there was pain, I was learning important lessons for my personal growth and, yes, for my character development as well. That painful time has passed for me—and the days are much brighter now. I am so thankful, and still, in memory I often recall that long drive. I remember those beautiful green, grassy hills; reflect that my Friend owns the cattle on a thousand hills and knows every bird in the mountains. How grateful I am to know that God. MYRNA MELLING

SEPTEMBER 27

Stay on the Trail

Whether you turn to the right or to the left, your ears will hear a voice behind you saying, "This is the way; walk in it." Isa. 30:21, NIV.

Our family loves hiking and backpacking. At the trail head we always stop to read the map and the hiking rules, and sign the register. One important rule says, "For your safety and the protection of the fragile terrain, stay on the trail."

Hardly had my husband and I finished making a trail from our home to the railroad tracks below when a family with five children visited us. They wanted to hike down to the tunnel. Delighted to share our beautiful bluff with them, I suggested, "Will you please help us protect the fragile hillside and the wildflowers? We have only two requests. Stay on the path, and don't pick the flowers. We want them to live and grow another year."

I led the way. Behind me I heard the father mumbling. "Switchbacks bore me. Such a waste of time when I can easily cut straight down and be at the tracks in no time."

Matching action with words, he leaped past me, making deep gashes into the hillside with his boots. His feet dislodged heavy rocks I'd lugged up the steep hill to reinforce the trail's outer edge.

Angry feelings welled inside me as I heard them clank when they hit the tracks below.

Later, when we came back up the trail, I felt sad picking up the wilting flowers his children had strewn everywhere, many pulled up by the roots.

You, like these visitors of ours, have a choice. Will the joys of the hike be lost in your mad rush to be first? As you dash ahead, will you spread disaster, leaving a mess for those who follow? What will you miss if you take shortcuts, or turn aside to go your own way? God has strewn life's pathway with so many surprises for those who will stop, look, and listen.

This year you and your heavenly Father can become great friends. You'll really get to know Him if you don't spoil your daily walks with Him. But if you choose to go your own way or run ahead, you may get lost. Don't make Him sad by lagging so far behind that you can't hear His voice calling, "This is the way. Walk in it." What a wonderful journey you'll have if you stay on the trail with Him. EILEEN E. LANTRY

SEPTEMBER 28

A Little Good News

Whatever things are true, whatever things are noble, whatever things are just, whatever things are pure, whatever things are lovely, whatever things are of good report, if there is any virtue and if there is anything praiseworthy, meditate on these things. Phil. 4:8, NKJV.

Hurriedly slicing a banana and pouring milk into a bowl of corn flakes, the pastor's wife, mother of teenage daughters, and executive secretary all bundled up into one person dashed to her car for the 50-mile commute to work early that fateful Friday morning.

Now, you may think it foolhardy to attempt to eat a bowl of cereal while driving, but this seasoned commuter was no novice at on-the-road breakfasting. She had managed this feat successfully for more than five years.

Perhaps she was attempting to soothe her troubled feelings following the impatient words she and her husband had just exchanged; or perhaps she just wished for a moment of respite from the unrelenting demands of life. Whatever the reason, for a brief instant she was more intent on savoring her breakfast cereal than on carefully maneuvering her automobile through the morning drizzle.

She came to her senses abruptly, however, when she saw, just a few feet in front of her, a black pickup truck stopped with its left-turn signal flashing. Although she hit the brakes, there was not enough time to stop, and she careened into the back of the 8-day-old pickup. Momentarily stunned from the impact, she sat watching sliced bananas slide down the milk-drenched windshield and wondered just how angry her unintended-victim would be.

The pickup driver *should* have been angry. This was a rude intrusion into his tranquil life. Now he would be late for work, and would have to take a day off to get his new truck to the repair shop, and obviously it was all because of someone's carelessness. But instead he was concerned for her. He asked, "Are you OK? Why don't you put your car in neutral so I can push it off the road out of the way of this traffic. Here's a quarter so you can call your husband. There's a phone booth right over there."

And that's not all! When she spoke with the police officer he informed her that Mr. Pickup Driver had requested that she not be ticketed, and she left the accident scene with her "perfect" driving record still intact.

I wonder, why aren't stories of compassion, generosity, and forgiveness just as newsworthy as stories about robberies, murders, and rapes?

Our text suggests that we concentrate on the good, the noble, and the lovely. Today, why not pretend to be a reporter looking for only the good, noble, and lovely stories, then report those stories at home, school, work, and anywhere you can get an audience!

LINDA KLINGER

SEPTEMBER 29

The Gift of Time

There is an appointed time for everything. Eccl. 3:1, NASB.

Imagine going into a bank in a new town and requesting to open a checking account. To your surprise, you are customer number 10,000,000, and as part of a national promotion your account will be one of a kind—unique.

The bank is going to give you money. $86,400 of it every day for the rest of your life. You will never have to deposit anything again. There is just one restriction. Each day you must find ways to spend all the money in your account. Any money left over at the end of the day will not be added to the next day's deposit.

By many standards you would be quite wealthy. An annual income potential of $31,536,000 is not to be regarded casually! Realizing the maximum benefits of this sizable, regular sum would require careful, prayerful, joyful planning.

Our high-tech world would make spending it easy. If you didn't have a computer, this new account would make it possible for you to purchase one and add software connecting you and your bank. All the necessary transactions for spending the money daily could be done from your home in minutes.

Imagine the joy you could bring to others with your newfound wealth! Your weekly $60,000 additional tithe income would make a remarkable difference in the ability of our world church to respond to the gospel commission. Setting up scholarships for worthy students would be exciting. Paying off bills would be a relief. Shopping for a new wardrobe would be fun. And the list grows.

As critical a role as money plays in our lives, however, we have something that God regards as even more valuable. 86,400 seconds each day are a gift from Him. One of my favorite Christian writers has said that our time belongs to God; that time is precious; and He will require a more strict account of how we use it than He will of any other talent.

This gift is not one you need fantasize about. You've been the recipient of it ever since birth, and in terms of time your wealth is quite real. Every morning a time deposit has been made in your name of 86,400 seconds to be used wisely by you. Prayer and Bible study provide the link between here and heaven as you seek divine guidance in planning the best use of the generous gift from above.

DAWN L. REYNOLDS

SEPTEMBER 30

Powerful Prayer

I will contend with him that contendeth with thee and I will save thy children. Isa. 49:25.

My grandmother died at 29, leaving six young children in unworthy hands. Ill with pneumonia, she suddenly felt death was near and called for her children. As they gathered around her bed, she spoke to each one earnestly, admonishing him to serve Jesus and meet her in heaven.

My father was eight months old at the time and had not seen her for a couple days. Joyfully bouncing with delight, he buried his hands in her hair and gave her slobbery baby kisses. With her face

in his neck she sobbed, "He will never remember his mother."
Seventy-five years later, on his deathbed he smiled and said, "Just
think! In what will seem to me but a moment of time, I will see my
mother."

She prayed for each child and had to leave them.

They grew up in adverse circumstances of poverty, brutality,
and evil. Through the years they often reminded each other of
"Mama's" concern for them. Somehow they all became solid,
dependable citizens, and each one, sooner or later, accepted
salvation. They died at various ages up into the 90s, all securely
expecting to meet their mother in heaven.

Dear Grandma,
>Your life was short and very sad
>And I have never met you,
>Six young children you had to leave;
>What agony it cost you!
>The things they suffered make us grieve;
>How tragic that they lost you!
>
>You pleaded with them on your dying bed
>That they'd meet you in heaven.
>You placed a prayer on each little head,
>And God held you close—all seven.
>
>Now all of them have gone to rest,
>All waiting in the grave.
>You taught them all to give of their best,
>And of their best they gave.
>
>Your dying prayer has borne fruit well;
>It gives courage to us others.
>Only the passing of time will tell
>What we owe to praying mothers.

LILLIAN LAWRENCE

OCTOBER 1

Terror by Night

*Thou shalt not be afraid for the terror by night . . . There
shall no evil befall thee . . ." Ps. 91:5, 10.*

Are you ever afraid at night? In these violent days, hardly anyone is fearless. But the year that my first child was born, I faced the most terrifying nights of my life. We had just moved into a new house in a Virginia suburb, and my husband had begun a job that required him to travel all week. True, he returned on weekends, but week nights were awful.

Our light, airy rooms were surrounded by curtainless windows that I draped with all the extra sheets I could find. As there were more windows than sheets, many were left bare. Our glass patio doors were the worst. They faced a deep woods, and at night my imagination conjured up thieves and murderers, peering into my house. The daily crime reports on the radio fueled my fears.

Every night I stacked glass canning jars in front of each outside door, hoping any intruder would be scared off by the crash. Then I would barricade myself in the bedroom, hold Sherri, and read, cry, and nurse her until daybreak, when we'd both fall into an exhausted sleep.

Determined to break this cycle, I began reading my Bible, underlining every single text that promised God's protection. Night after night I would reread the texts and search for more. Gradually, my faith in God's protecting powers was restored, and I began to sleep again.

Then one day our church paper arrived. I read it eagerly, as usual, but to my dismay the author of one article pointed out that sometimes people think God has promised physical protection when, in fact, the Bible promises only spiritual protection, the keeping of our souls from eternal harm!

The rest of that week was a nightmare! To make things worse, a serial killer was on the loose. That weekend we attended a spiritual retreat with H.M.S. Richards, Sr. At his first meeting he offered to talk privately with anyone who had special problems. I was one of the first to sign up.

When I related to him my experience, I couldn't help bursting into tears. I wanted protection for myself and my baby—body *and* soul!

Elder Richards shook his head. "Let me tell you something, Fern," he said, peering over his glasses in the kindest way. "I believe the Bible is inspired, but I do not believe everything in the church paper is inspired!

"I am also afraid at night when I travel in dangerous places. I like to jog, and I frequently jog right down the middle of a deserted street rather than on the sidewalk near alleys that might hold a mugger. I claim those same promises that you have underlined, and the Lord has never let me down. I think we must be prudent and cautious, of course, and when we have done that, we can rest in His protection free of fear. Now let's pray for His protection right now." And we did.

Such a peace and comfort his prayer brought! As we rose, he went to his briefcase and brought out a small metal door-bracing device that he used when traveling and gave me the address so I could order some for my external doors. How practical was his concern!

Never again have I been so afraid, although I've traveled the world, been in riots and revolutions, and had a madman walk into my home. I have claimed His protection for the past 30 years, and I continue to put my trust in Him. Not only has He taken care of my body, but He has even sent one of His faithful servants to straighten out my twisted thinking and remove the terror from my nights. What a God!

FERN GIBSON BABCOCK

OCTOBER 2

This Is My Life

This is the day the Lord has made; let us rejoice and be glad in it. Ps. 118:24, NIV.

One of the joys that my husband and I find in being parents is that of continually learning lessons from our children.

One such lesson came several years ago when our daughter Terril, a nurse, was totally exhausted from working nights at a hospital, taking six hours of college work, and teaching a prenatal class. She called to tell me that she was sick of the lifestyle she was caught up in and that she was going to drop one of her classes. She intended to get more sleep and have more fun.

Her sage observation was: "This is my life." She went on to say that we begin living, not after the next project is completed, but now. She was by no means diminishing the wise idea of planning ahead or of working toward goals. What she was saying was that the quality of our life as we extend ourselves and stretch forward needs to be positive and fruitful—and happy. She was combining the philosophies of "Today is the first day of the rest of your life" and "Take time to smell the flowers."

When I hung up from talking with her, I had an immediate attitude change. It was as if a light had turned on in my buzzing, busy brain. And the light that turned on wasn't a purple-pink psychedelic light. It was a calm, serene, blue light. The light was as blue as a Minnesota lake on a bright October day. Immediately I began "scheduling" some fun things—some times to be with friends. Immediately I began forcing away the guilt that usually erupted if I lingered too long on my morning walk or stretched out a precious moment of meditation.

I'm not naive. I know that there will be times when I absolutely have no control over a disrupted day or even a week. I know there will be times when I will be more or less moved with the current of activities—many times against my will. I intend to stay busy, and I abhor the idea of ever being considered lazy or undisciplined. But what I can control I will, with God's help. Some of the things I can control are my attitudes. I also will no longer let people take from me the things that I know are important to my physical, mental, and spiritual well-being.

Maybe David had reached some of these same conclusions when he wrote, "This is the day the Lord has made; let us rejoice and be glad in it."   BARBARA HUFF

OCTOBER 3

Only One Road Home

Strait is the gate, and narrow is the way, which leadeth unto life, and few there be that find it. Matt. 7:14, NIV.

We've all heard people ignorantly argue the point that all roads lead to heaven. A fatal deception! When Christ said that He is the way, we know He is the *only way* to heaven. But not only is Christ the only way to heaven; He is the only way to get through this "veil of tears" called life on Planet Earth. And His life insurance policy is out of this world! It's an eternal life insurance policy none of us is safe without.

You may have heard the story I'm about to paraphrase. It's about a husband and wife returning to their homeland after working tirelessly for the Lord on foreign soil for many long years—decades, in fact. On their ship was a famous dignitary. As they sailed into the busy harbor, the red-carpet treatment was afforded this dignitary, with throngs of people roaring, cheering him home. The fanfare on his behalf was phenomenal.

The missionary husband turned and said with deep sadness to his wife, "Look how the crowds are thronging around him! But no one, not one person, is here to welcome us home after all our toil and hardship these many hard years!"

His devoted wife, no doubt just as saddened, rose above her own sorrow to comfort him: "But honey, we're *not home yet!*"

Dear friend, remember that the way to our heavenly home is "strait" and narrow, and only a few will find it. You may feel like those returning missionaries—you are doing all the work, and someone else is reaping all the glory.

Lift up your weary chin, and know that there are other faithfuls out there too, working tirelessly like you, to reap a rich harvest for our lovely Jesus. Just remember that all the earthly glory others may be achieving here on earth for their own selfish pursuits doesn't hold a candle to the thrill that you, dear faithful soldier, will have when you wing your way into our heavenly home. It will be worth it all, I guarantee you, to have insisted on taking the *only way* home. Christ and His magnificent throng of brilliant angels will be there to welcome you like you've never been welcomed before! Home at last! Home at last! What a thrill it will be, to be *home at last!*
JUDY COULSTON

OCTOBER 4

Words of Intercession

I exhort therefore, that, first of all, supplications, prayers, intercessions, and giving of thanks, be made for all. 1 Tim. 2:1.

There are no atheists in foxholes," quipped the preacher. When one's life is threatened, the almost universal reaction is to pray, a desperate pleading for help from any god who will hear. No, there is nothing unusual about prayer for self.

But prayer for others is another matter. Or as Mark Twain commented when lauding the U.S.A.'s involvement in the Spanish-American War: "It is a good thing to fight for one's own freedom; it is a sight finer to fight for another man's."

The apostle Paul would agree; he exhorts Christians to pray for others, prayers of intercession "for all."

My father knew he was dying. In the reality of contemplating his funeral, he asked that he be buried in his old gray suit and that his new black one be given to my brother, his same size. Unusual, this thinking of *others* when facing death. Unusual, this thinking of others—period.

My office mail usually contains book advertisements, seminar announcements, and informative but often boring interoffice memos. Consequently, any handwritten letters get opened first, welcomed personal messages to break the business routine. Sandwiched between a literature brochure and a page of some committee minutes was a letter—"You have been chosen by our prayer group to be the object of special intercession next week. We will be asking God to remember you especially during that time." The note was signed by a friend who had moved away, yet who still remembered me in his prayers. It was comforting, reassuring.

Anyone who does consider others, pray for them, intercede for them—that person has the example of Christ. His whole life was by nature one cosmic intercession, one divine attempt to bridge the gap of sin. "Never lived there among men another so weighted with responsibilities. Never another carried so heavy a burden of the world's sorrow and sin" (*The Ministry of Healing*, p. 51).

The lives of millions hung with Him on that cross, their eternities made certain by the intercession of His blood. Although aware of the eternal significance of His death for millions, yet when dying Jesus still could pray for the *individual*: "Woman, behold thy son!" (John 19:26).

Excruciating pain, emotional and physical, pressed down: "Behold thy mother!" (verse 27). The thief died with hope; Jesus' tormentors were forgiven.

But we Christians are not Christ; we face no cosmic cross.

"Bury me in my old gray suit," my dad asked. And maybe that's the best a human can do; maybe that's all Paul meant: "I exhort . . . prayers, intercessions . . . be made for all."   WILMA MCCLARTY

OCTOBER 5

Words of Human Need

I thirst. John 19:28.

The story broke in a city a few miles away, so I wasn't surprised when local papers featured it for several days. But when my friend several states away told me she had read it in her newspaper, I began to realize the national human interest level of the little girl's plight.

The 5-year-old's story unraveled in a series of sickening episodes, told in graphic detail. As is so often the case in child abuse, weeks—even years—of neglect, harassment, or torture can go on unchecked, the youngster's age and size, which permitted the abuse in the first place, preventing his or her going for help.

Lucy's two adult tormentors would make the small tyke walk around and around the living room endlessly for hours, beating her if she stopped.

Exhausted, frightened, and thirsty, Lucy would beg, "I'm so thirsty. Please, may I have something to drink?"

And they would say, "Sure, here's some hot taco sauce." Her

protests would bring just more torment—walking, beating, thirsting.

Yes, the whole nation heard Lucy's cries, reacting in disbelief and then anger.

And what must Jesus have thought? Do you suppose He had a flashback to Calvary? He who bore a cross on a beaten back, who asked for something to drink—"His tongue was parched, and He said, 'I thirst.' They saturated a sponge with vinegar and gall, and offered it Him to drink; and when He had tasted it, He refused it" (*The Story of Redemption*, p. 224).

Poor little Lucy! The whole nation felt sorry for her, trying to imagine her misery. But Jesus needed no imagination to empathize, only memory. "See Him in His agony upon the cross, as He exclaimed, 'I thirst.' He had endured all that it is possible for us to bear. His victory is ours" (*The Desire of Ages*, p. 123). And Lucy's victory too . . . and the victories for all the sin-abused Lucys of the world.

"I thirst"—words of human need spoken by the Son of God. Oh, incomprehensible irony—the *Water of Life* thirsted that all might drink forever from the cup of His salvation.

WILMA McCLARTY

OCTOBER 6

Words of Peace of Mind

And the peace of God, which passeth all understanding, shall keep your hearts and minds through Christ Jesus. Phil. 4:7.

The Declaration of Independence guarantees to every American citizen life, liberty, and the pursuit of happiness as unalienable rights. That's the good news.

Now the bad news. Where are the instructions on how to pursue this happiness? And what does happiness mean in the first place?

One of the most popular parlor games ever manufactured is Trivial Pursuit, a game that intrigues its players by demanding recall of insignificant or at least easily forgotten facts. Categories such as history, geography, and entertainment serve up hundreds of questions such as the following: "Who led the victorious forces at the Battle of Hastings?" "What's the world's largest suspension bridge?" "Who sang the 1963 hit 'It's My Party'?" Do you know the answers? Does it make any difference either way?

Maybe one reason for the success of the game is that its purpose—to answer trivia questions—correlates with people's lives being pursuits of trivia. For many the pursuit of happiness has become trivial pursuit, with everyone searching in the wrong places for the wrong things for the wrong purposes, finding answers to questions that don't matter to begin with.

Life for the masses resembles the passengers on an airplane whose pilot told them, "I have something good to tell you—we're making excellent time. Now I have something bad to tell you—we're lost."

Too many people have confused temporary gratification with the eternal peace of mind that Paul spoke about to the Philippians. And so the pursuit of happiness has degenerated to a mad dash through life, trying to stay alive in the fast lane. The human "race" has become just that—a purposeless race to a trivial end.

Monopoly, another best-selling table game, has a card that says: "Go to jail. Go directly to jail. Do not pass Go. Do not collect $200." Often men and women spend their lives in search of temporary happiness, rarely finding even that—to say nothing of true peace of mind. They end up—no goals having been reached, no vast sums of money having been earned—in the prison of their own trivial pursuits.

Peace? Peace? What is it and how to get it? The peace that God gives never promises wealth, power, or even the temporary type of happiness. It offers something much better.

Paul in his time, Isaiah before him, and Ellen White after him would agree, all with their own Declarations of Peace of Mind Independence: "And the peace of God, which passeth all understanding, shall keep your hearts and minds through Christ Jesus" (Phil. 4:7). "Thou wilt keep him in perfect peace, whose mind is stayed on thee: because he trusteth in thee" (Isa. 26:3). "If you are faithful, the peace that passeth all understanding will be your reward in this life, and in the future life you will enter into the joy of your Lord" (*Testimonies*, vol. 8, p. 34).

God's peace of mind is a truth for *all* times, the unalienable right of all citizens of His kingdom. Thank God for His words of peace.
WILMA McCLARTY

OCTOBER 7

His Precious Jewels

And they shall be mine, saith the Lord of hosts, in that day when I make up my jewels. Mal. 3:17.

It was late October, and I sat alone lingering over a scrumptious breakfast. Although the food was pleasing, it was not the aroma, taste, or sight of it that caused me to linger a little longer. No, my leaving the table was delayed by the arrival of a small package that had just been pressed into my hands.

I was attending the New York Conference women's retreat. It was Sabbath morning, and as I started to leave the table, this small box was given to me. Inside was a crystal clover-shaped prism. As I held it up to the light, the prism reflected the colors of the tablecloth and of the pretty pink napkins. I sat as one entranced because it was so lovely.

Suddenly I was aware of the presence of another. Miriam Miller had quietly sat down beside me and was watching me watch the prism. I did not know that Miriam had been a diamond cutter. As I turned it this way and that, letting it catch the rays of light, Miriam began to describe how a prism must be cut and shaped in order to catch the light, just as a diamond must be cut and polished and recut and repolished again and again until it stands brilliant and multifaceted, picking up and reflecting rays of light all around it.

I sat there utterly fascinated as Miriam told me of the care taken in cutting and polishing each stone. My mind turned to Jesus, the Master Diamond Cutter, and to how He takes loving care to cut and polish us, His diamonds in the rough, His jewels, His precious jewels who are being outfitted to shine for His glory.

The diamond does not feel the cutting and the polishing, but we do. The process by which we are turned into jewels often hurts. We cry and feel bruised. Oh, if only we would remember that the Master Craftsman will never chip or mar us in the process. Oh, if only we would yield ourselves to His polishing, then we would come forth from His hands as a jewel fit for His precious crown.

> Here we are, all His jewels,
> Treasures from the night;
> Glowing in His light,
> He has gleaned us from the mines of earth,
> And claimed us as His own.
> Precious jewels we are,
> To brighten up His crown.
> There we were deep in the mines of sin;
> Torn and dirty, useless pebbles in the ground.
> Then Christ picked us up with His own hand,
> And cleansed us with His blood.
> Now we're precious jewels to brighten up His crown.

I met Miriam again at a little church at which I was singing for the worship service. After services we spoke again of the prism, the diamond, the Master Cutter, and of ourselves. Miriam added this postscript to the story of the cutting-polishing process. She said you must remember that the light that is reflected comes from the inside out, not from the outside in.

Women of the Lord, invite Jesus into your hearts so that He may shine out and so that others will be attracted to this marvelous sight, the marvelous jewel reflecting and refracting the Light of the world—Jesus.   JUNELL VANCE

OCTOBER 8

Groomed for Service

You say, "I am rich; I have acquired wealth and do not need a thing." But you do not realize that you are wretched, pitiful, poor, blind and naked. I counsel you to buy from me gold refined in the fire, so you can become rich; and white clothes to wear, so you can cover your shameful nakedness; and salve to put on your eyes, so you can see. Those whom I love I rebuke and discipline. So be earnest and repent. Rev. 3:17-19, NIV.

My 6-year-old grandson and I were driving home after a day at White Water Park. Mulling over the great events of our special day together, he reached over, patted my arm, and said, "Grandma, I really do love you."

"I'm glad, Scottie."

"In fact," he added, "I love every part of you."

"Is that so, dear?" I asked.

"And you know the part I like best?"

"Tell me."

"I like your floppy muscles that jiggle when you move your arm."

Now, that's acceptance! That's the dimension of love that looks beyond the wrinkles, the trifocals, the floppy arms. Maybe grandmas are supposed to look like that. In any event, Scottie is satisfied.

Is this somewhat like God? Does God accept me just the way I am, wrinkles and all? In the physical world, yes, God accepts me. If I've done the best with what I have, perhaps He gives me a passing grade.

What about the spiritual world? I believe that in my spiritual life God accepts me just the way I am too. He sees the dimness of my spiritual eyesight. He notes the wrinkles of harmful habits. Surely He recognizes the spiritual tone to muscles that are prone to temptation. Like Scottie, God loves me just the way I am, but unlike Scottie, He loves me too much to leave me that way.

God wants to give me a strong, steady step to go on His errands, to walk confidently in His paths. He is both able and willing to strengthen my spiritual perception so that I can see the beauty of His character, enabling me to reflect it to others more clearly. He is eager to firm up my spiritual muscles to resist evil, developing power that Satan cannot match. My Father wants to condition me for heaven, in the meantime grooming me for fuller service while I am here on earth. He longs to make me a whole, beautiful person. He loves me far too much just to leave me as I am.

LORABEL HERSCH

OCTOBER 9

Do Not Fear

So do not fear, for I am with you; do not be dismayed, for I am your God. I will strengthen you and help you; I will uphold you with my righteous right hand. Isa. 41:10, NIV.

This promise from Isaiah was printed in a box in a magazine I was reading. I thought it was so beautiful that I cut it out and slipped it into the frame of the mirror on my dresser.

Some months later my grandmother became very ill with cancer. As the weeks and months wore on, my mother realized that Grandmother would not recover. One day Mother confided to me, "I don't know how I'm going to hold up. Her suffering is getting unendurable. I can hardly keep from breaking down in her presence." She was trembling and wiping tears as she said it.

This frightened me. I was 19, and an untried Christian. I thought, *If Mother can't weather this storm of sorrow, how can I?* I also trembled. I went upstairs to my room. My eyes fell on the promise on the mirror. As I read it, an indescribable peace enveloped me. I will never forget it. I loved the promise the first time I read it, but its real value I experienced when I really needed it.

My heart still aches, though, when I remember that I did not show the promise to Mother, who needed its comfort even more than I did. No doubt God led me to it in order for me to pass it on to her. God's promises are so precious. We should be, not only acquainted with and grateful for them, but ready to pass them on to others at the opportune time.

MARCEDENE V. WOOD

Breaking or Building?

Therefore encourage one another and build each other up.
1 Thess. 5:11, NIV.

His little not-quite-2-year-old frame quivered as I looked down on him and continued to accuse and reprimand. He sucked in his lower lip, his eyes grew large, but he wasn't going to cry. The frightened blue eyes looking up at me belonged to the little boy for whom I had spent many hours crocheting the pieced, multicolored alphabet rug that he and I now stood on. Now he trembled before me. It rather shocked me as I stopped for a breath and saw his bodily reaction. Were my words really that powerful?

John Wycliffe once said, "The tongue breaketh bone, although the tongue itself have none." Is it really that strong? How will I harness and direct it? It is so tempting for a frustrated, tired young mother to react with angry words to the mishaps of the day. It is so tempting, with friends around you, to add to the funny stories by making fun of your best friend's habits and idiosyncrasies. It is so easy to blame someone else for the embarrassing, silly mistake you made at work.

Yet how beautiful and strengthening words can be. Gentle words of truth, kindness, acceptance, encouragement, and understanding. Words of confession and grace that speak of the wonder of God, of His love, and His wisdom. Words of welcome for the stranger, and words of commitment to a friend. How truly magnificent when there is personal integrity and verbal expression perfectly matching Christlike actions.

One glorious day God will change us, even our speech. Zephaniah 3:9 promises, "Yea, at that time I will change the speech of the peoples to a pure speech, that all of them may call on the name of the Lord and serve him with one accord" (RSV). What a wonderful day to look forward to, but even now we can claim God's power for a disciplined tongue to praise and honor Him. A tongue that will build up others rather than destroy them. A tongue that, with each word, speaks life and hope to all who hear it.

EVANGELINE LUNDSTROM

Solder of Society

A true friend sticks closer than one's nearest kin. Prov. 18:24, NRSV.

Society is changing, and it is affecting our personal relationships. In the past, relationships were continuous and long-lasting; but in today's superindustrialized society, many seem to be caught up in their own busy world feeling the need for self-sufficiency. This has made it so easy to push aside interaction with friends, loved ones, and neighbors. Feeling fragmented and crushed from our already overcrowded schedules, we withdraw, crying out, "This is enough—I cannot encompass another person or thing!"

In her book, *The 25-Hour Woman*, Sybil Stanton warns, "Worse than overcommitment is the other extreme of distancing yourself from people to avoid intimacy and vulnerability. We need closeness for our emotional health and growth . . . the trend toward self-sufficiency has perpetuated an 'I don't need anyone' attitude, which encourages some to avoid commitment and avow independence."

Jesus' life clearly portrays the importance of social interaction. He was social in His nature. He interacted with people on the streets, on boats, in the synagogue, and along the lakeshores. From attendance at the marriage of Cana to His visit to the home of Zacchaeus we come to understand that while Jesus enjoyed social interaction, the purpose of it was to help prepare people for citizenship in His kingdom. His presence and power in turning the water into wine added joy to the happy marriage occasion while also strengthening the faith of His mother and His disciples, and His social visit to the home of Zacchaeus transformed a life.

Why not reevaluate your busy schedule? Consider priorities and adjust your day's activities. Become acquainted with your new neighbors by taking them a baked casserole, or offering to care for their children while they unpack. Write a note of thanks to the person who did something special for you, or write a department store, praising a certain salesperson for his or her helpfulness. Join a prayer or Bible study group. Plan a time in every week when you and the family or a friend can enjoy a special time together. In relaxing your schedule for interaction with others, you just might lower your stress level! Taking a new look at sustaining relationships doesn't mean we take on all the world and its problems. It does mean we take time to relax, renewing our strength while lifting the burdens of others and influencing them for Christ. As with the Australian boomerang, the happiness we bring to others comes back to us.

How true are Robert Blair's words of wisdom: "Friendship! mysterious cement of the soul! Sweetener of life, and solder of society!"   MARIE SPANGLER

OCTOBER 12

We All Have a Chance

There is neither Jew nor Greek, there is neither slave nor free, there is neither male nor female; for you are all one in Christ Jesus. Gal. 3:28, NKJV.

In October of 1992 I had one of the most wonderful experiences of my life. I spent one week in Israel. Our hotel was on the slope of the Mount of Olives facing Jerusalem. Every day I could feast my eyes on the city and the surrounding area, for Jerusalem is 2,500 feet high.

Every day brought a new adventure for me. On one particular day we spent eight hours touring the old part of the city. Every important happening recorded in the Bible has some sort of church commemorating that spot. The site of Solomon's Temple has the Dome of the Rock mosque, where the Muslims meet to worship. Five times a day you can hear the mournful wail calling Muslims to stop what they are doing and go to the mosque to pray. Greek Orthodox, Armenian, Catholic, and other churches are all over the city. Everywhere I went there were church services being conducted. Sometimes small groups of tourists were gathered together to study and worship right at the place we were visiting. And there seemed to be praise-filled songs all over Jerusalem.

Because our visit was early in the season, before most Americans go to Israel, the songs were sung mostly in languages that I did not know, but I did recognize many of the melodies that I heard. It gave me a warm feeling to realize that people from around the world were here to share with me where my Jesus had been, even if I could not understand what they were saying or singing.

My most favorite church was in Bethlehem, built by the Canadian Catholics, situated on top of the mountain overlooking the fields of the shepherds. It was light and airy, and the priest officiating at the service radiated happiness as he shared the good news with his congregation.

Those who came to pray at the Wailing Wall were so reverent

334

that when they had finished their prayers or left their messages pressed in between the cracks of the stones in the wall, they backed away a respectful distance before turning to leave the area. There was always an attitude of respect in every church or holy place that we visited.

Your life can never be the same after you have visited the Holy Land. There is so much to see and even more to think about. I saw so many different forms of worship, heard so many songs of praise, even on the top of Masada. I went down and touched the Wailing Wall and stood with the worshipers there. I watched a Jewish man form his own prayer closet using his prayer shawl, watched the priests sprinkling incense, and clothed myself properly to enter a Muslim mosque.

And what impressed me the most was that all were worshiping the same God. How wonderful that God sees no differences between us. We are all His children. How reassuring to know that He hears our praises, hears our requests, and knows the secret messages pressed into the walls of our hearts. In the end, whether Jew or Gentile, male or female, we all answer to the same God.

SHEILA BIRKENSTOCK SANDERS

OCTOBER 13

Please Give Me Strength

God is our refuge and strength, a very present help in trouble. Therefore we will not fear, though the earth be removed, and though the mountains be carried into the midst of the sea. Ps. 46:1, 2, NKJV.

My idea of wilderness had always been influenced by books I had read about the Lewis and Clark expeditions. Imagine my surprise when I traveled through the wilderness of Judea and found mountains with absolutely nothing on them but rocks. I didn't even see a weed in some places.

One warm October day I went to the top of the mountain plateau called Masada, which overlooks the Dead Sea. I got there the easy way—by tram. On the top of the 200-acre hilltop I listened to the story of the few against the many.

In the latter part of the first century A.D., 12,000 Roman soldiers and 60,000 Jewish slaves began building a ramp to the top of Masada to wipe out the last vestiges of rebellion against the Roman government by about 900 Jews living on the top of Masada. When these Jews saw that it was impossible to stop the advance of the Roman soldiers, they decided to kill themselves rather than surrender. Each man killed the members of his own household. Then those remaining drew lots, and 10 were selected to kill the others. The 10 remaining men drew lots again, and one man was chosen to kill the nine, then to fall on his sword when all were dead. All the buildings were destroyed except the storehouses, which were left full of food so that the Romans would realize that they had not been driven to suicide because of starvation.

It was a somber story told in a desolate area, and I could not help wondering and speculating about the people living at that time. That death was going to be the final solution, whether by the hands of the Romans or their own, was evident. But what a terribly painful solution to have to kill your own wife and children. How they all must have suffered over the decision that they made. There is no doubt in my mind that they called on God for strength under such adverse circumstances.

How wonderful to know that they and we can pray to the same God, ask for help, commitment, or deliverance, and He will answer our requests with the appropriate response. My daily prayer is that I can live my life fearlessly, facing whatever may happen, with the same singleness of purpose, the same strength or belief, and the same confidence in God as my refuge, as did those living on Masada almost 2,000 years ago. SHEILA BIRKENSTOCK SANDERS

OCTOBER 14

A Lesson in Humility

For by the grace given me I say to every one of you: Do not think of yourself more highly than you ought, but rather think of yourself with sober judgment, in accordance with the measure of faith God has given you. Rom. 12:3, NIV.

One of the greatest blessings God has given us is the blessing of friends. This blessing is even more precious when our friends are members of our own families. What a thrill it is when one son telephones us from college "just for a chat" or when the other wants us to share in the fun with his friends. We thank God every day that we have a good relationship with our sons; that we can talk together, share things, and relish each other's company.

A few years ago I learned how precious this closeness can be. Since my mother died I have always been the one to "fix" things in our family. No matter what went wrong, my father, brothers, and sister turned to me, and invariably I was able to solve the problem.

Sometimes I had to ask God's help, but often I was able to cope alone.

Now, however, I was faced with a problem I couldn't solve. My father, who has Alzheimer's disease, was living with us. The doctor wanted him to go into the hospital for an assessment. His subsequent opinion was that my father needed full-time psychiatric care. I couldn't accept the verdict. Everything in me revolted against him going into the hospital permanently. I wanted to care for him. I wanted to cope. I wanted to "fix" things, as I had always done.

As we left the hospital my tears flowed freely. The past few days had been a nightmare, and my mind was in rebellion to all I had been told. Suddenly my son took my hands and, looking deep into my eyes, said words I will never forget. "Mother, all through our lives you have taught us to take all our problems to God; to rely on Him for guidance and to follow His leading." Gently but very firmly and with great emphasis he said, "I think it is time you took your own advice."

The words of my child stopped me in my tracks, and I realized he was right. I was saying all the right things to them, but in my own life I was all too often relying on my own strength. There and then I gave the problem to God. The pain didn't go away immediately. I still hated the thought of others doing what I couldn't for my father, but I was able to allow God to direct my thoughts and to make decisions according to His will.

Now, although I still wish it could be otherwise, I can see that my father is cared for in ways I could never have managed. There is peace in my heart when I look at him, and thankfulness that I was taught a valuable lesson before my self-sufficiency became too great.

No longer am I able to "fix" things. Oh, I admit, sometimes I try. But when I am tempted to do so, I remember the words of my son and turn the problem over to my heavenly Father. In doing so, I am thankful that my son, as my friend, was able to point out that I was in the wrong. Friendship brings responsibilities, and one of these is not being afraid to point out error in a gentle, loving, but firm way.

AUDREY BALDERSTONE

OCTOBER 15

He Loves

Jesus wept. Then the Jews said, "See how he loved him!"
John 11:35, 36, NIV.

The mother of twin boys whom I had known since birth recently asked me to write to them on the occasion of the brutal and untimely death of their father. Because their relationship with their father had not been the best, I struggled to find something of value to say to these sons, now in their early 20s, that would ease their pain at such a time. This is what I wrote:

"No one has a perfect parent, yet we all have a vision or dream of what that perfect parent might be for us. Somewhere in our subconscious we each keep hoping that one day our parent, while still alive, might miraculously turn a new page and give us the unconditional love and nurturing for which we long—and actually need in order to thrive.

"When the relationship with a parent is damaged or dysfunctional and that parent dies, we then have lost hope of that miracle ever taking place; all hope of that perfect, loving, nurturing parent has vanished. Not only do we need to grieve for our parent and whatever his or her role was in our lives, but we also need to grieve for the perfect parent for which we longed. This process may be more painful and more difficult than grieving the death of a parent with whom we had a wonderful relationship.

"Grieving now is essential nevertheless. Grieve the loss of what you had; the loss of what you might have had. If you do not grieve at the appropriate time, the unresolved grief will come back to haunt you at a later time in unexpected, often exaggerated, and sometimes frightening ways.

"Take time to be with your sorrow and experience it as a normal part of the life process here on this planet. Feel the pain, acknowledge it, talk about it if you can, and in so doing you will heal and grow. Remember to celebrate the happy times you shared with your dad. Look to a Power greater than you, for there is One who knows your sorrows—who will comfort you in your grief."

How comforting that Christ, our role model, set us an example in grieving—Jesus wept.

MYRNA MELLING

OCTOBER 16

Extraordinary Power

Every good gift and every perfect gift is from above, and cometh down from the Father of lights, with whom is no variableness, neither shadow of turning. James 1:17.

God is always ready to listen to us and to answer favorably our requests on condition that we address Him with faith and in the name of Jesus Christ!

I would like to tell you briefly how God revealed Himself to me personally in the days of distress. Above all, it is an experience that edified me spiritually. Prayer is a powerful arm that all of us ought to use whenever we are assailed by the trials of the enemy.

It was in 1988 that all my family went to Uganda, where my husband was to study theology. While my husband and children were in school, I was occupied with domestic duties and a small child who at that time was not yet of school age.

One day my husband was struck by malaria, and his condition worsened incredibly. We did everything we could to assist his healing, but in vain. His condition became worse and worse. This situation troubled me greatly. The whole family was worried, and all the more since we were in a foreign country. The doctors truly spared no effort and finally counseled me to transfer him to another hospital because the case seemed to be beyond them and had become more and more alarming. You can imagine how I was reacting in the face of this situation: I grew cold from fear and trembled.

I began to make preparations for the transfer, but aside from my husband's sickness what worried me the most was the language, because I could not communicate. Neither my English nor my Swahili could help me in this situation. It was a bête noire for me because my husband was now unconscious.

Just before our departure for the hospital I heard a soft voice coming from I don't know where, asking these two questions: "Why are you crying? Why are you discouraged and desperate? Pray!" Immediately I knelt down and began to pray: "O God, it is You who created us and who have everything at Your command. It is You who by Your strength healed the mother-in-law of Peter while she was in all likelihood suffering from the same sickness as my husband. I am always trusting and counting on Your wonderful power. Lord, if it be Your will, heal my husband of this malaria, or teach me a language to enable me to communicate with the doctors of the hospital to which I am preparing to go tomorrow morning, because all knowledge comes from You, Lord. You can do everything, Lord. I implore You to answer my prayer that comes from my heart, that I address to You in the name of Jesus Christ, Your Son. Amen."

After this prayer I went to bed. Nevertheless, I woke up from time to time to check on my husband and give him a drink. Astonishingly, toward midnight he began to speak and told me that he felt relief from the headache and that his temperature was beginning to go down! The next morning the patient himself raised his voice to say that he no longer saw the necessity of going to another hospital, because he was beginning to feel better!

The All-powerful healed my husband. I am an eyewitness. The Lord answered my prayer without delay. It is I who confirm it. Following my sincere prayer my husband was not long in going back to his studies after total healing from malaria. Our family will never forget the experience. Truly the Lord hears and answers.

In conclusion, I would like to assure all of you who read this that there is an extraordinary power in prayer, as was the case with Elijah, Moses, Joseph, Anna, and others. Let us talk to the Lord, and He will answer us. This is our assurance by Him who does not change, with whom, as James affirms in his Epistle, there is no variableness or shadow of turning.

ESTHER SIMBAYOBEWE

OCTOBER 17

In His Service

And whatever you do or say, let it be as a representative of the Lord Jesus, and come with him into the presence of God the Father to give him your thanks. Col. 3:17, TLB.

A few years ago, while I was working as a medical assistant for an urgent-care facility, a woman in her 30s came in to see the doctor. After being treated and released, she was instructed to return within a few days if she wasn't feeling any better.

After she left, my coworkers and I settled back to enjoy a few relaxing moments before the next emergency. Our break was short-lived, as someone stumbled through the door—it was the same woman we had just discharged. At first she stood silent and expressionless in front of the desk. Then she burst into uncontrollable weeping.

Unable to move, I watched her standing there, sobbing, body limp and trembling, concentrating on keeping herself erect. "I've been mugged!" she exclaimed suddenly. "I've been mugged!" she repeated, crying wildly. We were all standing motionless for what seemed like hours, listening to the paralyzing words.

Finally I was able to shake off my stupor to walk around the desk to where she stood and place one arm around her. Slowly I guided her into a treatment room. I listened sympathetically as she poured out the details of her ordeal. Occasionally I would interject words of comfort as I held her hand or nodded my head. After a while she regained her composure, and the atmosphere changed to laughter and small talk about our lives. She thanked me generously for my help, and she kept in touch with me by phone a few times after that memorable day.

It seemed a small thing to offer a soothing word and a listening ear, hardly much to warrant such deep appreciation. And yet God had given me the opportunity to be a "representative of the Lord Jesus" to someone in need, not only to bless her but to bring blessing on myself and honor to the Father. Christ's call to service can surprise us in the least-expected moments of life—what's important is not to lose that opportunity when it comes our way.

JAMISEN MATTHEWS

OCTOBER 18

Fishing on the Other Side of the Boat

He said, "Throw your net on the right side of the boat and you will find some." When they did, they were unable to haul the net in because of the large number of fish. John 21:6, NIV.

Jesus loves to prepare food for us. He does this when it is least expected. When the disciples went fishing (to meet some of their physical needs after Christ's crucifixion), they fished all night without results.

Jesus was there on the shore. He showed up quite unexpectedly, preparing breakfast for them. He called out, "Friends, haven't you any fish?"

"No," they answered.

Then Jesus told them to throw their nets on the other side of the boat, and when they did this, they got a large number of fish.

I don't think the disciples were praying, "Lord, please help us catch fish." But Jesus read their hearts, and I think the heart message was: "Jesus, how will we ever be able to do the work You have called us to do? We can't even catch fish!"

It's at a time of desperate need that Jesus comes and tells us how to catch fish, and then He prepares a table of food for us that others know nothing about. Jesus referred to this food when talking with the woman at the well (John 4:32).

When I felt God calling me to full-time ministry, I struggled for months before coming to a decision. I was afraid to leave my place of work. My job gave me a sense of security. It was my place of witness. But I felt God tugging at my heart. I had a consuming passion to lead people to Christ. I wanted more and more people to know Him and have hope.

341

Early one Friday morning Jesus surprised me with food prepared by Him, and He asked me to fish on the other side of the
boat. The side of faith, the unknown. "Lord," I said, "help me
make a right decision. I need Your peace." As I prayed, I opened my
Bible to Genesis 15:1, then turned a few pages to Exodus 14:13,
then a few more to Numbers 14:9. As I continued turning pages,
the same four words spoke to me as if they were the only four
words on the page: "Do not be afraid."

As I continued reading, I saw these same four words 20 times
in just a few minutes. The last verses I read dealt with priorities:
John 6:27-33; John 4:34-38; Matthew 6:25-34. What peace I had
as I ate the food Jesus prepared and was strengthened to make a
decision.

After I quit work, the Lord affirmed my decision with a large
catch on the other side of the boat. The first month God blessed me
with 17 decisions to follow Him—people God brought into my life
by divine appointment!

When Jesus prepares food for us, it's always special; it strengthens us and increases our faith. I don't know what God is calling you
to do, but whatever it is, do it with all your might. "Do not be
afraid!" HAZEL BURNS

OCTOBER 19

Thankful for What?

Do not be anxious about anything, but in everything, by
prayer and petition, with thanksgiving, present your re-
quests to God. Phil. 4:6, NIV.

My tearful face was unsettling my surgeon, who was also my
friend. But this was serious business.

I thrust my arm out like a signal for a left turn. "Look at this
fat arm," I sobbed. "Why? Why now, after all this time? I've been
perfectly normal—even healthy—for a whole year. I don't understand . . ." Tears dribbled down my chin.

"Sometimes it happens this way after breast cancer surgery."
His voice was calm and kind. "It can happen even after two or three
years. But it's a circulation problem, and it's not fatal." He looked
at the arm. "Besides, it's hardly noticeable."

"Hardly noticeable! Well, I notice it. It's full of needles and pins
that never go away. It bothers me all the time; I can't keep my mind
off it."

He handed me a card. "Get an elastic bandage from Orthotics

to wear in the daytime. Keep it elevated as much as possible."

I wasn't comforted.

"Cheer up! You'll get used to it." He was smiling.

"*Get used to it!* You mean I have to carry this ugly, uncomfortable thing around for the rest of my life?"

As I walked to my car I was filled with visions of an arm getting bigger and bigger, turning purple, then black, then gangrenous. I knew better, but I couldn't help it.

I grieved. I pounded the pillows. I considered a concession on Kleenex. This was harder to take than the lump in my breast. At least that was something I could get rid of.

Pieces of Scripture eddied about my mind. *"Don't be anxious . . ." "In every thing give thanks . . ." "The Lord has chastened me severely . . ." "Stop grumbling . . ." O God, help me!*

One day it occurred to me that I did have another option. My surgeon could cut the thing off.

I looked at the offending arm with new eyes. It was all there, working just fine, serving me well. Actually, I was very attached to it.

"Hey, praise the Lord! I have a usable arm!"

Yes, I have gotten used to it. Sometimes I can forget about it for several hours at a time. And it hasn't gotten bigger, or purple, or gangrenous.

"Thank You, God. This is a wonderful arm."

AILEEN LUDINGTON

OCTOBER 20

The Former Things Are Passed Away

And God shall wipe away all tears from their eyes; and there shall be no more death, neither sorrow, nor crying, neither shall there be any more pain; for the former things are passed away. Rev. 21:4.

February 23, 1990, will remain forever in my memory. It was a sunny, crystal-clear, but very cold day in northern Michigan. My husband and I were driving south for the wedding of a nephew. We were taking a leisurely scenic route, enjoying the beauty of the glistening snow on the tall pine trees. The bright sunshine made each snow crystal fairly dazzle.

As I drove, my husband read to me from our newest book, *Thoughts From the Mount of Blessing.* He had read the first 13 pages, which included the section on Matthew 5:4, "Blessed are they that mourn," when I asked him to stop reading so that I could quietly think about what he had read.

At that very moment, in His infinite wisdom and love, God was preparing us for the most traumatic experience of our lives. The next 24 hours would be indelibly impressed upon our hearts and lives forever.

At very nearly the same hour that we were reading together in the car, the lives of our oldest daughter, her husband, and their 2-year-old daughter ended abruptly in an automobile accident in Virginia. We did not get the news until noon the next day.

Horrendous. That word was in my vocabulary for several months. I could not speak of their deaths without using that word over and over.

What was it like to have three loved ones snatched from our lives so abruptly, you ask? It was unspeakable pain, endless numbness, loss of sleep, appetite, and even reason at times. For a long time the question "Why?" hung over us like a black cloud, nearly suffocating us.

Yet as I look back on those first nightmarish days I can still recall the feeling of being "wrapped in soft cotton" by everyone around us. Family, relatives, and friends provided financial assistance for our trip to Virginia. As we made the journey, we were forced to stay overnight with my family in Indiana because of a bad winter storm. The Lord knew we needed that time to gather strength for the days ahead.

Prayers, prayers, everywhere, everyone. Pain, pain, intense, throbbing pain. Over and over our anguished cries, "Jesus, where are You? Why? Why? Why?" Seeming silence! "Jesus loves me, this I know" was the part of the funeral service for Kari, who was only a baby. Even now it brings me pain to hear it or to sing it.

But soon, very soon, the great Life-giver Himself will call our children forth from their graves on a mountaintop in Virginia. Then together we will all go home! Then He will answer the whys. Our tears will be dried forever, and the pain will be gone forever, "for the former things are passed away." "Even so, come, Lord Jesus."

BETTY R. BURNETT

Anywhere With Jesus I Can Safely Go

For . . . you must learn to know God better and discover what he wants you to do. Next, learn to put aside your own desires so that you will become patient and godly, gladly letting God have his way with you. This will make possible the next step, which is for you to enjoy other people and to like them, and finally you will grow to love them deeply. The more you go on in this way, the more you will grow strong spiritually and become fruitful and useful to our Lord Jesus Christ. 2 Peter 1:5-8, TLB.

In the past 24 years I have seen Christian literature placed in thousands of homes. I will be forever grateful that the Lord allowed me to be a spectator as He prepared the hearts of the people to accept this literature.

It has been a lifelong series of unforgettable experiences. He has taken me deep into Catholic convents where I had never been before. He has taken me to large mansions and to humble shacks. He has taken me up to the tops of high rises and down to the depths of valleys. I've walked in mud up to my knees because my car could not go any farther. He has taken me to college dormitories and behind state penitentiary walls, to pastors of all denominations, to college professors, to the blind, and to those who could not hear.

He has taken me to plantations and to servants' quarters. We've gone across creek bottoms to an Amish farmer who said it was humanly impossible to get there.

We've gone into bars and taverns. We've gone far back in the mountains, through the large cities, to the rich and to the poor. To the people of all nations. To the learned and to the illiterate. To the 33-year-old young woman who asked, "Can you teach me to pray? I don't know how!" To the lady who said, "I can't listen now. My heart is so heavy because my children have no food and are hungry." To the young, to the old. To the sick, to the lonely. To the young woman possessed by demons and delivered from oppression.

We have been in scorching heat and in blinding snowstorms. On roads and sidewalks covered with thick ice, where I had to climb down a mountain on my hands and knees after visiting with a grandmother who wanted our books for her grandchildren.

We've gone to a young man studying to be a warlock. To a Hare Krishna temple, where we sat cross-legged in a circle and watched as a plant was worshiped instead of the God who made the plant. To the man by the side of the road with the sign "I'll work for food"—and as I circled back to give him my lunch, I looked into his eyes. To me, they looked like the eyes of Jesus. I quickly turned so he couldn't see my tears. For many days his eyes haunted me. In my mind I had truly seen Jesus that day.

Always at the end of the day, wherever I've gone, I can truly say I walked today where Jesus walked, and felt Him close to me.

SANDY LEE BETKE DANCEK

Truth

And ye shall know the truth, and the truth shall make you free. . . . If the Son therefore shall make you free, ye shall be free indeed. John 8:32-36.

As a child I read an abridged rendition of Nathaniel Hawthorne's *Scarlet Letter*. Last night I read a critical edition. Now I know that Hester Prynne is one character who greatly shaped my life responses to imposed silence and aloneness. Now I know the others in the story as well.

I have been Hester, walking alone, my great sin lying in consenting to the lie, in not being true to myself. But I will, by the grace of God, turn that silence into a ministry of listening and caring. And I will hope, as did Hester, for a prophet one day who *will* be heard.

I have been Arthur Dimmesdale, dying alone for lack of one piece of knowledge, sensing the presence of dreadful evil very near but not knowing where, unable to discern friend from foe because of my sin of consenting to the lie. But I will tell the truth now, be the cost what it may.

I have been Roger Chillingworth, greatly wronged, and aware that I contributed to that wronging by giving myself to a system that could never love me. But I will choose to give up the vengeance rather than to let it eat me alive, alone.

I have been Pearl, a child of the forest and a mystery to my parents, crying out for the truth about the identity of the origin of my life's evil, the one who with increasing intensity and decreasing subtlety refused to acquiesce under the alienation and aloneness imposed on her from birth.

The only way of escape for any of my characters lies in climbing the scaffold of truth. Then we will find we are no longer alone.

WILMA ZALABOK

God's Lovingkindness

We have thought of thy lovingkindness, O God, in the midst of thy temple. Ps. 48:9.

My only son had a job that necessitated his traveling over several states. He had no direct address to receive mail or phone calls. Sometimes he would call me or just show up at home, but often there were long stretches of time that I did not hear from him. When this happened and I could not bear it any longer, I would go to the piano or organ and play, "Where Is My Wandering Boy Tonight, Does Jesus Care?" It never seemed to fail that I would hear from him right away. I did this often because of the longing in my heart to know he was OK. I know that the Lord cares about mothers and their children.

One time when we were living in Idaho, I went to Boise to a literature evangelist institute for a week in January while my husband and son stayed home. When I was ready to return home on the bus we had a big snowfall, and the roads were impassable. The bus was not able to get through until the snowplows had cleared a path on the highway, which took a couple of days. When I finally arrived at my hometown, it was night. My husband and son were at the bus station waiting for me, and together we began the half-mile walk home in the freezing cold. I had caught a cold while gone and was tired from the trip, and the blowing wind had chilled me to the very bone. I longingly anticipated my warm house and a nice warm bath.

As I was thinking about the warm bath I would soon be taking, my husband broke the silence. "I don't know what we'll do, but I know we're going home to a cold house. I've ordered coal for the furnace, but the delivery truck hasn't been able to get through because of the snow." My heart sank at the very thought of a cold house, but I began to pray earnestly.

When we arrived at the house, the coal bin was full! Soon we had a good fire going and a season of praise to our wonderful Father for His lovingkindness!

When I find a promise in God's Word I like to put a "TP" in the margin by it for "Try to Prove"; then I pray and watch for it to happen.

LOIS BARKER

God Does Lead

You chart the path ahead of me, and tell me where to stop and rest. Every moment, you know where I am. Ps. 139:3, TLB.

I sat numbly, anguished and weary with the pain of an abusive marriage. I was too depressed to pray, unable to share the facts of abuse in my marriage. Totally unaware of the reasons for my discouragement, the pastor could say little to lessen my pain or to make things better for me. But just before he left, he suggested that I read Psalm 139.

Because of my inability to find passages that would reach through my pain, it took me some days to reach for a Bible to read the chapter. Through the fog of depression a faint glimmer of hope reached my heart as I read the words.

Years have passed. I still cannot understand the whys of those painful years. But I do know the Lord carried me through. No, the pain did not suddenly end when I was finally able to leave the marriage safely. But I was able to earn a graduate degree and obtain very wonderful support from my classmates and family as I went through the court system to prevent further sexual abuse of my children by their father. Counseling and time have brought healing to our family. The hurt and anger have subsided. Now we are going on with joy in our new life.

Why did God allow those painful years? I don't know. But the Lord does lead. Psalm 139 is precious now as I look back at His miraculous leading, ending those painful years in the very best way for us. Whatever His reasons, I now understand the pain of other women in similar circumstances. I can be a support and a role model in a unique way.

Are you hurting? Your hurting years can end. Don't let go of God . . . He *is* with you. If you can't read the Bible for yourself, read a Bible story to a child. If you can't pray, read the words of a hymn, or just rest in the prayers of others. Begin little steps toward a better life. God knows where you are, and He loves you. He *will* bring you slowly and tenderly to better days. Help is available. Take advantage of it, and God *will* lead.

Maybe life is good for you. Are your friends happy too? Don't be too sure. I wore my mask of "dutiful mother and happy wife" to church each week. I denied my pain if some perceptive person asked questions. It is very likely that you know someone who also wears a mask to cover pain. Pray for your friends, and share promises from the Word. Share your discouragements, opening the door for your friends to share too. Familiarize yourself with community and church resources for hurting women. God can use *you* to alleviate the pain in other women's lives in a way no one else can.

ANONYMOUS

OCTOBER 25

A New Heart

I will give you a new heart [I will give you new and right desires] and put a new spirit in you; I will remove from you your heart of stone [sin] and give you a new heart of flesh [love]. And I will put my Spirit in you and move you to follow my decrees and be careful to keep my laws. Eze. 36:26, NIV.

My brother-in-law, Bill, is a budding authority on astronomy, and I love to see the excitement on his face as he describes the latest article in his journals about some new equipment or discovery. On a clear summer night he will spend hours searching the starry heavens to see the rings of Saturn or some other specific wonder in God's night array.

What an awesome thought that the great constellations, the Milky Way, the Big Dipper, and all the billions of stars and planets are there because God spoke—He commanded, and they appeared.

That same God, who is the same yesterday, today, and forever, speaks to us and tells us He wants to do something very special and beautiful for us. "I want to create in you a new heart."

At a recent Christian women's retreat Alice came wearing a facade of smiles and laughter, but underneath there was an ache that would not go away. On Friday night we were all asked to write a short prayer to God—to tell Him why we had come to the retreat, what we were really feeling inside, and what we would like for Him to do for us.

Reluctantly she wrote her thoughts on paper, hardly daring to believe that God was willing to speak to her troubled heart and to meet her needs. As the weekend progressed, she began to feel the pain slide away, and to feel a cleansing and a peace filling her heart. She left that weekend with a "new heart."

What a powerful yet personal God! He who created the sun, moon, and stars says to us, "Come boldly into My presence. Come, let's talk this over." Then He gives us this incredible promise: "I will give you a new heart."

RUTHIE JACOBSON

So Can You

But God is faithful, who will not suffer you to be tempted above that ye are able; but will with the temptation also make a way to escape, that ye may be able to bear it. 1 Cor. 10:13.

If I can do it, Gertrude, so can you!" I was speaking to my 65-year-old volunteer in the medical library. She had been given a prescription from her doctor to "do some volunteer work" to take her mind off herself and her depression. She was a Jewish lady who had recently lost her husband from cancer, and partly because of his death and partly because of the holocaust that had occurred in Europe during World War II, she no longer believed in God, and could see little reason for living. I had "inherited" Gertrude from the volunteer office.

"If I could survive the death of my mother when I was 4, the death of my stepmother when I was 10, the death of my brother when I was 14, the death of my baby when I was 22, the death of our 28-year-old daughter, and the death of my father two years ago, you can survive the death of your husband." I never realized how difficult it would be to console or encourage someone who did not believe in God. I couldn't use Christ as an example, since she wasn't a Christian, but I couldn't even use God this time. We who take for granted the "blessed hope" find it hard to understand when someone has no hope at all.

Gradually, over a period of six months, I had the joy of seeing Gertrude change from a depressed, unhappy person to a lovely, enthusiastic woman. The last I heard, she was still there, volunteering.

I would not have chosen to lose any of my loved ones, but God can bring good from it, as evidenced by Gertrude. He has told us He will not give us more to bear than we are able, but will give us the ability to cope with it. This He has done, and He has even provided others for me to help, by the use of these experiences. So if you too have had many tragedies in your life, turn them around, with God's help, and help someone else to find that hope also.

LORAINE SWEETLAND

God's Promises Are Sure

*For no matter how many promises God has made, they are
"Yes" in Christ. 2 Cor. 1:20, NIV.*

After a difficult time in our family life and a period of marital
separation, the family was reunited and we were all rejoicing in
our precious times together. We had been to visit family in Arizona,
and the day had been stormy with dark, fierce clouds, rain, and
hail. As we were driving home through a lonely stretch of desert I
was recounting the amazing story of God's grace after the flood of
Noah, and how worried they were that this devastation might
occur again. And so God, in His wonderful love for His children,
made a solemn promise to them that He would never cover the
whole world by water again. And so that they wouldn't fear when
the raindrops fell, He gave them His promise, the beautiful rainbow
that we so often see after a storm. As we talked of this Bible story,
I commented that I could not recall ever seeing a completely whole
rainbow that spanned the sky, where both ends could be seen
touching the ground. I assumed that this is the way that rainbows
are supposed to look, as that's the way they are always painted in
picture books.

Just then something prompted me to look out the back
window. As I glanced out I saw a rainbow, and I started shouting
to our oldest son, who was driving, "Stop the car! Stop the car,
quick!" He slammed on the brakes and pulled the car over to the
side of the road, all the while wondering if Mom had lost her
marbles. I jumped out of the car, and there was my rainbow—a
complete, whole rainbow spanning the sky, with both ends touching the earth. If I hadn't looked behind at that moment, I wouldn't
have seen what I had never seen before. And for me, that is so true
of life. Sometimes I can see God's promises in my life only by
looking behind, at the way He has led me, and trusting that there
will be rainbows in my future too. JANIS VANCE

A Good Word

Anxiety weighs down the human heart, but a good word cheers it up. Prov. 12:25, NRSV.

Pregnant, facing certain banishment from continuing her education, she dropped out of academy to marry. She felt no pride in the pregnancy, only the shame of her fear and stupidity. Still, was she not a person?

That summer she wheeled her newborn across the uneven ground at camp meeting. Though ashamed of the circumstance of his birth, she felt immense pride in her child. Leaving school had meant abandoning all friendships with fellow students. She accepted that. Her life no longer existed on the same plane as theirs. But somewhere in the adult society of the church, the only society she knew and valued, must come an acceptance of her son.

Spotting her favorite teacher near the pavilion, she timidly approached. "Do you want to see my baby?"

The woman looked at her coldly. "You should be ashamed," she muttered, and walked away.

Wrapped in a mist of pain, the young mother slowly turned from the meeting place and headed aimlessly across the campground, pushing the bulky carriage. She looked up at no one.

Suddenly a voice called, "Wait a minute! I want to get a look at that young man."

Through blurred vision she watched the academy principal striding toward her. The principal: a man feared and revered by students; a man respected by the community; a man so gifted with words he could shred a person to pieces if he chose, but also a man with incredible insight into human need. This man stooped and lifted the infant from his carriage, held him high, proclaimed him beautiful and wonderful, and cradled him in his blessed arms.

It took hardly more than a minute, but that and his public smile of affirmation and acceptance lasted a lifetime, making more difference than he could have imagined.

Grace Observed

> I watched her there,
> a child too young
> for burdens she must bear;
> head low, with world

of weight upon her spine.
And then a word, a smile;
I knew not the content
nor the cause,
but what I witnessed
gave me pause,
for from a child
to woman she transformed;
her back drew straight,
her head raised high.
I saw life's radiance
in her eye.
What words she heard I cannot know,
but Father, teach me to speak so.

Dear Lord, You called us not to be judges of one another, but to be ministers of Your love. Help me speak the helping words to set someone else's life alight for You or ease a heaviness of heart. You shower me with kindness; teach me, please, to pass it on.

LOIS PECCE

OCTOBER 29

Good News

And the angel said to them, "Do not be afraid; for behold, I bring you good news of a great joy which shall be for all the people; for today in the city of David there has been born for you a Savior, who is Christ the Lord." Luke 2:10, 11, NASB.

Before the birth of our daughter I meticulously made out two lists of people who should be notified after her arrival. I gave one list to my mother, who would be at the birth, and I gave the other list to my husband. On my husband's list I had included the names of several of our close friends who waited fervently with us for the "overdue" entrance of our child. "Should the baby arrive in the middle of the night," I carefully explained to Curtis, "wait until morning to call these people." My sister, who had given birth to her daughter only a short time before, had called us at 12:30 a.m. with the news of the birth, and I found it impossible to return to sleep. Birth is an exciting event!

Not surprisingly, Kimmy arrived at 1:39 a.m. on a Sunday morning. Exhausted from labor, I fell into a deep sleep at about

2:00 a.m. My husband and my mother, I assumed, went home and also fell asleep. It was not until several weeks later that I discovered the true course of events. A friend, whose name was on my husband's list, told me laughingly that he had received the good news at 2:30 a.m.! Shocked by this, I stared in disbelief at my husband. As if to answer my look of amazement he calmly replied, "With such good news, how did you expect me to go home and sleep?"

Although my husband had two other children, he was still so excited by the birth of our daughter that he had come home and called every person on his list at 2:30 in the morning! Rising to my husband's defense, our friend confessed, "After Curtis called me, I called the unit [the hospital ward where he and I both worked evening shift] so they could announce it at the morning meeting!" Good news is meant to be shared!

When God sent His only Son to this world, He also could not contain His joy. The angels sang out the message. Jesus Christ has arrived! Now, that was good news!

Is the precious message of Jesus Christ exciting to you today? Jesus came for each one of us; it is the most breathtaking birth in history. "For God so loved the world, that he gave his only begotten Son, that whosoever believeth in him should not perish, but have everlasting life" (John 3:16). Call someone today and share the precious news of Jesus.

CAREL CLAY

OCTOBER 30

I Deserve It

I have loved you with an everlasting love; I have drawn you with loving-kindness. Jer. 31:3, NIV.

Fridays were my favorite days. Friday meant clean sheets and extra cooking, as in cakes, puddings, and such. My pre-school job was to help with the cooking; my younger siblings had chores of lesser stature.

For me the capstone of all the kitchen hubbub was scraping out the batter bowl. However, it was my duty to divide it in thirds, then call the others in for the lickin's.

One day I apparently had worked especially hard. After the pumpkin pies had gone into the oven, I began tunneling the three divisions in the bowl. "Lorabel," my mother said, "you don't have to share it today. You deserve it all." Angel voices could not have sounded sweeter! I was getting it all! Self-worth soared. I not only got all the lickin's, but I deserved it. I was being rewarded for faithful performance.

Now, I must tell you, at the risk of losing friends, that I still have the disgusting habit of licking out the batter bowl. I don't need it and I don't deserve it. I just like it. I never do this if anyone is watching. It's one of my secret vices, one of those dark peccadillos I'm loath to claim. Then why am I admitting it? I'll tell you.

God fills my batter bowl of life with blessings that never end. He doesn't deal with crumbs and scrapings. His gifts are abundant, both temporal and spiritual: affordable groceries, a comfortable mattress, a clear conscience, unending patience with me. What have I done to deserve these and many other gifts? Not one thing. Nothing I do could ever qualify me for His rich expressions of love and care.

Then where does my self-worth come in? Because I am God's child. I have no other claim. He calls me to His "batter bowl" and bids me, "Take all of it. It's yours. You deserve it. You are My child."

LORABEL HERSCH

OCTOBER 31

To Be Like . . .

Beloved, we are God's children now; what we will be has not yet been revealed. What we do know is this: when he is revealed, we will be like him, for we will see him as he is. 1 John 3:2, NRSV.

Everyone needs someone as a role model. In our lifetime most of us cross paths with someone we would like to follow, to emulate. This person usually has thoughts and ideas similar to our own. We hold on to what that person says as if our very lives depended on it. We copy his or her mannerisms, speech, and style of dress, and begin living similar lives, if we are able. That isn't always bad.

I have a good friend who seems to be everything that I would like to be. I've never seen her with a hair out of place. She looks great in a business suit, has a professional "air" about her, and has a warmth about her that draws others to her. She is an excellent public speaker with a lovely smile, and the Lord's presence is seen in her life. Even though she is a "grandmother," her posture is just perfect. I think she is beautiful.

I came home from a women's retreat, after being around this friend of mine, and wanted so much to be like her. It's funny the things we do, even when we are grown women. I wanted to change my style of dress, to be more like "her." I went to the hairdresser and changed my hairstyle so that I would look perfect. At least that's how I thought I would look.

It's hilarious when I think about it! I made a dress with a straight skirt, and I couldn't get it down over my hips. Although my hair looked great after the hairdresser got done with it, I wasn't able to do a thing with it after washing it myself.

In my frustration the Holy Spirit spoke to me, saying, "She's human. She's just like you." I was led to a quote on page 71 of *Steps to Christ*, by Ellen G. White, which read, "Christ in His matchless love—this is the subject for the soul's contemplation. It is by loving Him, copying Him, depending wholly upon Him, that you are to be transformed into His likeness."

Meditating upon this quote has been a wonderful blessing to me. I'd still like to possess the many fine qualities that my friend has. I still want to improve my hair and clothing, to learn to smile more, to have a warmth about me so that others will be drawn to me. But most of all, I want an experience with the Lord. This is what makes a person truly beautiful.

I want to be like Jesus! MONICA STOCKER TAYLOR

NOVEMBER 1

Do You Not Know?

But those who look to the Lord will win new strength, they will grow wings like eagles; they will run and not be weary, they will march on and never grow faint. Isa. 40:31, NEB.

Once I would have replied, "No, I don't. I've wanted to know. I've tried to know. I've acted as if I knew. I've even taught others skills to help them know. But finally I have had to admit it. I do not know. Not completely."

* * *

I am the offspring of offspring of offspring—going back to the second, third, and fourth generation and more—who never knew how to teach females how to fly along the cliffs, mastering updrafts and downdrafts and the winds of storm. As a fledgling in the nest I was never shown flight for females: they just pushed me out over the abyss and hoped my wing feathers would support me and I would get the hang of flight and gliding. And I seemed to, for a while.

When I flew around the rest of my peers and my parents' peers, I was careful to fly "right," by imitating the flight of older females. But something seemed to be lacking, so I would fly away and practice on my own. In the beginning I crashed a lot, but usually only when I flew in secret. Once upon a time, everyone thought I had flown away from home and wasn't ever coming back, but I had damaged my struts when I dared the cliff winds in another canyon than the one in which I grew up, and I had to wait for my wings to mend.

Oh, my parents wanted me to fly, but only so high. They wanted me to soar, but only for a safe distance. They wanted me to have strong wings, but only if I didn't venture too far. They wanted to protect me from the skies of the wild blue yonder. They didn't want me to get caught up in the winds of change that ride before a storm. They didn't want me to learn bad habits from other fliers of other flocks.

With the entire sky before me, I was hedged by invisible walls, barriers that distinguished themselves only if they were crossed. Eventually, however, I crossed those barriers with increasing frequency, exceeding the limitations imposed upon me. But as free as I pretended to be, I flew fettered still, because nearly all my flight was taken a distance from, in spite of, and in opposition to my elders, as well as my own more conventional peers.

In the early days, whenever I flew home I tried to recount what I had seen, where I had flown, what I had learned, how exciting the wild blue yonder was. But my tales made those who stayed safely at home uneasy. Even though I am now mostly among the flock, I don't fly quite the way they do. Storms don't terrify me as much, it seems, nor do the winds of change, and far distances, or drafts of any kind. Still, a quick shift in wind can throw me from a lazy circling soar to a beating up of wings against a downdraft.

The challenges I face and accept seem foreign to the flock, at least for females. The males have always flown thus.

I wish I knew more adventuresome females from whom I could learn the techniques of strong, audacious, soaring flight. Somehow it doesn't seem right to imitate the flying style of males, for I am not wholly like them, though we are equal.

I stand on the edge of my tall aerie, my mate behind me. He nudges me with a wing and invites me to share daring flight. As we fly together, sometimes I copy him, sometimes I do what I learned when young, and sometimes, somehow, I seem to be flying in my own style . . .

* * *

I awaken. It was a dream. My Bible rests open upon my supine breast. I read once more those familiar words:

"Do you not know, have you not heard? The Lord, the

everlasting God, creator of the wide world, grows neither weary nor faint; no [man or woman] can fathom [God's] understanding. [God] gives vigour to the weary, new strength to the exhausted. Young [men and women] may grow faint, even in their prime they may stumble and fall; but those who look to the Lord will win new strength, they will grow wings like eagles; they will run and not be weary, they will march on and never grow faint" (Isa. 40:28-31, NEB). KATIE TONN-OLIVER

NOVEMBER 2

Bloom Where You're Planted

And be content with what you have; for he has said, "I will never fail you nor forsake you." Heb. 13:5, RSV.

There were three mesh bags by my knees; one marked red, one white, the other yellow. I knelt on the ground in the front yard and carefully held a tulip bulb in my gloved hand while I tried to visualize a design that would be attractive around the light pole next spring. My trowel loosened the soil, and carefully I slipped each little tulip bulb into its earthen winter bed.

The spring sunshine beckoned to the spark of life in the little bulbs, and gradually each red, white, and yellow tulip assumed its place in the design around the light pole. The cheerful tulips brightened my days, and I was pleased that God had programmed them to bloom where they were planted. The little bulbs had had no say over soil type, amount of rain, or amount of sunshine, yet they responded with every degree of energy they possessed.

I'm not always like that. Through the years I've relocated a number of times with my minister husband, and although we've never moved against my will, my heart hasn't always arrived with the moving truck.

It's not only following a move that we're tempted to be discontented. Sometimes the marital status, living arrangement, or employment opportunity can be less than ideal, and we can find ourselves in a downward spiral of self-pity. When Paul wrote to Timothy, his advice was "But if we have food and clothing, with these we shall be content" (1 Tim. 6:8, RSV). ROXY HOEHN

Lovely as a Tree

There is a time for everything, and a season for every act under heaven. Eccl. 3:1, NIV.

The first thing I see when I open my eyes in the morning is a tree. This morning its golden autumn leaves were bathed in an ethereal light that almost took my breath away. Throughout the year "my tree" never fails to turn my thoughts to God and to His goodness, and when I gaze on it I feel baptized by beauty.

As the seasons come and go, so the tree changes. In the spring it is a picture, with pink blossoms clothing its limbs and carpeting the ground beneath. Then the bright-green leaves appear, and in their delicate airiness there is life and joy. In summer the leaves are dense and green, providing shade and coolness under the spreading boughs. Before they fall in autumn, we are treated to sights of constantly changing colors as the leaves cling tenaciously to life.

All too soon, however, the winds come, and the leaves, which today are so beautiful, will lie discarded on the ground. Then I shall see only stark branches against the morning sky, but they too have their beauty. The early-morning light or the shades of sunset often throw into relief the delicate tracery of the twigs against the sky, and when the frost and snow come the tree is breathtakingly beautiful once more.

My tree often reminds me of life, and teaches me that in all seasons and at all times God can make our lives beautiful. When we are young we seem to dance in the breeze with scarcely a thought for tomorrow. The little ones and the youth bring joy with their vitality and enthusiasm, but all too soon they too have to grow up. Sometimes trials come, and often we can become bowed down with cares. It needn't be like that. With God's guidance we can use our trials and experience to give "shade" to others. We can empathize with them, draw them to Jesus, and together stand under His protection.

Those who are more mature can keep bright, active, and interested in all around them. If they do, it seems that God bathes the autumn of their lives in an ethereal glow that draws others to them. Our older members have much to teach us, so we should cherish them and learn from them.

All of us, at some stage, have to face the stark reality of death. It is hard to see beauty then, but if we allow Him, God will bring to mind the precious memories we have. They are like the twigs highlighted against the winter sky, and just as the frost and snow make the stark tree beautiful, so time will soften the pain and allow us to look forward to that day when sin, sorrow, and parting will be no more.

I know that after the winter my tree will blossom again. It will be the time and the season, and God has ordered it so. Just as I have confidence that spring will follow winter, so do I know that soon we will be reunited with those we have lost, and an endless spring will have begun. "Even so, come, Lord Jesus."

AUDREY BALDERSTONE

NOVEMBER 4

Mother's Trust in God

Others went out on the sea in ships. . . . They cried out to the Lord in their trouble, and he brought them out of their distress. . . . He guided them to their desired haven. Ps. 107:23-30, NIV.

When I was 9 years old, my mother and I made a trip back to America from Brazil for medical reasons. Our ship, the *Pacone*, had developed problems even before we boarded. When the port pilot had brought the ship into harbor, he had collided with the dock and badly damaged the rudder, which had necessitated several days of repairs before the ship was considered seaworthy again.

On board, the problems continued. Three days after leaving for New York City, we ran into a storm in the middle of the night, and the ship pitched violently after the heavy rudder fell off completely. Everything loose came tumbling down. The night cook was badly burned when boiling water splashed over him. The crew spent the rest of the night shifting cargo to balance the ship. Without a rudder, the *Pacone* drifted toward Africa.

After several days of drifting, one of the passengers, a devout Catholic woman, excitedly told my mother that a group of angry men were planning to kill the captain because he had not yet provided for the passengers' rescue. She begged my mother to go "calm them down." Pausing to ask for divine help, Mother went. When the men finally spoke to the captain, they found that the ship's telegraph equipment was inadequate to reach land from where we were. But God had foreseen our need and had already provided a rescue.

It turned out that a telegraph operator had boarded our ship at

Ceara—with salvaged telegraph equipment from his ship that had been abandoned after it had struck a sandbar. He was able to patch equipment together and reach Bermuda—asking for help. Four days later a tug located us as we drifted along. What a welcome sight! Our troubles were not over, however.

The *Pacone* needed to be headed in the opposite direction before it could be towed, and the crews of both ships worked all night without success. The next morning when my mother heard of the dilemma, she said confidently, "God can turn this ship around," and went to our cabin to "talk to Him about it."

When Mother returned, she noticed that the direction of the wind had changed, and thought this was how God had chosen to turn the ship around. But much to her surprise, she found that the ship had turned while she was still in prayer. Four days later we were taken off the *Pacone* at Bermuda and placed on another ship headed for New York City! (The *Pacone* made only two more trips before going down!)

How close heaven really is to us. How low God bends to hear our prayers. How it pleases Him when we express our needs to Him. What enjoyment it gives Him to grant our petitions!

ENOLA DAVIS

NOVEMBER 5

Remember to Say Thanks

Give thanks to the Lord. 1 Chron. 16:8, NIV.

Wow! We were lucky!" If Kristi and I had been average college students returning to school, that's probably what we would have said after traversing the treacherous wintry roads between Boise, Idaho, and Walla Walla, Washington. But we did not credit our safe journey to luck.

"Mindy, would you pray again?" Kristi said these words several times on that trip. We fishtailed more than once on the icy roads, and we had to stop and buy chains for the tires less than halfway into the trip. Visibility was bad and the driving tedious.

We made it back safely, but no, we were not lucky. God was watching out for His daughters that day!

When we finally arrived at school, we made a list of all the bad things that did not happen and the uncanny good things that did. For instance, that police officer who stopped to help us put on our chains—what happened to him? We know he did not stay parked on the roadside, but why, when we looked back after two or three miles, could we not see him in our rearview mirror? He did not pass us, and neither of us remember seeing a place to turn around. Maybe he was an angel; maybe not. He was definitely sent by God! Why was the car undamaged and why were we not hurt when it plowed into a snowbank? We could have hit a signpost, a guardrail, or any number of things.

God definitely took care of us, for which both of us are thankful, but the lesson I learned was not the theme of Psalm 91. It was a lesson of basic manners. It is important to thank God! My family's tradition has always been to pray for safety before embarking on a journey, but I do not remember thanking God for safe travels. I'm sure He enjoys hearing "Thank You" when He protects us and answers our prayers.

I would challenge you to recognize God's hand in your everyday life, and thank Him for it. It does not need to be something major, like getting the job you wanted, giving you safe travels, or healing a family member from a life-threatening disease. He does little things for us every day in addition to tending to the bigger issues. It might be a helpful nighttime exercise to jot down things that went right instead of wrong during the day, and thank God for them. Most people would attribute a green light instead of a red light when they are late for work to luck, but take the opportunity to direct your thoughts heavenward and be a thankful child.   MINDY RODENBERG

NOVEMBER 6

We're Polishing His Treasures

Set your heart first on his kingdom and his goodness, and all these things will come to you as a matter of course. Matt. 6:33, Phillips.

The contemporary-styled lounge in Creation Studios is a relaxing place to catch a breather from the exhilarating but tiring recording process. And in my many breaks I've formed an unexpected but delightful friendship with the manager. It's not every day that her clients bring their whole family to the studio, and she noticed more than just the foreign aroma of dirty diapers. Things like seeing my patient husband baby-sitting our children while dashing in and out of the control room to give me input and moral support, and me taking a break to be with my family for evening worship and cuddles before bedding the kids down on the floor, certainly did catch her attention.

I'm a young Christian mom and she's a yuppie in the seemingly exciting field of professional recording. She deals in a world of rock stars, glitzy album release parties, and Emmy Award banquets. My world includes diapers, memory verses, and comforting kids with owies. Although her lifestyle sounds interesting to me, I'd never trade with her. But she often looks misty-eyed as I share details about my world with her. You know, like Charles putting peanut butter on Kymbrelee's nose.

We've had many talks about my recording. She finds the topics intriguing. She's asked me much about our lifestyle and child-rearing philosophies. I vividly recall our conversations about family worship. She thought the idea of a family singing, praying, and reading stories about Jesus together sounded loving, fun, and cozy—like a dream come true.

We moms and dads should take the opportunity to renew our commitment to the Lord and to our children. Schedules are not always convenient, but we must gather our family together to learn of Jesus. Make worship a looked-forward-to time of the day. Remember that God isn't stuffy—He'd love to see your family acting out Bible stories, doing experiments with water ("my cup overflows" [Ps. 23:5, NIV]), trying to see the wind (the Holy Spirit is like the wind [John 3:8]), and hunting for things that He has made. Read from Bible story books with lots of pictures and learn memory verses and recite them for each other. The important thing is coming together to meet the Lord. He'll bless with ideas and love and coziness.

As parents we must be secure in the Lord in order to deal gently and consistently with our children. This requires a commitment to a personal devotional life, which isn't necessarily easy. Many times I have been awakened by my children saying, "Mommy, why are you sleeping in the living room with your Bible?" But make a commitment to take at least a few quiet minutes before the troops awaken and then to meet the Lord at other convenient times during the day also. At naptime, instead of flying at the housework, take the time to study and pray, and the rewards will be greater than a good housekeeping badge.

We have a once-in-a-lifetime chance to be on the cutting edge with young minds that will readily soak up the dynamic truths of God's love—if we take the time to water them. And these little people are the very tools that God uses to shower us with the realization of our own great need to be filled by God.

I'm heading for the studio again soon, and I'll be reminded of the contrasts between our two worlds. But I think mine is the glamorous one because I work with the King—we're polishing His treasures.

JANICE R. SMITH

Half-filled Baskets Are No Good

There is a boy here who has five loaves of barley bread and two fish. But they will certainly not be enough for all these people. John 6:8, TEV.

He had finished speaking. But the people seemed reluctant to move. Perhaps it was the soothing breeze of the evening air or the orange glow of the setting sun or the memory of His voice that mesmerized them.

A small group of men huddled around Him now. While He appeared calm and unperturbed, they were anxious and agitated. Some in the group kept pointing to us, shaking their heads, and then looking back at the Man for some kind of guidance.

The Man talked quietly with them. After a while, the men began to walk slowly among the people. "Food" was the whisper that rippled through the crowds. "The Man wants food."

My hands tightened on the little basket that rested on my knees. I had food—five barley loaves and two fish.

The men were milling around nearby—should I tell them about the food? They must have wanted it for the Man. He looked weary and hungry.

I studied the Man. His face portrayed qualities I had never seen in one person—I felt compelled to give Him all I had!

Slowly I stood up. Holding my basket in front of me, I called out, "I have food." The crowd hushed. "This way," beckoned one of the men. Peering into my basket, he exclaimed, "Oh, no, only five loaves and two fish. Definitely not enough to feed all these people."

I felt foolish. Some laughed at me. I stooped to sit down, but this time the Man beckoned me. "Come," He said tenderly. "What you are giving is all I need."

As I stood in front of the Man, He took my tiny basket and offered it to God. Then my basket began overflowing with fish and bread too numerous to count.

* * *

As women we must sometimes feel like that boy. Much of our time is spent in taking care of the needs of others, after which we feel we can offer Jesus only the equivalent of two fish and five loaves in service to Him. Many of us cling to our "baskets," embarrassed to give the Lord the few remaining hours of time we have or the talents we are too weary to use properly. Often we compare ourselves to others and feel that what we have to offer God is too insignificant, or perhaps we look at the enormous needs around us and feel that what we offer God is so useless.

But this story teaches us two things:

1. God isn't interested in the amount or the quality of talents we give Him, but whether we are truly giving all that we have. He cannot use us fully when we are keeping some loaves and fish to ourselves.

2. When we give our "basket" to God, we must let Him use it His way, not ours! Most of us have preconceived ideas of the way we want God to use us. However, it is only when we give ourselves with no strings attached that we can truly be useful to God.

We then can have baskets that are topping over with the joy of service to God.   MARY BARRETT

NOVEMBER 8

Remembering Things That Count

If you turn away your foot from the Sabbath, from doing your pleasure on My holy day, and call the Sabbath a delight, the holy day of the Lord honorable, and shall honor Him, not doing your own ways, nor finding your own pleasure, nor speaking your own words, then you shall delight yourself in the Lord; and I will cause you to ride on the high hills of the earth, and feed you with the heritage of Jacob your father. The mouth of the Lord has spoken. Isa. 58:13, 14, NKJV.

I'm a minister's daughter and the middle one of five children. My parents had the vision that each of us had been lent to them by the Lord. Their task was to train us for service.

As I think back, I know they enjoyed the challenge. Our home was filled with the atmosphere of love and praise.

I don't remember ever missing church. We always went. I guess if any of us were sick, it's been long since forgotten. During those growing-up years, I attended large churches and small churches.

It's funny the things I remember. We often went to the larger church in the morning, but in most instances I couldn't say whether the membership was 100 or 300. Mostly I remember friends—adults and children, finding babies to love between Sabbath school and church, and sometimes leaving my own division and helping out in another.

I also have fond memories of happy singing with my family, for family worship, at Saturday night socials, and, as I grew older, choir practice.

Many weekends, after a hurried lunch, we'd set out for the day's second service. This trip wasn't a drudgery; we thought of it as an adventure. A time of family togetherness. At times my dad had four churches, so the afternoon churches were often different and up to 45 miles away.

But standing out in my memory are the people. How glad they were to see us. Sometimes there were only a few. One church had only one man, and he worked hard—but all the women also took part and did their best in the positions they held.

My older sister loved the pump organ in one of the churches. I loved it when a small church had some young couples—that meant babies! I would immediately lure a baby away from a mother (she probably prayed I'd come and give her a moment's peace) and then practice my art of loving children.

We made up many games for these trips. Often we were soul winners—one baptism for each electrical wire we saw or for each cow in the field. (Come to think of it, at times we baptized the dishes we washed during the week.)

But the best part was the singing. We'd start out with a song like "Heavenly Sunshine," then on to "There Is Sunshine in My Soul Today." That would lead to "Sunshine and Rain." We picked a word from each song to lead us into another song.

Heaven became our favorite subject to sing about. We'd sing about it for miles. Sometime during the trip we'd sing the sad song "Were You There?" but then go on to our favorite, "Lord, Build Me a Cabin in the Corner."

What are your family's spiritual memories? Is that special day of worship a delight or a burden? It's a taste of heaven, you know. Make it the best day of your week. GINGER MOSTERT CHURCH

NOVEMBER 9

Letting Go

Where is the wise man? Where is the scholar? Where is the philosopher of this age? Has not God made foolish the wisdom of the world? For since in the wisdom of God the world through its wisdom did not know him, God was pleased through the foolishness of what was preached to save those who believe. 1 Cor. 1:20, 21, NIV.

It takes no strength at all to give up and let someone trample your rights. It takes more strength to fight for what you want and stand guard over it. It takes the most strength of all to let it go into the hands of Jesus and trust in His almighty power. The third looks much like the first to the world, but the results are a testimony to the difference! CHERI SCHROEDER

Jesus Knows a Mother's Burdens

I have loved thee with an everlasting love: therefore with lovingkindness have I drawn thee. Jer. 31:3.

Sometimes it seems to a young mother that no one shares her burdens or drinks of her sorrows. Her work is often solitary and can seem thankless. Exhaustion dogs her steps after wakeful nights filled with pitying care. Feeling alone, burdened, and weary, she longs for comfort and encouragement.

"Jesus knows the burden of every mother's heart. . . . He . . . is touched today by the mother's sorrow. In every grief and every need He will give comfort and help" (*The Desire of Ages*, p. 512).

Let me share one little example of how God has drawn me with His kindness and brought comfort and help. I love flowers. They start my heart singing and set me to work more energetically. The simple wildflowers and fragrant lilies are of course the very best. Spring violets are one of my favorites, but even dandelions are beautiful when lovingly brought by a little hand. Set to float in a shallow dish, they can brighten any table. But more than anyone else, God knows that I love flowers.

It so happened that one day this past November I paused to look at my flower bed. The tiger lilies were long gone and their dead stalks had been cut back. The few remaining partly bug-eaten daisies, which I had covered tenderly during the first few frosts, were doing their best. But to my amazement I discovered that my violets were blooming! This may not seem so amazing to those living in warm climates, but it was approaching Thanksgiving in Iowa!

My heart was singing, for my heavenly Father had sent them just for me. There weren't very many, and the violets way out in the yard weren't blooming at all. The heavenly Father had sent comfort and was drawing me with lovingkindness.

God sees each one of us. He knows our needs and sorrows. "If God so clothe the grass of the field, which to day is, and to morrow is cast into the oven, shall he not much more clothe you" (Matt. 6:30) and comfort you, and encourage, strengthen, and help you?

JULIANNE PICKLE

My Father's Daughter

Behold, what manner of love the Father hath bestowed upon us, that we should be called the [sons and daughters] of God. 1 John 3:1.

In Iceland, the country of my birth, children are given their father's name, and even when women marry they continue to use their father's name. Although customs change from culture to culture, we all recognize that whether or not we retain our father's name throughout our lives, we often take some of his character traits with us long after we've left home. Before birth, we inherit our parents' genes. We may notice early in life that we have our father's eyes, his smile, or perhaps some other physical trait. But more important than inherited physical traits are the character traits we take on. I have been told many times that I'm just like my father.

It's true. We bring either honor or shame to our Father's name when people know whose child we are. When we accept Christ, we call ourselves Christians. We have chosen to be identified as one of His children. From early childhood or at the time of conversion, we have assumed our Father's name. From that point on, He has sent His Holy Spirit to help us emulate His character as well! I want to bring honor to my Father. I don't want any selfish conduct to dishonor Him, because I claim to be His.

In the Middle East, where I live today, all the people claim to worship the same God. I have many Muslim neighbors, and they have taken the name of their prophet Muhammad. I observe how careful they are to avoid dishonoring his name in any way. I see in their daily lives how they follow the teachings of their prophet to the letter of the law. In most cases they are willing to defend his reputation with their very lives. When I discern this all around me, I often ask myself, "What do these people see in me? Is my love for my family, my siblings, my fellow believers, evident and consistent with my claims of being in Christ, or do others see an impatient me, or a person who lets small misunderstandings take their toll on valuable relationships? Do I try to force everyone into my mold, or with my heavenly Father's help do I exhibit forbearance and a willingness to see others' perspectives?"

I realize that I have been fortunate, but I can't ever remember being pushed away by my earthly father when I came to him to say I was sorry for something I had done. Instead, his arms would unfold to draw me close to him. The miracle of this is that I know my heavenly Father loves me even more. His love is without measure, unconditional and everlasting, and I want to bear not only His name but His blameless character, too! ANNA JOHANSEN

NOVEMBER 12

Priorities

In all thy ways acknowledge him, and he shall direct thy paths. Prov. 3:6.

Most of us think we have our priorities straight, but I wonder. Evaluate this past week's activities. If you wrote down everything you did each day of the week, would you be proud of what you accomplished? Would time with God in study and prayer even appear on your list?

All of us struggle to keep our priorities and lives in balance. But we must remember to put God first. To start each day with Him in meaningful study and prayer will assist us in getting other priorities straight.

But how to handle the other things that scream for our time and attention. Most women make a "To Do" list, a never-ending list of tasks that press urgently on us. The list is much too long for any normal person to complete in a week, and yet we keep adding to it. At the beginning of the day we attempt to work our way from top to bottom, scratching off things as they are cared for.

At the end of the day two, three, or more things may have been crossed off, yet many more important things have been left undone.

I believe there is a better way. I keep a weekly list of everything that I need to do that week, to which I may add things as I think of them. All week I work on my list. But I evaluate what is important for me to complete that day. Many tasks do not require that I complete them right now. Other more urgent matters may need attention today. I find that I am more likely to use my time wisely if I have all tasks on one list for the week. That way I can work on tasks of varying length according to when I have time.

I still may have a daily list, but I have learned to stop through the day and reevaluate. How important is it that I get this done today or tomorrow? Will my day and my family be better served if

I wait to do this? Can I break it into two parts rather than exhausting myself all in one day? This process of making lists and prioritizing jobs is the secret for being able to serve God and my family more effectively.

God has a plan for each day of my life. He is a God of order and wants me to use my time wisely. He has given me the intelligence to evaluate the priorities in my world. When I do this daily, I am better prepared to deal with the unexpected major and minor crises that come my way. This paves the way for me to make more effective use of my time for myself, my family, and others.

What about you? Do you need to take a look at the priorities pressing for your attention today? Attempt to accomplish what is most important. Then save some time for yourself, your family, and others. You're worth it!

CARLENE WILL

NOVEMBER 13

The Parable of the Good Seed

But the fruit of the Spirit is love, joy, peace, longsuffering, gentleness, goodness, faith. Gal. 5:22.

My husband had completed the full course of radiation therapy for a recurrent malignancy and was doing well. We then had a 6- to 12-week wait before we could expect the blood marker to be back to the "normal" range, indicating that the radiation had destroyed the cancer cells.

As the weeks of waiting dragged by, I realized I was experiencing the uncertainty of the waiting time as impatience. I knew I needed patience, but how to acquire it eluded me. One day during that time a Lutheran pastor friend called. I told her of my need for patience and asked her to remember me in her prayers. She prayed with me on the phone. Then she asked, "Margaret, what is your image of patience?" At once I realized that I had no such image in my mind, and at once I also knew that such an image was the key that could unlock for me the Holy Spirit's store of patience!

Later, when I sat down with my Bible and a concordance, I found the Old Testament entries unde *patient* and *patience* useless to my quest. But as soon as I read the parable of the good seed, the old gardener in me knew I had discovered my image of patience. For the seed in good ground must also wait in darkness, and I must trust God's provision for the warmth and moisture it is unable to provide by its own efforts. In the good seed I recognized that patience is not something I work to provide for myself. I need to

trust the Lord to provide patience for my inmost need as an aspect
of that fruit that grows by the Holy Spirit's presence in my life.

MARGARET TURNER

NOVEMBER 14

Unselfish Love

*Love knows no limit to its endurance, no end to its trust,
no fading of its hope; it can outlast anything. It is, in fact,
the one thing that still stands when all else has fallen.
1 Cor. 13:7, 8, Phillips.*

Meeting his son at the door in the middle of the night, the father
exclaimed, "We have had enough of this! Continually you
keep us awake worrying about you and your drugs. We are tired of
listening to your rock music and all that goes with it. Get out, and
don't bother to come back again!"

What a contrast to the story of the prodigal son in the father's
willingness to forgive and accept his wayward son. You are
thinking, *But the prodigal son was sorry for his sin.* Notice Luke
15:20. "But while he was still a long way off, his father saw him,
and felt compassion for him, and ran and embraced him, and kissed
him" (NASB). Before the father knew of his son's repentant
attitude, he forgave him and accepted him back.

A contrast to the father above is the father who said to his
wayward son, "We love you and care enough about you to know
you are safely home. Your activities pain us deeply, but we love you
just the same. Your mom and I have always loved you, even before
you were born. Nothing you do will keep us from loving you. You
are our son."

This demonstrates the love God has for us. While we were yet
sinners, He died for us (see Rom. 5:8). This does not mean we
accept any kind of behavior. God does not. But He doesn't reject us.
He doesn't give up on us!

After the mother gave birth to twin sons her mind snapped. She
was institutionalized, and the husband raised the boys, faithfully
visiting his wife even though she did not know him. He was advised
to remarry since his wife was like a nonperson, but he felt he had
married "for better or for worse, in sickness and in health, until
death do us part." What a devastating experience; but he did not
give up! He continued to love his wife, visit her, and pray for her.
God honored his unselfish love. After 35 years she was helped,
through medical research, and reunited with her husband.

John the revelator reminds us that "love is of God; and every one that loveth is born of God, and knoweth God" (1 John 4:7). God is the source of all love and gives it freely as a gift to His created children. Not only does God love us supremely, as demonstrated in the gift of His Son, but He loves us unconditionally. He doesn't love us because we are good or for something good we may have done. He loves us no matter what our performance. And it is our acceptance of God's unconditional love that changes our lives, affecting our attitude toward others. If God loves us as much as that, "surely we, in our turn, should love each other" (1 John 4:11, Phillips).

The secret of happy relationships is unselfish love, a love that "seeketh not her own." It is the glue that binds us together in a caring, accepting attitude of each other.   MARIE SPANGLER

NOVEMBER 15

Sneaker-proof

Before [her] downfall, a [woman's] heart is proud, but humility comes before honor. Prov. 18:12, NIV.

Have you ever done something stupid, really stupid? If you were to ask me, I'd have to answer, "Which time?" There's a kid in me that refuses to grow up. And every now and then, this kid gets me in trouble. Let me tell you about one of those times.

My husband, Richard, our two girls, Rhonda and Kelli, and I camped at Capitol Reef National Park for the weekend. The first night the girls opted to sleep in a pop-up pup tent beside our travel trailer. Now, I like everything about camping except for getting up in the night and stumbling to the restrooms. Inevitably, no matter how well I plan ahead, nature will call.

Sure enough, about 3:00 in the morning, I awoke. After arguing with myself for 10 minutes or so, I climbed out of bed, struggled into my faded and well-worn terry cloth robe, slid my feet into my white tennies, and padded the distance to the women's restroom. I'd barely locked the door of my stall when I heard someone else enter the facility and step into the stall next to mine. That's when I spied the familiar green-and-orange sneakers.

Just before this vacation, my daughter Rhonda came home from shopping and showed me the ugliest pair of sneakers I'd ever seen. Trapezoidal in shape, the green-and-orange canvas-topped shoes could have passed for an alien spaceship.

Every time I saw her wearing those hideous creations, I cringed.

This time was no exception. Being a born pest, I saw an opportunity to play a prank on my elder daughter. After all, I knew who she was, but she had no idea who I might be. Peeling a few sheets of toilet paper off the roll, I wadded them into tiny balls. Then one at a time I flicked them over the divider. I waited for her response. None came. I chuckled to myself at what she must be thinking, and threw a few more. Nothing.

H'mmm—I must have missed. I restocked my arsenal and tossed the entire supply over the wall at once. Again no response. I couldn't believe it. How could she just sit there and say nothing? At the least I expected an aggravated "Mom!" or something. Anything!

Exasperated but unwilling to admit defeat, I stretched my foot and stomped on the toe of her brand-new sneaker. Not a sound, not a cry—total silence except for the sound of scuffing as the green-sneakered foot jerked to the other side of the stall, safely out of my reach.

I frowned. *What's the matter with her? Why isn't she . . . ? Oh!* A new thought entered my mind. *No! It can't be! No! No! There can't be two pairs of spanking-new green-and-orange sneakers, shaped like space shuttles, in the wilds of Utah—no!*

Mistaken identity? Before my mind could accept the possibility, my victim rushed from the stall to the sink, leaving me to do the only thing I could. I giggled. In fact, there was no containing my laughter.

I rushed out to explain my mistake to the poor woman. As I rounded the corner of the end stall, she froze, paper towel in hand. She backed away from me. Terror filled her eyes.

I reached out to her to assure her that I meant no harm. "Look, I'm terribly sorry. I thought you were my—tee-hee . . ."

Oh, no, I'd started giggling again and couldn't stop enough to explain my actions. And the more ludicrous the situation became in my mind, the harder I laughed. I leaned against the wall to catch my breath. Spotting her moment to escape, the terrified woman made a run for it—out the door and into the night.

Even as I stumbled back to our trailer, I could hear my laughter ringing off the canyon walls, which made me laugh all the harder—a symphony of stupidity. Lights popped on inside nearby camping trailers. The entire campground must have been awakened by my outrageous laughter. As I passed my daughters' tent, I heard Kelli say to Rhonda, "Oh no, Mom's at it again."

Once inside the trailer, I tried to explain, between bouts of laughter, to my now-wide-awake husband what had happened. It took me 20 minutes or more to regain my composure.

As luck would have it, the next morning when I awoke and headed for the ladies' restroom, whom did I meet coming out, just as I was going in? My victim. The woman's eyes widened with recognition and fear. Like a wild colt, she bolted out the doorway and down the trail behind the closest row of trailers, her gray hair blowing in the breeze. You know, for a 65-year-old lady, she sure could run.

There was no doubt—when I first saw those sneakers in the next stall, I knew it had to be my daughter. I was certain. I knew beyond a doubt. I could have sworn it was Rhonda in that bathroom stall.

It wasn't that I didn't have any facts to go on. I recognized the sneakers. I knew Rhonda owned green-and-orange sneakers. I considered the odds of there being another pair of the ugly shoes for a couple hundred miles. From that point, I logically deducted that the person in the next stall had to be my daughter. But the truth remained: I was wrong; wrong and humbled!

A silly mistake. Unfortunately, not all my mistakes are of the humorous variety. Sometimes my leaps in logic bruise, maim, and destroy the ones I most love. When that happens, refusing to admit I was wrong would compound my mistake. It is only by my asking for forgiveness that the wounds I've inflicted can begin to heal and my tears of repentance can restore honor between me and those I love.

"Before [her] downfall, a [woman's] heart is proud, but humility comes before honor." A diet of pride is empty calories. It inhibits spiritual digestion and starves the soul. But a slice of humble pie is nutritious for any woman's diet from time to time.

KAY D. RIZZO

NOVEMBER 16

Flowers

Yet we have this assurance: Those who belong to God shall live again. Their bodies shall rise again! Those who dwell in the dust shall awake and sing for joy! For God's light of life will fall like dew upon them! Isa. 26:19, TLB.

Over the past few years I have acquired a number of various houseplants. My favorite of the foliage that now lines my windowsills and occupies sunlit hanging spaces in my home is my African violet. My mother gave it to me about 10 years ago.

African violets were Grandma Dancek's favorite. The one that Mom had given me had been started from Grandma's line. My own little piece of family heritage. At the time that Mom gave it to me, the plant was full of beautiful blossoms.

It was not very long after the violet became mine that the flowers all faded and died. I couldn't figure out why. The plant itself was still green and healthy, so I persisted in giving it plenty of warm sunshine and quenching its thirst with the proper amounts of water.

Week in and week out I cared for my plant for *three years* with no sign of a bud. I often wondered why it didn't respond to my tender loving care, and tried not to get upset. I would just give it another flowering plant spike and place it back on the sunny sill.

Then one day when I was doing my routine watering, as an afterthought I checked for any sign of a bud. To my surprise I found not one, but two *stems* of buds slowing rising from the base of the plant! I couldn't believe it. I picked up the pot and hurried to show my mother.

"Flowers!" I yelled. "I've finally got flowers!" Mom just giggled and said how proud of me she was. I even ran to show Dad. "Flowers!" I yelled. "I've finally got flowers!" I even showed Max, my cat.

After three years of perseverance, the feeling of satisfaction that swarmed over me at that moment gave me such peace that it was worth all the time and effort spent to get the desired results.

I believe that Jesus has spent three years, 15 years—lifetimes—nurturing many of us with loving care. Patiently watching and waiting, week in and week out, for the rise of even a single blossom. How He longs for the day when He can run to His Father and exclaim, "Flowers! I've finally got flowers!"   SHARI DANCEK ELDER

NOVEMBER 17

Stewardship of God's Resources

Gather up the fragments that remain, so that nothing is lost. John 6:12, NKJV.

We had a drawer in my grandmother's house in which we kept neatly folded used gift wrapping paper of all designs and sizes. Each sheet lasted for years, as we "recycled" it every Christmas.

When I was a child we reused paper and plastic bags, and refilled empty bottles rather than discard them. We turned off lights when we exited a room. We brought our own reusable shopping bags to the grocery store to transport our groceries. We often created new meals from leftovers. I saved broken pens to create new ones from the separate parts of different pens.

Sometimes my friends make fun of me when I pull down a single paper towel in a public restroom and carefully unfold it to wipe my hands dry. "You're supposed to use at least five sheets at a time; don't scrimp," they tell me.

I still find it hard to tear off the paper wrapped around a gift. I still feel guilty when I have to throw an empty container out. I insulate my house more to conserve energy than to keep the electricity bill low. I don't encourage my students to write on every other line, and I do encourage them to "recycle" by printing their essays on paper that has already been used on one side.

My attitude has nothing to do with how much money I have or how frugal by nature I am. I conserve my resources, recycle what I can—myself or through the county pickup program—because I hate waste.

Why is it that 20 years after I have been making these daily choices naturally, there is a sudden worldwide self-conscious concern for the environment, for conserving our resources, for recycling? Why did anyone ever come up with the idea of styrofoam in the first place? It seems that in our attempts to "develop" modern conveniences, we have created destroyers, vandals of nature, wasters, and people who scorn those who reuse an item, describing them as "cheap" or "miserly."

Jesus did not believe in waste. After the multitudes ate the loaves and fishes, He made sure the leftovers were not wasted. His instructions to the disciples were clear.

According to different translations, the Bible uses the words "destroyer," "vandal," and "mistreats" to describe someone who wastes. Are we like the prodigal son, who squandered everything he had? Are we too embarrassed to save paper to reuse? Are we too lazy to rinse out containers and recycle them? Do we buy products that cannot be recycled? Do we care enough about the world God put us in to conserve it?

We can claim the promise in Isaiah that "violence shall no longer be heard in your land, neither wasting nor destruction within your borders; but you shall call your walls Salvation, and your gates Praise" (Isa. 60:18, NKJV).   MICHELE BEACH

NOVEMBER 18

Thirty-Year Prayer

If you call to me I will answer you, and tell you great and mysterious things which you do not understand. Jer. 33:3, NEB.

Gregorio, what a fine job you did putting that puzzle together. And you finished your math and spelling! Why don't you go to the reading corner and listen to a story tape and 'read' the book?"

The puzzle consisted of a picture, laminated and cut into three pieces. The math assignment—six problems (1 + 4 = _____ , 5 + 1 = _____ , etc.); the spelling lesson was the word "car" written five ways: in clay, like a rainbow with crayons, with a pencil and a picture drawn, with felt-backed letters, and with letters cut from a newspaper. The effort had taken most of the morning. Now he could listen to his favorite story, and he got three checks for good behavior.

Gregorio headed for the back of the room, kicking Timmy on the way, and shoving Sally's chair to make her lash out in anger. I prayed a silent prayer and claimed Jeremiah 33:3: "God, this child is a mystery. Teach me what I do not understand."

Gregorio, oldest of three children and son of migrant farm-workers, was a major discipline problem. Eight years of age, he could read only a few words. No teacher had been able to handle him. He was so emotionally disturbed that psychologists could not get an IQ.

My assignment was one of several experimental classrooms in southern California targeted for emotionally disturbed children. I had accepted the challenge of 13 very difficult children. For Gregorio it was the last resort before assigning him to a classroom for the mentally retarded.

Later that day I visited Gregorio's home. "Mr. Gonzolas," I said through an interpreter, "Gregorio has improved at school. He finishes all his work."

"He is stupid," his father said, picking up his beer can. "His brother is smart, gets good grades. His sister is smart. Gregorio is stupid!"

"Mr. Gonzolas, do not call Gregorio stupid. Gregorio needs your love. And Mr. Gonzolas, I don't want you to hit Gregorio ever again. If I hear of it or see any more bruises, I will report you to the authorities. Will you promise?"

Mr. Gonzolas growled, "I'll try."

I put on a stern look.

"OK, I won't hit him anymore."

Last week, now almost 30 years later, Gregorio, a handsome correctional officer for the California men's prison, sat in my living room. He had brought flowers and candy, and introduced his beautiful Mexican wife.

"Mrs. Appleton, I was a bad kid, but you were firm and kind. You gave me confidence and hope. I was proud to finish six grades in my three years with you. Now I have many officers under me and I'm in charge of 400 prisoners. If it had not been for you, I would be in that prison. Thank you for praying for me."

BERTHA APPLETON GLANZER

Peaceful Rest

Come with me by yourselves to a quiet place and get some rest. Mark 6:31, NIV.

I was on my way home. It had been a wonderful Sabbath with my family of choice. We had celebrated Thanksgiving dinner early because of our varying schedules later that month. Driving along, I realized how rested I felt.

Rest is such a precious gift from God—and we receive many different types of rest. There is the rest we treasure when we lay our heads down on our pillows at night. There is the rest of death—a rest that some of my elderly acquaintances are actually looking forward to. With John they believe, "Blessed are the dead who die in the Lord." "They will rest from their labor" (Rev. 14:13, 14, NIV).

Other types of rest came to mind: the special Sabbath rest that I had learned to treasure over the years; the ultimate rest in the new earth, when we will be released from the stress of life as we know it in this world. I watched the fading sunset and gradually the following words took shape in my mind:

> The sky has turned to gold and red,
> Creator puts His world to bed.
> Long hours were spent in meeting needs,
> Of daily chores and thoughtful deeds.
> Our head upon the pillow lay
> At end of this long weary day.
> And we by God have been so blest!
> He gives with joy this peaceful rest.
>
> A week has passed, the vespers chime,
> Comes Friday's special sundown time.
> God beckons us at eventide
> To put all earthly cares aside.
> We greet the Sabbath day with prayers,
> And spend it with a God who cares.
> And we by God have been so blest!
> He gives with joy this peaceful rest.
>
> Shaky hands, a frame that is bent,
> A silv'ry head shows life is spent.

Years of a lifetime slipping by,
We face at last the hour to die.
Our Maker looks upon our soul;
He grants that death shall take its toll.
And we by God have been so blest!
He gives with joy this peaceful rest.

The Advent cloud in eastern sky
Declares that Christ's return is nigh.
With triumph shout and trumpet blast,
He'll take His people home at last!
This sinful world will be no more,
We'll thrive upon a heavenly shore,
And we by God will be so blest!
He'll give with joy this peaceful rest.

LORNA LAWRENCE

NOVEMBER 20

The Fragrance

But thanks be to God, who in Christ always leads us in triumph and through us spreads the fragrance of the knowledge of him everywhere. 2 Cor. 2:14, RSV.

A few years ago when I was visiting my son and his new wife in a quaint little town in eastern Colorado we decided we would go shopping. We did just that. We went to the only "department" store in town, a little building consisting solely of one floor and an old-fashioned balcony. As we entered the store we noticed a sweet-smelling aroma wafting from one corner of the building. Of course, this attracted our attention right away, and we discovered what was bringing this pleasant scent to our noses. Everyone who came into that store was instantly allured to a large display of bright, colorful potpourri. The fragrance it exuded was irresistible!

"If we are following Christ, His merits, imputed to us, come up before the Father as sweet odor. And the graces of our Saviour's character, implanted in our hearts, will emit around us a precious fragrance" (*Testimonies*, vol. 5, p. 174).

Just as the colorful display of potpourri drew customers to its charm, so will the grace of Christ in our lives draw people to us. They will savor being in our presence because we show Christ's character in being long-suffering, kind, and gentle. Our conversation will be different, and our actions Christlike.

Is it evident that we have been with Jesus? As we go out into the work world or endeavor to create a haven at home for our families, is this sweet perfume of God's love permeating our lives and emanating this fragrance? Is this fragrance irresistible to those who see us? Only as we spend time with Jesus can we become potpourri for Him!

PEGGY TOMPKINS

NOVEMBER 21

Taste and See

No eye has seen, no ear has heard, no mind has conceived what God has prepared for those who love him. 1 Cor. 2:9, NIV.

My car moved slowly down the long driveway and turned onto the street for the last time. It was loaded down with household odds and ends. Moving day. I was leaving the little dollhouse that had been my home for more than 30 years. What memories those walls held, and yet I was eager for a change!

My new home was just a couple blocks away. I rounded the corner, and there it was. Tall pillars flanked the front door; mature trees hovered nearby. It was almost too good to be true. I could hardly believe that it was really mine. Never had I imagined such a lovely place in which to continue my retirement.

Once again my heart overflowed with gratitude as I looked around the spacious interior. Not only was there plenty of room for all my earthly belongings, but friends and family could visit and stay over! With the psalmist I could truly say, "Taste and see that the Lord is good" (Ps. 34:8, NIV).

As I carried one of the boxes into the house, my thoughts sped forward to my new home in heaven, the place prepared especially for me by my heavenly Parent. In my mind's eye I could just see the tall pillars, the arched doorways, the verdant foliage; the large windows overlooking fadeless flowers, bountiful fruit trees, a flowing stream, and my own little vineyard. Of course there was a study, too, where I could continue to learn the mysteries of the universe forever—and never grow tired!

Many of us, if we spend time meditating about the new earth at all, tend to etherealize the concept. We may think about meeting Christ face-to-face, but so often we miss the tasting in our mind's eye of the wonderful tangibleness of heaven's marvels. God knows each one of us and is preparing a place that will suit us individually and perfectly. It will be thousands of times lovelier than the best of the best on this earth. After all, don't earthly parents know how to give good gifts to their children (see Matt. 7:11, NIV)? How much more our heavenly Parent!

Back out to the car for a last load of dishes, I waved to my new neighbor across the street. "I will do this in heaven, too," I mused. "I will wave to my neighbor across the street. I will call out, 'Come over and visit. I have plenty of room. Just wait until you see what God has built into my house.' "

Won't you meet me there?

LEONA GLIDDEN RUNNING AND ARLENE TAYLOR

NOVEMBER 22

Giving Thanks in All Things

Rejoice in the Lord always. I will say it again: Rejoice! Let your gentleness be evident to all. The Lord is near. Do not be anxious about anything, but in everything, by prayer and petition, with thanksgiving, present your requests to God. And the peace of God, which transcends all understanding, will guard your hearts and your minds in Christ Jesus. Phil. 4:4-7, NIV.

Have you ever been in jail? Imagine yourself locked into a small concrete cell. There's nothing else, except for a few rats. You decide to write a letter to your friends back at your home church. What will you say? Will you write of the joys of prison life? Or will your response be "Help—get me out of here"?

Most of us haven't been physically incarcerated, but all of us at times feel imprisoned by life's circumstances. Financial dilemmas, family problems, uncomfortable relationships at school or work, loneliness, or poor health can cause you to feel like a prisoner of life.

Is your consistent response to the less-than-ideal circumstances in your life joy? If you're human, probably not. Do you sometimes feel chained by unmanageable problems, frustrated because you're not in control as you'd like to be? Are mountainous difficulties blocking joyful sunshine from your life?

Paul found a way to live as a free man, even a joyful man, while physically imprisoned and in the worst of circumstances. In his letter to his friends at the church at Philippi, written while he was in prison in Rome, Paul outlines the formula he used to maintain a sense of joy while a prisoner of life (Phil. 4:4-7, NIV).

Paul's joy formula begins with a command: "Rejoice in the

Lord always. I will say it again: Rejoice!" This might seem like an impossible command. Paul goes on to explain how it can be done.

Part 2 involves relating to all people (even surly jailers) with a noncondemning gentleness. He says to do this because "the Lord is near," i.e., "Jesus is coming soon."

Part 3 is simply: Don't worry! Instead (part 4), continually bring your cares before God with confidence and thanksgiving. Paul promises that if you will follow these steps, God's peace, transcending all your previous combined experiences of peace, will stand guard to protect you from all discouragement. This peace will so comfort and soothe you that you will find ample reason to rejoice continually!

As the year-end holidays usher in this year's grand finale, I would encourage you to focus on Philippians. Think thankfulness every day. Love gently and generously. Don't worry! (Be happy!) Allow God's peace to surround, soothe, and support you. And finally, remember, no matter how difficult your circumstances, find some reason to rejoice! I'll say it again: Rejoice!   SALI JO HAND

NOVEMBER 23

Unnoticed Waves

Oh, that men would give thanks to the Lord for His goodness, and for His wonderful works to the children of men! Ps. 107:15, NKJV.

That warm Indian summer afternoon was perfect for grocery shopping. I worked through the preparation process:
Nathan dry and reasonably clean—check
Car seat secured in car—check
Grocery bags, coupons, and list collected—check
Stocked diaper bag in hand—check
Keys—?
Now, where could those keys be? I searched all the familiar places they might be, in addition to all the places I could imagine where a 17-month-old might have put them. My search yielded only frustration. I finally located my husband and discovered that in his haste that morning he had taken the keys to both cars with him.

Somehow through my frustration, the Lord still spoke to me. He reminded me of the smallness of this trial; it really was nothing to become unglued over. And so I sat down on the front doorstep, read the mail, leisurely wrote a long letter, and absorbed the autumn sun and breezes while Nathan toddled about the yard, waving sticks and sampling questionable berries.

Every so often a vehicle would whiz past us, and soon I noticed something peculiar: Nathan was waving at the cars and trucks. As our home is set back off the road, no one probably even saw him, but he persisted in his waving.

That's when it came home to me: how many times has someone "waved" to me and I never even noticed? The warmth of a hug at church from a typically reserved member, the extra minutes my husband makes for us on a very full day, the same faithful folks who set up potlucks month after month, Nathan playing contently on a Friday afternoon when company is coming—how many times have I simply expected these "waves" from others?

Of course, those extras are only crumbs compared to the gigantic good things from my God. Far too many of those things I've come to expect, too. I'm ashamed to think of all the earnest prayers I petitioned, and He graciously answered, that I didn't even remember to acknowledge. Then there are the daily surprises He sends that somehow become just "nice things," not the valued gifts He intended them to be.

This Thanksgiving season my prayer is that of David's: "Praise the Lord, O my soul, and forget not all his benefits" (Ps. 103:2, NIV).

COLLENE KELLY

NOVEMBER 24

I Am Thankful

But earnestly desire the higher gifts. And I will show you a still more excellent way. 1 Cor. 12:31, RSV.

The whole house was alive with the sounds of happy voices and hurrying feet. It fairly bulged with the aroma of delicious food. My little French grandmother had flown all the way from California to visit us, and because she couldn't stay until the real Canadian Thanksgiving, we were celebrating early. (My father's parishes were seldom located near relatives, and her visit was such a treat!)

My dad, a towel wrapped around his waist and onion tears streaming down his face, had operated the old-fashioned food grinder until the traditional gluten roast was ready to pop into the oven. He had punched down the bread, too. Six round loaves, baked in recycled smooth-sided juice cans, stood proudly on the drainboard.

My mother, tendrils of black curly hair clinging to her temples, had mashed the potatoes until they were as smooth as silk. Grandma, from a recipe written only in her mind, had created pumpkin pies that were out of this world.

My brother and I had set the table, grated the carrots, snitched black olives off the tray, and generally gotten completely underfoot—in a determined attempt not to miss anything.

At last we were all seated around the table. "Before we pray," Dad said, "let's each mention something for which we are thankful." Joining hands, we each took a turn. My brother was thankful he had a new three-speed bike; I, that Grandma Rose was present—and that she had given me my first real watch, a delicate pin-brooch timepiece. (I still have it!)

Then it was Grandma's turn. In her soft, slightly accented voice she said, "I am thankful for the ability to learn to do something in a better way." What a strange thing to be thankful for, I mused. Because I adored her, however, I filed her words away in my memory bank.

They no longer seem strange to me. In fact, they evidence a wealth of understanding far beyond her limited formal schooling. How often I had taken that gift for granted—the ability to learn to do something in a better way.

Then one day Grandma was gone—and I wrote:

> Laid to rest,
> Grandmother—
> Yet more like mother.
> Gone, but not forgotten.
> Still deep within my heart
> The cherished mem'ries
> Of her gentle love
> Help reduce the pain.
>
> Gone, yet always near.
> Silent, except for
> Echoes on the wind
> And whispers in my mind.
> Through fading sunset rays
> The music lingers.
> Grandmother,
> Laid to rest.

Innovation, a God-given ability, enables us to develop healthier behavioral patterns; to create positive outcomes with our own unique talents; to enrich our own lives and the lives of others. We can learn a more excellent way—including implementing the new commandment that we should love one another (see John 13:34). Thank you, Grandma Rose, for teaching me to be thankful for the ability to learn to do something in a better way. May I more fully utilize it! ARLENE TAYLOR

Give Me Joy

The joy of the Lord is your strength. Neh. 8:10, NIV.

Do you ever enjoy a good gripe session? Do you find relief from spilling all your miserableness out on the table for others to examine? I confess, sometimes I gripe about anything, sometimes everything—about money problems, about school, the children, and even about my husband being away from home. It's not that I want to gripe, but I do. Do you? Perhaps if we knew we were starting into a gripe session, we'd stop ourselves. Even in the middle of a gripe session, it's not too late to stop. Unfortunately, many times we recognize only what we've said after the damage has been done. After the shadows have settled on our spirits and those who listened.

I need frequent reminders that I was born to reflect God's message of hope, that I am the reason He sent His Son to die. In response to such unspeakable love I want to spend my life praising Him. This should come so easy when I think of all the ways He blesses my life. I sing "His banner over us is love," and I want my life to show this love.

So how do we rid ourselves of the nagging habit? One thing that can make the difference between a good day and a bad day is praising God as soon as you wake in the morning. Praise Him for the challenges you feel certain will come your way. Praise Him for promising to provide solutions to these challenges. Praise Him for being an all-wise God who knows what's best for your life. Tell Him out loud that you want to be a joyful daughter! Praise Him for victory over the gripes!

The Lord wants our days to be filled with happiness, love, laughter, and praise! If you aren't experiencing these positive emotions yet, take matters into your hands and do something to change the situation. One sure cure is to focus on someone else's needs.

Recently I met a woman new to our south Texas town. The stacks of boxes in the front room attested to that. She confessed to me that she hoped that someone in the church would invite her to celebrate Thanksgiving with their family, but when an invitation didn't materialize she chose not to have a pity party among the boxes. Instead she piled the boxes in an adjoining room and invited another lonely family to spend the day with her. Together they found joy, laughter, and time to praise God.

Trials and pain make their tracks across all of our lives, but when we learn to praise God instead of grumbling, we begin to see life from a whole new point of view! HORTENSIA BRYCE

Promised of God

For we are labourers together with God. 1 Cor. 3:9.

It might have been a dreary day, but somehow she arose anyway. Perhaps the sunshine was absent from her heart as well; the end seemed close enough to view. Maybe she tidied the few things remaining in her little home while fighting back a tear or two. Poverty, poor, destitute—what word can fully describe the intensity of her crisis? Yet, she had determined to be the best mother possible for her only son. He was such a good child. What more could she do? Ever since her husband had died, life had been a daily battle that had dwindled to the point of desperation.

Today, she silently and reluctantly admitted, *I will feed myself and my son for the very last time*. Surely her thoughts must have raced over her life—the joys, the sorrows—slowly being embraced by imminent death.

Not so very far away, the same heavy, gray day was being encountered by a man—a man similarly desperate for food, a man with no home to call his own, but a man with a living knowledge of an all-powerful God who cared for his every need. As the needs of both this widow and this man escalated beyond their human capacities, one faced a bitter end while the other faced a new beginning. Calling upon God, the man was told to go to a city, whereupon he would see a woman—indeed, the widow—gathering sticks to prepare her last meal; certainly a critical collision of life and death. This woman would sustain him with her meager, humble means! And not only him, but herself and her son as well (1 Kings 17:9-16).

I think God had confidence in this woman. Why? Because even before she set out on her course for that day, God had announced to Elijah where she would be and what she would be found doing. Even when she could not imagine her life beyond her next meal, while choking back tears as she gazed into the eyes of her dear, precious son—even then God could say that she would be there.

Have you ever wondered why God may have asked you to move at a particular time, or to go to a specific place at a peculiar time, or to take a certain job? Maybe He has already announced your presence or your coming to someone in need. Perhaps He wants you there to catch a falling soul. What a wonderful thought—we can be God's promises! He has not made any mistake in creating each of us exactly the way we are. Every request He makes of us is an invitation to work with Him "for such a time as this" (Esther 4:14). What an honor and a privilege for God to have confidence in us and promise us to others! "For we are labourers together with God." I wonder what God may have already announced to someone about you?   CHERRYL A. GALLEY

Take Action: Ask, Seek, Knock

Ask, and you will receive; seek, and you will find; knock, and the door will be opened. For everyone who asks receives, [she] who seeks finds, and to [her] who knocks, the door will be opened. Matt. 7:7, 8, NEB.

That's easy for *you* to say," I muttered to Matthew. "You walked and talked and followed the literal, physical Christ. You were not a woman, either."

I slammed the Bible shut and went about my day . . . with recurring thoughts of this powerful promise, and one of its modern counterparts: "Nothing ventured, nothing gained."

How can one ask (I asked myself and God) when one is terrified to ask? And how can one seek, when one doesn't know what to look for? And as for knocking on a door, any door, the idea itself seemed too bold and audacious to consider.

If anyone had asked, I could have given a bunch of personal reasons for not asking, seeking, or knocking, but all of them came down to one—an outgrowth of a strong belief: boldness and venturesomeness were traits for only males to exercise. I feared to make mistakes. Yet asking and seeking and knocking are needful actions one takes for many reasons: to find work, to locate housing, to discover one's talents, to choose a mate, to be a writer. Such actions often require the risk of mistakes, of errors in judgment, of failing, of rejection—so it was easier to venture nothing. But even though I avoided the pain of rejection, I also avoided the joy of acceptance. And when I avoided the failures, I also avoided success.

Matthew's recounting of Christ's words have lately taken on

new meaning for me. Because I desire to succeed, to have positive results from the efforts I put forth, I have been observing and reading about people who have not only succeeded but also have been following their dreams. Their success exceeds that of material gain; it is success of the spirit.

Without exception, these individuals have in common the ability to perform these three actions of Christ's promise. They are able to overcome their fears: to ask for help, for information, for support; to seek, even in the most unlikely places; and to knock on every door behind which opportunity may await them.

Certainly they "fail." They may ask, seemingly endlessly, and not receive answers to their questions. They may seek everywhere they can think to look, and find nothing. They may knock, and find door after door barred or slammed in their faces. But to these intrepid ones, apparent failures are perceived as feedback—nothing more, nothing less. Courageous people don't give up, even when they are afraid. They will modify their questions and seek answers from different sources. They may refine the definition of what they seek, and learn to spot what they look for. They may learn to knock only on doors that are slightly ajar or almost open, or doors that, inexplicably, seem to beckon. Such people take action, gain feedback, refine and redefine their plans, and then do it over and over until they receive the fruits of their efforts.

I now believe these two verses are a statement of spiritual law. In my own experience, this set of spiritual laws has never failed, as long as I can overcome my fears and act in the light of these promises. But I must be patient and persistent, continuing to ask, seek, and knock until the promises come true and the laws are fulfilled.

Do you have a dream? Place it before God in the light of these promises. Ask for help (for questions display wisdom, while being ashamed to ask displays ignorance). Look for what you want, and learn to be skilled in recognizing it. Knock on the doors of opportunity, and keep on knocking even if the door is shut, for it may even be the right door, but one for which you may not be quite ready.

These spiritual laws, as recounted by Matthew, clearly show that we must take action. Just as a child learns to walk by walking and falling, so also we learn to create the dreams of our hearts by risking, by asking, by seeking, and by knocking—over and over and over and over—until we receive, find, and walk through open doors.   KATIE TONN-OLIVER

Nuts

She openeth her mouth with wisdom; and in her tongue is the law of kindness. Prov. 31:26.

As I walked across the campus Squirl darted on to the sidewalk ahead of me. She eyed me, and with a blink of her eye decided it was safe to continue on her quest. She headed straight for the huge pecan tree by the sidewalk. By the time I was next to the tree, Squirl was going up the trunk, peeking at me from one side and then the other as she worked her way up the back side of the tree. Squirl was still stopping every few moments to check on me, until I could hardly see her. She was 20 to 25 feet up when I heard an awful squawk and whir of wings and leaves. Squirl now ran and jumped with abandon. I saw Byrd swooping down and landing a peck with each pass. Squirl ran to the far side of the tree. Byrd chased her back to the center. Squirl darted down the trunk and raced across the sidewalk behind me. But before she had time to disappear into the bushes, she was soundly tweaked by Byrd, who stayed fluttering and scolding the bush that had swallowed Squirl.

So much like people. Each with a goal, an agenda. Each preoccupied with harvesting more nuts. Each feeling it necessary to cross into the other's area in order to get all the nuts desired. Each sure that his or her approach to gathering and eating is the best. We have all seen it, in the playground, in the business world, in the church, in the home, where sharing and caring ceases because someone needs more nuts and/or more area in which to gather nuts. Some want them to eat now. Some want them to store. Some work their way from the bottom up; others are born at the top and fight others who try to get there. Some are silent as they work; others squawk for all to know what they are doing. The world has nuts enough for all to gather, but some insist that all the tree is theirs. I can't tell you if Squirl ever made it up that tree, but it doesn't matter now, because later the wind blew and the nuts came down close to Squirl's bush.

God, who watches the sparrows, also takes care of the squirrels. One lives "hand to mouth"; the other saves for a "rainy day." God, who made the nuts and the need for nuts, provides space and time for all to meet their own needs. Shouldn't we be as gracious and allow others space and time to gather their nuts in their style, without squawking about how they go about it or pecking them when they cross "our" boundaries? EVELIN GILKESON

By Faith Sutchie . . .

*And the life which I now live in the flesh I live by the faith
of the Son of God, who loved me, and gave himself for me.
Gal. 2:20.*

I met him in a large government hospital in Victoria, Australia. He
was a patient in the men's ward in a big six-story block. I was the
evening supervisor, and I have to admit, I became quite an admirer
of the old man. He was 98 years old and had been a tall, well-built
man, but now he was emaciated and scrawny. He had a beautiful
smile, even though he was reduced to what looked like skin drawn
over a bony skeleton—a mere shadow of what must have been a
stately frame. His mind was clear, however, and he never failed to
amaze me with snippets of Shakespeare or Dickens. He had
"willed" his body to the University of Melbourne for scientific
study, a practical token of his continuing interest in helping science
and humanity.

Alas, he had a major health problem. His right foot was
gangrenous. It required strictly regular dressings every four hours.
The old man hated these occasions, even though painkillers were
administered before each dressing was done. He continually suffered a great deal of agonizing pain, and particularly so each time
his foot was touched.

From time to time I would tell the male nurse in charge of his
care that I wanted to be present when he did the dressing, so I could
see if there was any progress. Whenever I came to his bedside, the
old man always looked up and said, "Please don't let them touch it.
It is looking good and doesn't need dressing."

I would reply, addressing him by a favorite name I had for him,
"Sutchie, it is more than my job is worth to let you miss one of these
dressings."

Occasionally he would signal extra pain with a pinch or a light
punch to the nurse doing the dressing. We then knew it was more
than he could bear and we needed to take it easy for a while. But
even with the best of care and in spite of the old man's courage, the
day came when Sutchie's aging body could take no more, and he
went to his rest.

As I went on duty that evening, a nurse came up to me and said,
"I thought you might like this poem written by one of your favorite
patients." I unfolded the crumpled page and read the words of a
man facing life's sunset after almost a century of living. It said:

My Testimony

Life's sun, which long has risen,
Is setting now, I know.
My mortal flame is flickering,
And burning very low.
The shadows, like things around me,
In solemn silence fall.
And soon I shall be listening
To hear the farewell call.
Why should I fear the dying?
The sting of death is sin,
And mine are all forgiven;
I've perfect peace within.
Death to me will bring sweet rest
And freedom from all pain.
Through Jesus I shall conquer,
For I shall live again.

Then I knew what made Sutchie different. He belonged to that noble band of believers whose faith was real and vibrant and grew stronger with the passing years. Yes, by faith Sutchie . . .

SYLVIA TAYLOR

NOVEMBER 30

Soft Moments

Be joyful always; pray continually; give thanks in all circumstances, for this is God's will for you in Christ Jesus. 1 Thess. 5:16-18, NIV.

Your female psyche needs softness. You don't deny it, for it seems as if you're ever seeking the gentle things. The softness may be in holding a newborn, wrapping yourself in a terry robe after a warm shower, or applying a powder puff to your nose. Then there's the softness afforded by the gentle touch of the sweet Spirit, knowing He is close by as you pray.

Prayer is a very special happening, even when it is entered into in public, because it's a conversation with Father. God's listening ear is with you. And the knowing that Jesus intercedes for you as you pray provides gentle joy. Certainly prayer adds to your feminine needs.

Sometimes your prayers may occur in the middle of a long, black maze, when you feel like spider snares surround you. But by reaching out to your Friend, who understands the zigzag pattern, you can find the softness of peace amid the harshness of turmoil. There may not be an immediate understanding about your dilemma—but the taken-care-of feeling comes, and endurance ensues. Prayer becomes a zenith communion, while talking it over with your Father.

"The opening of the heart to God as to a friend," which Ellen White writes of in *Steps to Christ*, tells you of the beautiful requirement you need in prayer, to come to God believing that His amazing grace will cover all your inadequacies. (I always take the hymn "Amazing Grace" as a personal prayer offering. His grace to me *is* amazing.) Belief in His grace adds another dimension to your gentleness. It provides you with a forgiving heart, when you might, by nature, issue a retaliatory action, rather than be gentled.

Prayer serves as a vital element in a Christian woman's life. Not only for your own needs, but for the concerns of others. Intercessory prayer widens your caring attitude, while prayers of thanksgiving declare God's graciousness. Prayer thereby serves as a loveprint. And a habit of prayer makes a delightful design—a spirit of tenderness. With a resulting supple nature, God uses you to do His bidding. He enables you to be His sympathetic representative in the home, work place, church, and community. Indeed, you become a gift to your surrounding world.

May soft moments be yours in abundance, especially as you please God with claim prayers. He longs to talk with you as you bow your listening ear with a listening heart. — BETTY KOSSICK

DECEMBER 1

Give Yourself Away

Let each of you look not to your own interests, but to the interests of others. Phil. 2:4, NRSV.

It's extremely easy to become so wrapped up in our own little world and the holiday season that we forget about people who are hurting. Many are in need of not so much a material gift as a gift of time—of yourself.

If you're like me, you probably have precious little time to invest. With family attentions, working, volunteering—all "musts" in my life—I find it difficult to squeeze in time for myself, my friends, or anyone else, for that matter. However, statistics show that suicides increase around Christmastime, and this means there are people who need us desperately.

For example, there is Jane, who this Christmas will be alone for the first time in her life. Her husband died last month. Money is not a problem, but companionship is. She's wondering how she'll get through the holidays without breaking down.

Or what about Kallie? She and her husband have recently retired and moved south for health reasons. Their children have decided they won't be able to join them this year for Christmas because money is tight.

And there's Marcie, a young college student who can't get off from her essential job to go home for the holidays.

However, most of us will be fortunate. We won't spend Christmas Day in a cold, bare institution. We won't eat Christmas dinner all alone in a restaurant. How then can we show we care?

Begin in little things. Charity starts with small steps—gifts of time and yourself to people who are near you every day. When making or purchasing Christmas presents, remember those who are alone. It's not the price that counts; it's the thought. And when planning a family dinner, always think of those who might be forlorn. Don't hoard your good times and family celebrations for just "you and yours." Share. Share yourself, your home, your meals, your gifts. The memories you give last a lot longer than you'd ever realize.

Why not give real meaning to the spirit of Christmas this year and give yourself away? Remember that God has shown us the supreme example of willingness to give. As we remember how He gave up His Son to come and live among us and die for us, let us reflect that spirit of love.

Giving yourself away is so simple, yet so hard, but it's the golden key to happiness at Christmas and all through the year.

MADLYN HAMBLIN

DECEMBER 2

Jewels

It shone with the glory of God, and its brilliance was like that of a very precious jewel, like a jasper, clear as crystal. Rev. 21:11, NIV.

It was still dark when I left for work. The sky was overcast, and the temperature where I lived (near the Canadian border) had dropped to near zero. I'm not much of a morning person, and my mood was much like the weather: dark, cold, and unpleasant.

As I drove along I started thinking about my problems, my pain, the losses and the financial worries that loomed so big, the whys that crowd into my mind, when almost imperceptibly I became aware of flashes of twinkling lights on the trees, grasses, and bushes lining the road. The sudden drop in temperature during the night had produced beautiful crystals of frost that sparkled like jewels when my headlights hit them. At first I just reveled in their beauty; then I thanked the Lord for this glorious display on such an ordinary day. Suddenly the frost crystals reminded me of the bright spots in this dark world. As I drove along I thanked God for every precious friend in my life, for my husband, my children, my church family, and for each person who adds richness and dimension and decreases the loneliness and pain that invade my life from time to time.

My heart was full that day, and all day long I was blessed by the thoughts of God's beautiful handiwork. I was reminded in a very unusual way that my Father is never far from me. My heavenly Father loves me and cares for me.   CAROL FOOTE

DECEMBER 3

Boundaries

When the Most High gave the nations their inheritance, when he divided all [humankind], he set up boundaries for the peoples. Deut. 32:8, NIV.

'Twas the week before Christmas, and it's been such a flurry.
    No one else can cook . . . I'll do in a hurry!

I took all the cares (wouldn't budget on the dinner).
Only I can prepare berry jellos that shimmer.

Family offered to help! I groaned as I faked it
"You—enjoy holiday scenes. All the dinner—I'll make it!"

I quake and I moan, I've done it—again!
Taken all of the slack, leaving none for a friend.

Am I ego-bedeviled? Will my talents be wasted?
I'll try sharing the load, so my death won't be hasted!

I've done it before . . . will I do it again? In the past, whenever there arose a need for a project to be done, for a large family dinner to be planned, for a location from all distant parts of my family to converge upon for Christmas week, for any project to be handled responsibly, I thought to myself, *Sure, I can do that!* I loaded myself up, not remembering the avalanche effect the deadline would bring. I could see myself as quite capable; as a good shoulder; as a caring friend. But when the overload hit, I'd sit in my muddle, feeling befuddled and usually a little angry at being used.

No change occurred until I realized that I taught folks how to treat me, that any overload was because I allowed it to happen to me. I learned to say "No."

A call to arms came in the form of a statement that I have adapted to make mine—"I have met the enemy and it is me." It's up to me to protect my person! I've inventoried my time, my talents, my goals, my energy. Now instead of blaming other people for all the work I have to do, I challenge other people to take on responsibilities they are capable of handling. They also can say "No," but an equitable distribution of energy requirements preserves my vitality for work that truly matters to me; that fulfills my need to be effective.

God sets boundaries. For each of us, this must be our example.

JUDI WILD BECKER

DECEMBER 4

Healed

To each one is given the manifestation of the Spirit for the common good. For to one is given . . . gifts of healing by the one Spirit. 1 Cor. 12:7-9, NASB.

I remember that day as if it had been yesterday.

I'd opened my eyes with joy in my heart that bubbled to the surface like an artesian well, and burst forth in delighted laughter with no listener to benefit. I'd surveyed my two hands and wrists, swathed in white. The numbness no longer pained my movements. My happiness knew no bounds.

"Carpal tunnel syndrome," my doctor had diagnosed the painful, tingling sensation I had increasingly experienced. He'd referred me to orthopedic surgeon Galen Hoover.

Dr. Hoover appeared confident and full of a peaceful joy. He confirmed my need for surgery after a terribly enervating and jarring shock test. To cheer me up he stated solemnly, "I wanted to be a tree surgeon, but I couldn't stand the sight of sap!"

Then he asked, "When shall we schedule you for surgery?"

I hedged. "Which hand to you plan to do first?"

"Whichever one the surgery nurses have draped when I get scrubbed up," he replied with a grin. "Actually, I intend to fix both tunnels during the same operation."

"But what if it isn't successful?" I worried.

I guess he thought he was reassuring me when he replied, "I've probably done this procedure a thousand times! I could do it blindfolded!"

"Please don't!" I said, and finally agreed that both hands should be done at the same time.

Lying there in the recovery room, feeling so surely the presence of the Great Physician "with healing in his wings" (Mal. 4:2), I grew philosophical. *Some part of our anatomy always wears out first,* I thought. With some it is the heart, and then all is sometimes over quickly—even this probationary life itself. For me the nerves of my wrists had deteriorated earliest. How overjoyed I was that the problem could be corrected!

Though all that happened 10 years ago, I still thrill with thankfulness for the skillful surgeon's work, for my rapid and total healing, for the comfortable use of my hands.

"To God be the glory, great things He hath done."

ROBERTA SHARLEY

DECEMBER 5

Come, Run With Me!

Cast me not off in the time of old age; forsake me not when my strength faileth. Ps. 71:9.

When was the last time you took the time to sit down and listen to someone with gray hair and wrinkles? Seniors may be slow of step, but they have a lot to offer us. For instance, lessons learned from long years of experience in a changing world, hardships borne, and patience perfected by the ups and downs of this life. However, many times the older generation feels rejected. But what joy comes from seeing an elderly person's eyes light up and realize that perhaps you have brightened a day that might otherwise have been long and lonely.

In *The Ministry of Healing* there's some good counsel on this subject. "There is a blessing in the association of the old and the young. The young may bring sunshine into the hearts and lives of the aged. Those whose hold on life is weakening need the benefit of contact with the hopefulness and buoyancy of youth. And the young may be helped by the wisdom and experience of the old" (p. 204).

I experienced this with a woman I met when I was doing some volunteer work at an adult day-care center. Mary was 90 years young; fragile but agile. One day as we walked along hand in hand, she told me about her life in Scotland, where she had owned a bakery. As long as she could remember, Mary had served her Lord in the Salvation Army. When she was younger her favorite sport was running. With a trace of sadness in her voice, she told me how she wished she could run, but no one would let her for fear she would stumble and fall. Running, she had been told, was not for persons her age.

Without much thought of the consequences, I gripped her hand a little tighter and said, "Come on, Mary, let's run!" She needed no second invitation. Together we ran, and she kept pace with me until we were both out of breath! Her eyes danced. Her face shone. For a few fleeting moments Mary had been young again, with the wind blowing through her hair and the ground passing quickly beneath her feet. Just a small, impulsive thing to do, but it made Mary's day.

Small kindnesses, spontaneous acts of empathy and love, make a big difference for those who all too often feel abandoned. Why not save a little time to "run" with someone who needs you today!

ALMA ATCHESON

DECEMBER 6

Cover Me, Lord

I counsel you to buy from me gold refined in the fire, so you can become rich; and white clothes to wear, so you can cover your shameful nakedness; and salve to put on your eyes, so you can see. Rev. 3:18, NIV.

We awoke this morning to a world wrapped in a soft blanket of white snow. The woods behind our house were transformed overnight from a tangle of nude branches into a wonderland of spotless white. As we slept, millions of snowflakes silently did their job. The evergreen by my window is now a perfect, glistening Christmas tree, naturally adorned in white.

I'm reminded of the robe of righteousness God has offered to me. Christ's purity and goodness—covering the tangle of my life. Somehow I've been waiting for the transformation to begin inside. Today I see that God wants to envelop me in a transforming blanket of love. If I am cold, I can wrap myself in a down comforter and soon be warm—from the outside inward. If I'm wrapped in His love, purity, and joy, soon I'll participate in that love, purity, and joy.

God has been in the covering business for a long time. When Adam and Eve distrusted His instructions and set up the first do-it-yourself business, God gently covered them with animal skins. Well, the death of those animals was hardly gentle, but I can envision the tender, loving, and gentle way in which God Himself prepared those first garments and covered His erring children. I can feel the sadness of that covering at the gates of Paradise.

In the desert sanctuary the atonement cover or mercy seat was the place where God's glory rested. It was the place where reconciliation between God and human beings took place. In fact, the Hebrew word for atonement means "to cover." The Day of Atonement was a day of "covering"—covering of sin, not as in hiding an evil, but as the blanket of white has transformed my world this morning.

David sang of the blessedness of the one "whose transgressions are forgiven, whose sins are covered" (Ps. 32:1, NIV). Not only do the piles of leaves and twigs at the edge of my woods not show anymore under this blanket of white; by spring they will be well on their way to becoming dark, rich soil. Undercover transformation! Not only of my leaf piles, Lord, but of me, too!

Another favorite psalm provides a further glimpse of God's tender covering. "He will cover you with his feathers, and under his wings you will find refuge" (Ps. 91:4, NIV). Last spring we watched a mother nighthawk raise her babies in a nest only a few feet from a busy campus sidewalk. Alert eyes on any movement near her, she stretched her wings to cover two balls of fluff. As they grew stronger and their urge to explore intensified, we found them each day a few feet from where they had been the day before. The mother moved with them during the night, always keeping them under her wings. A similar promise, given to God's people through the prophet Isaiah, reads "I have . . . covered you with the shadow of my hand" (51:16, NIV).

As I write, a well-known hymn comes to mind—first the melody, then the words:

"Look upon Jesus, sinless is He; Father, impute His life unto me.

My life of scarlet, my sin and woe, cover with His life, whiter than snow.

Cover with His life, whiter than snow; fullness of His life then shall I know."

Even so, Lord Jesus, cover me with Your white robe of love, forgiveness, and rightdoing! NANCY VYHMEISTER

The Broken Wall

But you will call your walls Salvation and your gates Praise. Isa. 60:18, NIV.

As our train was about to enter a certain railway junction, I looked through the window at the wall on my right. I noticed a large gaping hole in the wall. That hole served as a convenient gateway for the people in the residential area close to the station. The railway had built the wall to protect adults and their children from the constant trains that come and go day and night, yet these people did not appreciate the protection. They preferred to take the shortcut across the rails to the other side than to go all the way to the overpass.

The moment the wall was made, they felt that it was a threat to their freedom. They dared not break the wall at once. So the wall came down slowly at first. It began with a small hole just for the children to peep at the fast-moving trains. Little fingers slowly started digging deeper into the wall. Soon even grown-ups helped to make the hole bigger for their own convenience. As a result, the hole grew into a large gaping opening. Everyone at the colony began to use it. Their trespass had become an acceptable practice. Was this gaping hole the reason we saw so many beggars with missing limbs, and frequently heard of lost lives as a result of crossing the tracks?

Sensible people don't understand others who risk their lives by rebelling against safety precautions. Yet how many of us do the very same thing? God has built a wall of protection around each of us. He has even put a sentinel on that wall to warn us of approaching enemies. But many of us do not heed the sentinel's warning. Like curious children we dig through the wall to see what is on the other side. We continue digging right under the nose of the sentinel. We say, "We only want to peek. There is no danger in peeking." Yet we forget that Christ regards "looking" as breaking one of His commandments (see Matt. 5:28). Even a small hole is enough to allow impurity in to pollute our soul.

Once a hole is made in the wall, it is easier to keep using it than to repair it. The gap grows steadily in size with little notice. We are cautioned, "There should not be one departure from reserve; one act of familiarity, one indiscretion, may jeopardize the soul in opening the door to temptation, and the power of resistance becomes weakened" (*The Adventist Home*, p. 404). Fortify the walls of your relationship today.   BIRDIE PODDAR

One Night in December

The angel of the Lord encampeth round about them that
fear him, and delivereth them. Ps. 34:7.

Night came early that evening of December 8, 1973, and by the time I left the warmth of our little church to walk back home, it was very dark.

The road I normally took had few buildings to overshadow it, and there was usually some traffic, but it was a roundabout way, and it was getting late. The alternative was to cut through the stadium, now dimly lit and almost deserted. I always avoided it after dark. However, earlier I had mentioned my fears to a friend, and she had asked me if I no longer believed in guardian angels. Now her words echoed in my ears. Ashamed of my lack of faith, I turned toward the stadium.

The roofline of the building was clear against the night sky, but the lower parts were in deep shadow. It looked foreboding, but there was still an occasional athlete hurrying here and there, so I started up the steps leading to the main entrance.

Suddenly I heard a whistle. Several youths were converging on the stairway. Preoccupied with my thoughts, I continued to walk briskly toward home, but soon their soft footsteps were punctuated by their heavy breathing immediately behind me. A hand closed over my mouth. A knee jabbed into my back, and I went down struggling with every ounce of desperate strength I could muster. Then suddenly my mind cleared, and I started to pray, "Help, Lord. Please help. There are too many of them. O God, help me!"

The concrete felt hard under me as I rolled and kicked. Their hands were everywhere, covering my eyes and mouth, pressing my shoulders into the unyielding pavement, pulling at my clothes. I could see nothing and hear only their breathing. Desperately I turned my head from side to side, trying to free my mouth. For a split second the hand slipped. "Help . . ." It clamped down again. Someone bit me on the forehead. *O Lord, where are You?*

Suddenly the pressure lessened, and seconds later I was free! As I looked around I could see shadowy forms disappearing fast into the darkness. From the opposite direction a young man was running toward me. He was a well-dressed man, and I realized he must have been the reason for the hasty departure of my attackers. Perhaps he would help me now.

However, without even a glance at my disheveled form, he passed in front of me and began to climb the slight incline leading to the road above. Confused, I followed a few paces behind. Reaching the top, I looked to see which way he had gone. The road shone like a ribbon of silver in the moonlight. It was deserted. He had disappeared.

A text flashed into my mind, and I felt a mixture of awe and excitement. "The angel of the Lord encampeth round about them that fear him, and delivereth them." I had seen an angel, my angel, and he had indeed delivered me in my hour of need.

REVEL PAPAIOANNU

DECEMBER 9

His Eyes Are Watching O'er Us

For the eyes of the Lord are on the righteous, and his ears are open to their prayers. 1 Peter 3:12, NKJV.

"Marge, put your book away," the chapel speaker said from the pulpit. My cheeks turned bright red, and tears filled my eyes. My sister Beth, seated next to me, shared my embarrassment too.

We were attending a private Christian school, near La Crosse, Wisconsin, in the 1950s. Every day the students were expected to attend chapel, and normally I enjoyed this worship period. But this particular day studying was more important to me, and I had my nose buried in a textbook when I got caught! Quietly I closed the book while 60 pairs of eyes were riveted on me. I wanted to slide under the seat in front of me and disappear from sight.

I smile now when I look back, but at the time this experience was humiliating. I must admit, though, it did teach me a valuable lesson. Ever since that day I've tried to give my full attention to speakers. Sometimes it's difficult, with children and grandchildren, but I try to put myself in a speaker's place. It must be very disappointing for a speaker, after all the preparation, to see people in the audience who aren't paying attention.

Does the Lord do things to get our attention when our mind wanders from what He wants us to hear? Learn from my experience to keep your eyes on Him. It will keep you from embarrassment and even tears.

MARGE MCNEILUS

Hang On to That Hope!

And I, when I am lifted up from the earth, will draw all people to myself. . . . While you have the light, believe in the light, so that you may become children of light. John 12:32-36, NRSV.

Somalia! That's where my son is at this writing.

Recently our small-town newspaper featured a story about my son when they spotted the door to the physical therapy department in the hospital where I work decorated for the holidays with Operation Restore Hope photos. The photos were of our U.S. troops, including my son Vincent. After all, what spoke more eloquently of the true meaning of Christmas than "restoring hope"? Isn't that what another Son had done almost 2,000 years ago?

Vincent wrote of his feelings when he and the other troops from the U.S.S. *Rushmore* were among the first to land on the beaches of Somalia on their mission of mercy. In one of his letters he suggested that I should be proud of how I had raised him! *Then why do I have all these doubts and fears?* I asked myself. Maybe because at times he seemed to reject the very faith values I had tried to teach him. It appeared that each of my three children had, at least for a time, chosen other more popular routes.

Am I, a Christian mother, alone in my concerns for my children? No, of course not! But how do I reconcile my children's apparent lack of desire for a heart experience with the Lord? Do I excuse it and chalk it up to the pain we all suffered from a painful divorce? No, I think not. There are eternal consequences at stake, and God loves my three children even more than I do.

The reality is that I have a divorced son who is making a career of the Navy; a divorced daughter searching for work and meaning in her life; and a third child, very young, but happily married and expecting a child. I love these children and suffer with them through their personal struggles to find peace in their lives. And I also have a powerful Partner who gave not only His Son, but the parable of the prodigal (see Luke 15:11-32), and the promise that if we train our children as He instructs us to do, they will not forget this training when they are grown (see Prov. 22:6).

Alas, *hope!* Have we become too sophisticated for the word? Not I! I cling to God's promises. As a mother I can intercede on behalf of my children before the Father and, because of that long-ago "Operation Restore Hope," leave them safely in His care.

Didn't I have to learn too? How many years and painful experiences did it take *me* to come to the heartfelt realization of His love and grace? At what point in my life was I able to internalize His love so that it became as natural as breathing? He patiently waited, watched, and picked me up when I fell. He even carried me when I needed to be carried.

So never give up hope! Pray for your children, yes! Be there for them, yes. But worry? No need! — BLANCHE ORSER

The Best Gift Ever

The Lord is close to the brokenhearted and saves those who are crushed in spirit. Ps. 34:18, NIV.

For most of us Christmas is a time of great celebration. A special time to share with those we love the most. Christmas is especially wonderful to experience through the eyes of children. Each morning Christine, our 2-year-old, awakens and, standing up in her crib, exclaims, "Christmas downstairs." At the bottom of the stairs is a gleaming Christmas tree, and her large blue eyes widen with delight as she dances and twirls around the tree.

To many of us the holidays signify happiness, but Christmas can be a time of pain. There are those who are experiencing loss through death, divorce, bitter disappointment, or separation from a loved one. Those who are happy are filled with even more joy at Christmas; but for those who are hurting, the holidays can be devastating.

Reaching out to those in need personifies the true meaning of Christmas. It's important for us to realize that although most people are smiling and may even be joining in the festivities, there are those among us who need an extra dose of love. A genuine hug or a simple note of encouragement could make a difference. And as you spend time alone with God, pray for them.

It wasn't but a few years ago that I came to view the reality of broken dreams at Christmastime. Just six months earlier our only son died. We tried to ignore the whimsical Christmas music and the bright decorations. We even ate spaghetti for Christmas dinner. But I discovered on *that* Christmas Day, as never before, that Jesus was my best friend. Suddenly it wasn't so bleak after all. Jesus *is* a trusted friend, always comforting and giving strength.

If you, my dear reader, are one who is hurting this Christmas, realize that God has not left you alone. He is ever drawing nearer to you. Jesus, who came as a babe in a manger, is close at hand to those who are brokenhearted. With Jesus at your side you do not have to be defeated by despair or self-pity. Look higher than yourself, and see the tears in His eyes as He cries with you. He mourns with those who mourn. Stop and feel His loving touch upon your shoulder. Jesus came to this earth so that we would never be alone again. When He comes to this earth the second time, His desire to eradicate suffering will be fully realized. Jesus came that first Christmas to give true peace on earth to those who receive Him.

So in spite of the pain, I found the true meaning of Christmas: God sent His only Son to be born for us, to die for us, so that we may receive His gift to us—eternal life and joy.

Thank You, dear Lord, for the best gift ever.   JULIE REYNOLDS

DECEMBER 12

The Influence of the Heart

And beyond all these things put on love, which is the perfect bond of unity. Col. 3:14, NASB.

Joseph was a very special child. I met him when I moved into his neighborhood. He was a handsome boy with big expressive eyes and rosy cheeks. What made him dear to me was the love he showed to everyone he met. Joseph was mentally deficient from birth. He was given a lot of love and encouragement from his family and friends. He learned that God loved him very much and that He had special plans for him, even though he had less ability than most children. Although he experienced many challenges and frustrations, he was usually an outgoing and secure child.

One day he excitedly told me about an incident that took place at school that day. One of his classmates was angry with another student and started to hit him. When the boys began to fight, Joseph intervened. He pleaded with his classmates to stop fighting. "You're only hurting each other, and we're supposed to love each other," he said. The boys stopped fighting and shook hands when Joseph suggested they do so. I was impressed with Joseph's story and assured him that his life was a special blessing to others because he "shines the light" God has given him.

I had another relevant experience recently when I took part in a Christmas concert. At the end of the program I was one of the choir members who left the stage to sing carols in the aisles while the audience sang along. The section where I stood was near a group of handicapped persons. As we all sang "Joy to the World," I heard their spirited voices singing in unity. They sang louder than any others in surrounding sections. Their faces beamed as they sang with real conviction. I could easily picture the angels singing along as the group sang, " '. . . and heaven and nature sing.' " I felt tears fill my eyes as I witnessed this beautiful lesson in life. Those who could be considered to have less to sing about were determined to praise God despite their circumstances.

Not one of this group hesitated to sing out for fear of what others might think. They sang from their hearts, just as young Joseph had been compelled to say what was on his heart. When we "shine our lights" of love, others will experience personal, spiritual growth, and it will expand our Christian witness; keeping our lights hidden stifles both. May God help us share His life-changing love with those around us.   Norann Cubberly Walker

DECEMBER 13

Don't Run From Me

The earth is the Lord's, and the fulness thereof; the world, and they that dwell therein. Ps. 24:1.

One might conclude that the whole of northern Sudan is totally desert, except for the Nile passing through it. As we drove along I shouted to my colleagues that Moses must have traveled in this land. Egypt is so close that few would argue whether or not Moses had indeed walked here. As we journeyed through the Nubian Desert, from Khartoum to Karima in the north of Sudan, we marveled at the vast desert stretching as far as the eye could see. I wondered whether life was possible in the desert, with the heat of the day and the extreme cold of the night.

After making half the 16-hour journey, driving through deep sand, we came upon a humble shelter that the desert people use as family homesteads. Not far from the shelter was a shrub from which smoke rose. When I saw the smoke, I asked the driver to go in the direction of the smoke. I was quite sure that I'd find some women to talk to. I was right. There were four women cooking a meal over the fire. As we approached them, stopping to leave the vehicle at a safe distance, the women looked up. As soon as they saw us approaching, they left the fire, scooped up their children in their arms, and ran from us as fast as their legs could carry them. I was perplexed. What had we done to cause this kind of reaction?

"Poor ladies," I muttered. "We must have frightened them." As the driver and I stood there wondering what to do next, I noticed that one of the women dared to come back to the fire just long enough to grab a baby that had been left near the fire when we surprised the group. Still frightened, she ran back to the other ladies as fast as she could, carrying the baby with her. Yes, we had scared these mothers. We hadn't meant to. We had wanted only to befriend them. But they didn't know who we were or why we had come, and they didn't dare take a chance. I couldn't help thinking how wonderful it will be when we can live in harmony in the new earth. Then there will be no missed opportunities for fellowship, for Isaiah 11:6 says that we will have no fear in heaven, for "the wolf will live with the lamb . . . and a little child will lead them" (NIV). Heaven will be free of fear!   SOLOME OMANYA

DECEMBER 14

What Can I Give?

For God so loved the world, that he gave his only begotten Son. John 3:16.

I don't know what childhood treasure you have saved, tucked away in an attic somewhere. Through all those years you may have kept a doll, books, old photos, a grandmother's locket, or even one of your baby outfits. If you have nothing tangible from your past, maybe you have a cherished bit of sage advice from a beloved aunt.

Whatever the "treasure," I'd like for you to imagine giving it to your child or to a child you love very much. Now imagine several responses to the offered gift. One: the child could reach for the gift with as much joyful anticipation as you have in giving it. Two: the child could respond with a halfhearted "Oh, thanks" and put the treasure aside. Three: the child could snatch the gift from your hands, throw it to the ground, stomp on it, and destroy it. Any of us would be greatly disappointed if the second scenario became reality. But we would be devastated, hurt, and angry if the child we entrusted our treasure with followed the third pattern.

During the Christmas season I have often wondered what kind of gift I can give to Jesus. And each time I come back to this thought: there is only one gift my Saviour desires, and that is for me to accept His gift joyfully.

Ponder for a minute how Jesus, the treasured gift of God, was treated. His life was threatened from infancy. The Gift was given to the children of God, and they rejected Him, accused Him of demon possession, spat in His face, and eventually killed Him.

How must the Father feel when I take His gift and "shelve it"? How must He feel when I deny the power of His gift? How must He feel when, in the person of my neighbor or sister in the church, I destroy His reputation with deadly gossip?

Truly the greatest gift we can give our Lord this Christmas season is the gift of joyful anticipated acceptance of His treasure. This year let us accept His gift more fully than we ever have before. Let us permit His gift to work its miracle of love in our lives. May we allow the fullness of recovery to be accomplished.

Indeed, the greatest gift that our God longs for is the gift of complete reception. When we fully receive His Gift, then we fulfill our Father's joy! And isn't joy a wonderful gift to give?

KAREN NICOLA

DECEMBER 15

The Meaning of Christmas

In Him appeared life and this life was the light of [human-kind]. The light still shines in the darkness and the darkness has never put it out. John 1:3, 4, Phillips.

The meaning of Christmas used to be simple. Simple and profound. The Love of the universe poured out on a needy world in the form of a newborn Baby. Wonder shining in the eyes of a child on Christmas morning. The newness of gentle snow falling on a quiet night.

But tonight the joy and pain of the past year—indeed, the past decade—crash together in my mind. Nothing is simple anymore. For the world has grown old and very sad.

This Christmas I share the grief of those who dread the first Christmas since their loved one died.

I hear the incongruency of "peace on earth" in broken families.

I sit in family togetherness at a bountiful table aware that thousands will die of hunger this very day.

I drink in the joy in the eyes of our little ones, hoping to shut out the pain-filled eyes of the children on the evening newscast.

This Christmas the baby I see is Natosha, a beautiful 5-month-old victim of sudden infant death syndrome. Natosha lies lifeless in the arms of her sobbing parents in the hospital chapel where I serve as chaplain. We are giving her back to God.

This Christmas the stable is made up of shacks on the other side of our lives where the homeless seek shelter from the cold.

Sometimes even the angels' songs seem far away. For the world has grown old and very sad.

I give, and my giving doesn't stop the pain.

I love, and my love is like tears falling in the desert of a vast world's need.

I'm overwhelmed. Needy myself.

Wearily I go again to Bethlehem.

I see the starkness of the stable. The pain of delivery. The young couple alone in their struggle. The newborn Son shivering in the cold of a Judean night and the cold of an unwaiting, unwelcoming world. He is named Emmanuel, God With Us.

I watch the God of the universe enter the tangle of humanity without pretense or protocol, almost without notice. A tiny Baby, dependent for life on a young Jewish woman. He enters the world through pain. He will die in 33 years, having experienced all of pain there is, the deepest depths of human grief. "My God, my God, why have You forsaken me?"

God With Us.

I kneel in wonder. The Love of the universe poured out on a needy world in the form of a newborn Baby! Look! "The light still shines in the darkness and the darkness has never put it out." Through my tears I touch the edge of the meaning of Christmas:

That pain and joy often grow together;

That God's power comes not through strength but through weakness;

That true greatness is in releasing rights, not achieving them;

That God With Us is for today—comfort and grace and courage, healing for brokenness, peace for pieces, soul hunger filled;

That God in Us is Life and Light and Love,

That a world so loved is not abandoned when it is old and sad, but will be changed when God makes "all things new" (Rev. 21:5).

The meaning of Christmas, simple, profound: Love, Wonder, Newness. LINDA LANE GAGE

DECEMBER 16

His Unfailing Love

Trust in the Lord with all thine heart; and lean not unto thine own understanding. In all thy ways acknowledge him, and he shall direct thy paths. Prov. 3:5, 6.

This scripture has always been very dear to my heart and has been such an encouragement in my walk with the Lord. We have been shown how important it is to start each day with Christ and to lay all our plans at Jesus' feet. But so often in our rush to get all the many things accomplished on our agenda, we have a tendency to put God on hold and take things into our own hands. If only we could realize that with Him at the helm, we could avoid many of the hassles that occur, we could accomplish our tasks in less time, and we would experience that complete peace that only He can give.

As I reflected on this thought my mind turned back to when my husband, Bob, and I were first married and still in college at Berrien Springs, Michigan. We had some errands to take care of just a short distance away. When we got in the car, I suddenly felt a strong urge to have prayer before we left. We always prayed for God's protection when we were going on long trips, but was it necessary for just a few miles? Yet when that still small voice speaks to us, it is important to listen. At the time I didn't know why I felt the sudden urge to pray, but after we had driven only a short distance I found out.

We were driving along unmindful of any danger, but as we reached the crest of a small hill, just in front of us on our side of the road was a car that had only moments before skidded and rolled over—in fact, the wheels were still spinning. The driver apparently was going too fast to make the turn, and the car lay in the road exactly where we would have been if we had just gone on our way that morning. We realized those few short moments in prayer had saved our lives. We were so thankful, and praised the Lord for watching over us and directing our paths.

Recently while reading from *Steps to Christ* I came across this beautiful thought: "We should keep in our thoughts every blessing we receive from God, and when we realize His great love we should be willing to trust everything to the hand that was nailed to the cross for us" (p. 104).

How comforting it is to know we have a Friend who loves us and never fails us. He is interested in every part of our lives, no matter how small. He will guide us safely through any storm. Let us be willing to let Him direct our paths today.   MARG KINNEY

I'm Not a Leftover!

Do you not know that your body is a temple of the Holy Spirit, who is in you, whom you have received from God? You are not your own; you were bought at a price. 1 Cor. 6:19, 20, NIV.

I was not looking forward to Christmas! My brother was bringing his fiancée, and my sister's boyfriend would be visiting too. I realized my reasons were selfish. I wanted to spend time with my family, and I wanted them all to myself. But there was an even bigger issue on my mind. I was haunted by memories of past family gatherings.

Whoever said "It's what's on the inside that matters" never went to high school. I was too smart, too fat, and wore thick glasses. These things mattered! When kids started pairing off, I was often left alone. It hurt. I felt rejected, unloved, and inferior to those who were considered better looking. Now it was happening all over again. This time it was my younger brother and sister who were growing up and pairing off with prospective mates, and I was still alone.

As I drove to my parents' home to join the family for the holidays, I felt depressed. I just knew that I would become a leftover and would be left out as new relationships were formed.

"God, why can't someone love me?" I sighed, not expecting an answer. But God did answer. "You are not your own; you were bought at a price."

"Bought at a price." And what a tremendous, immeasurable price! Here it was, Christmas, a time for celebrating Christ's birth. A time to remember the Incarnation, the miracle of Jesus coming to redeem a sinful people. How could I have forgotten? How had the true meaning of Christmas gotten lost in the rush to be "ready" for the holidays?

My depression soon evaporated. My feelings of worthlessness began to lift. In God's sight I had infinite value! Jesus loved me and valued me enough to come to this earth to die for me.

It turned out to be one of the best Christmases ever! Not because there were lots of presents and good times with family. It was because I'd been reminded that these new relationships in our family didn't take anything away from me. They didn't make me any less important or less loved by my family and especially by my heavenly Father! CHRISTINA ENNIS

Lord, Make Me an Evergreen

The righteous flourish like the palm tree, and grow like a cedar in Lebanon. They are planted in the house of the Lord; they flourish in the courts of our God. In old age they still produce fruit; they are always green and full of sap. Ps. 92:12-14, NRSV.

I never tire of the evergreens. Standing beneath one gives me a sense of strength and serenity. I like to rub the tree's slender needles between my hands, bruising them to release their tangy sweet essence, and inhale deeply. It's invigorating!

God speaks in His Word of the cedars of Lebanon, in both Psalms 92 and 104, as flourishing, spreading their boughs as a shelter for those seeking refuge beneath and for the fowls of the air above. He says that if we are planted in the house of the Lord, we shall be fresh and flourishing, bear fruit into old age, be full of sap (the Holy Spirit), and be a refuge. What an invitation and blessing!

In order to flourish, the evergreen sends down a lengthy taproot far beneath the surface to gain sustenance and strength to withstand the blasts of winter. It sheds its old needles, letting them fall silently to the ground without notice; while new ones are added, old ones form a carpet below.

My prayer is "Lord, make me an evergreen. Help me to dig deeply in the rich soil of Your Word while Your Son sends the rain of His Holy Spirit on my life. I want to absorb its life-giving nutrients to empower me for the storms of life and the last great blast of Satan's fury.

"Help me to let go of my old sinful character traits and put on new ones from the hand of my Re-Creator. When I am bruised and broken, help me to exude the sweet essence of the Lord Jesus.

"Fill me with Your power and strength so I can offer shelter and hope to those who seek refuge from their sins, that I may lift my boughs heavenward, pointing them to You. Help me to tread silently and softly on the old needles of their sins as they struggle to put on new ones. If I should fall, let others tread softly on me, pick me up, and find some life-giving use for me.

"As the farmer banks strawberries with fallen needles to hold in moisture and keep down weeds, so even in my most useless, lifeless state, help me to hold in the life-giving moisture of the Water of Life to nourish others as I hold down the weeds of sin in their lives.

"Lord, make me an evergreen. If not a tree, then a bough; if not a bough, then a branch; if not a branch, then a twig; if not a twig, then a sweet-smelling, tangy needle; but never as spiritually dead as the silent carpet beneath my feet.

"Lord make me an evergreen!"

May we stand like evergreens in the storms of life, firmly anchored to the Rock. May we be evergreens in the winter of someone else's life, too.   EMILIE ROBERTSON

DECEMBER 19

Sensing His Presence

Fear thou not; for I am with thee: be not dismayed; for I am thy God: I will strengthen thee; yea, I will help thee; yea, I will uphold thee with the right hand of my righteousness. Isa. 41:10.

Have you ever *felt* alone—powerlessly alone and overcome by the crippling, immobilizing fear that usually accompanies that "helpless aloneness"? Such was the experience of Elijah very soon after he had accomplished great exploits for God on Mount Carmel. The feelings of abject loneliness that overpowered him are reflected in his words "I, even I only, am left" (1 Kings 19:10). And then with fearful emphasis he adds, "And they seek my life, to take it away."

I too have had my Elijah experience. I remember only too clearly the feelings of utter loneliness and intense fear that gnawed at my being after an unforgettably traumatic experience in the South American country in which my husband and I worked. I had been recently married and had just moved with my minister husband to our first pastoral district. Everything seemed to be going well: I was enjoying my teaching at a nearby high school; our church members were open and welcoming; our new neighbors were polite and helpful; and our 10 church congregations were on fire for God. Ours was a Mount Carmel experience.

And then it happened. One December evening, just a few days before my first Christmas as a wife, an armed intruder crept into our home—and swept the peace out of my life. Miraculously, the burglar left without robbing us materially or harming us physically, but he succeeded in planting within me an intense fear of being left alone at home. That fear became so intense and irrational that every time my husband walked out the door I would crouch behind a piece of furniture and remain there motionless for as long as five hours! I had become a slave to fear.

One day, while visiting with another minister's wife, I found the key to the peace I so desperately needed. As her kind eyes surveyed my dark-circled eyes, sunken cheeks, and gaunt frame, she said softly, "Lena, why don't you claim God's promise? He wants to be with you. Make Isaiah 41:10 your verse. Repeat it over and over as you go through the day, and soon you will sense God's presence and experience His peace."

I took her wise counsel. The dark circles around my eyes disappeared, but more important, I had learned that acknowledging the reality of God's abiding presence is the secret of lasting peace. Ellen White affirms this: "Only the sense of God's presence can banish the fear that, for the timid child, would make life a burden" (*Education*, p. 255).

Do you feel alone and powerless in the face of discrimination, abuse, or injustice? Are you fearful because of failing health, wayward children, uncertain job prospects, or advancing age? Thank God we have the answer. Like Elijah, we may still discern God's still small voice reassuringly saying: "Don't be afraid, My child; you are not alone, for *I am with you*." LENA G. CAESAR

Light Comes to the Stable

Love one another; as I have loved you, so you are to love one another. If there is this love among you, then all will know that you are my disciples. John 13:34, 35, NEB.

When God wrapped His Son in a tiny bit of humanity to send Him to this dark world, He could have come to a carefully prepared palace. But He chose a stable, probably a cave, dark and dirty, cold, cluttered, disorganized, and unprepared.

Why? Why would God choose a stable? Maybe to show us that He comes to the darkest places, to show us grace, to allow us to experience love. Maybe to teach us that when Jesus is born anew in our hearts He is born in the cave of our lives.

As Christians we readily invite Jesus to the palace—a quiet place inside ourselves where everything is more or less tidy, and we can offer God a semi-clean space from which to rule our lives.

We are familiar with the palace. But we want to deny the cave: the place of our pain and our need. In the cave, if we allow ourselves to go there at all, we face our fear, our loneliness, our brokenness. We face our sins, too, and our powerlessness to change ourselves.

We run away from the cave, yet this is where Jesus longs to come. For in the cave we see Him best.

All my life Jesus lived in the palace I had prepared for Him. But the day He came to the cave He showed me startling pictures of the struggler I am. First was my stubborn, resistant self. A workaholic, trying yet often failing, because in this deep inner place I had not fully surrendered.

I also saw a codependent woman, living for many years on the praise of others, an anxious rescuer skilled at denying what she did not want to face. And I saw a frightened child, unable to dance and play.

I wrote about the images, trying to understand. Suddenly I noticed that Jesus did not enter into my discussion or analysis of my inner self. He simply held me, hugged me, soothed me. He had showed me myself. Now He loved me just as I was. His love covered me, and my shame disappeared. I saw Him as I had never seen Him before. And in His eyes I saw healing for each part of me.

At Pentecost all the disciples had failed their Lord. The palaces had been stripped away. Only the caves were left. The truth of their need was all they had. Their need and His promise. There, in that very place, grace and love accepted their brokenness and began the change in them that changed the world.

Then, and only then, could Jesus' desire for them be lived out. Because we can never really love one another as Jesus loves us until we experience *how* He loves us. We don't know how He loves us in the palace—only in the stable. LINDA LANE GAGE

DECEMBER 21

Away in a Manger

She gave birth to her firstborn, a son. She wrapped him in cloths and placed him in a manger, because there was no room for them in the inn. Luke 2:7, NIV.

I lay in the labor and delivery suite of our local maternity hospital. Our firstborn child lay in my arms, all bathed and clean, and wrapped in a cotton blanket. The room was spotless, white and bright, filled with every latest gadget to relieve pain and to ease delivery. An empty, transparent crib waited in the corner, the shelves underneath filled with diapers, creams, powders, and fresh changes of bedding.

I gazed with wonder at the baby I had loved for so long already. I thanked God for a safe delivery and for the modern technology that has made having babies so safe. It was not so long ago that childbirth was a life-threatening experience.

Bethany was born a few days into January, and when I was taken to the postnatal ward I noticed the Christmas decorations, still sparkling along the corridors. A wooden crib scene was arranged on a table filled with flowers.

I thought about that other birth 2,000 years ago. I thought of Mary in a smelly stable. No pristine crib with every accessory—just a manger full of hay and some torn rags to wrap the baby in. How terrible! How could God put Mary through such an awful experience?

But then, was it so bad? What was the alternative if Jesus was to be born in Bethlehem, so far from His parents' home? Only an overcrowded inn with people everywhere. No privacy—just mats on the floor wherever you could find a space. And I wondered where I would rather have given birth.

I would have wanted somewhere quiet and private, somewhere where I wouldn't have to worry about disturbing others' sleep with my labor pain, somewhere where I could just be alone with my husband and away from inquisitive eyes and the embarrassment of having to expose my body in public.

The stable was the perfect place. Sheltered, hidden away, peaceful. No worries about making a bit of a mess—no one would mind out here. But in the inn it could have been awkward. The hay would make a softer bed than the hard earth floor of the inn. The cries of the baby wouldn't bother anyone, and the manger would make a safe and quiet sleeping place, away from lots of bustling people with their noise and crush.

And so God knew what was best for Mary. He knew where she would be most comfortable; He knew how to preserve her dignity. He knew where she and the Baby could both find peace. And now I understand why such an apparently inappropriate place was the very best Bethlehem could offer to the King.   KAREN HOLFORD

DECEMBER 22

A Gift for the Baby King

When they saw the star, they were overjoyed. On coming to the house, they saw the child with his mother Mary, and they bowed down and worshiped him. Then they opened their treasures and presented him with gifts of gold and of incense and of myrrh. Matt. 2:10-12, NIV.

I walked up and down the aisles of the department store pushing my 4-year-old grandson, Ryan, and his 2-year-old sister, Heather, in a shopping cart. The store was crowded with shoppers, and my daughter was trying to make a few last-minute selections before Christmas. Now, if you've ever tried to keep two small children corralled in a shopping cart for any length of time, you know that 30 minutes can seem like 24 hours! For when you've managed to capture one child's attention, the other is precariously straddling the cart in an attempt to examine something you can ill afford to take home in one piece, let alone a hundred.

That day I discovered that one of the safest aisles in the store was the one displaying brass items. While my grandchildren sat like little angels surveying the passing merchandise, I tried to keep the cart moving fast enough to prevent them from grabbing anything and yet slow enough to make the trip down this particular aisle last as long as possible.

Ryan wanted to examine a decorative brass French horn. I saw no harm in his request, and after a few imaginary blasts on the horn he put it back on the shelf. Beside it, though, was a lovely octagonal-shaped brass box with a delicately pierced cone-shaped lid. "Oh, Grammie," Ryan cried out with a sound of awe in his voice. "Look, it's just like the box at the manger, isn't it?" he said, pointing at the brass container.

I had to admit that he was right. The ornamental brass box did look like something a Wise Man might have brought to Bethlehem. "You're right, Ryan," I said, picking up the box to examine the detail. "It does remind me of the gifts the Wise Men brought the baby Jesus."

With a sense of wonder Ryan traced his little fingers over the design, seeming to want to prolong the moment. When he was through examining it, we carefully placed our newfound treasure back on the shelf and continued down the aisle. I leaned over the cart and gave that little boy a big hug. For it was he who reminded me that the true spirit of Christmas is not long lists of to-do's, busy shopping malls, and plastic credit cards, but a celebration of the arrival of the greatest Gift of all—Jesus, our Lord and Saviour.

ROSE OTIS

Which Master?

No one can serve two masters. Either he will hate the one and love the other, or he will be devoted to the one and despise the other. You cannot serve both God and Money. Matt. 6:24, NIV.

Matthew, the Jewish tax collector. How fellow Jews must have hissed his name! Because he was a Jew-turned-tax collector, other Jews avoided him as if he were a pestilence. Jews ostracized those Jews who collected the Roman poll and land taxes because (1) paying the poll tax was to concede to Roman subjugation, and (2) paying the land tax was to insult God, whom they "regarded as the real owner of the land and the dispenser of its bounties. It was considered bad enough to pay the Romans taxes, but infinitely worse to assist the Romans in collecting them" (*SDA Bible Dictionary*, pp. 891, 892).

To irritate the insult further, each tax collector was to exact more than the required assessment in order to make a living. No wonder Jews could well have uttered Matthew's name as a curse. No wonder then that Matthew must have stood amazed as Jesus invited *him* to be one of His disciples.

Thus it was that Matthew, the tax collector-turned-disciple, must have listened to Jesus' sermon on the mount with all the ardor of the newly converted. Surely the words in Matthew 6:24 conveyed a special meaning to him whose life not so long ago had been tyrannized by money. But now Matthew's fortune no longer depended upon the extra he could demand. From the second he heard Jesus' voice breaking through the vicious circle of hate that imprisoned him, Matthew ceased lining his pockets with ill-gotten gain and began storing his treasure in heaven, where "moth and rust do not destroy" (Matt. 6:20, NIV).

This holiday season, as the media perpetuates its blitz against your bank account, will Jesus' words mean as much to you as they did to Matthew? Advertisements with their catchy jingles blare into our ears from the radio and television, while glittering store windows and savvy magazine advertisements glare into our eyes. All are designed to make us believe that we will be miserable if we do not spend our money on this, that, or the other thing. But what soul misery of yours has the Saviour's soft voice broken through to empty your heart of traitorous coinage? This Christmas, upon which master will you focus?   LYNDELLE CHIOMENTI

A Dual Answer

Before they call I will answer; while they are still speaking I will hear. Isa. 65:24, NIV.

One Christmas Eve my family had to work around an unexpected event. The gas company had scheduled the installation of gas in our home some days before. However, because of a snowstorm the rescheduled date happened to be on Christmas Eve.

I was told that we would not have water or heat for a while, but that by 5:00 p.m. everything would be completed.

At 4:00 p.m. the man in charge of the installation announced his job was finished, yet there was no heat or hot water. He informed me that the gas company had to send someone to turn on the main switch. On regular days it was four to six hours before the person was able to come, but today, because of the extremely cold temperature and the holiday rush, it might not be until early the next morning. Furthermore, this meant someone would have to be home to let the person from the gas company in.

I lashed back, "You said everything would be finished by 5:00. We have a family gathering planned, and now it will be spoiled because someone will have to be home the whole evening. Because of the sunlight the house is still warm. In less than an hour it's going to be sunset, and the parrot and orchids are going to freeze because we have no heat."

"I'm sorry, ma'am, but it can't be helped," he responded.

That morning during my devotion I had specifically prayed for things to go well and for divine help to be like Jesus in my responses and interactions. I had asked God to search my heart and help me to recognize hidden sin. Now, feeling extremely frustrated, I tried reflecting on my morning prayer. Suddenly I was struck with a thought. *Why am I so upset? Why am I making such a big issue out of this?* The realization of how impatient and intolerant I was of small annoyances and inconveniences was stark. How easy it was for me to vent my negative feelings and blame someone else.

I turned to God. "Lord, please forgive me for being so impatient and so insensitive. At least I have a space heater that works. There may be someone with children without any type of heat in this very cold weather. I am getting upset over a party when it may be life or death to someone else. And Lord . . ."

I was interrupted by the doorbell. There stood a stranger. "I'm from the gas company. I'm here to turn on the gas."

I felt joy, relief, but most of all, rebuke. "Lord, why did I not trust You? Why did I allow myself to become so upset when You had everything all worked out? You not only answered before I called; You gave me another glimpse of how unlovely I can be when I allow my feelings to take first place in my life."

NORMA JEAN PARCHMENT

DECEMBER 25

Unwrapped Christmas Gifts

But grace was given to each of us according to the measure of Christ's gift. Therefore it is said, "When he ascended on high he led a host of captives, and he gave gifts to men." Eph. 4:7, 8, RSV.

Have you ever wondered what Jesus would give as a Christmas gift?

Although the very question is remarkably redundant since Jesus is the Reason for the season, the underlying thought expresses a curiosity about the type of gift Jesus would give at the holidays. After all, we are commissioned to live our lives as Jesus would. So, facing the gift-giving season, what do you think Jesus would give?

Can you picture Him running from store to store frantically buying presents, as we often find ourselves doing because of our procrastination? Can you envision Christ getting a gift for one of His disciples only because that disciple had gotten Him one? Maybe you feel more comfortable thinking that He used His carpentry skills to make something special for His family or His friends.

When I reflect on Jesus' life on the earth, I find He did not give material gifts. However, the spirit of gift-giving that we feel at Christmas is what He carried with Him all year through.

I soak in all the feelings, sights, sounds, smells, and tastes of Christmas that I possibly can. It's no surprise that it is definitely my favorite time of year. But with all there is to love about the season, the highlight for me always is the look on the faces of my loved ones as they open the carefully wrapped presents I chose for them.

The Christmas spirit of gift-giving, in eager anticipation for the look of delight in the faces we love, is what I'm sure Christ had as He healed the lame and the blind, or comforted the grieving, or believed in the hopeless. Christ consistently gave gifts to others by showing them what they could be, instead of condemning them for what they were.

At this holiday season there are gifts more precious than those you can wrap a ribbon around that are definitely in your budget to give. Look in the eyes of your loved ones as they recognize how you consistently demonstrate your unconditional love for them. Feel the warmth in the hearts of those you encourage. Watch the smiles grow from corner to corner on those you show you believe in. Search for the teardrops on the cheeks of those you touch with your kindness and tenderness.

You'll find it as rewarding as Jesus did when He gave those same gifts, and you'll find yourself celebrating Christmas all year long! LAURA PASCUAL DANCEK

DECEMBER 26

Like Best Friends

No one has greater love than this, to lay down one's life for one's friends. You are my friends. John 15:13, 14, NIV.

Sunlight flows out of winter skies, spilling big droplets of gold onto the kitchen windowsill. Curly leaves play tag on the front lawn. Blue skies—no white Christmas, but our house is filled with the Christmas spirit anyway.

My youthful, smooth hands are in unison with the aging, weathered ones beside me. I'm washing breakfast dishes with Mom again. I feel far away from the college campus. Far from the endless round of term papers, cafeteria mush, new faces, old rooms . . . so nice. I tell Mom all about my life at college—the little things. The plant that died over Thanksgiving break, the color of the carpet in my dorm room, the number of times I do laundry every week, the guys—the cute ones, the rude ones, the ones I cry over—and together we laugh.

Then it's time to walk the dog. We walk together for the longest, shortest time. Just Mom, me, and Fluffie. Through curling leaves, under skies spilling golden droplets on our cheeks, with a snippy wind kissing our noses. We talk. About life's big issues—life, death, love, and God. And I ask her why there is so much hurt in the world, why all must suffer. I listen. She gives the wisest answer: "Only God knows," she says. I wonder where she got that answer. I ask her. We laugh.

Then she says, "You know, we're more like sisters or friends than mother and daughter." We laugh, like sisters. So nice to be home again, like friends. No need to say it, she already knows. And I realize she's always been that to me, a sister, a friend; like God, I think. It's more than enough, like a sister, like a friend.

Then it's time to go home. Laughing, chasing Fluffie through the leaves, under the late-morning skies spilling gold droplets to the earth, with a sister, a friend at my side. So much to do when we get home. Christmas dinner to cook, whole-wheat bread to bake, bookshelves to dust, fresh sheets to slip onto beds, Dad's shirt to iron; but so much more fun with Mom, like having a sister, a friend.

It's a merry Christmas.

Then it's time to leave. I walk alone for the longest, longest time, just me. To the silver-winged bird that will fly me above the curly leaves, to the skies spilling golden drops to the earth below; back to it all: papers, people, problems, just me . . . and God to face it all together. Just like sisters, like friends, like Mom and me, we talk about the big things, and about the little things. I ask Him questions, he gives the wisest answers—I don't have to wonder where He got them. We laugh, just like sisters, just like best friends.

SHARON FUJIMOTO

DECEMBER 27

Spirit-filled Magnets

For the flesh lusts against the Spirit, and the Spirit against the flesh, and these are contrary to one another, so that you do not do the things you wish. Gal. 5:17, NKJV.

My eyes almost popped out of my head as I peered into the gift with my name on it. "You've got to be kidding," I said under my breath! Unbelief and anger welled up inside me. I had been looking forward to getting a gift from my secret pal, but the contents of the gift bag were not what I had been hoping for.

Ever since the women's ministries director had suggested that we choose secret pals, I had thought it sounded like fun. We agreed that we would all share little love gifts from time to time, to encourage one another. I love to get gifts, especially surprises!

After several weeks of seeing other women in the church receive their gifts, I approached the designated dropoff spot on top of the basement piano to read the names on the packages. Finally, there it was, the gift I had been anticipating. I opened the gift bag to see what delightful treasure waited inside, and I was stunned. At the bottom of my bag were some fruit-shaped refrigerator magnets! "How could she do this to me?" I muttered, closing the bag before anyone asked to see.

A war began to rage in my mind. The carnal nature warred against the spiritual. I prayed that God would forgive me for being so ungrateful, but I had expected a pretty little notion to appease my thirst for things. Almost immediately I began to recall all the pretty things that others had received, and I conjured up plenty of justification for my indignation.

On the way home from church my husband asked me what I had received. I just opened the gift bag and let him look for himself. His reaction was the same as mine: "You've got to be kidding." But then he reminded me that perhaps my secret pal could be one of the poorer women in the church—like the new immigrant woman. My husband questioned me about why I felt the way I did. I told him that I wasn't at all pleased with the way I had reacted to my gift. Frankly, I was ashamed of myself.

Suddenly, with insight that only God could have given, my husband said, "I know—they are spiritual fruits!" My jaw dropped at his astounding insight (he's a new Christian), and I began to laugh and praise God in my heart for this amazingly subtle way of disciplining me, His daughter.

Proverbs 3:11, 12 says, "My child, do not despise the Lord's discipline or be weary of his reproof, for the Lord reproves the one He loves, as a father the son [or daughter] in whom he delights" (NRSV).

The Lord showed me that this was indeed the precise gift I needed to stimulate my spiritual growth. For after all, He is my best Secret Pal. He wants to give me the best gift: a gift that is priceless, the gift of eternal life. He also promises to change my carnal nature, and He never stops striving with me to give me victory over this fallen nature that wars within me.

How grateful I am now to my secret pal who gave me the Spirit-filled magnets. Now every time I enter my kitchen, my refrigerator door has a message for me from both my secret pals.

LAURA LEE SWANEY

DECEMBER 28

Heritage of Faith

Your statutes are my heritage forever; they are the joy of my heart. Ps. 119:111, NIV.

Great-grandmother regularly gathered her family in the front parlor of her New England farmhouse to read the Bible. No doubt it gave her comfort when she was widowed with five daughters and three sons, as well as the wisdom to raise them singlehandedly.

In order to teach her two older sons a trade, Great-grandmother established a printing business in her basement. For nearly 20 years the family did small printing jobs and published two locally circulated journals that reported community news and promoted religious, temperance, and social causes.

When old age and other responsibilities brought Great-grandmother's printing career to an end, she sold all the equipment except the large slate imposing stone on which type was made ready for the press. A stonecutter carved the Ten Commandments on one side and 1 John 1 on the other. In 1927 the tablet was mounted by the roadside a few yards north of Great-grandmother's home. Since she lived on the main road to Wachusett Mountain, a local tourist attraction, the stone often caught the attention of families driving up the mountain for cool breezes and an inspiring view.

Although moved to a less-conspicuous spot when the road was widened in the 1950s, the Ten Commandments stone still stands on Mountain Road in Princeton, Massachusetts. It's merely a curiosity to those who never knew Great-grandmother. But Princeton's old-timers know that she lived her life by its principles. They knew her heart belonged to God and her hands served her family and her community. And when they forgot it was her Sabbath and stopped by the farm to buy apples or milk or eggs, she would graciously say, "Take what you need, but since today is the Sabbath, there'll be no charge." Few took advantage of her; most returned later in the week to pay what they owed.

Living once again in Great-grandmother's part of the world, I often walk past the Ten Commandments stone and am reminded of the women of faith who have gone before us, leaving us a heritage to be proud of—and to follow. JOCELYN FAY

DECEMBER 29

Sunlight Pure

You will receive power when the Holy Spirit comes on you; and you will be my witnesses in Jerusalem, and in all Judea and Samaria, and to the ends of the earth. Acts 1:8, NIV.

Sam gazed out the window at the wide expanse of deep-blue ocean beneath the plane. The only indication they were nearing their destination was the sound of the engines cutting back. He had to admit that it would feel good to get home to Los Angeles after the long flight from Sydney, Australia. Flying wasn't his favorite activity. He glanced over at Elaine in the seat next to him. She sat with her eyes closed and the airline headset firmly in place. Listening to the classical music station was her way of coping with flying.

Having recently become Christians, Sam and Elaine had developed the habit of holding hands and praying together on all takeoffs and landings during the extended holiday to the South Pacific. Sam reached over and took her hand. She opened her eyes and smiled just as the engines cut back further.

"Do you want to have prayer now?" Sam asked. "You go first."

She nodded and bowed her head. "Dear Father, we know You love us and care for us. We come to You once again to ask for Your divine—"

Sam tapped her arm anxiously. She opened her eyes.

"Sh!" he hissed and pointed toward his left ear.

She frowned. "Sam, I'm praying!"

Her husband noted the sideways glances they were receiving from the other passengers. He removed one of her earphones. "No, dear," he patiently whispered, "you're witnessing."

Embarrassed, she lowered her head and her voice for the rest of her prayer. We may chuckle at the story, but without realizing it Elaine discovered the purest form of witnessing—the unconscious witness.

So many times in our lives we do the right thing because it is the best way to accomplish our goals. For example, when I find myself and my luggage trapped in the middle of an airline's worst nightmare, I have discovered that by remaining calm, courteous, and understanding, I receive much better treatment—e.g., a meal voucher, paid hotel accommodations, or a first-class seat. It is in my best interest to behave like a Christian, to be a good witness.

Shopping in the grocery store, waiting in the turning lane, dealing with bureaucratic red tape—so many times I find myself living by the adage "You catch more flies with honey than with vinegar." While there's nothing wrong with being courteous and patient, I can't help wondering if I'm doing the right thing for the wrong reason. Is this what the Good Book means when it calls my good deeds nothing more than filthy rags?

Is it possible that when my witness is encumbered by the ulterior motives of receiving human praise, filling quotas, or just feeling satisfied, all I'm actually serving is myself? One writer describes a true witness as being as pure and transparent as sunlight. I like that. No muddiness, no personal gain, no hidden agendas—just the love of Jesus bubbling from my soul, spilling on everyone I meet, as natural as breathing.

I know that such a witness is impossible without the Holy Spirit. Yet when He dwells within me, the love, the joy, and the peace of heaven are mine. And believe me, the world will notice. I will be the sunlight-filled witness Jesus desires.

Mother Teresa was once quoted as praying, "Lord, make my life a window for Your light to shine through and a mirror to reflect Your love to all I meet. Amen."

To her prayer I add, "Come, Holy Spirit, fill me today."

KAY D. RIZZO

Someone Touched Them Long Ago

Jesus turned and saw her. "Take heart, daughter," he said, "your faith has healed you." Matt. 9:22, NIV.

She pressed through the crowd, sick and alone.
Would she never reach Him? Should she go back home?
Just a few inches more, she touched His robe,
His strength filled her body, she was made whole!
 She touched Someone long ago.

He was born blind; he never saw the sun, the trees, the
 sky
Till a Man took his hand and put some clay upon his eyes,
And told him to the Pool of Siloam to go.
He washed his eyes, and then he praised
 The One who touched him long ago.

She lay there dead, her little body so cold.
Her family was weeping, the story is told,
But Someone took her hand and said, "She's only sleep-
 ing, you know."
She sat up and smiled into the face
 Of the One who touched her long ago.

He blessed the children on His knee.
He said, "Bring the little ones to Me."
He fed the thousands with fish and bread,
He calmed the storm and raised the dead.
He healed the sick and made them whole.
He made the lepers clean, you know.
 Someone touched them long ago.

He will guide your life and calm your fears,
Solve your problems and wipe away your tears.

He will forgive your sins and save your soul,
And make your heart as white as snow,
That same Someone who touched them long ago.

LILLIAN MUSGRAVE

Endings

The end of a matter is better than its beginning. Eccl. 7:8, NIV.

I'm so grateful for stopping points.

The end of a day. Dick is reading in bed. I've gone to each child's room to say goodnight and give a hug and kiss. The cat is out; the dog is in. Moving through the quiet house, I savor my privacy.

The end of a week. Unfinished work is laid aside, and the Sabbath is welcomed. Strains from Dick's guitar call us to the living room where we sing favorite choruses and read the Bible. Tensions disappear in these sacred moments.

The end of a month. It pleases me to flip another page on the calendar and to wonder what a new month will bring. What should I accomplish? What goals should I set? I pray that I'll relish this month's special days.

The end of a season. It is as satisfying to put away heavy coats and fleece-lined boots at winter's end as it is to dig them out again when cold winds blow. I am as happy harvesting squash and potatoes in October as I am picking new lettuce and radishes in May. When summer is over, it feels good to get indoors; but once bright days return, I can't wait to be outside again.

The end of a year. I understand God's leading better now from another year's perspective. Some of the things I'd hoped to do are still only phrases on paper, but those plans seem unimportant now. I see new directions in which God has guided and new areas He has opened.

Tasks finished. People touched. Prayers answered. Beginnings represent exciting possibilities, but endings make me want to whisper, "Amen."

CHERRY B. HABENICHT